THE **SINO-SOVIET** ALLIANCE

The New Cold War History

ODD ARNE WESTAD, EDITOR

THE SINO-SOVIET ALLIANCE

An International History

AUSTIN JERSILD

The University of North Carolina Press *Chapel Hill*

Designed and set in Arno and Calluna Sans types by Rebecca Evans

The paper in this book meets the guidelines for permanence
and durability of the Committee on Production Guidelines for
Book Longevity of the Council on Library Resources.

The University of North Carolina Press has been a member
of the Green Press Initiative since 2003.

Complete cataloging information for this title is available from the
Library of Congress.
ISBN 978-1-4696-1159-4 (cloth: alk. paper)
ISBN 978-1-4696-2983-4 (pbk.: alk. paper)

FOR **HEATHER**

CONTENTS

ILLUSTRATIONS

The specter of an emerging alliance of Russia and China in response to American unilateralism and "hegemony" in the wake of the collapse of the Soviet Union has attracted the attention of numerous observers of contemporary international affairs. The new "strategic partnership," as it was called in the 1997 Treaty of Good Neighborliness, Cooperation, and Friendship, has since then featured border agreements, the growth of small-scale trade, arms sales, joint military exercises, exchange in the strategic and sensitive area of natural resources, and the emergence of the Shanghai Cooperation Organization. The two countries again share common suspicions about America, the presumed maker and beneficiary of a unipolar world, and its promotion of NATO expansion, preventive war, the campaign in Iraq, and the abrogation of the 1972 Antiballistic Missile Treaty. Both countries are especially sensitive about what they perceive as intrusive American criticism of their supposed human rights violations.[1] This relationship, however, far from an alliance, is a far cry from what was known as the "Great Friendship" established by Joseph Stalin and Chairman Mao in Moscow on 14 February 1950. The two societies and economies in their current form cannot possibly reproduce anything close to the forms of collaboration and cooperation once characteristic of the socialist world. The shared perception of America as a threat is significant but less important than the shared hope of greater trade and participation in the global economy. If anything, the relationship borders on what both sides once denounced as the traditional diplomacy characteristic of the world of imperialism and capitalism, the antithesis of socialist "internationalism." Minus the Chinese purchase of Russian oil, the current relationship is more reminiscent of the earlier history of the Sino-Russian frontier, with its series of treaties clarifying borders, regulating trade, and resolving settlement disputes.[2] The lofty rhetoric and complicated practices of "proletarian internationalism" belong to the past.

The study of this past required fellowship support, advice, and intellectual camaraderie from a wide variety of institutions, friends, and colleagues, and I am grateful to have the opportunity to recognize some of them here. I began research on this project a decade ago, but it occupied some corner of my imagination many years before then. As part of an exchange between St. Olaf

College and East China Normal University, I taught English in Shanghai in 1986–87, where I had the opportunity to meet many Russian-speaking Chinese with distant memories of their experiences in the Soviet Union in the 1950s. As a graduate student at the University of Michigan and at the University of California, Davis, I was fortunate to learn about Chinese history and politics from Kenneth Lieberthal, Michael Yahuda, Donald Price, and Kwang-Ching Liu. More recently, I started archival work in Russia in the spring of 2004, with the support of the American Councils on International Education, and continued archival work in Moscow, Prague, Vladivostok, Berlin, and Beijing with additional support from the Fulbright Program in the Russian Federation, the Fulbright Program in the Czech Republic, the National Council on Eurasian and East European Research, the Old Dominion University Faculty Leave Program, and the ODU Summer Faculty Research Program.

This list of those I wish to acknowledge and thank is surely incomplete, but let me start with Karolína Šimůnková, Pavel Baudisch, and Jiří Bernas of the National Archive in Prague; Zuzana Pivcová of the Central Military Archive in Prague; the highly professional archival workers of the Russian Federation; Sylvia Gräfe of SAPMO in Berlin; the International Department of Far Eastern Federal University in Vladivostok; Anthony Koliha, Marina Bezrukova, Valentina Gruzintseva, Hanna Ramboukovska, and Muriel Joffe of CIEE and the Fulbright program; Graham Hettlinger of American Councils; Dean Charles Wilson, Vice Provost Chandra DeSilva, and former Department of History chair Annette Finley-Croswhite of Old Dominion University; Cui Yan of Beijing University; Dean Guo Yingjian of Minzu University of China in Beijing; Michael Carhart, Martha Daas, Kurt Gaubatz, Jin Hailstork, Maura Hametz, Erin Jordan, Lorraine Lees, Jane Merritt, Katerina Oskarsson, Kathy Pearson, Heidi Schlipphacke, Steve Yetiv, and Ren Zhongtang of Old Dominion University; Tomaš and Marketa Reiner in Prague; Lola Rakhimbekova and Elena Larina in Moscow; Detlef Pohontsch in Berlin; the Kuhn family in both Norfolk, Virginia (Sebastian and Kathrin), and Berlin (Susanne); and Zhihua Shen, Dai Chaowu, Ron Suny, Rex Wade, Willard Sunderland, and Brantly Womack. Conference presentations and seminars highly useful to the evolution of this book included those organized by Eric Lohr and the Russian History Workshop at Georgetown University; Charles King and the Center for Eurasian, Russian, and East European Studies of Georgetown University; Maura Hametz and the Associates Writing Group at Old Dominion University; Yoko Aoshima and the Davis Center for Russian and Eurasian Studies of Harvard University; and Priscilla Roberts and the University of Hong Kong.

I am grateful to Christian Ostermann of the Cold War International History Project for making possible my participation at this last event, dedicated to "Mao's China, Non-communist Asia, and the Global Setting, 1949–1976." In Hong Kong I was fortunate to meet Sergey Radchenko and Qiang Zhai, both of whom were extremely helpful and insightful readers of an earlier draft of this book. My thanks to them and to Yafeng Xia for encouraging me to go to China for research, and to work in the Ministry of Foreign Affairs archive in Beijing in particular. I am especially grateful for the scholarly inspiration and intellectual encouragement provided over the years by Odd Arne Westad. It was an honor to work with a series and a press that has taught me so much about the Cold War, and I am grateful for the insight and hard work of Chuck Grench, Sara Jo Cohen, Alison Shay, Paula Wald, Alex Martin, and their colleagues at the University of North Carolina Press.

My deepest thanks go to my family—my parents, Paul and Marilyn Jersild; my children, Annika and Kira; and my wife, Heather. I was fortunate to have my father read an entire draft of this book, part of an ongoing conversation that extends back as far as I can remember. Annika and Kira are especially brave, and they taught both of their parents quite a bit about the virtues of resilience and flexibility in response to the challenges of travel and dislocation. And finally, this book is dedicated to Heather, whose spirit of adventure and curiosity has inspired not just this book but so much more in our shared lives.

Portions of this work appeared as part of an article titled "The Soviet State as Imperial Scavenger: 'Catch Up and Surpass' in the Transnational Socialist Bloc, 1950–1960," published in February 2011 in the *American Historical Review*. I would like to thank the editor of the journal for permission to include the relevant material from the article in this book. The illustrations are reproduced with the permission of the Russian State Economic Archive and the State Archive of the Russian Federation in Moscow. In the text and the notes, the transliterations from Chinese conform to the pinyin system, and those from Russian follow the Library of Congress system, except in the case of a few names that are generally familiar to English readers (for example, Mikoyan rather than Mikoian).

The following abbreviations are used throughout the book.

AUS-VN	Armádního uměleckého souboru Víta Nejedlého (Víta Nejedlého Army Cultural Group)
CC	Central Committee
CCP	Chinese Communist Party
GDR	German Democratic Republic
GMD	Guomindang
GUES	Glavnoe upravlenie po vneshnim ekonomicheskim sviaziam soveta ministrov (Main Administration of External Economic Ties of the Soviet of Ministers)
OKSD	Obshchestvo kitaisko-sovetskoi druzhby (Society for Chinese-Soviet Friendship)
OVS	Otdel vneshnikh snoshenii (Department of External Relations)
PLA	People's Liberation Army
SEV	Sovet ekonomicheskoi vzaimopomoshchi (Committee on Economic Mutual Assistance)
SSOD	Soiuz sovetskikh obshchestv druzhby (Union of Soviet Friendship Societies)
VOKS	Vsesoiuznoe obshchestvo kul'turnoi sviazi s zagranitsei (All-Union Society for Cultural Relations with Foreign Countries)

THE **SINO-SOVIET** ALLIANCE

The Imperial Question Transformed

The Socialist Bloc as International History

At the present time the [Chinese] government is experiencing an
extraordinarily large need for civilian cadres, which we have not
been able to meet because of the circumstances of the war.
—Liu Shaoqi to Nikolai V. Ros chin, October 1949

[The Chinese are suspicious of us because] the Chinese people
suffered more than 100 years from foreign imperialism and therefore
distrust foreigners, and because . . . the people do not understand
the nature of the Soviet Union, not understanding the fundamentals
of the new type of relations among socialist countries.
—Nikolai G. Sudarikov to Nikolai T. Fedorenko et al., February 1958

Pavel Iudin and the Soviet Empire in Eurasia

Soviet ambassador to China Pavel Iudin liked to talk, usually about obscure
matters of Marxist theory and history. In part this was his job, as before he became ambassador he was well known within the bloc for his expertise in matters of official ideology and the related question of potential deviation from official ideology. He enjoyed the patronage of Joseph Stalin and Andrei Zhdanov
through the 1930s and 1940s as he worked for the Central Committee (CC),
directed the Institute of Red Professors, and served on the editorial board of
the theoretical journal *Bol'shevik*. Zhdanov, of course, was the presenter of
the famous "two-camp" speech to describe the developing Cold War at the
Cominform conference in Poland in September 1947, and Iudin remained his
close assistant until his death in 1948. Iudin's career in sensitive Belgrade, where
he edited the Cominform newspaper *For Lasting Peace, For People's Democracy*,
presumably prepared him well for the China post, the culminating episode of
his long diplomatic career.[1]

China was simultaneously promising yet dangerous to the socialist bloc countries and their many advisers who worked there through the 1950s. The Chinese Communist Party (CCP) had successfully combined revolution, victory in a civil war against the Guomindang (GMD) and its American ally, and success in the struggle against the invading Japanese. Their victory in 1949 and the signing of the Treaty of Friendship, Alliance, and Mutual Assistance with the Soviet Union in February 1950 placed China squarely in the world of socialist bloc exchange and collaboration, and subject to a vast advising program. Unlike the Central and Eastern European parties, the CCP was not beholden to the Soviet Union, or dependent on the successes of the Red Army. The Chinese communists had substantial Soviet support, especially in the Northeast, but their experience left them feeling far more confident about the indigenous sources of their revolution than did their Eastern and Central European counterparts. Could Chairman Mao be trusted? In 1956, Iudin conceded to Mao himself that rumors about him as a "Chinese Tito" were common in 1950.[2] This was a sensitive charge, of course, as it raised a host of issues pertaining to insubordination and betrayal that were politically unacceptable in the early years of a Cold War struggle that demanded bloc "unity" against the "imperialist" threat. Iudin's role was to ensure that this difficult history would not be repeated, and in part the task at hand was perceived to be one of maintaining Marxist-Leninist ideology. Before he became ambassador, Iudin was in China in 1950 and 1951 working on the production, publication, and translation of Mao's *Collected Works*.[3]

Preoccupied with Marxism-Leninism, the Soviet ambassador was oblivious to a heritage of empire in Russian history that continued to complicate relations within the supposedly new world of socialism. Iudin was characteristic of a confident and even arrogant Soviet officialdom in the bloc, and his long theoretical digressions illustrated a Soviet obliviousness to the contemporary events that mattered in China.[4] Most essential to the Chinese was the very history of European colonialism that Iudin even in his personal life was unable to address. Longtime embassy official V. P. Fedotov described the appointment of Iudin, the "well-known philosopher and academic," as a "colossal mistake." He was excessively preoccupied with rank and hierarchy in a way that reminded the Chinese of precisely what bothered them about the Soviet system. Iudin the "Soviet baron," recalls Fedotov, had expectations about service and servants that impressed even European colleagues in China.[5]

Such a bearing was likely to bother the Chinese, whose long struggle against European colonialism was fresh in the minds of builders of the new revolutionary state. This was the central issue of modern Chinese history, and the rise of the CCP was one aspect of the broader response to years of frustration marked by losses to the British in the Opium Wars, the French and the British jointly from 1856 to 1860, the French in 1884, and the Japanese in 1894–95. In response, reformers sought to transform traditional China so it could compete with more advanced foreign powers and end an era of poverty, backwardness, and national humiliation.[6] China is in "imminent peril," warned scholar Kang Youwei in a discussion of the "Society for the Study of Self-Strengthening." "The Russians are spying on us from the north and the English are peeping at us on the west; the French are staring at us from the south and the Japanese are watching us in the east."[7] The slogan to "save the nation [*jiuguo*]" first emerged in the wake of the concessions granted Japan in 1895, and anti-Japanese frustration and sentiment was further inflamed by the Twenty-One Demands presented by the Japanese in 1915. The May Fourth Movement (named for the student demonstrations in Beijing on 4 May 1919), gave voice to numerous radical sentiments in culture, personal life, and politics but above all emerged from the competition between China and the outside world, and the related dilemma of foreign imperialism in China.[8] Reformers, nationalists, and revolutionaries, among them Kang Youwei, Liang Qichao, Sun Yatsen, Jiang Jieshi (Chiang Kai-shek), Chen Duxiu, and Mao Zedong, shared a belief in the necessity of a Chinese "awakening" that would end the special privileges and concessions enjoyed by the imperial powers and restore China to its rightful place in the world.[9] Socialist bloc advising, or the system of *komandirovka* (work-related travel) that serves as the background to this book, was but the most recent episode in China's long history of unequal interaction with foreign powers.[10]

Like many other Soviet officials and advisers in China, Iudin believed Soviet experience and revolutionary internationalism made the painful history of European colonialism irrelevant. In early 1955, in total seriousness, Iudin approached Chinese foreign minister Zhou Enlai about the absence in Lüshun (Port Arthur) of a monument to General Stepan Makarov, the prerevolutionary explorer and conqueror of the Russian Far East. The Soviets after all, had placed a large statue of Makarov prominently looking over the bay in Vladivostok, which still stands today.[11] That Iudin could be so insensitive about such symbolism in a strategically valuable warm-water port, historically host to Russian rivalry with the Japanese over control over Northeast China, is astonishing. The question of Soviet influence in the Northeast was highly sensitive, yet alone coupled with a tendentious and explicit reference to a prerevolutionary Russian conqueror of the Far East. The Soviets were reluctant to part with strategic ports such as Lüshun and Dalian, as well as the Changchun Railway, in both the 1945 and 1950 treaty arrangements with the Guomindang and the CCP, and Chinese domestic critics were quick to remind the CCP of this sensitive history.[12] As Peng Zhen confided to Soviet ambassador A. S. Paniushkin in January 1953: "A majority of the intelligentsia in China openly refer to the Soviet Union as imperialist," he said, "asking things like, why until now has the Chinese Changchun Railway been the property of the Soviet Union."[13] Even party members in the immediate wake of the revolution posed the question, "Is the Soviet Union an imperialist power or not?" Scholar and professor Chen Haoling, with five children in the CCP, was representative of numerous Chinese intellectuals in his awareness of the many "predatory acts on the part of the USSR."[14]

As Serhii Plokhy puts it in his recent study of the Yalta Conference, Soviet leaders acquired gains and privileges that the "tsars could only have dreamed of."[15] The Soviets were remarkably direct with GMD officials after 1945, eager to maintain not just access to ice-free ports in China but also control over property and industrial equipment left by the retreating Japanese ("war trophies"), buildings in Shenyang (Mukden), resources, and railroads.[16] GMD foreign minister Wang Shijie pleaded with the Soviets to be more sensitive to the "psychology of the Chinese people," who after all were only recently "liberated from foreign oppression."[17] Resource exploitation was the norm in the war, however, and the Soviets behaved in a way similar to the Axis powers that preceded them.[18] After 1945 in the Northeast, Soviet officials carefully studied and translated materials concerning the Japanese export of resources and goods from the region in the 1930s.[19] In Central Europe the situation was "catastrophic," reported a Czech official about the activities of the Red Army in 1945, a "deleterious influence on the economy, legal system, schools, and everything else in the region."[20] The Russians clearly did not possess a vision of future productivity for the region and routinely rejected German, Czech, and Polish requests to allow trade, exchange, and other measures to revive the economy.[21]

Wartime practices shaped the early history of the socialist bloc. The "joint" or "mixed" companies (*smeshchannye obshchestva*) were designed to facilitate the continuing expropriation of resources from the region that began in the form of reparations and war "trophies." The companies facilitated, for example, the exploitation of oil ("Sovrompetrol"), uranium ("Sovromquartz"), and metals ("Sovrommetal") in Romania; bauxite, aluminum, the oil-refining industries, and coal mining in Hungary; metals and civil aviation in Bulgaria; and uranium and coal mining in the German Democratic Republic (GDR).

In most of these cases, the companies were administering former German assets and German-run companies, meaning that these early Soviet institutions were a direct outgrowth of the earlier expropriation of "war trophies" and the ongoing collection of reparations. In Hungary this included more than 200 former German firms, including 82 devoted to mining and manufacturing. In Germany itself the Soviets established 31 such firms to exploit the resources and productivity of 119 German plants and factories.[22] The enterprises, as the term suggested, were presumably collaborative and joint-owned; representatives from the bloc country and the Soviets together administered the business at hand. In part they were to facilitate the standardization and uniformity of production practices throughout the bloc. Industrial machinery planned and produced in one country, for example, would be interchangeable with similar goods produced in another country.[23]

The Chinese were again introduced to practices from Eastern and Central Europe. One of the smaller agreements accompanying the Treaty of Friendship, signed 27 March 1950, was the setting up of joint companies in China similar to those in Eastern and Central Europe. Firms were established to mine precious metals, minerals, and oil in Xinjiang and build and repair ships in Lüshun and Dalian.[24] While the Chinese were initially highly complicit, as Charles Kraus points out, in their willingness to take on the joint exploitation of the resources of Xinjiang in the form of companies such as the Sino-Soviet Nonferrous and Rare Metals Company and the Sino-Soviet Petroleum Company, they remained highly sensitive about Soviet interest in their country's resources. [25] Mao jokingly told Andrei Vyshinskii that he could now relax about the need to fulfill the next Five-Year Plan, as China's contribution of resources would make the difference.[26] He continued to make pointed references to Soviet interests in resource extraction in places such as Xinjiang and the Northeast through the spring of 1950.[27] Translator Li Yueran recalls a pushy exchange between Soviet advisers and Bo Yibo: "Can't you get [Chinese officials at the joint companies] to hurry up [the shipment of tin]?[28] Zhou Enlai and Wang Jiaxiang in vain pushed for the right at least to tax the materials and resources sent to the Soviet Union.[29]

The early history of the bloc centered on reparations, the Soviet exploitation of resources, and security and political arrangements designed to protect against the revival of Germany, and only gradually did Soviet officials more carefully consider the possibilities of exchange and cooperation. The reparation payments were reduced by 50 percent for Bulgaria, Hungary, and Romania in 1948, for East Germany in 1950, and eventually eliminated for Hungary,

Poland, Romania, and Germany in the early 1950s.[30] The Soviet zone in Germany was on its way to becoming the GDR. The nature of future bloc collaboration, however, was far from clear, and tension between needs of the local or national economies versus the broader needs of the bloc persisted throughout the entire socialist era. In these early years it was not even clear if the bloc had much of a collaborative purpose, beyond these exploitive measures designed to serve Soviet security and economic needs. There was not a central coordinating plan to industrial development or sufficient attention to the regulation of foreign trade, exchange rates, and intrabloc exchange generally, which was ironic in a system that glorified economic planning.

Recent scholarship on international history fittingly explores the geopolitical dimensions to the conclusion of the war and the early Cold War, as well as the heritage of the Russian empire.[31] Contemporary scholars from mainland China especially emphasize the imperial dimensions to Soviet foreign policy. Chinese scholars direct attention to the enduring Soviet willingness to sacrifice China's interest for the sake of the broader struggle against America and its new ally, Japan, the Soviets' manipulation of the terms of the 14 August 1945 Treaty of Mutual Alliance with the GMD that accompanied the Yalta agreements, and their determination to acquire territory such as the Kurile Islands and southern Sakhalin Island.[32] Stalin's primary objective, argues Xue Xiantian along with many other Chinese historians, was "the continuation and development of tsarist Russian policy" in Xinjiang and the Chinese Northeast.[33] Port Arthur for the Russians resembled the ports at Vladivostok and Sovgavan', which facilitated trade in the East, served as defense against the Japanese, and facilitated access to the Pacific and the important natural resources of Sakhalin and Kamchatka.[34] The Chinese knew how to reassure the Soviets on this score, which became a way to emphasize their own value to the Soviets. When Peng Zhen was in the Soviet Union in October 1956, coinciding with the precarious "events" unfolding in Poland and Hungary that fall, he exclaimed, "The Far East is secure, as China is a reliable friend to the Soviet Union."[35]

The domestic Soviet situation was equally as unpromising. The problem of empire was evident within the Soviet Union and the broader bloc, and the two issues were related. The Soviet Union "projected itself as a postimperial form of power," notes Mark R. Beissinger, "a civic multinational state that aimed to transcend national oppression in the name of class solidarity."[36] Nikita Khrushchev spoke with enthusiasm in a *Pravda* article of 27 March 1959 about the future emergence of a "single world system of the socialist economy" and the disappearance of state borders: "In all likelihood only ethnic borders will

Chinese youth observe the sculpture *Ninochka* in the Hall of Culture Soviet exhibit in Beijing, 1954. (RGAE f. 635, op. 1, d. 291, l. 350b.)

survive for a time and even these will probably exist only as a convention. Naturally these frontiers, if they can be called frontiers at all, will have no border guards, customs officials, or incidents."[37] This vision grew out of the multinational community of the Soviet Union itself, marked by the conventions of the nation (republics, cultures, flags, literary heroes) but supposedly moving toward the socialist future of a world without nations. "As all nations become equal and their lives are constructed on a single socialist foundation . . . the borders between the union republics within the boundaries of the USSR more and more lose their former significance," explained nationalities theorist M. S. Dzhunusov in a history journal in 1963.[38]

In practice, however, Soviet nationalities policy as well as many other policies could hardly serve as a model for the bloc. The emergence of Russian culture as "the most progressive culture" and Russia as the "first among equals" within the Soviet Union was well-established by the time the bloc emerged in the postwar era. As Terry Martin explains, by 1938 the notion of the "Friendship of Peoples [*druzhba narodov*]" had become the "officially sanctioned metaphor of an imagined multinational community," in part as a consequence of the failures and dilemmas of the "affirmative action empire" established as a result of Lenin's version of Wilsonian national self-determination. Russia,

Russian culture, and the Russian Republic played the decisive role in maintaining the "friendship of peoples." "Indeed, great and mighty is the language of Pushkin and Turgenev, Tolstoi and Gorky," proclaimed the newspaper *Uchitelskaia gazeta* in 1938.[39] The model of Russia as the "leading people" of the socialist world, eventually contested in the Soviet Union itself, was even more unlikely in the competitive world of intrabloc exchange and relations.

The heritage of the Russian past continued to shape the Soviet Union. Typically, this did not deter Pavel Iudin, who enthusiastically told Chinese officials of numerous episodes and events in Soviet history suitable for emulation by China.[40] Before Chairman Mao in July 1955, Iudin tried to put into perspective the activities of Gao Gang, the ambitious Politburo member and leader of the Chinese Northeast who was purged in February 1954 for "conspiratorial activities" and forming an "anti-Party alliance."[41] Gao Gang "never actively suggested merging [*sblizhenie*] with us," Iudin tried to reassure Mao.[42] The use of the term itself is telling. In the nineteenth-century Russian empire, "merging" was a common notion entailing the ethnic assimilation of the non-Russian peoples by the presumably superior Russians. The term was also, perhaps more ominously, used by imperial state-builders to describe the administrative incorporation of frontier regions and their institutions into the general system of administration from St. Petersburg. Iudin was not a proponent of "merging," of course, but that the topic was on the minds of both Russians and Chinese in the 1950s points to the limitations of a Soviet model inevitably shaped by the heritage of the Russian empire. Zhou Enlai suggested as much in a May 1956 exchange with Iudin, reminding him of the potentially dangerous implications of Russia's past: "Russia was an imperialist country, a country that exploited other nationalities."[43]

The transformative promise of the Marxist-Leninist tradition contributed to the problem of empire, as it suggested to both the Chinese and the Soviets that the Soviet presence in China by definition was not and could not be imperialistic. For the Soviets, the new concepts associated with socialism even contributed to the eventual deterioration of the relationship, as Soviet assumptions about their perpetually progressive project left their representatives in China—diplomats, instructors, advisers, professors, musicians, and others—oblivious to their own nationalistic and even chauvinistic tendencies. The definition of "friendship" was what served the needs of the bloc, including practical matters such as the control of oil, coal, the salt industry, electric power stations, chemicals, and paper production in the Northeast after 1945. "Imperialism" referred to the other side in the Cold War, a disastrous mix of

"American money, Japanese specialists, [and] Chinese soil," as embassy official V. Vas'kov put it in early 1949.[44] If Soviet aid, Soviet programs, and even Soviet behavior were all by definition inspired by "internationalism," how could they possibly stand accused of what Mao and others eventually referred to as "great-power hegemony [daguozhuyi]" and "chauvinism [shawenzhuyi]"? Among "friends" in the bloc the Soviets could do no wrong, as the Soviet Union was by definition the center and foundation of the broader collaborative effort to oppose imperialism and capitalism. Both of the great powers of the twentieth century, the United States and the USSR, promoted their own values and customs abroad in a way that reminded the rest of the world of nineteenth-century colonialism.[45] In Soviet foreign policy, even the use of these terms was hopelessly compromised. An "internationalist," noted Stalin in 1927, "is one who, unreservedly, without wavering, without conditions is ready to defend the USSR."[46]

China's Transformation of the Imperial Question

The makers of the alliance associated imperialism with the West and especially the Americans, even as the experience of socialist bloc collaboration suggested otherwise. The Chinese temporarily chose to ignore the accumulating evidence of Russian imperialism. Mao himself famously swallowed his pride during the uncomfortable exchanges surrounding the negotiation of the new Sino-Soviet treaty in Moscow in December–January 1949–50.[47] "Lean to one side" (the decision to ally with the Soviet Union in the Cold War) did not signify a close relationship with one of the powers that formerly extracted special concessions and rights from China but instead was a decision "to stand against the imperialist camp," as Liu Shaoqi wrote to Stalin in the summer of 1949.[48] The revolution and the new alliance was supposedly the culmination of this long struggle, the successful resolution of China's "some 100-year opposition to imperialism."[49] CCP officials repeatedly emphasized publicly the meaning and significance of socialism and related concepts such as "internationalism" and "friendship" that shaped the relationship with the Soviet Union, and the supposed transformative promise of Marxism proved useful to this effort. The October Revolution "changed everything," declared a Renmin ribao editorial in October 1949; the Soviet Union under its own initiative revoked the privileges once held by tsarist Russia.[50] New Friendship Society branches throughout the country went to considerable effort to clarify and explain the nature of the Soviet advising program. "Why does the Soviet Union help the Chinese people?" was a topic for public discussion at exhibits and discussions sponsored by the Friendship Society in Shenyang.[51] The Soviets could be trusted to be "faithful" and reliable friends to China, a "most intimate friend," argued Guo Moruo, who generously shared their own resources and expected nothing in return.[52]

Everything about the socialist bloc (its currency, centralized planning, the training of specialists, housing for workers, employment practices, and access to culture, leisure, and consumerism) was supposedly an improvement on the practices and norms found in the West.[53] This new world, incomprehensible to "people with old bourgeois views," supposedly even redefined international relations, or the world of traditional diplomacy characterized by imperialism, coercion, exploitation, and a multitude of other sins. The future of the socialist bloc was a world of "internationalism," declared Liu Shaoqi on 5 October 1949, shaped by "people of a completely new type, until this time unknown to history."[54] The agreements that initiated socialist bloc exchange were themselves understood not as traditional state treaties but as programs outlining the future course of "Friendship." A familiar propaganda mural in both the Soviet Union and China showed Joseph Stalin, Mao Zedong, and their happy witnesses at the signing of the 14 February 1950 Treaty of Friendship and Mutual Aid. Traditional "international relations" belonged to the past, or to the West. Deng Xiaoping noted this distinction between diplomatic work among socialists versus relations with the broader world in a discussion with Soviet ambassador Stepan V. Chervonenko in 1959. "Diplomacy" itself referred to exchange with the capitalist world. "Of course, for us it is not diplomacy but party work," he explained. "[Ambassador] Liu Xiao in Moscow also is not engaged in diplomacy but is conducting party work. Iudin in Beijing for us also was not a diplomat but was in party work."[55] For the Soviets, this distinction explained away the continuing Chinese fears of Soviet "imperialism" in China. The critics were ignorant of the "nature of the Soviet Union, not understanding the fundamentals of the new type of relations among socialist countries."[56] The Marxist-Leninist heritage encouraged the Soviets to ignore and discount their critics, and encouraged the Chinese wishfully to believe the Soviet presence in China was by definition divorced from the history of colonialism.[57]

The promise of socialist bloc collaboration and the mission of the advising program intersected with China's vast needs in the wake of war and revolutionary struggle. The ruling parties of the Soviet Union and China shared a vision common to developing societies ruled by ambitious state-builders determined to overcome archaic social structures, a history of agrarian poverty, and the

The Signing of the Treaty of Friendship, Alliance, and Mutual Assistance, 14 February 1950, mural. (RGAE f. 635, op. 1, d. 409, l. 110b.)

consequences of war and social breakdown. "Thirty-two years ago, imperial Russia was a backward country," noted Liu Shaoqi soon after the founding of the PRC, but Soviet Russia had proven capable of countering threats from the "imperialists" and "reactionaries" who now opposed China.[58] The Soviets were also a model in the matter of reconstruction in the wake of the devastation brought by war, again germane to Chinese needs in 1949. Wang Jiaxiang, who became China's first ambassador to the Soviet Union, developed this theme upon his arrival at the Moscow train station in late October 1949.[59] Soon after, he emphasized to Ministry of Foreign Affairs official Andrei Gromyko that "the Soviet Union is China's teacher, [and] Chinese people should become pupils of the Soviet people."[60] The ambassador was drawing on the ideas of Chairman Mao himself.[61] China was eager to benefit quickly, Liu Shaoqi wrote Stalin, from the "excellent organizational work of the experts," or the many advisers who quickly came from the Soviet Union and most of the socialist bloc countries to help in China's reconstruction and development.[62]

The subsequent tensions and spectacular polemics characteristic of the early 1960s make it easy to forget the shared challenges and goals faced by postrevolutionary state-builders in countries such as the Soviet Union and China.[63] Officials of the Beijing Municipal Administration, for example, were significantly inspired by their counterparts in Moscow, evident still today in spite of the extraordinary changes of the past two decades. Delegations from Beijing went to Moscow to study urban planning, the water supply system, housing for workers, transportation, parks, educational systems, museums, hospitals and preventive medicine, architecture, socialist realist painting, propaganda, and numerous other areas. They were impressed by recently created working-class districts, educational programs for workers linked to the experience of factory production, and a city plan already completed for the upcoming year.[64] "Backwardness" was a real concept to state planners and educated people in the Soviet Union and China, and they constructed vast pedagogical societies designed to address a problem that to their minds was obvious and evident even in everyday forms of culture and behavior.

Red Experts

The socialist bloc advisers on *komandirovka* in China ultimately looked to reproduce themselves, and they found many enthusiastic Chinese state-builders eager for help in the making of a new Chinese elite. Russians and Chinese shared a belief in the crucial importance of a technically trained, politically reliable, and empowered technical intelligentsia to the process of state-building and social transformation. Young "red experts," in tune with the technological and education achievements of the West but not shaped by the traditions, values, and generally Western orientation of the old prerevolutionary intelligentsias, were crucial figures in the centrally planned economies of the socialist bloc. They provided not only knowledge and expertise but also leadership and guidance to societies perceived by the state to be in need of transformation from above. Their role extended to matters of culture, propriety, and behavior, where guidance as well was required to facilitate the dissemination of culture and new socialist values to the broader and less educated population. Both regimes endlessly exhorted their new intelligentsias to new discoveries and accomplishments in natural science, technology, and industrial production. Stalin even encouraged the East Germans to address the problem of their "brain drain" to West Germany by creating a reliable technical intelligentsia.[65]

In the reproduction of a new and politically reliable intelligentsia the Soviet aid project appeared to have a clear purpose. Help in the development of "national cadres" throughout the bloc was a common Soviet justification for the bloc's very existence, "one of the concrete forms of the multifaceted and selfless aid" rendered by the Soviet Union to the "fraternal" countries and then also to its new allies in the postcolonial world.[66] One of the primary purposes of the Soviet-bloc advisers on *komandirovka* in China was ultimately to contribute to the Chinese reproduction of their own administrative elite, which again would aid in the struggle to compete with the Americans. The appeal of the accomplishments of Soviet science "beyond the borders of our Motherland" was an especially crucial matter in the ever-present business of "catch up and surpass," wrote A. Mizerov in a Vladivostok newspaper in 1951.[67] By 1962 A. I. Arnol'dov claimed success in the formation of new intelligentsias throughout the bloc: "bourgeois scholars," he claimed, now hoped to "catch up" to the USSR in the "area of the preparation of specialists and in a variety of crucial areas in science and technology."[68]

Chinese officials were genuinely grateful and serious about the significance of Soviet support for their efforts to develop their own technical intelligentsia throughout the 1950s, and even in the early 1960s they continued to hope for the continuation of this aspect of the exchange. Liu Shaoqi and other Chinese leaders often pushed for more Soviet specialists and were not shy about admitting to the "low cultural level of [our] cadres" in discussions over Soviet aid.[69] "At the present time," Liu Shaoqi told Nikolai V. Roshchin in October 1949, "the [Chinese] government is experiencing an extraordinarily large need for civilian cadres, which we have not been able to meet because of the circumstances of the war."[70] Liu Shaoqi was well-known as an enthusiastic state-builder enamored with the Soviet model, but he was far from alone in this concern. Numerous Chinese officials pushed the Soviets for more rapid and significant help in this area as the dilemmas of administering the country quickly unfolded before them after October 1949.[71] Before the revolution, the situation was similar in the Chinese Northeast, where Zhou Enlai in frustration informed the Soviets that many military and party cadres were unable to operate equipment provided by the Soviet Union.[72] Chen Yun attributed Chinese inadequacies to the heritage of European colonialism, which now left "backward China, enslaved for centuries by imperial states," in need of Russian help to navigate the "vast road of socialist construction."[73]

The rural origins of Chinese communism further encouraged Chinese officials to turn to the Soviets for help in administering the vast cities of China's more developed East and South. Some of the new communist officials recently arrived from the Northeast were perceived as "tactless, and sometimes even crude," Professor Chen Haoling informed P. Shibaev in September 1949.[74] Liu Shaoqi described for Roshchin illiteracy rates of some 70–80 percent among cadres within the Communist Party from the "poor peasantry."[75] Officials throughout the Chinese bureaucracy made their case for Soviet help in their diverse areas of expertise. Ministry of Foreign Affairs official Huang Hua looked to train new diplomats for the foreign affairs bureaucracy who were not from the "petty and middle bourgeoisie," Ambassador Wang Jiaxiang wondered how China would even staff its embassies and consulates, General Zhang Zhizhong complained about similar problems in the financial sector, and Feng Wenbing of the New Democratic Union of Youth of China described a "severe shortage of cadres from among the youth."[76] Numerous officials in Xinjiang pushed their counterparts in Beijing for more trained cadres and hoped to increase Soviet Central Asian emigration to their region.[77] Here was an area where Soviet administrative and managerial experience seemed like a perfect fit for China's needs as it faced the work of reconstruction and development after 1949.

The Chinese made a similar plea for Soviet help in military-related industrial enterprises. Chinese embassy official He Zhangguang, military attaché Qi He, trade official Xiang Zeming, and others expressed their gratitude for Soviet support in aviation, the navy, heavy industry, automobile production, and the military during their trip to the Soviet Union in February 1951.[78] Zhu De described for V. V. Kuznetsov in April 1953 a "serious deficiency" in the "lack of qualified cadres" in key areas of military production such as aviation and tank production.[79] General Zhang Zhizhong had been making a similar case to Soviet colleagues beginning in the fall of 1949.[80] As late as 1957, People's Liberation Army (PLA) officials at an Artillery Academy adopted the traditional manner of presenting and explaining their urgent requests for help: "We still do not have any experience." In this case, Chinese pilots were being injured and even killed during training exercises.[81]

The new state-builders also viewed their inherited technical and scientific intelligentsias with a suspicion that was often mutual. The "mood" and orientation of most of China's cadres in science, industry, and culture, complained Guo Muruo to N. V. Roshchin in 1952, was "strongly pro-American and pro-English."[82] Chen Yun similarly described some 20,000 engineers who were "reactionary, and pro-American" in their political views, especially in the financial and banking sectors. Sixty-two of the seventy engineers at the crucial Anshan Steel Factory in Manchuria were Japanese, "hostile to the Chinese in general and especially to the Chinese communists."[83] L. Kutakov, a teacher for two years at the Beijing Diplomatic Institute of the Ministry of Foreign Affairs, still in July 1957 complained that Chinese intellectuals continued to rely on "bourgeois" authors and "international bourgeois information" for insight into international relations and global affairs.[84] As Peng Zhen put it, the "majority of the technical intelligentsia received their education in the USA [and] formally agree with Soviet methods of work, but in fact do not support [these methods]."[85] The party had to devote enormous efforts to "ideological reeducation," he explained to Soviet ambassador A. S. Paniushkin.[86] Peng Zhen held out more hope for the younger generation and the prospect of their proper education and orientation to the building of a new China. In a much more extreme way, this became part of Chairman Mao's tragic vision during the later Cultural Revolution.

The advising program in China grew out of the existing military collaboration in the Northeast before the revolution, and the effort to reconstruct the Changchun Railway. The group that traveled to the Soviet Union in June 1949 to develop more concrete plans for the future collaborative projects was led by Liu Shaoqi, head of the North China Bureau of the Politburo from 1948, Gao Gang, the head of the Chinese Northeast, and Wang Jiaxiang, the future ambassador to the Soviet Union. They procured $300 million in credit from the Soviet Union, at the favorable rate of 1 percent interest over five years, and returned to China with a Soviet contingent of 50 engineers, 52 technicians, and 220 advisers in administration, finance, transportation, education, law, culture, and other areas, headed by Stalin's important envoy, Ivan Kovalev.[87] The initial arrangement called for the Soviet Union to provide assistance in 50 different construction projects. In March 1953 another 91 Soviet aid projects were announced, followed by another 15 in October 1954, for a total of 156 projects over the period of the First Five-Year Plan. Anastas Mikoyan announced an additional 55 projects during his trip to Beijing in April 1956, and eventually the exchange included 256 industrial projects altogether.[88]

The 156 initial projects host to bloc advisers included enormous factories and excavation projects in iron and steel (7), nonferrous metals (14), electric power stations (24), industrial and agricultural machinery (63), coal (27), oil (2), chemicals (5), and other industries. Huge joint efforts included the tungsten plant in Anyang, a tin combine in Kochiu (Yunnan province), aluminum and shale processing plants in Fushun, and the Changjiang (Yangtze) Bridge at Wuhan. Harbin possessed new factories dedicated to aluminum, electrical engineering, turbine manufacturing, and boiler manufacturing. There were huge steel plants in Anshan and Wuhan.[89] Well-known projects included the Harbin Flax Factory, which was the largest linen mill in the country; Xian Electrical, a heavy electrical equipment plant; Luoyang No. 1 in Henan province, the largest tractor factory in the country; and Luoyang Bearing Plant, the largest ball-bearing plant in China.[90] The Shanghai Diesel Factory and the

Shanghai State Factory of Electrical Equipment were collaborative enterprises modeled on the Soviet experience.[91] There were huge collaborative efforts between ministries dedicated to the construction of nationwide systems in industries such as communications, geological surveying, urban planning, and metallurgy. The Soviets and Chinese collaborated in the construction and operation of chemical equipment, veterinary hospitals, medical institutes, clinical hospitals, electricity stations, and radio stations.[92] Beginning his count in 1947, Zhihua Shen identifies some 20,000 Soviet advisers and experts as veterans of the China exchange, dispersed through numerous Chinese ministries and institutions.[93]

Sino-Soviet Relations

New scholarship on Sino-Soviet relations and international history, most notably from Lorenz Lüthi, Sergey Radchenko, Chen Jian, Zhihua Shen, Danhui Li, and Yafeng Xia, significantly adds to the work of an earlier generation of scholars who relied principally on newspaper accounts and official party pronouncements, or "symbolic evidence from Communist media," as Donald Zagoria put it many years ago.[94] This book draws extensively on such scholarship but is also inspired by the work of scholars of Sino-Soviet relations who have tried to broaden and enhance our notions of diplomacy and international relations in their exploration of the advisers, educational programs, cultural exchange, film, and other topics.[95] The use of adviser, embassy, and ministry reports from the lower levels of the exchange allows for a more nuanced understanding of the bloc as a transnational community. The study of bloc exchange and collaboration even complicates the very notion of "Sino-Soviet" relations. Poles, Czechoslovaks, East Germans, and Hungarians are very much part of this study of "Sino-Soviet" relations, suggesting that, at least for the 1950s, the idea of "Soviet foreign policy" was itself problematic. This book describes a regular and complicated series of exchanges between the Central Europeans and the Chinese. Each side, for different reasons, was very interested in the other. In part all these countries were struggling with the curious position of the Soviet Union, the heir to the backward Russian empire that in the twentieth century was somehow the "leading people" in a vast alliance that stretched from Berlin to Hanoi. The focus on the lower-level dimensions of Sino-Soviet collaboration illustrates emerging tensions and frustrations that made cooperation unlikely over the longer term and explains basic impediments to

Nikita Khrushchev and Zhou Enlai at the opening ceremony of the Soviet exhibit in Beijing, October 1954. (RGAE f. 635, op. 1, d. 291 l. 60b.)

the "friendship" beyond changing strategic calculations, ideological disputes, or personality conflicts between Khrushchev and Mao.[96]

What the Chinese did not understand, and what they chose to describe as "revisionism," "capitulationism," and other epithets part of the later public and high-level polemics, was that the Central Europeans by the late 1950s were highly invested in the evolution of Soviet society and the broader bloc toward something different from the "scavenger" state that initially characterized the Soviet Union on its frontiers.[97] As small peoples on the edges of larger empires learn to do, the Central Europeans made a series of compromises that allowed them an important role within the socialist world. The Soviet Union was changing in the 1950s and eager to participate in international politics in a new way. It was determined to "catch up with and surpass" America in the numerous forms of competition that made up the Cold War, which included consumerism, standards of living, and related areas foreign to the historical experience of backward Russia.[98] The Central Europeans turned out to be crucial to the overall project of "catch up with and surpass." They welcomed the transformation of the bloc and were determined to carve out space for themselves to develop their consumer economies, trade with the West, acquire technology and industrial expertise, and honor and cultivate their many links to European cultural tradition. The Czechoslovaks, as they liked to remind the Soviets, had long played an important role as a "bridge" to Europe, and there were numerous other such voices from the region.[99] The Central Europeans were threatened in this effort by the prospect of outright opposition to Soviet rule, of course, and hence the example of Yugoslavia, the instability of 1956, and eventually the direction of China from the fall of 1958 were all dangerous matters that threatened the position they carefully maintained within the bloc.

The Chinese were highly interested in the Central Europeans as well, for other reasons. Central European technological expertise and industrial development was no secret to the Chinese, and they hoped to benefit, as the Soviets did, from greater access to this world. "Your military technology and training is modern," Chinese defense minister Peng Dehuai told visiting Poles in 1957.[100] The Chinese especially valued Czechoslovak and East German industrial and technological advice, and they admired their political stability and orthodoxy in the difficult year of 1956. Chinese exposure to the practices of the Soviet Union left them sympathetic to emerging Central European claims about Soviet "great-power chauvinism," and they contributed an important voice to this debate about the advisers, industrial practices, and even Russian cultural attitudes that were all part of the background to the precarious year of 1956. As China set on its own "path" toward communism, it never lost interest in potential support from the Central Europeans, even as the relationship was well past vitriolic with the Soviets. After the withdrawal of the advisers in the summer of 1960, the Chinese immediately appealed to the Central Europeans to stay and strengthen their relationship. Khrushchev's ouster in 1964 offered yet another opportunity for the Chinese to at least hope for support from the Central Europeans.

The Socialist Bloc as International History

The countries of the socialist world in the 1950s were engaged in complicated and contentious "foreign" policies with each other. They had policies, conferences, Ministries of Foreign Affairs, embassies, diplomats, and the other practices and institutions scholars of foreign policy and affairs generally study.[101] Newspaper articles and public pronouncements from communist party Central Committees and congresses, however, only hint at the much richer internal discussion and disputes that form the background for important notions such as "peaceful coexistence," diverse "paths to socialism," the "cult of personality," and so on.[102] These formulations were the final packaging and outcome of the remarkably sensitive but surprisingly candid world of intrabloc exchange and debate. In many cases dissenting voices continued to dispute and challenge policies formulated in Moscow for quite some time. The exploration of this world demands attention to sources beyond the crucial material now available in Moscow archives. This book is based on archival materials from four different countries (the Soviet Union, China, Czechoslovakia, and East Germany, three of which no longer exist), and in many cases the material pertains to other bloc countries as well. The documents come largely from Ministries of Foreign Affairs and their embassies, the Central Committees of the communist parties (which controlled the various International Departments and Liaison Departments heavily involved in bloc affairs), large industrial and cultural ministries (most of which contained specific sections on bloc exchange), and miscellaneous federal and municipal archival collections.

The socialist countries' foreign policies, toward each other and toward the broader world, cannot be studied in isolation from one another. The makers of the socialist bloc talked about this constantly—if only to clarify their mutual commitment to each other and to the virtues of what they called "internationalism," "unity," the "socialist community," or even what the East Germans liked to call the "socialist world economic system."[103] The institution of *komandirovka*, the source of many of the adviser reports useful to this study, originated in the Soviet Union, was extended to Eastern and Central Europe in the wake of the war, and was understood by its participants to exemplify the very notion of "internationalism."[104] Both the ideas and practices of socialism served as sources of integration in this transnational alliance. This book also crosses the borders of the socialist world to follow three different regional histories that turn out to be related because of the character of the socialist bloc: (1) the enduring problem of Russian imperialism, or practices and attitudes perceived by the other peoples of the bloc to be reminiscent of this history; (2) Chinese frustration with Russian imperialism, or what they and others called "great-power chauvinism," coupled with a recovering national pride over the course of the decade that resulted in a significant leadership challenge to the Soviets; and (3) the role played in China by the Central Europeans (East Germans, Poles, Czechoslovaks, and Hungarians), who had their own ambitions for the evolution of the socialist world, goals that demanded a careful compromise with the Soviet Union.

International history should be more than a reminder of the dangers of the study of foreign policy as yet another exercise in "nation-centered" exceptionalism, or an argument about the close connection between domestic and foreign policy.[105] The former issue has been especially sensitive among Americanists, while the latter issue is explored most consistently by scholars of China. Several generations of China scholars have described domestic change and its relationship to China's evolving foreign policy since 1949. Mao's primary concern in foreign policy was to "maintain and enhance the inner dynamics of the great Chinese revolution," suggests Chen Jian, which in part explains CCP motivations for both the alliance and the subsequent split.[106] The usefulness of the study of international history, however, is its promise of complicating the very history of topics and issues that we thought were well understood. The "events" in Poland and Hungary in 1956, for example, mattered in China in ways impossible to understand in depth before the opening of the archives. The Chinese estimation of what was going wrong with socialism, specifically in places like Poznan and Budapest in 1956 but then more generally in the entire bloc and the Soviet Union itself, provides the context and background for the unfolding of key events in Chinese domestic history such as the Hundred Flowers campaign, the subsequent "antirightist" movement, and the Socialist Education Movement.[107] Some scholars prefer the related term of "transnational" history to describe this method of exploring themes, motifs, movements, and people that cross borders. "The claim of transnational methods," suggests Isabel Hofmeyr, "is not simply that historical processes are made in different places but they are constructed in the movement between places, sites, and regions."[108] The socialist bloc, then, did not just feature the same problems unfolding simultaneously in different countries (the leadership cult, reform, methods of socialist construction, etc.); rather, these issues and their history were a product of this interconnected community. They are only comprehensible when studied in this transnational or international context. Other matters, such as the debate over consumerism and standards of living, also a matter of contention between the Soviet and Chinese communist parties, intersected with the world of the opposing "camp" in the Cold War.[109]

Soviet history and foreign policy deserve similar attention. The vision of socialism, the "camp," and the American threat important to former foreign minister and Politburo member Viacheslav Molotov complicated the efforts of reformers such as Nikita Khrushchev, and the communist parties of the broader bloc were very much involved and invested in the outcome of these endeavors. The Chinese were engaged in intense and focused discussions with all the bloc parties on matters such as the interpretation of Stalin and his rule, and a running dialogue on this and numerous other issues endured through the early 1960s.[110] The issue is not just that again, as in China, domestic and foreign policy were interconnected, or that there was an enduring "China factor" in Soviet politics and culture, as Georgi Arbatov noted.[111] The bloc itself was a transnational community that complicated the making of the foreign policy of any one particular state, and even proclaimed the end of traditional forms of "foreign policy," a term they reserved for the "imperialist" powers of the past and their contemporary capitalist heirs. Significant policies and innovations traditionally understood to make up the history of the Soviet Union and Soviet foreign policy (peaceful coexistence, de-Stalinization, the suppression of reform in Hungary in 1956, etc.) cannot be studied without attention to the broader dimensions of a socialist bloc which importantly included China. The recent work of Sergey Radchenko on the Sino-Soviet relationship in the 1960s illustrates this issue, for both countries. When Mao addressed Soviet ambassador Stepan Chervonenko, explains Radchenko, he was also communicating with his domestic rival, Liu Shaoqi; when Khrushchev attacked "bourgeois culture" in the Soviet Union, he was simultaneously addressing his Chinese critics, in the "spirit of Lei Feng," a CCP campaign designed to oppose Western influence and culture.[112] International history enhances our understanding of domestic topics too often studied in isolation. In the study of Russian and Eastern European history, current work on transnational influences, institutions, and experiences is simultaneously the revival and rethinking of what was once called Soviet foreign policy.[113]

The Shape of the Study: Mao's Trips to Moscow

Mao's two trips to Moscow, the only foreign trips of his life, frame the organization of this book. The first trip was the December–January 1949–50 visit, resulting eventually in the signing of the Treaty of Friendship, Alliance, and Mutual Assistance with the Soviet Union. Mao subsequently described his unease with the terms of the treaty and the tenor of the relationship, but at the time the Chinese were eager to "learn from the Soviet Union [*xuexi sulian*]," as the slogan went. The three chapters of part 1 describe the socialist bloc's advising relationship to China, with attention to its tensions, contradictions, and transnational character. The Soviets and the other bloc advisers were eager to share their advice, and the Chinese were eager to take advantage of the new possibilities of collaboration. The tensions and calculations evident even in the "honeymoon" of the relationship offer insight into the limitations of "proletarian internationalism," as chapter 1 explores. The subsequent two chapters introduce the important role of the Central Europeans in the bloc, as well as

China's effort to limit its own exposure to the consequences of socialist bloc interaction.

Part 2 offers a series of chapters on the very different climate of roughly 1956–64, characterized by a more assertive China determined to recast the character of the alliance. The "events" of 1956 (de-Stalinization and the rebellions in Poland and Hungary) form the background to this transition, as chapter 4 explores. Mao's new role and the Chinese conditional affirmation of Soviet leadership over the bloc was on display at the November 1957 International Conference of Communist Parties in Moscow, for which Mao made his second trip to the Soviet Union. Mao was proud of his role there and optimistic about the growing strength of the bloc.[114] The event was attended by sixty-four communist parties, he noted upon returning home, and some 3,300 party members from around the world, including members of the thirteen socialist parties in power in the bloc. This, of course, was the site of his well-known "east wind" reference, and he continued to communicate such confidence. The bloc now possessed a huge population, military successes in Korea and against the French in Vietnam, and Soviet technology that was supposedly superior to that of the Americans. The English had lost Pakistan and India, and soon would be overtaken by the Chinese. "I think imperialism is afraid of us," he concluded.[115] A careful equilibrium in the bloc was established in 1956–57, soon to be broken by the more radical developments in China that made up the Great Leap Forward, begun in the fall of 1958. This time socialist bloc advisers and diplomats saw little advantage to maintaining the equilibrium that affirmed China's important role in a bloc led by both the Soviets and the Chinese, and instead recoiled from the implications of the radical currents that made up the Great Leap Forward and the emergence of the people's communes. Chapter 5 draws on the raw reporting of the advisers and diplomats in China on the changes under way there beginning in 1958. Chapter 6 describes China's radical refusal to retreat from its notion of Soviet "revisionism," consistently evident in its continuing overtures to the Central Europeans and even the inhabitants of the Soviet Union. The last chapter describes the transformation of the Friendship Society by the Chinese from what was initially an organization dedicated to Russian-language study and the propagation of information about the Soviet Union to a vehicle for the propagation of Chinese views about Soviet "revisionism" and what had gone wrong with the Sino-Soviet relationship. The transformation of the institution reminds us of China's consistent ability to recast foreign traditions and ways to serve its own needs. This historical theme, along with many others, shaped the supposedly unprecedented practices that made up the world of "socialism."

One practice that did not disappear from socialist China in the 1950s was the rickshaw, symbolic of everyday European colonial privilege on the streets of China. Some of the socialist bloc advisers in China on *komandirovka* enjoyed the custom in such an ostentatious fashion that it came to the attention of the Soviet embassy in Beijing. Advisers were "behaving in a far too 'European' manner," complained an alarmed Soviet official, V. Akshinskii. They rode rickshaws, carried on loudly in restaurants and on streets such as historic Huahai Street in Shanghai, insulted Chinese service people in shops, demanded free entrance to entertainment, and so on. It is "indistinguishable whether these people are from bourgeois countries or the people's democracies," complained Akshinskii. He attributed the worst behavior to the most "European" members of the bloc, the Czechoslovaks and East Germans: "The difference between the behavior of these two groups of specialists [Russians and Czechoslovaks] is striking."[116] Russians still remained, he assumed, divorced from the history of European imperialism in a way that provided them with a special mission and purpose in Asia. Akshinskii's assumptions about a special Russian mission in China distinguishable from the predatory behavior of the West drew directly from the history of Russia on its frontier in the nineteenth century.[117] In this case, however, the misbehaving "Westerners" in China were the socialist Czechoslovaks and East Germans. Iudin was alarmed enough to bring the matter to the attention of Nikita Khrushchev, who in turn alerted high officials in both Czechoslovakia and East Germany.[118] The colonial heritage endured in China, but the Russians imagined themselves to be divorced from this history and the Chinese proved able to focus on larger goals and needs and thereby to overlook the reappearance of the rickshaw. Socialists in power perpetually talked about the creation of new societies and institutions, while the experience of socialism and the study of the three primary themes explored here (Russian imperialism, Chinese ambition, and Central European pragmatism) remind us of the continuing impact of the past.

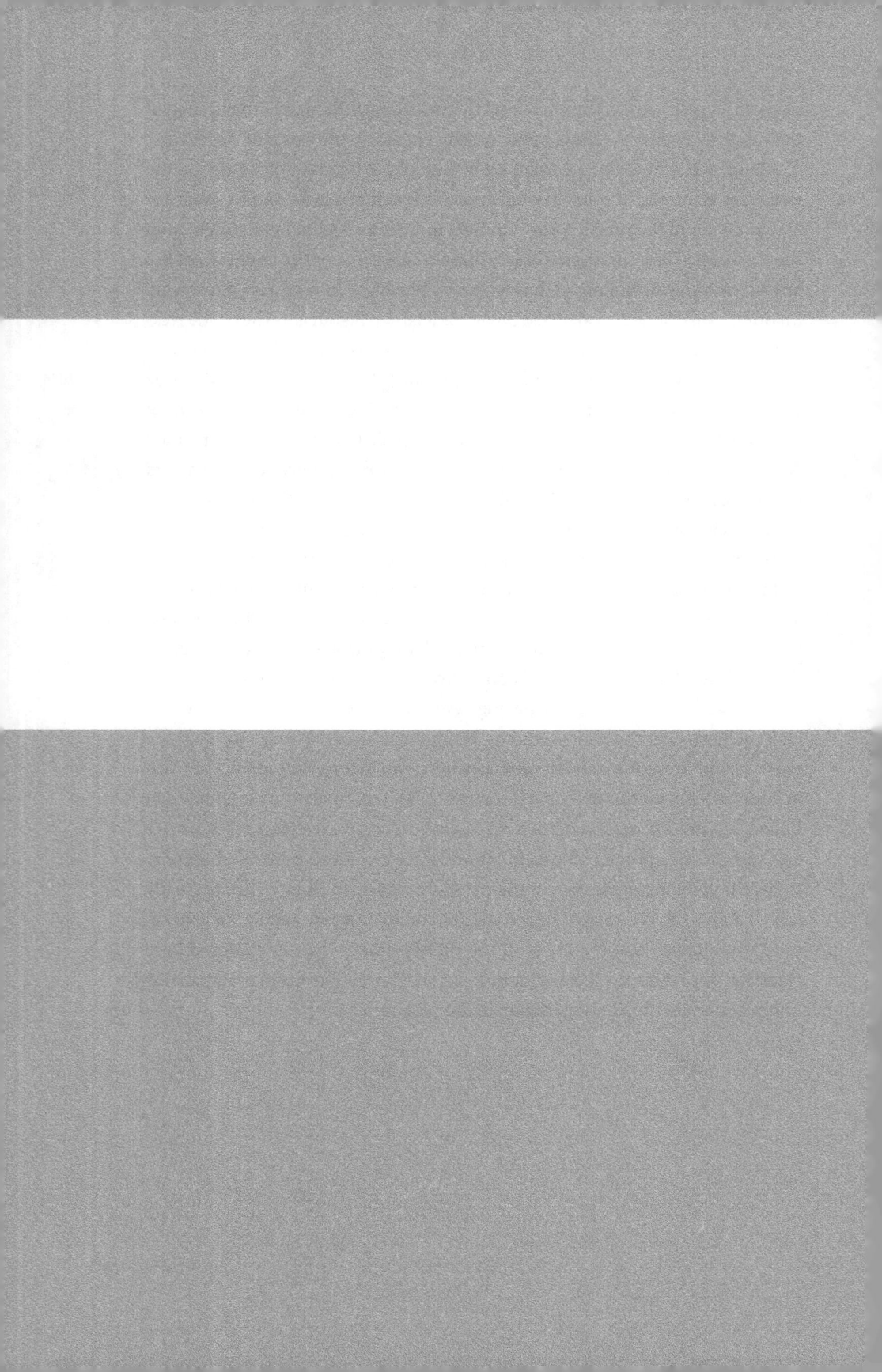

PART 1

Mao's First Visit to Moscow

December 1949–January 1950

CHAPTER 1

Proletarian Internationalism in Practice

Pay, Misbehavior, and Incentives under Socialism

Unfortunately many Muscovites do not want to understand the
simple fact that the PRC is still a young and poor republic, and that
their economic regime is not a matter of idle talk; and the voracious
eating, sleeping in luxury rooms, and traveling in the international car
at the expense of the PRC is not helping things.
—Aleksei Stozhenko to Andrei M. Chekashillo, 1956

The study of the distorted economic incentives of socialism has attracted the
attention of scholars of both the Soviet economy and intrabloc exchange.[1]
The topic is especially interesting for its striking contrast to the many public
discussions about the virtues of socialist bloc exchange, which extolled the
great accomplishments achieved by bloc "unity" in the struggle against "imperialism," the rational use of resources and people that served as a contrast to
the world of capitalism, and the virtues of new forms of consumption and economic activities. This chapter ignores the grandiose claims about socialism and
instead explores the messy and contested business of adviser pay and behavior,
Soviet ministerial practices, disputes over contracts, and related matters in
China. New archival materials, largely in this case from Moscow, also offer
insight into disputes over resources, such as the transfer of blueprints from
the bloc to China, that constituted an important part of the advising program.

All of these issues illuminate Chinese frustration with the exchange and the
supposedly "selfless" Soviet aid. Colonial inequality and Chinese sensitivity
to it again inform the background to the disputes and frustrations described
here. The Chinese were far from simply victimized, however. The issue of blueprints, for example, reminds us of Chinese duplicity about their own role in
the relationship, and hypocrisy concerning their own frequent rhetoric about
"self-reliance." The straightforward copying of blueprints is tempting for a less
developed society struggling to modernize—why not just import the entire

industrial product and skip the process of indigenous development? As the discussion of the Changchun Automobile Factory suggests, their claims to "self-reliance" notwithstanding, numerous Chinese industrial officials active in intrabloc exchange expected to use the socialist bloc advising program in this way for their own benefit. The everyday practices and experiences of bloc exchange were far removed from the many sentimental proclamations about the virtues of "proletarian internationalism" and socialist bloc "unity" against "imperialism."

Komandirovka as a Transnational Institution

The system of komandirovka (work-related travel, or the dispersal of advisers throughout the bloc) was interestingly similar to the administrative practices of the empire of the Russian tsars.[2] Imperial Russia also covered the vast multinational territory of Eurasia and devised administrative distinctions and practices that did not conform to national or ethnic borders. Its system of sosloviia (estates) also functioned as a transnational administrative institution, which also clarified the important distinction between those borderland figures loyal to Moscow and those serving a competing power. Imperial officials in the borderlands were eager to cultivate a local elite who would prove worthy of the responsibilities of "subjecthood [poddanstvo]" to the Russian throne, which included forms of privilege and high status that went along with association with the highest soslovie.[3] In a time of peasant emancipation and general social reform in the 1860s and 1870s, officials continued to value the estate system and especially the privileged estate as a source of stability and order.[4] Reform was for officials an opportunity to incorporate newly educated and capable non-Russians, assuming they were at least from "respectable" families, into the imperial administration. In many cases officials decided to grant high status to those historically not part of the highest soslovie but deserving in their view because of their "service to the State."[5] Officials and commentators thought of the concept in different ways, but in part the notion suggested an occupational category or function, with related expectations about service and responsibility. Importantly, the notion and practice was divorced from national identity. The institution of soslovie was attractive to the state not simply because of the importance attached to privilege in an old regime society but because of its enduring usefulness as a transnational institution of administration, distant from the developing and threatening national question of the imperial era.

The communist party elite of the bloc shared some similarities to the multiethnic service elite that formerly served the tsar in the sprawling and multi-ethnic empire ruled from St. Petersburg. High-level communist party officials in Eastern and Central Europe now cast their lot with their new rulers from Moscow, "self-Sovietizers" in the formulation of John Connelly, eager to carry out the transformations of their own societies while aligning themselves to the new system of rule from the Kremlin.[6] Privilege, opportunity, and security often accompanied the new form of political loyalty.[7] There were new bureaucracies, militaries, and national security committee departments to staff and manage. Local communists were eager to benefit from their collaboration with the Soviets, and Soviet officials had a strong hand in the emergence of the new postwar elite and its "psychology," as a collection of Russian scholars explains.[8]

The Soviets functioned as administrators of a patron state in its relation to its client parties and administrative elites, inviting them to the Soviet Union for vacations at fancy resorts such as "Sosny" and "Pushkino" on the outskirts of Moscow, to sanatoriums in Gagra and Sochi along the Black Sea, or for special medical treatment at privileged hospitals. There they socialized with party and state officials from other countries in the socialist "camp." Eastern and Central European communists on holiday enjoyed "delicacies and drinks obtained by phone from Moscow," as T. V. Volokitina and her colleagues put it.[9] The bloc administrative elite frequently experienced these privileged forms of socialization, with Eastern Europeans mixing with Soviet winners of the Stalin prize, members of the Supreme Soviet, engineers, professors, and trade union officials.[10] Leftist figures from around the world sometimes visited.[11] Maurice Thorez of the French Communist Party flew to Moscow for medical treatment in November 1950.[12] Czechoslovak official Karol Tomášek received special ophthalmology treatment in Moscow in 1957.[13] Cultural figures were similarly privileged. East German writer Günter Simon enjoyed four weeks with his wife on the beaches of the Black Sea in May 1954 and assured his hosts that the experience had prepared him for future literary work.[14] Leading administrative families within the socialist world took these practices for granted. Kim Il Sung of North Korea personally intervened to rearrange study arrangements in the Soviet Union for the son of one of his top officials.[15] The wife of the Mongolian minister of internal affairs spent seven months in Soviet sanatoriums and resorts in 1955.[16] Relatives of communist party figures from Lebanon, Syria, Iran, Cameroon, and Finland, among others, inhabited this world.[17] Sometimes socialist families even intermarried. Stalin's daughter Svetlana I. Allilueva was married to an Indian communist until his death in 1966.[18]

The Chinese were now exposed to similar opportunities and privileges.

Party cadres, especially those weary from "many years of revolutionary struggle," enjoyed month-long stays at health resorts and spas in Karlový Vary in western Bohemia (historically "Karlsbad" to the Germans).[19] Zhu De's military delegation spent time in a resort there in January 1956.[20] Liu Shaoqi spent a month on the beaches of the Black Sea after attending the 19th Party Congress in October 1952, as did Deng Tuo, the editor-in-chief of *Renmin ribao*, in the summer of 1955.[21] Those who had lived in the Soviet Union sought opportunities there for their children.[22] Liu Shaoqi sent his fourteen-year-old son, Liu Yunbin, to the Soviet Union in 1939, where he eventually became a doctoral student in chemistry at Moscow State University, a Soviet citizen, and a party member in 1948. In 1950 he married Margarita S. Fedotova, also a chemist from Moscow State University, and the two of them returned to China to participate in the exchange in 1955. They left behind a three-year-old daughter, Sofia, with Margarita's parents.[23] Before their return to China, they enjoyed an extended stay at an exclusive sanatorium in the Soviet Union, where they were granted all the privileges due "foreign party and social activists."[24] Sophisticated medical treatment for high Chinese officials was also sometimes an option. The future ambassador, Wang Jiaxiang, came to Moscow for this purpose in early 1947, as did the future minister of defense, Lin Biao, in October 1950, also finding time there to address Sino-Soviet planning for the Korean War.[25] Yang Shangkun and several other Central Committee secretaries found care in Moscow in the summer of 1952.[26] Jiang Qing, the wife of Chairman Mao, almost traveled to Moscow to receive cobalt treatment for skin cancer. Instead, she sent her doctor, Yu Aifun, who returned to Beijing in 1956 with a collection of top doctors, radiologists, and professors.[27]

The Soviet notion and practice of *komandirovka* sent advisers, experts, managers, and party officials around the bloc engaged in the collaborative construction of "socialism," which resulted in the extension of Soviet norms to lands far from Moscow. These figures were not as privileged as the leading cadres of the communist parties, of course, but they too were privileged, politically loyal, and engaged in matters of social and political administration. Most but not all of them were communist party members, especially the most skilled and educated. In China the advisers enjoyed the resorts generally reserved for Chinese cadres in Qingdao and Lüshun, special schools for their children in Beijing, and special shops and forms of transportation. The "Friendship Stores," today a curious relic long made irrelevant by China's dynamic economy, were originally created in 1955 to provide special goods for the advisers and bloc visitors.[28] The advising communities in Shenyang and Anshan were

Soviet engineers in China.
From *Suzhong youhao, no. 5* (1959).

served by accompanying Soviet physicians.[29] In contrast to leading political figures, the advisers at least possessed actual credentials, skills, and educational attainments that they put to use in the far reaches of the bloc. Especially on the China exchanges, many of them possessed a sense of adventure, a desire to travel, and an inclination to share their skills with what they perceived as the needy Chinese. Like "reliable" figures from "respectable" families in the nineteenth century, they were both dependent on the state for their privileges and status and crucial to the state's administrative goals and projects. Their goal was to facilitate a bloc cohesion and "unity" that transcended traditional national borders, and they functioned with the support of a series of transnational organizations and institutions.

Advising was by definition a transnational institution and affair, with China host to not just Russians and other peoples from the Soviet Union but Poles, Hungarians, Czechoslovaks, Bulgarians, and others. Like nineteenth-century administrators traveling and working in the frontier areas of the Russian empire, advisers on *komandirovka* in China filed reports about their experiences, with suggestions designed to improve current collaborative projects and identify potential forms of exchange. This format was followed by pianists on a one-month trip to a music conservatory in Shanghai and mechanical engineers on a two-year trip constructing a bridge in Wuhan. In both the nineteenth and twentieth centuries, Russians placed themselves at the center of vast contiguous space and transnational communities designed to be something other than the modern nation-state. In both cases officials and advisers routinely addressed the political dimensions or potential dilemmas of their relationship with peoples on the edges of empire, and always with an eye to the broader international implications. In the nineteenth century, borderland officials worried about whether or not potential collaborators were "reliable [pochetnye]" and likely to remain "subject [poddanye]" to the imperial system; Soviet security officials compiled detailed biographies and "character reports [kharakteristika]" on those potentially engaged in collaborative bloc activity.[30] The advisers from the Soviet Union, like their imperial predecessors, were pleased to have the opportunity to extend the fruits of modern industry and culture to eastern lands that in their view were historically dormant and distant from civilization.

The transnational institutions that facilitated the work of the advisers were themselves an outgrowth of the "all-Union [vsesoiuznaia]" institutions of the Soviet Union itself. The Soviets established "Friendship" agreements with the bloc countries for diverse projects and advisers, generally first with the enemies and victims of Hitler (Czechoslovakia on 12 December 1943, Yugoslavia on 11 April 1945, Poland on 21 April 1945) and then with his allies (Romania on 4 February 1948, Hungary on 18 February 1948, Bulgaria on 18 March 1948).[31] "Friendship," interestingly, was also the term used to describe interethnic cooperation within the Soviet Union (i.e., the "Friendship of Peoples [druzhba narodov]"). The Treaty of Friendship signed with the Chinese on 14 February 1950 was part of this tradition. The Soviet institutions that lent themselves well to expansion included the information organization Sovinformbiuro (the Cominform), the press agency TASS, the media organization Radiokomitet, the trade organization International Books, and the All-Union Society for Cultural Relations with Foreign Countries, or VOKS (Vsesoiuznoe obshchestvo kul'turnoi sviazi s zagranitsei), which included the "Friendship" Societies. VOKS often worked with and was aided by the Komsomol, the Academy of Sciences, the Antifascist Committee of Soviet Women, and the Soviet Committee for the Defense of Peace.

Industrial exchange and enterprise collaboration in the bloc was facilitated by the expansion of the main ministries based in Moscow. Most ministries established a Department of External Relations (Otdel vneshnikh snoshenii,

OVS), which directed affairs in the "external" (not foreign, or *zagranichnyi*) areas of the socialist "camp," coordinated by a bureaucracy called the Main Administration of External Economic Ties of the Soviet of Ministers (Glavnoe upravlenie po vneshnim ekonomicheskim sviaziam soveta ministrov, GUES). A series of Scientific-Technical Commissions facilitated technology exchange and the movement of advisers ("experts"), equipment, and blueprints among the peoples of the bloc. The vast cultural bureaucracies (culture, mass consumption, higher education) also established Departments of External Relations. As in industry, cultural advisers and pedagogues traveled on *komandirovka* to universities, high schools, newspapers, journals, conservatories, and so on.[32] The socialist bloc exhibit was another well-known Soviet institution that functioned within the broader bloc, serving the needs of both industrial and cultural development and collaboration. Although organizers of the exhibits assumed and hoped that positive feelings and meaningful cultural exchange would result from the diverse exchanges, these were not just exercises in learning and mutual understanding. Ministries, enterprises, factories, universities, and other institutions were attempting to cooperate, collaborate, and integrate their activities and operations toward the common end called "socialism." Even the security agencies of the respective bloc states attempted to communicate with each other.[33] Another important institution of exchange and coordination was the Committee on Economic Mutual Assistance (Sovet ekonomicheskoi vzaimopomoshchi, SEV; often rendered in English as Comecon), an organization that routinely struggled to encourage forms of production and specialization that served the needs of the bloc as a whole rather than those of a particular nation.

Paying the Advisers

Adviser pay and financial responsibility for their work was a source of tension from the very start of the Sino-Soviet alliance. The Soviets saw the specialists as a resource, on loan to China in the form of a "gift." After the Sino-Soviet split of 1960, advisers, officials, and scholars routinely portrayed the Chinese as ungrateful for this generous expenditure of funds, skills, and human capital. For Soviet industrial managers, the labor being provided was another resource, potentially in scarce supply and hence to be hoarded in order to fulfill a future plan. Consequently, from the perspective of the bloc, the Soviets were supporting and parting with a valuable resource. "Experts" were part of the technical intelligentsia, produced and formed in order to serve the regime and its "construction of socialism." The Soviet advisers were still administratively connected to their ministries, on leave from their positions in the Soviet Union, and still receiving a salary as if they were at home. Sending them to China and other parts of the bloc was understood by Soviets to be a key part of the country's "selfless aid." Thus ministries at home frequently complained when the Ministry of Foreign Affairs ordered the dispatch of engineers to China. Too many of his skilled engineers were "abroad," lamented A. Romanov in the Ministry of Mechanical Engineering in 1953, by which he meant the socialist bloc.[34]

Soviet managers such as Romanov complained about their losses, and the other nations of the bloc were compelled to provide compensation. The notion was that the "country receiving the help" should pay the expenses of the specialists, the costs associated with the necessary equipment, materials, and documents, and a monthly fee to the domestic Soviet ministry in question.[35] According to a 1951 Soviet-Czechoslovak contract, for example, this included housing, translators, any necessary materials, labor help, transportation, medical aid, apartments, heat, and electricity for visiting Soviet specialists. The Czechoslovaks also paid for the visitors' train travel, luggage, and salary in transit, and they were compelled to reimburse the ministry in question for its "losses" resulting from the specialists' absence. In spite of these outlays from the non-Russians, the Soviets remained in charge. Officials in Moscow retained the right to choose and change the specialists or to extend their stay.[36] The situation was similar in Romania and other parts of Eastern and Central Europe.[37]

The Chinese also bore these financial responsibilities for this part of the exchange. They paid the train fare for the specialists and their families to and from China, numerous expenses in China, the monthly salary for the one-month vacation granted to experts who stayed in China for more than one year, and a 1,500–3,000 ruble monthly payment to the Soviet government, depending on the qualifications of the specialist.[38] The April 1950 arrangement with the Ministry of Mechanical Engineering called for the Chinese to provide the Soviets with paid vacations, satisfactory conditions at work sites, "heated apartments with furniture," qualified translators, health care, and exemptions from any Chinese taxes. At work sites the Chinese were obligated to cover transportation costs, any needed Chinese labor, and the cost of transporting equipment within China. If the time period for the project in question was extended, the Chinese were obligated to cover the additional costs associated with the extension.[39] The constant Soviet proclamations that the advising program was a "gift" and an example of selfless Soviet "internationalism" cannot be taken too seriously. The initial figure presented by the Soviets to Liu Shaoqi, Gao Gang, and Wang Jiaxiang in the summer of 1949 for the Chinese subsidy to the Soviet government per specialist was 2,000 to 4,000 yuan per month.[40] The Soviets again presented these figures to Zhou Enlai in Moscow in February 1950, but Li Fuchun, Wang Jiaxiang, and Wu Xiuquan later negotiated them down in the 22 March additions to the treaty. Interestingly, the Soviets also floated the idea of Chinese payment for this aspect of the exchange in American dollars, a reminder to the Chinese of the real source of economic power in the postwar world and of the dilemmas of intrabloc autarky and exchange. The Chinese did not want to have anything to do with the dollar, but they did pay in internationally convertible currency.[41]

From the start, the Chinese posed uncomfortable questions about the financing and organization of the expert exchange, and things only got worse.[42] Soviet terms were changing, the Chinese complained, even in the short time between Liu Shaoqi's visit in the summer of 1949 and the treaty discussions in February and March 1950.[43] The imperial question was perpetually part of the background to this exchange. Liu Shaoqi publicly noted in early October 1949 that bloc specialists would be paid like Chinese technicians and specialists, "in contrast to the past and the privileges of English and American engineers."[44] And the question of just who was helping whom also made the constant Soviet expectation of bloc gratitude for their "selfless" support somewhat delicate. Soviet advisers traveled throughout the bloc with particular concerns, as we will see in the next chapter, germane to the needs of the Soviet economy. Since we know from Soviet managers themselves who were stationed in China that one of the chief attractions of the China exchange was the opportunity to become familiar with Western industrial plans and literature left by Europeans in China before 1949, one wonders about the value of Chinese exposure to these same industrial managers and their methods. And some advisers were, of course, less than serious, eager to engage in "scientific tourism," or worse.[45] Wang Jiaxiang suggested to Gromyko in the initial discussions surrounding the February 1950 treaty that the Soviets support financially those experts in areas and enterprises proposed by them, while the Chinese would cover the expenses of the experts they had specifically requested. Gromyko declined the suggestion, however, referring to the general practices of the bloc and the matter of *komandirovka* within the Soviet Union itself.[46] Moscow would decide who needed what. And the Soviets were not shy about presenting the bill. Every six months the Ministry of Finance bluntly informed the Chinese Ministry of Foreign Affairs of the cumulative figure for the monthly reimbursement to the Soviet ministries ("losses to Soviet organizations"), complete with an account number at a bank in Moscow.[47] Fraternal enthusiasm about proletarian internationalism did not mean the bills could go unpaid.

By the late 1950s, an increasingly sensitive Chinese nativism posed a series of questions about the insufficiently "mutual" nature of the relationship. In the area of technical cooperation, the Chinese were frustrated that their support for Soviet advisers was not reciprocated in Soviet support of Chinese specialists in the Soviet Union. Chinese specialists received training in the Soviet Union, and like the graduate students who studied there, they paid for most of it. According to the 9 August 1952 agreement, the Chinese were to pay 50 percent of the cost of the living expenses of some 38,000 students and technicians who eventually studied in the Soviet Union. They also provided stipends of 500 rubles monthly to undergraduates and 900 rubles to graduate students for some 8,000 people. The Soviets kept careful records of all costs associated with the Chinese in the Soviet Union, and possibly inflated them. Zhou Zhengmin, for example, was trained at the "Elektroapparat" factory according to the following schedule:

Russian language study, 200 hours × 15 rubles	3,000 rubles
theoretical study, 750 hours × 15 rubles	11,250 rubles
managerial practice, 150 rubles per month, × 24	3,600 rubles
miscellaneous consultations	2,500 rubles
program and study plans	300 rubles
study texts and supplies	400 rubles

The total was 21,150 rubles.[48] A group of eleven Chinese engineers in the Soviet Union for two years, from November 1951 to November 1953, ran up the following bill from the Ministry of Electrical Industry:

theoretical work, 3,100 hours × 20 rubles	620,000 rubles
Russian language study, 1,500 hours × 15 rubles	22,500 rubles
industrial study, 11 × 24 months × 140 rubles	36,960 rubles
administrative fee	3,600 rubles
15.8 percent tax	19,760
study materials	2,400

The total in this case was 147,220 rubles.[49] A similar report left in files of the Ministry of Electrical Industry describes a 143,640 ruble program for the technical training of fourteen Chinese technicians, twelve workers, and two engineers for twelve months in 1955–56.[50] In contrast to the Chinese support for the numerous expenses of the Soviet advisers in China, the Chinese covered transport, travel within the USSR, food, accidents, medical problems, translators, and other expenses within the Soviet Union.[51] And for their money, the Chinese were treated to a thorough exposure to the inefficiencies of the Soviet system. Factories with Chinese trainees, for example, were often not properly compensated by the sponsoring ministries, or they ran out of money before the exchange was concluded.[52] As the personnel director at the Electro-Mechanical Factory in Kharkiv put it, such lack of support put him in a very "uncomfortable situation" in his relationship to the Chinese.[53] The situation was even worse at the tractor factory in Kharkiv, where the visiting Chinese were subject to something less than "normal living conditions."[54]

From the very start, notes historian Zhihua Shen, the Chinese were made aware of the hierarchy of relations within the socialist bloc. Throughout the decade, the Chinese were frustrated by the vast discrepancies in remuneration between the Soviet experts and their own specialists and workers, in spite of their complaints about this issue, initially brought up by Bo Yibo and Zhou Enlai in Moscow in February 1950.[55] The manager of the Soviet specialists in 1955 at the Changchun Automobile Factory, for example, earned twice the salary of the Chinese manager of the factory.[56] Russian teachers at People's University were paid much more than their Chinese colleagues, and many of them were housed in style at the Beijing Hotel and the International Hotel.[57] Soviets in Korea were also paid more than Chinese specialists, even when engaged in the same tasks and possessing similar qualifications.[58] Czechoslovak experts sponsored by the Academy of Sciences received higher payments than their Chinese counterparts in Czechoslovakia, which the frustrated Chinese began to complain about by 1958.[59] In the 18 January 1958 agreement the Chinese added a provision to the earlier agreements stipulating that they were not obligated to pay expenses for specialists they had not formally invited, returning to their concerns initially raised in 1950.[60] They realized by then that they were sometimes supporting exotic vacation trips for fortunate and trusted Soviet cadres and members of the managerial elite. They also began paying more attention to the advisers' inflated expense reports.[61] These concerns of the Chinese and Soviet advisers themselves eventually compelled embassy and International Department officials to explore these matters, but there were many more Soviet voices determined to concede nothing on this score.[62] They felt their experts deserved more money, better conditions, more respect and gratitude, and they wanted greater compensation to reimburse ministries and enterprises for their loss of labor and expertise.[63] Their monthly pay, complained Soviet officials in a quiet but intense argument with the Chinese over this in 1959, represented a "gift from the Soviet Union to the PRC, which, however, is never recognized."[64]

The overall equality and nature of the exchange is, of course, difficult to assess. Total Soviet economic assistance to China from 1946 to 1960 might have been as high as $3.4 billion (U.S.), a figure that does not include the adviser salaries and stipends to Chinese students in the USSR.[65] The aid, however, came with strings attached, as we have discussed. Even everyday exchanges were routinely disputed within the socialist world. What was the actual value of Soviet technical material provided in this form of collaboration to allies who were not allowed to shop around in the broader world of expertise and technology transfer? The Czechs and Poles had similar disputes over the exchange of technical documentation, as when the Czechs simply refused to alter and update material requested by the Poles in 1954 until adequate payment was in hand.[66] The longer-term consequences are even more difficult to determine. Soviet experts helped increase Chinese coal production by 60 percent by 1952, points out Zhihua Shen, and perhaps saved the Chinese decades of work on coal exploration and excavation. Similar gains were made in oil production, irrigation works, forestry, livestock production, mechanical engineering, and the railways.[67] Significant portions of China's automobile, truck, and hydroelectric turbine production were a product of the exchange.[68] The ability and capacity to refine oil, produce machine tools, and forge metals such as aluminum and zinc outlasted the Sino-Soviet split, of course.[69] The Chinese would have their own atomic bomb by 1964. The complexity of the exchange, the quality of the aid, the overall character of bloc cooperation, the assumptions that shaped Soviet economic management, the difficulties of estimating the nature of the long-term Soviet contribution to Chinese industrial development, and the political dimensions to the relationship make it very difficult to estimate the program's much debated costs and comparative advantages.

Insulting the Chinese

Privilege did not disappear under socialism, and neither did traditional Russian cultural attitudes about the significance of their presence in an "Eastern" land such as China. Soviet advisers in China witnessed tension over these issues, which were suggestive of the broader dilemmas of socialist "friendship"

A Soviet mechanical engineer instructs Chinese observers at the Soviet exhibit in Beijing, 1954. (RGAE f. 635, op. 1, d. 291, l. 15)

and the bloc itself. Aleksei V. Stozhenko, a geography professor and deputy chair of the Far Eastern Branch of the Academy of Sciences, was remiss in writing home about his experiences in China because "there was not even time to dream." He spent some six weeks in the Northeast, working in Beijing, Harbin, Shenyang, and several smaller cities in the region. Stozhenko was enthusiastic about China and the great potential of the Sino-Soviet relationship. He was elated by the intense activity of the trip, which, however, was not for tourism "but to work, and there was always an extraordinary amount of work." Stozhenko believed the work he and his colleagues did was crucial and valuable in the East. One of his colleagues, B. T. Bykov, continued on a similar trip to North Korea. In China they worked closely with Chinese hydro-technicians, geologists, soil scientists, forestry specialists, agricultural specialists, and their institutes. The group was successful in formulating and sharing plans, establishing ties, and exchanging materials and programs. The Chinese "literally snatched up" and "quickly translated" their manuscripts, blueprints, and written materials.[70]

The Chinese "made an enormously astonishing impression on us," wrote Stozhenko to his friend and colleague Andrei M. Chekashillo. "They have placed before themselves the task of catching up to global science (including our own) in twelve years. But everything suggests that they will accomplish this even sooner." Stozhenko was stunned by Chinese progress in the building of diverse research institutes and laboratories in the Northeast. "In four years they have constructed several times more than what Akademstroi [Academy of Construction] has done in twenty years of its existence," he claimed. The institutes were enormous, well-constructed, and equipped with the most modern forms of technology and equipment from West Germany, the GDR, and Czechoslovakia, "about which our institutes can only dream, including even those in Moscow." The opportunities for productive and satisfying work were thus greater, he implied, than in the Soviet Union itself. "What is most extraordinary about all this," he reported, "is that all of these institutes have been built and equipped and set up under the leadership of our advisers. Our scientists have realized their dreams on foreign soil." The scale of everything in China was unimaginable, said Stozhenko. Each institute was inhabited by countless students, teachers, and engineers. "Even when they take a collective photograph, they [assemble] at least some 500 or 1,000 people," he wrote. "But the most valuable thing in China is the Chinese themselves." Stozhenko enthusiastically described the Chinese:

> They are hardworking and disciplined (in some forty days I saw not a single loafer or drunkard or gambler, even as I was among the most provincial people), highly talented in all the sciences, decisive and active, with initiative, polite and courteous not only to us Russians but to each other, and the main thing is that they are honest to the very last one of them. You can forget your camera in a store or a coatroom (as happened with us), and they will return it to you within an hour, a day, a week, or whenever they find you. All internal financial accounting is done orally. Someone going on *komandirovka* is given money without receipts. They spend it as they choose. When they return they turn in the remaining [money], attaching the report as pro forma. No one criticizes them for the amount they spent. But the main thing is that not one person on *komandirovka* would think about wasting a single ruble. Professor Lu Zuzhu was given 60,000 rubles for an expedition (he went for two months). He spent 4,600 rubles. The remainder was 55,400 rubles. And indeed the "expenditures" were calculated precisely according to our norms.[71]

Stozhenko's enthusiasm for China served as preface to his disappointment. Too many of his own colleagues, he argued, threatened the health of the exchange and the broader Sino-Soviet relationship by callously misusing the generosity and kindness of their Chinese hosts. "Unfortunately many Muscovites do not want to understand the simple fact that the PRC is still a young and poor republic, and that their economic regime is not a matter of idle talk; and the voracious eating, sleeping in luxury rooms, and traveling in the international car at the expense of the PRC is not helping things." Stozhenko discovered that it was possible politely to reject Chinese forms of hospitality without threatening "to complicate things internationally." He tried to offer guidance to other advisers about how best to behave so as to promote "internationalism." Stozhenko's group insisted to their host that they liked simple Chinese food, would pay for their own meals, and preferred to travel in the hard seats on Chinese trains, as it was "more interesting to travel with the public and get to know the Chinese comrades than to sit in luxurious prisons." His Chinese hosts were pleased and relieved, "as for them too it is more interesting to be in the public areas and play cards, rather than be bored with us," and a mutually beneficial form of cultural exchange was the result. "We quickly learned the rules of their games, and taught them some of our own."[72]

Stozhenko's report found sympathy and concerned supporters in the Central Committee's International Department, which was accumulating information from diverse sources. "It is time," wrote Boris Polevoi on 26 November 1956, "to think seriously about the organization of the work of the Soviet advisers in Chinese industry." In many cases, Polevoi conceded, Soviet advisers were "very intelligent" people capable of "[handling] themselves well." Too often, however, the visitors were far too comfortable in a relationship that seemed disturbingly colonial. "The Chinese comrades offer them excellent conditions, pay rates, travel throughout the country, stays in the most expensive hotel rooms, feeding them well in restaurants [chefanakh, from the Chinese chifan, to eat food], hosting them at banquets, and so on. The Chinese are a very economical people. It is not a secret that they live simply, and their modesty is evident even in their work style." Soviet advisers were insufficiently sensitive about the "privileged position and good fortune that they find themselves in." Polevoi suggested further study of the problem and instruction for the advisers that they do not have the "duty to accept the good fortune that has come to them, and that they should live modestly and not compel the Chinese to make luxurious expenditures, and be content with their salary, which, it must be said, is very high."[73]

Boris Polevoi was a well-known figure in Soviet culture long before his trip to China. "A real frontovik," as Alexander Werth wrote, Polevoi served as a

A Soviet adviser explains the function of the E 505-A Excavator to Chinese observers at the Soviet exhibit in Guangzhou, 1955. (RGAE f. 635, op. 1, d. 307, l. 32)

wartime correspondent in the struggle against the Nazis.[74] His long career as a journalist and writer allowed him to glorify shock workers, soldiers, and the builders of Soviet socialism generally—"real people," as an approving literary commentator put it, in reference to the title of one of his novels.[75] In his interview with Werth in 1960, Polevoi continued to marvel at the "sacrifices" made by the Chinese people for the construction of socialism and romanticized "a kind of spontaneous iron discipline in China" long absent from the Soviet experience.[76] The socialist realist writer from the Stalin era apparently found what he was looking for in the China of the 1950s.

Like Stozhenko, Polevoi was concerned about the general problem of inequality in the diverse exchanges, which betrayed a Soviet failure to promote the study of China in the same way that "learning from the Soviet Union" was promoted in China. In part the problem was the cultural attitude of Soviet advisers, who were similarly criticized in other parts of the bloc (as were Russians in the Soviet Union) for their failure to take an interest in the "names of well-known writers, artists, and scholars who make up the pride of the nation."[77] At the airport in Novosibirsk, Polevoi was horrified to see Chinese visitors pondering an enormous map and display titled "The USSR—The

Leading Socialist Power in the World." Columns to the side of the giant red map of the bloc listed, in alphabetical order, the countries of the bloc. "Thus China [*Kitai*] in this list comes after Albania, Bulgaria, Hungary, and the GDR. The Novosibirsk comrades, seeing this map, are completely devoid of a sense of humor, even as the following is written on the large map: population 200 million people, and on the small map—China—600 million. We ourselves have seen the amusement of foreigners as they look at this map."[78] Polevoi hoped to see local party officials in Novosibirsk address the matter immediately. Reflexive Soviet assumptions, in this case from the provinces, about the importance of the Soviet model for the rest of the bloc were painfully insulting to the Chinese, which in this case was well understood by writers and professors such as Polevoi and Stozhenko. Officials from Ministries of Foreign Affairs and other high ministries of diverse countries, as we will see in chapter 4, were at this very moment engaged in a complicated debate about Sino-Soviet relations and the "leadership" of the bloc. Similar sentiments of concern to Polevoi emerged from diverse parts of the exchange. Advisers could be overbearing, as was the educational adviser in Beijing who admonished the many teachers who do not even "read the newspapers themselves" or "concern themselves with socialist construction."[79] A Chinese Defense Ministry report from February 1957 referred to the "self-satisfied and chauvinistic feelings" of visiting Soviet advisers.[80]

Misbehavior

"Ninety-nine percent of [the advisers] are good men," Mao affirmed to the visiting Khrushchev in the summer of 1958. "Just a few are bad."[81] This was Mao's way of simultaneously addressing and ignoring the frustrated reports circulating up through the Chinese bureaucracy about the behavior of some of the bloc advisers. The Chinese were exposed to more than Soviet technical incompetence and hierarchical pay scales that reminded them of the history of colonialism. Soviet specialists sometimes drank too much, failed to show up for work, or even attracted the attention of local police. This was a problem throughout the entire bloc and, perhaps most seriously from the Chinese perspective, appeared to be an outgrowth of the Soviet system itself. After his 1956 trip to the Soviet Union, Peng Zhen noted administrative "shortcomings" in the Soviet party, including "cadre drunkenness."[82] N. Smeliakov, a Soviet official in the Ministry of Mechanical Engineering, conceded in November

1956 (regarding Czechoslovakia) that behavior was lax, and that "[we] have not taken any measures toward the oversight of the work of Soviet specialists."[83] Soviet air force technicians and officers often "systematically drank" in North Korea. One technician even killed his wife under the influence of alcohol.[84] The situation was similar in Poland, where the behavior of the specialists often "discredits us before the local population," as investigating official S. R. Savchenko informed the Ministry of Internal Affairs. Chauffeur V. A. Poteriaev of the Ministry of Heavy Industry murdered a driver from the Turkish embassy, then fought with the investigating Polish police. Thirty of the 4,200 Soviet experts in Poland with the Ministry of Heavy Industry in 1952 were found to be either current or former criminals.[85] Some 80 percent of the almost 2,700 Soviet laborers at work on a Palace of Culture were between ages nineteen and twenty-five, a recipe for disaster, concluded Soviet officials at the embassy. There were numerous incidences of public disorders, drunkenness, and fights in restaurants.[86]

More educated specialists fought in their own way. On the diverse edges of the bloc they competed with each other for opportunities, or for professional and administrative control over work sites.[87] Sometimes they accused each other of errors and weaknesses by writing Stalinist-style denunciation letters.[88] They could be careerist and materialistic, no doubt contributing to Chinese fears of consumerism and the related "revisionism." In Europe diplomats often flaunted their access to Western consumer goods, while in the East chauvinist specialists liked to complain about their comparative deprivation, as expressed dramatically by the wife of a ship commander in North Korea: "There's nothing for us to do here; it's their homeland; let them defend it and get us out of here; they've sent us to an impoverished country and existence, and we're starving and tortured."[89] In Shanghai the Polish general consul, K. Biernácki, accused the wives of Czechoslovak diplomats of befriending the English for the sake of shopping trips to Hong Kong. The Czechs returned to their apartments in Shanghai loaded with consumer goods from beyond the bloc.[90]

The Chinese were now exposed to these aspects of the Soviet system. Russian sailors in the seaports of northeastern China were especially notorious for their misbehavior. Iurii D. Rostov, who routinely "drank himself into oblivion" in Dalian, was known as "Stepan Razin" for his assaults on Chinese citizens.[91] After L. A. Korzhov and M. P. Glushak, from Magnitogorsk, were detained by the Chinese authorities for their drunken marauding, they insulted the police and behaved "like an English sailor." Captain Novoselov of a fishing boat was known as the "King of Vodka." Sailors stole cameras and other consumer goods, destroyed restaurants, and obtained goods from Japanese ships to resell in the Soviet Union.[92] There were even cases of rape and murder.[93]

There were similarly many instances of "moral decay among the [Soviet] workers" and specialists chosen for the China exchange. Radio operators were prone to drunkenness, intimate relations with each other that led to abortions, sexual activity by managers that "undermine[d their] authority as a leader," and intimate relationships with "the suspect local population." Air Force commander P. P. Sidorov arrived drunk in China, having already created a disturbance at the Omsk airport as he left. G. A. Zhdanov was censored for promoting one of his drinking companions to inspector of cadres. A Comrade Kniaginichevyi was famous for issuing severe commands to the Chinese, such as, "Go and stand in the corner" and "Don't set up a bazaar. I'll order you where to go as necessary." An air force pilot drunkenly murdered a radio operator, and Soviet officials in China covered up the event. Another radio operator used her sexual relationship with an air force commander to obtain the use of a private car for numerous trips around Beijing.[94] The Ministry of Coal Industry sent an adviser to Shenyang with severe psychological problems.[95]

The air force colonel who headed the investigation of these abuses was especially disturbed by the lack of attention in the selection process to the background of many advisers in China. Their previous performance records, he emphasized, should have made them ineligible for such a sensitive post abroad.[96] A January 1951 investigation into 466 air force advisers and specialists in China led to the immediate return of eighty-two of them to the Soviet Union, for, among other things, drunkenness, "immoral behavior," and inappropriate liaisons with foreigners. Aeroflot workers were particularly incompetent in China and throughout the socialist bloc. The coordinator of a related investigation, another air force colonel, emphasized the civilizing influence of the family: "Sending workers abroad without their families creates an inclination toward moral decay and [the deterioration of] everyday life, and hence drunkenness."[97] By 1953 far more families accompanied the advisers. Ministry of Communication reports from January 1953 list 475 workers, accompanied by 259 spouses and 306 children. About one-half of this group stayed in China for one to two years, with the other half there for two to three years, and even three to five years.[98] The behavior and activities of the vast Soviet advising program throughout the bloc had become a sensitive foreign policy issue, as was evident from the interest of host-country security officials. In China security officials were particularly alarmed by the propensity of their compatriots to fraternize with the remnants of the Russian émigré community in the Northeast.[99] There were foreign policy implications to the well-known Russian fondness for alcohol. In July 1959 the Chinese refused to supply hard liquor at official social occasions for visiting advisers, limiting them to wine and beer.[100]

Struggling over Blueprints

The exchange of industrial blueprints eventually became a focal point in the dispute, used by the Chinese as a means to challenge the Soviets about their assumptions, their previous practices, and the financial side of "proletarian internationalism." While the Europeans paid for the delivery of blueprints, the Chinese were supposedly the beneficiaries of Soviet largesse regarding their specialists and also their blueprints.[101] Soviet scholars such as L. V. Filatov, writing in 1980 and still prone to anger about China's manipulative "betrayal," counted some 8,547 diverse sets of blueprints provided to the Chinese from 12 October 1954 to 19 June 1961, at 1963 prices of 9.2 million rubles, of which the Chinese only paid 1,050 rubles.[102] The Chinese did, however, help cover the cost of producing the materials that were part of the exchange, and they paid to prepare, print, and bind the blueprints. The blueprints were a mixed blessing, like most other Chinese encounters with the Soviet system. According to particular exchanges and contracts with China, factories in diverse locations of the Soviet Union received commands to supply industrial documentation to particular factory locations, ministries, or other sites in China. Plan fulfillment and the procurement of materials and labor outweighed any response to demand. The Soviet system left managers without the necessary incentives to provide careful work at the drawing table to the Chinese, and Chinese frustration with frequently shoddy technical documentation became a very sore point in the relationship. F. Kleimenov, the scientific secretary of the Soviet part of the Scientific-Technical Commission for China, was also frustrated by this aspect of the exchange. Worried about Chinese discontent, he reminded the Ministry of Communications in 1959 that technical documentation was to be well-presented, properly bound, and printed on "good paper, with clean and clear blueprints, without any distortions."[103] Thus, while the value of this component of the exchange is difficult to estimate, it was not exactly "free."

The Chinese, to be sure, were convinced by the end of the decade that they had been victims of abusive Soviet practices. When I. V. Arkhipov, longtime veteran of Sino-Soviet exchange, returned to China in February 1961 as head of an economic delegation, he was greeted with a series of complaints about the financial component of the technical exchanges. The Chinese argued that their financial contribution to the exchange of technical documentation, equipment, and miscellaneous expenses had been calculated in a way advantageous to the Soviet side. This reflected their notion that their overall contribution to the exchange had been insultingly underestimated by the Soviets. The Soviets were also guilty, as Wang Zuzhuan argued, of inflating the "actual cost of [their] documents," and overcharging the Chinese 8.55 times the actual value of what they had been sending to China. They had also taken advantage of the generous nature of the Chinese, whose ministries and organizations had been routinely providing smaller contributions along the way but without proper compensation.[104] Soviet officials were aware by the end of the decade that the Chinese would sometimes reduce components of particular exchanges because they worried about the expenditure of foreign exchange.[105] In June 1961 the Chinese suddenly suggested that documents on scientific-technical cooperation would be presented in the "language of the granting side," that is, they would not make the effort to translate their own material from Chinese into Russian. Soviet officials recognized immediately that this would be a problem and pushed the Chinese informally to continue to offer translation help into Russian.[106]

In part the financial dispute was an inevitable feature of the socialist planned economy, where prices did not represent information about demand but instead appeared to be determined arbitrarily in a way that could be interpreted as advantageous to the other party. I. Dudinskii, an economist studying intrabloc trade, admitted as much when he suggested that the "international" (bloc) price of a good was determined by the "quantity of socially necessary labor" that produced it, which was likely to be viewed one way in Warsaw and another in Wuhan.[107] The Chinese charged the Soviets with underestimating the value of Chinese exports and overestimating the value of their own diverse contributions. From 1957 they complained that the ruble-yuan exchange rate (approximately 1:1 from 1950 to 1957) was weighted in favor of the ruble (it was adjusted to 2:1).[108] A 30 November 1961 meeting of the Scientific-Technical Commission reflected the continuing Chinese frustration over the issue of money, which now went to the heart of the very nature of "proletarian internationalism." The Chinese were enraged by the relentless Soviet propaganda claims about their "gratis [*bezvozmezdno*]" rendering of technical materials to the Chinese. In the technical exchange agreement they wanted to eliminate the paragraph that proclaimed Soviet generosity and clarify that they were responsible only for the "actual costs" of the organization and transport of the material. The Soviets again refused to concede, claiming that the "word 'gratis' and that paragraph of the act emphasizes that scientific-technical collaboration is an example of fraternal mutual aid and fully corresponds to the spirit of proletarian internationalism."[109] It was very important to clarify just who, and to what extent, was to be grateful to whom. The Chinese went ahead with their new version of the exchange, which the Soviets reluctantly accepted as a "compromise decision" at the twelfth session of the Sino-Soviet Scientific-Technical Commission in June 1962.[110] Regarding Sino-Soviet trade generally, as Lorenz Lüthi points out, Chairman Mao himself was determined to repay quickly China's total debt to the Soviet Union (800 million transfer rubles) after the withdrawal of the advisers in 1960.[111] He attempted to clear Chinese debts quickly with the other peoples of the bloc as well.[112]

The unilateral Chinese revisions to the scientific-technical agreements had immediate financial consequences. For example, the Chinese now wanted to send on material pertaining to a production of a turbogenerator consisting of forty-four pages of documents and two diagrams at a cost to the Soviets of 2,133 rubles and 70 kopecks; according to the old agreement the cost to the Soviets would have been 337 rubles. Metallurgical equipment information (ten pages of material, seventy-seven drawings, five photographs) now cost the Soviets 108 rubles rather than 69 rubles, 90 kopecks.[113] In part this explains their continuing eagerness to fulfill and even overfulfill the terms of the exchange, as certain arrangements were now increasingly lucrative. The Soviets, by contrast, were inclined to end a relationship that was now costing them significantly more. In 1961 the Soviets sent on 364 (72.8 percent) of a planned 500 sets of blueprints, while in the first quarter of 1962 they fulfilled only 13 (18.6 percent) of a planned 70 different programs. The Chinese, by contrast, fulfilled 67 percent (163 of 240) of their planned program in 1961, and 85.2 percent (29 of 34) in early 1962.[114] The Chinese actually increased their rate of fulfillment in these troubled times, both to collect on the more favorable terms of payment and to ensure that blame for the breakup would rest with the Soviets. Soviet technical commission officials were well aware of the political pitfalls of their disputes and advised caution to their colleagues so as to avoid any Chinese accusations. The Soviets sent on 186 plans to the PRC in 1962, but only 65 in 1963. The real slowdown came after 1962, in the years preceding the outbreak of the Cultural Revolution. The Chinese sent to the Soviet Union only 69 different projects between 1962 and 1966.[115]

Red Imperialism: The Shenyang Cable Factory

Russians managed to combine several trends regarding the conduct of intra-bloc exchange, all increasingly disputed by the Chinese: the universalistic assumptions about "proletarian internationalism"; the traditional Russian civilizing mission in the East; and the practices of industrial administration drawn from the Soviet Union. Confidence about their traditional role in Asia led many industrial advisers simply to assume that Soviet norms and practices obviously were superior to those they found in China. Chinese egalitarianism in Tianjin, concluded a group of visiting Soviet labor specialists, was some sort of a relic from the premodern past, and they proceeded to instruct the Chinese on a pay scale properly linked to specialization and qualifications, and on a promotion system for engineers. "Wage-leveling [*uravnilovka*]" and the failure to distinguish between "qualified" and manual labor had still not been "liquidated," the Soviets complained, and they were condescending about pointless Chinese meetings informed by the "so-called 'democratic path'" of discussion.[116]

To their minds, Soviet norms were universal norms, especially applicable and useful in the Far East. Soviet industrial managers and economic officials were remarkably oblivious to national borders and thought of China as simply another series of work sites within the vast Soviet system. From their perspective, the particular Chinese factory, institution, or ministry in question was simply the "*zakazchik* [customer, or placer of the order]" with an "order number" who could just as well have been located somewhere in provincial Russia or Soviet Central Asia.[117] The Soviet factory or ministry identified to fulfill an "order," in this contractual language, was the "supplier [*postavshchik*]." The language of socialist bloc exchange at the lower levels was surprisingly formal, testy, and contractual, a far cry from the numerous and public theoretical discussions, or the journalistic stories of sentimental bloc managers and their "fraternal" enthusiasm for fulfilling production requests from the distant corners of the bloc.[118] Lower-level factories and their managers in diverse parts of the Soviet Union might find themselves engaged in only a single transaction with a distant factory in the Chinese interior, while the larger construction and industrial ministries generally were extending their previously developed ties in Eastern and Central Europe to new eastern sites like North Korea and China.

This was the Soviet industrial system in practice, now extended to the bloc. The behavior of lower-level managers, as Julie Hessler and others have explained, was a response to the unique system of rewards and incentives characteristic of this famously hierarchical Soviet world.[119] Industrial managers and their ministries in the Soviet system were surprisingly powerful and capable of exerting their independence from the center.[120] "If their careers were to flourish and if they were to avoid punishment," points out economic historian Evgenia Belova, "party-member managers had to produce results, even if they had to act against the higher interests."[121] The interests of "party-member managers" did not always coincide with the senior officials making the better-known foreign policy arrangements. The signing of the 1950 Treaty of Friendship led to a slew of orders or administrative commands from the very top that revealed to the Chinese the practices and assumptions of this system. What this meant further down in this system remained to be seen.

One distant location where all these issues were evident was the Shenyang Cable Factory. Early directives in 1950 from the Ministry of Mechanical Engineering requested proper documentation and supply of "technological equipment for a cable factory according to order No. 023710732," as I. Sharshakov referred to the location of Shenyang.[122] Five Soviet specialists arrived from the ministry in the summer of 1950.[123] Located on the site of a prerevolutionary factory destroyed by the GMD during the civil war, the Shenyang Cable Factory was to serve as an example of China's new successful industrialization and of the merits and benefits of the "friendship." A product of collaboration between the communications ministries, the factory eventually produced copper and aluminum wires, bare cable, long-distance telephone wires, and several types of insulated wires. Technical work on the factory started in 1954, and the mechanical repair shop was completed by June 1955. By March 1956 many of the specialized wire, cable, copper, and blacksmith workshops were in operation.[124] The 1953–57 five-year plan called for a Chinese capital investment in the plant of over 77 million yuan.[125]

Numerous problems quickly emerged in the reconstruction of the factory. By August 1956 cost overruns had already compelled the Chinese to spend over 80 million yuan, and tensions emerged when the Chinese suggested that the Soviet advisers could more effectively limit the spiraling costs by recycling and reusing more material from the original plant. Chinese engineers Cheng Gongzheng and Liu Dingzhu faulted the Soviets for their late delivery of plans and materials for the assembly of high voltage equipment, the excessive speed of construction, the absence of parts for a ten-ton crane, inadequate gas generators, and the absence of a wood-finishing shop and a technological laboratory. The entire project was slowed by the general "lack of coordination between construction and assembly organizations and the factory," they complained.[126] Too much construction material was ordered by the Soviet advisers in certain areas and not enough in others. Engineers Sun Huafeng and Dian Guochen attributed responsibility for the insufficient gas pressure in the blacksmith shop to the Soviets, whose design failed to account for the limited gas pressure at the site.[127] Cheng Gongzheng and Liu Dingzhu suggested that the Soviet advisers wasted (Chinese) money because of their lack of knowledge of local prices, supplies, and the state of secondhand material, and the two Chinese engineers hoped to provide more input into future planning in order to remedy such problems.[128]

Reports from Soviet specialists suggest this Chinese criticism was quite accurate. The Soviet brigade leader Ignatov faulted the Ministry of Chemical Engineering for its failure to come through with plans and documentation for nonstandard equipment necessary in Shenyang, which compelled his Ministry of Communications group to spend an enormous amount of time developing blueprints and plans for things like a metal rolling shop. Frustrated by the ministerial confusion, Ignatov recommended to his colleagues that they turn to the East Germans for quick help. Ignatov also faulted the Chinese, however, who in his view were slow to provide the necessary preparatory information about specifications, measurements, and conditions.[129] Other Soviet reports from Shenyang are suggestive of the practices and incentives characteristic of the Soviet industrial system. B. Gusev, for example, resident at the factory at this same time period, perfunctorily filed numerous and meaningless reports about successes in the fulfillment of diverse plans.[130]

Contract fulfillment was a messy business in the Soviet Union generally. Contracts for the cable factory were verified by a chief accountant, Z. K. Sokolov, as well as a GUES commander, P. R. Stepanov, also attached to the Ministry of Mechanical Engineering. They worked with the firm Tekhnoeksport and its directors and accountants, which handled contracts for diverse "external ties" for a variety of ministries. Their chief interests concerned shipment dates, payment deadlines, the number of required train cars, the identification and quantity of the equipment, a confirmation from the Chinese by telegraph, and so on. The contracts usually stipulated that the condition of the delivered equipment was to be satisfactory, but the Soviets took extraordinary measures to protect themselves from matters they considered beyond their control, such as damage in transit or at the Chinese work site. The Soviet managerial elite worked hard, responded to the incentives, limitations, and possibilities of their world, and exhibited little interest in the fate of world revolution or the construction of socialism. Because neither side could utilize the pressure of either an alternative supplier or alternative buyer, both sides perpetually haggled over responsibilities for damage incurred in transit or the quality of the delivered material. Since the Soviet ministries and factories were responding to production commands from above rather than a satisfied customer at the other end of the exchange, they possessed few incentives to ensure the careful and attractive delivery of the product. Consequently the contracts devoted inordinate attention to the resolution of conflicts resulting from disputes over the character and quality of the delivered material.[131] None of the Soviet officials showed any interest in ideological or political questions and instead worked diligently to protect the interests of a particular ministry.

There were other problems at the factory. Labor conditions for Chinese workers at the site were atrocious, but neither Russian nor Chinese officials were particularly concerned. The work pace was harrowing and even dangerous. In late 1955, there were 3,933 people working at the Shenyang Cable Factory, including a Chinese labor force of 2,704 workers, 432 engineers, and 296 service workers.[132] For the period from early 1955 until August 1956, there were fifty-four serious accidents, including the blinding of one worker in both eyes and the loss of another worker's hand. Small fires were frequent, including a serious one that started in an electric motor in the rolling metal shop. Eventually a permanent fire prevention force of twenty-five men was established. There were 176 smaller accidents and incidents among the labor force that resulted in injury and loss of labor time.[133] The planned 12,500-meter dormitory, new dining hall, and day-care facility for the workers and their families had still not been built by the end of 1956 and were clearly priorities secondary to factory production targets.[134] There was no medical attention to the needs of women, and the dining hall was unable to accommodate the dietary needs of Muslims. The lack of living space separated many workers from their families. "Several workers want to get married, but they are unable to receive a room."[135]

The primary problem at the factory concerned the most basic of matters. In heavy rains the city sewage system was backing up into the basement, which included several important workshops such as the copper and rolling shops. Workers were futilely attempting asphalt and mortar repairs to the basement floor to hold back the sewage through the summer of 1956, but the situation only worsened after a huge storm on 23 August 1956. The approximately 120 square meters of floor space covered in water created an excessive amount of moisture throughout the building. Unrelated ventilation problems in the new building did not help matters, and the smell of sewage enveloped the entire structure. The sewage, as Cheng Gongzheng and Liu Dingzhu put it with considerable understatement in September 1956, "obstructs the normal process of production."[136]

Chinese Duplicity: The Changchun Automobile Factory

The Changchun Automobile Factory was deemed Automobile Factory No. 1 in China, a huge plant designed for the mass production of approximately 30,000 cars and trucks per year. Every aspect of the factory, one of the original 156 Soviet-sponsored projects, was planned in the Soviet Union and included contributions from twenty-four different ministries. The primary corresponding site for planning, blueprints, and instruction for visiting Chinese was the well-known Stalin Automobile Factory in Moscow. The Changchun factory possessed a functioning instrument shop and repair shop by early 1955, thermal and metal shops for the production of the chassis and steel framework by August 1955, and shops for engine and exterior metal production by early 1956. On 1 October 1956, in time for the celebration of the seventh anniversary of the Chinese revolution, the first truck came off the assembly line. Although Soviet managers and industrial officials engaged in reformist discussions about their weaknesses in regard to global standards, when facing east they remained confident: "every aspect of the [production] process is informed by the experience of the Soviet automobile industry over the past twenty-five years."[137]

Numerous Chinese traveled to the Soviet Union to facilitate the emergence of a Chinese automobile and truck production program. The factory director, main engineers, and technology specialists at the Changchun plant all spent time at the Stalin Automobile Factory. Many Chinese from the ball-bearing factory in Luoyang joined workers and engineers from Changchun for extended stays in Moscow. Their professed goal was to be treated and trained like Soviet specialists, exposed to similar problems, and to acquire similar skills.[138] A group of forty-two Chinese arrived in Moscow in early 1954, another thirty-six arrived in April, and the group eventually reached several hundred.[139] The exchange reproduced in China another well-known result of the Soviet revolution: the emergence of an upwardly mobile technical intelligentsia presumably loyal to the new regime. Hang Gui, for example, an uneducated twenty-six-year-old who had been a metalworker in Shenyang for thirteen years, became a shop boss after the revolution and was now studying in Moscow. Similarly, twenty-eight-year-old Gong Wuige had been a metalworker for ten years, and Dian Youtong, twenty-seven, had eleven years of similar work experience in a factory and only three years of primary school. Party affiliation was also part of the equation, with thirty-one of the first forty-two possessing membership in the Communist Party, eight others in the Komsomol, and only three without a party connection. For some the Soviet experience was part of upward mobility in party and administrative work. Liu Denyun, thirty-two, was the party secretary of a district committee and identified as a future candidate for "political administration." Hang Zhizhen, thirty-two, was a deputy for the administration of cadres for southern China from 1950 to 1953.[140] The exchange thus reproduced the formation of a Soviet-style technical intelligentsia in China, one of the professed goals of the relationship, and for many Chinese was a path of upward mobility and opportunity. Their wages at the factory, however, remained substantially less than those of their Soviet counterparts. The highly trained Soviet specialists made as much as eight times the salary of their Chinese colleagues at the Changchun plant. Soviet managers of groups of specialists made roughly 750 yuan (1,275 rubles), Soviet engineers made 625 to 675 yuan (1,063 to 1,114 rubles), while Chinese shop managers earned just 120 to 150 yuan (204 to 255 rubles), and highly qualified Chinese workers earned 60 to 70 yuan (102 to 119 rubles).[141] As we have seen, the inequality in pay between the visiting advisers and the Chinese was a sensitive matter throughout the 1950s.

The Changchun Automobile Factory suffered from many of the same inefficiencies and difficulties as the Shenyang Cable Factory, but its experience also illustrates another issue that was part of the broader Sino-Soviet relationship. The Chinese were determined simply to copy and reproduce the Soviet automobile and light truck production industry in their country. Factory director Zhao Bing even put pressure on I. P. Gusev, the Soviet OVS commander in the Ministry of Automobile, Tractor, and Agricultural Mechanical Engineering, to facilitate this wholesale reproduction of a Soviet-style plant. On one occasion Zhao Bing pushed Gusev to send quickly a certain Sigachev from the Soviet Union to oversee key decisions in the production process, but Gusev chided Zhao Bing for the reluctance of the Chinese to make their own decisions and develop their own expertise. In spite of subsequent Chinese preoccupations with "self-reliance" and Russian colonial behavior, in this case we have a Soviet official suggesting that it would benefit the Chinese to produce more automobile parts themselves with their own people, and the Chinese factory director explicitly arguing that certain specialized products and technologies were simply easier to purchase and transport from the Soviet Union. Gusev recommended that the Chinese "bravely resolve problems" themselves and produce more portions of the automobiles and tractors in China.[142] Advisers in other forms of exchange similarly pushed the Chinese to pay more attention to developing their own specialists and their own local forms of production.[143]

In practice the chief Chinese aim seemed to be the wholesale and rapid reproduction of an industry rather than the gradual accumulation of Chinese skills and capabilities that would allow for "self-reliance" and "independence." The Chinese also seemed to feel that they were owed something from the bloc and the Soviet Union, as if they were to be financially compensated in this way for their membership in the alliance. Charles Armstrong notes a similar tendency in North Korean perceptions of obligations owed them by the socialist bloc countries.[144] Trade adviser Liu Fang joined Zhao Bing to emphasize to Gusev and other Soviet officials in January 1955 that Chinese reluctance to be more "self-sufficient" in Changchun was because the original contract called for the Soviets to provide the materials and plans in question.[145] Yet the Chinese in this regard seemed to present ulterior and self-interested motives in this automobile production exchange, as if they were eager to take advantage of the industrial secrets of a more advanced society for the sake of quick gains and rapid industrialization at home. Chinese official Cheng Cutao, also present at exchanges with the Soviet Automobile Ministry officials, "asked us to speed up the granting of technical documentation" for a related tire factory to be built in Harbin.[146] Other exchanges between these same officials reveal the Chinese side pushing the Soviets for more contracts, more blueprints, and greater plans for the wholesale import of plans and equipment for the Chinese construction of cars, trucks, and agricultural equipment.[147] The Chinese pushed to receive, as quickly as possible, as much as was possible according to the technical stipulations of the original contract, which did not seem to be a particularly "friendly" maneuver.

The practice also countered the original goal of the advising program: eventual Chinese self-sufficiency. Zhou Enlai admitted as much in a conversation with East German, Polish, and Czechoslovak officials in February 1955. China's inability to coordinate the use of labor, machinery, and resources, he reasoned, made the import of finished machinery and other industrial products preferable and logical.[148] In the wake of the split, this led many former Soviet exchange participants as well as scholars to suggest that the Chinese had taken advantage of Soviet "internationalism" for the sake of serving their own nationalistic interests. In this rendition the Soviet Union again appears not as aggressor but as victim, this time of the Chinese "betrayal" of the many "selfless" advisers and their aid projects.[149]

Conclusion

"Proletarian internationalism" perpetually promised something new, something divorced from the past, different from the world of the West, and far from the heritage of colonialism in China. The advisers themselves were at the front line of intrabloc exchange and understood themselves to represent the very notion of "internationalism." In practice, however, the heritage of the past shaped the experience of intrabloc exchange and the Sino-Soviet relationship. The tensions of the advising program were numerous, evident in the disputes over pay, privilege, technical competence, colonial attitudes, cultural insensitivity, misbehavior, and payment for blueprints. In the world of "proletarian internationalism" there were bills to pay, contracts to fulfill, and goods to deliver. These were the issues that made up the daily experience of industrial advisers, economic managers, financial accountants, and numerous figures that were part of the advising program in China, matters far more pressing than speculation about Marxist-Leninist tradition and theory.

Like the general system of *komandirovka*, industrial exchange in the bloc emerged out of Soviet practice and tradition in a way that inevitably raised Chinese concerns about imperialism and "great-power chauvinism." The system had its origins and source of authority in Moscow and drew on not just Soviet but even nineteenth-century imperial practice. Given the incentives and structure of the Soviet industrial system, the practices of economic exchange that we have come to call "socialism" were rational and comprehensible within this world. They were not efficient, however, and they especially lent themselves to cultural insensitivity and chauvinism. These were the practices that shaped the world of intrabloc exchange. The system was gratifying to the Russians. As in the nineteenth century, officials on the distant eastern frontier found themselves of service to the industrial, political, and security needs of the imperial center. They were pleased to have the opportunity to extend the fruits of modern industry and culture to eastern lands that in their view were historically dormant and distant from civilization.

The grand Chinese effort to "learn from the Soviet Union" also possessed a practical dimension that frequently conflicted with the many public professions of gratitude. The stated goal of self-sufficiency and a future of independent and indigenous development was instead sometimes simply an effort to absorb as much Soviet industrial technology, expertise, and even trade secrets as quickly as possible. The Chinese attitude in this matter was sometimes openly cavalier, as if somehow the Soviet Union and the bloc owed China this sort of support, presumably as gratitude for a Chinese decision to "lean to one side," which had important demographic and geographic ramifications in the Cold War. The motives and practices of both sides in this complicated relationship were thus frequently suspect, all of which was hopelessly complicated further by the inefficiencies of the socialist system.

CHAPTER 2

Learning from the Central Europeans

Authority and Expertise in the Era of Reform

Right now the Soviet Union has extensive new technical experience
unknown to the rest of the world.
—Liu Shaoqi, 5 October 1949

The virtues and necessities of "learning from the Soviet Union [*xuexi sulian*]"
was a constant refrain in China after 1950. Soviet advisers, argued I. Dudinskii
in a prominent theoretical journal, represented "leading technical and organizational experience."[1] Public discussion, however, often did not correspond
to private practice or sometimes even to the obvious. Everyone knew that the
Central European countries were the most technologically and economically
advanced in the bloc. This chapter explores the implications of this reality for
the socialist bloc during the 1950s. The emerging experience of reform, which
accelerated after Stalin's death in March 1953, further directed the attention of
the bloc to the Central Europeans, whose technological achievements, industrial development, and greater access to the West became even more important
in the effort to compete economically with the West and America in the Cold
War. The evolution of the Soviet Union over the course of the decade provides
the important background to this new orientation in policy, with direct consequences for intrabloc exchange and the Sino-Soviet relationship.

The "Leading People" and the Central Europeans

Among themselves, even high-level officials acknowledged the real source
of industrial expertise in the bloc, since borrowing from the East Germans,
Czechoslovaks, Hungarians, and Poles was an important component of these
officials' plans and projects. The Chinese certainly saw it this way. "You have
progressed much further than we have," Mao exclaimed to a visiting Hungarian
delegation in September 1954.[2] Your "industry is very well-developed," Peng

Dehuai told a Polish military delegation in the fall of 1957, and "your military technology and training is modern."[3] The "high level of industrial mechanization" in East Germany and Czechoslovakia was especially important to the Chinese economy, noted embassy officials in Prague.[4] Countless examples can be produced from the Chinese Ministry of Foreign Affairs archive—from ambassadors in the bloc capitals to top leaders in Beijing such as Zhou Enlai, Li Fuchun, Bo Yibo, and Li Dequan—that illustrate respect for the economic and industrial achievements of the Central Europeans and gratitude for their contributions to China.[5] The disjuncture between this reality and the constant refrain about the importance of the Soviet Union was frequently sensitive, of course, raising complicated issues for the Chinese as they gradually learned more about the Soviet Union and became more confident of their own potential contribution to the "construction of socialism." It was frustrating to Central Europeans themselves but viewed by party and state elites as a compromise still necessary in the wake of the horrific war. Poland was "not a big country," a Polish military official told Mao, and "without the protection of the Soviet Union we could not construct socialism."[6]

Soviet advisers themselves were sometimes frustrated with the situation, as they found themselves and their country frequently the subject of derision and scorn. Eastern and Central Europeans regularly complained about comparative Russian underdevelopment, idle factories, and poorly designed equipment. Soviet engineer Ivan Korotin identified a consistent problem that he experienced in Romania, Czechoslovakia, and Hungary: the Europeans frequently excluded Soviet specialists from the important discussions where work plans and projects were formulated. Their first preference for collaboration and advice, he noted with chagrin, was clearly with the West.[7] Hungarians were generally "oriented to the capitalist West," added A. Fedorov, a visiting Russian history professor at the Lenin Institute in Budapest from 1952 to 1954 (the institute would produce significant intellectual dissent in 1956). Eastern and Central Europeans in the bloc were proud of their cultural heritage, well aware of their comparative advantages in technology and industrial development, and, of course, experienced at borrowing from the West. Czechoslovaks, Hungarians, and Poles as recently as 1947 had depended almost entirely on trade with the West for numerous resources and goods.[8] Fedorov, a self-described "member of the CPSU since 1929," struggled to cope with Hungarian "hostility to Russians and other peoples of our socialist fatherland."[9] East Germans in particular frequently complained that they were providing the bloc more in knowledge and expertise than they were receiving.[10]

From the Soviet perspective this was part of the plan, however, and the small countries of the region should still be grateful for their "liberation" from the Nazis and their "imperialist" successors still threatening the socialist world. Both the Soviets and the Chinese were eager to learn and borrow from the region. The Central Europeans and the Chinese were more enthusiastic about developing trade and exchange with each other than they were with the Soviets, and they complained about the initial need to use Moscow as an intermediary in their emerging exchange.[11] Bohuslav Laštovička, the Czechoslovak ambassador in Moscow, made plans to send Czechoslovak specialists to the Chinese Northeast in the spring of 1949, until foreign affairs official Anastas Gromyko pronounced this "still premature." Laštovička continued to propose the exchange of Czech and Chinese delegations and specialists that summer.[12] Embassy official E. Štefan pushed Gromyko on 30 September 1949 for details about the impending Soviet recognition of the new Chinese state, and he requested transit visas across the Soviet Union for a Czechoslovak trading delegation.[13] Officials from foreign affairs ministries throughout the bloc quickly established diplomatic relations with China in early October.[14] The Czechoslovaks were the first socialist bloc country after the Soviet Union to sign a Treaty of Mutual Alliance with China and to set up a consulate in Shanghai.[15] The Poles, Hungarians, East Germans, and others from the region followed close behind.[16]

The Chinese were eager as well. In December 1949 Wang Jiaxiang informed Mao of the prospects for trade with countries such as Poland, Czechoslovakia, and East Germany.[17] A month later the Chinese prepared for the Czechoslovaks a list of goods "required by new China" in the process of reconstruction.[18] Historically trade between Central Europe and China was limited, of course, slowed by the geographic distance and the political instability in China, but by 1953, 70 percent of Chinese foreign trade was conducted with the bloc. The first trade agreement between the Chinese and the Czechoslovaks was signed on 16 April 1950 and was followed by a larger agreement between the two countries signed on 15 July 1952 in Prague.[19]

The Czechoslovaks exported to China construction materials, compressors, cars, buses, tractors, telephones, turbines, boilers, telecommunications equipment, diesel motors, and other goods in the early 1950s. They received iron ore, wolfram, molybdenum, tungsten, zinc, oil, wool, leather, tobacco, fish, meat, seeds, beans, rice, poultry, and other agricultural products.[20] This was more or less the nature of the exchange with the East Germans, Poles, Hungarians, and other European bloc countries as well. The East Germans sent optical equipment and helped with radio, cement, and sugar-processing factories; the Bulgarians sold electrical equipment. Hungarian trade with China rose by 50 percent from 1952 to 1953.[21] The Czechoslovaks were also heavily involved in sugar-processing and cement factories, as well as several of the larger electrical power stations in China. They were also important suppliers of military equipment for the Korean War, including almost 100 airplanes (such as the MiG-15, the IL-14, and the Aero 45), plane equipment and engines, and 90 million 7.62 mm machine guns. Aleš Skřivan estimates the total value of this "special material" for the military from 1953 to 1961 to be worth 340 million crowns (korunni).[22]

The Soviets as well were eager for exchange with Central Europe and frank about the potential benefits to their economy of socialist bloc "proletarian internationalism." Soviet specialists in areas such as industrial auto design and construction especially valued trips to the GDR for the purpose of procuring not just experience but also copies of blueprints and other information.[23] The Ministry of Metallurgy sent its officials to Czechoslovakia to study the numerous components surrounding the production of aluminum casings and their transport, storage, and safety. Ministry officials accepted the reality of superior Czechoslovak expertise and experience in this area and demanded careful work and reporting practices from their experts during their stays there.[24] Ministry of Trade officials carefully listed and described any American-made accounting equipment they came across in Bulgaria.[25] While critical of standards of organization, management, and cleanliness at the Kolarovgradskii Machine-Tool Construction Factory in Bulgaria, V. V. Gushchinn, a machine-tool engineer from a factory in Gor'kii, was excited to find equipment whose design was "entirely original and very simple, and [that could] be successfully adopted in all of our factories."[26] A significant part of the Soviet advising program was the identification of superior methods of technology, organization, and industrial practice that might benefit the Soviet Union, which was not industrial espionage because it served the broader and justifiable program of the "construction of socialism."

The Chinese noticed all these trends. They also noticed that Soviet advisers viewed the heritage of colonialism in China as an opportunity to gain access to the West. S. Martsenitsen relished his work at Beijing Central Telegraph precisely because it gave him the chance to experience the latest in scientific debate and exchange. "I composed a list of literature that interested us so we can have it sent to the Soviet Union. I brought home nine albums of material about American and German equipment, and I made photocopies of material. . . .

These new developments interest us very much."[27] As in Eastern and Central Europe, Soviet advisers routinely and carefully documented technological equipment likely to be useful to the Soviet Union and tried to obtain it. P. Lysov, for example, noted the existence of a series of powerful water-cooling electric rectifiers from Germany at the Beijing Scientific-Research Institute, and D. V. Zheltukhin was pleased to obtain synthetic fibers from Harbin useful to the Soviet chemical industry.[28] S. F. Laptev scoured Chinese research institutes for help with the production of lead oxide, tin, antimony, manganese, and cobalt.[29] In Shanghai, reported one adviser, the Soviets found a factory that had been "built by French and English firms and [was] fitted with equipment very different from that of Soviet factories." "The technological process also has a series of advantages," he continued, and the finished product is of "high quality and exceeds that of our own."[30] Also in Shanghai, Soviet experts at the Electric Machine Construction Factory were excited about the financial potential of repackaging Chinese versions of large turbogenerators for foreign export.[31] On Hainan Island the Soviets were hopeful they might learn how to produce cars and trucks competitive for export to tropical climates.[32] Czechoslovak advisers were especially interested in industrial firms left behind in Shanghai, previously home to many "foreign imperialists," and they compiled descriptions of lathes, turbine generators, boilers, and other machinery left by a prerevolutionary power plant in Guangzhou.[33] Martsenitsen expressed intellectual excitement at this exposure to the broader world, but even he unwittingly subverted the premise of the "friendship." His experience in China was an opportunity to escape the stifling intellectual and professional climate of Stalinism and learn of international trends and research in communication networks. His comments, however, confirmed certain Chinese suspicions about the qualifications of the Soviet "teachers," as well as the opportunities and strengths the Chinese brought to the relationship.

As the Chinese began to notice the intense Soviet interest in Western technology and began to wonder about the comparative level of Soviet technological development, the Soviet advisers became embarrassed and extremely sensitive on this score. The comparative weaknesses of Soviet industry and technology were especially difficult topics in lands to the East, where the traditional Russian civilizing mission was an important subtext to the exchange. Many Chinese still remembered education and expertise before the revolution, which especially in the Chinese coastal cities entailed significant exposure to the practices and knowledge of the West. The frequent admonitions from the advisers together with the Chinese authorities illustrates a level of skepticism on the part of the Chinese specialists and workers.[34] "Old Chinese technical workers" in particular were likely to question the authority of the Soviet experts.[35] Others "arrogantly do not heed as they should the Soviet specialists."[36] A Comrade Chernenko from the Ministry of Communications especially feared being unable to respond to Chinese queries concerning current technological developments in communications, and he was frustrated that the OVS and the ministry could not provide him with up-to-date scientific literature. For A. S. Smirnov the ineptitude of his colleagues in the Soviet Union left him in an embarrassing position vis-à-vis his Chinese counterparts. "It's a good thing that I understood the matter [concerning a postal service]. If it had been another comrade, he would have found himself in an uncomfortable situation before the Chinese comrades." A Comrade Oganov complained that the "Chinese comrades receive the very latest technical literature, and I haven't read it. The GUES library does not have such material."[37] Sometimes the Soviets were sending to China literature from the 1930s.[38] The Yugoslavs' eagerness to bring attention to the comparative weaknesses of Russian technology in global terms enraged bloc officials in China.

Smirnov subsequently advised his Soviet colleagues not to air differences of opinion about technical matters in front of the Chinese. Instead, they were to resolve matters in private and present a united front so as to avoid "distrust and alarm among the Chinese comrades." His advice suggested a climate of frequent tension prompted by the routine Chinese intellectual challenges to the matter at hand. "The Soviet specialist should patiently illustrate each of his conclusions, and with pencil in hand convince by the logic of evidence, practice, and experience."[39] A. Fedorov in Budapest described similar scenes, at one point admonishing his colleagues for their long and boring lectures, and for public fighting in front of the "Magyars."[40] The idea that the Soviets were the "leading people" of the bloc was a bit of a fiction, and the Chinese knew it. Both the Soviets and Chinese valued the Central European societies for numerous reasons, including their ability to procure advanced technology from the West.

Soviet Paranoia and Inefficiency

To complicate the matter further, the preoccupation with security and the paranoia that was long part of Soviet culture posed additional impediments to bloc coordination and exchange. The Soviets especially feared the edges of their bloc, those areas "bordering capitalist states."[41] This prevented the Soviet

Union from serving as a useful coordinator of exchange, or even from fulfilling its function as the "center" of the socialist world. Soviet officials feared their own allies: visiting Czechoslovaks had to be warned not to allow their notes and materials accumulated in the Soviet Union from falling into the hands of "people from other countries in the Czechoslovak Republic"; the Soviet Ministry of Agriculture sent peach, almond, and cherry seedlings to other agricultural ministries with a warning that they were not intended for anyone beyond the borders of the bloc; and officials at the Stalin Metallurgical Factory in Leningrad wondered if it was appropriate to let visiting Czechoslovaks inspect a condensation turbine.[42] In part this was a socialist version of the copyright struggle. Officials at the Ministry of Mechanical Engineering pointedly reminded the Chinese that the blueprints and technical plans for an air compressor could not be passed on to a third party or country, and could not be "patented or published for any purpose."[43]

The Chinese along with the rest of the bloc were increasingly frustrated and even mystified by these Soviet tendencies. Bloc advisers and officials found themselves badgering Soviet officials and ministries for more information, responsiveness, and coordination on matters from precious metals development and automobile production to urban planning and apartment construction.[44] The Soviet Union appeared incapable of serving as the coordinator of bloc-wide systems of communication and exchange, and perhaps was not even interested in doing so. Czechoslovak officials at the Central Scientific-Research Institute pushed for deeper and more diverse forms of cooperation throughout the bloc, beyond simply "the exchange of technical material."[45] The Chinese added to the chorus of East German, Bulgarian, and Hungarian complaints about bureaucracy, unanswered letters, scientific isolation, and poorly organized exchanges. East German scholars found it ironic that they could more easily get Soviet books from West Germany and Denmark rather than through the cumbersome Mezhdunarodnaia kniga (International Books).[46] Czechoslovak industrial experts arrived in the Soviet Union with numerous practical questions about "cost-accounting [khozraschet]," planning, and production problems but were instead treated to a series of theoretical seminars about "socialist property," "politics and economics in a socialist society," and "economic laws under socialism" from the Ministry of Mechanical Engineering.[47] For further edification the Russians recommended a long list of readings from Marx, Engels, and Stalin, as well as a 1945 book by Viacheslav Molotov called *The 28th Anniversary of the Great October Socialist Revolution*.[48] In Prague, airline transportation specialists such as František Novák were forced to evoke the problem of basic public safety in order to elicit a response from his Soviet counterparts concerning the standardization of airport equipment between the two countries.[49] The Chinese were similarly frustrated at this very practical level. "Where can we find statistics on the development of the economy from 1938 to 1955?," queried Chinese officials in July 1956. "They do not exist," answered Soviet officials, "other than what you can find in the yearly volumes of *The National Economy of the USSR* [*Narodnoe khoziaistvo SSSR*]."[50]

In China both Soviet advisers and their Chinese colleagues were frequently stymied by these basic problems of communication and coordination. The records of the economic exchanges chronicle their almost desperate attempts to elicit responses and cooperation from their colleagues at home. S. G. Kraelov, working to improve a radio station in Shanghai, found himself saddled with equipment from the Ministry of Communications that arrived in an "unsatisfactory condition," technical documentation that did not correspond to the plan, and inaccurate machinery instructions.[51] A group of advisers at the Shanghai Boat Construction Factory reported receiving boxes from the USSR with miscellaneous items: "a collective [labor] agreement from some Leningrad factory, unnecessary bolts, garbage, and so on."[52] A. S. Smirnov and others in communications complained about the long delays in the receipt of technical literature from GUES, and the inability to develop direct ties with the pertinent economic ministries. A. P. Sorenzon, a teacher at the Beijing Communications Institute, in desperation wrote directly to an official in the Ministry of Foreign Affairs' Far East Department to complain that "in spite of my repeated reminders to the Ministry of Communications, at the present time I have not received A SINGLE ONE of my requests for scholarly collections."[53] A certain "N" at the Luoyang Ball-Bearing Plant sent numerous pleas ("Did you receive my first two [letters]?") to the Ministry of Automobile Production: "Just send all the blueprints you have, and we'll choose what we need here."[54] Numerous other specialists complained that progress in China was significantly slowed by confusion over which industrial ministry was responsible for what.[55] Or sometimes ministries would make agreements with China that their own factories could not fulfill in a timely fashion, making the Chinese victims of the basic practices of the Soviet industrial system.[56] These hierarchical and excessively bureaucratic practices formed the background to the criticism of the Soviet system emerging in the thinking of higher officials in the Chinese Communist Party.

At the lower levels, many Chinese contributors to the projects were disturbed by the situation. Tan Wai, an official in the Ministry of Mechanical

Chinese examine agricultural equipment at the Soviet exhibit in Beijing, 1954.
(RGAE f. 635, op. 1, d. 291, l. 26)

Engineering, asked his counterpart P. S. Bulgakov to arrange for more direct communication between Chinese and Soviet institute directors, factory managers, and specialists. He hoped for greater flexibility in the Soviet response to issues and problems in China, direct communication at the lower levels of the exchange without the involvement of the industrial ministries, and "mutual consultation about accounting reports and research work."[57] Ling Xueqing waited for months to receive an answer to his queries about the sources of corrosion in the lead casings of communications cables installed with the aid of a Soviet expert who was long gone and inaccessible in the Soviet Union.[58] Soviet preoccupations with security inhibited such exchanges as well. Chinese embassy officials in Moscow were frequently frustrated at their inability to organize what they considered to be the routine and vital trips of Chinese specialists to factories and other work sites.[59] The eventual calls for Chinese "self-reliance," long a touchy issue because of the history of colonial dependency, emerged with new rigor because of this more immediate and direct dependency on the Soviet Union.

Reform and Intrabloc Exchange

The Soviets' recognition of their comparative backwardness within the bloc gained ground with the advent of reform under Khrushchev, which again directed attention to Central Europe. This Soviet form of self-criticism was more sensitive than it might appear, as the Soviets had invested so heavily in the notion that they were the "leading people" and country of the bloc, the "liberators" of Eastern and Central Europe, and the makers of the first socialist revolution. Like de-Stalinization generally, things moved quickly after the dictator's death in March 1953, which in the case of the advisers and intrabloc exchange meant a lively debate on industrial management in the Soviet Union itself. "Reform" should not be misunderstood in this context: industrial managers were interested in not so much an exposé of the dictator as the improvement and greater efficiency of their traditional strategies for competing with the powerful West. Stalin-era secrecy, autarky, and suspicion in the view of many industrial managers was preventing them from doing their jobs, which they perceived as above all improving the country's efficiency and strength in order to compete with the West. The Central European countries were linchpins of this mission. Factory managers and industrial planners were at the forefront of the Soviet administrative elite, and they felt little need to apologize or take personal responsibility for the practices of the past. They were unafraid of security and foreign affairs officials, in part because they were confident that the improvement of their work was in the interest of the country and the bloc in the Cold War against the Americans.

Industry administrators and experts spoke openly and adamantly about their dilemmas in gaining access to the most modern methods in order to improve their efficiency and productivity. A factory director in Podol'sk, for example, pushed for upgrades in sewing machines and related equipment in 1955 by reminding officials in the Ministry of Mechanical Engineering that the 1-A machine was heavy, outdated, and "possesses the look of about 1886." His factory, the primary producer and developer of sewing machines and their related technologies for the entire Soviet Union, suffered from a "complete lack of information about sewing machine construction abroad." He estimated that Soviet technology in this area would lag behind that of the West for a good ten to fifteen years, and he suggested that the ministry sponsor his factory specialists and engineers abroad, in both Western and Eastern Europe, for months at a time in order to update their knowledge.[60] Managers and economic administrators demanded change and more flexibility in order to pursue more efficiently their agenda of the imitation, reproduction, and even theft of technological innovation. Their concerns about local initiative and horizontal relations among enterprises eventually percolated upward, to be expressed in the economic reforms common to most of the bloc countries by the late 1950s.[61]

A revived effort to compete with the West again directed the attention of the bloc to Central Europe. Lagging behind not just the West but also the people's democracies, economic managers frankly argued, Russia needed to pay more attention to its practices and norms. Iu. S. Muntian, an engineer working on oxygen compressors in Czechoslovakia, suggested in September 1955 to the Ministry of Mechanical Engineering that in order to make goods more desirable in Eastern and Central Europe, the Soviet Union must "carefully study the particularities of [the foreign] market and its traditions." Soviet goods and industrial plans, while "sufficient for our domestic conditions," were "completely incomprehensible for other countries."[62] A Ministry of Communications engineer wrote in September 1956 that machinery, technology, and industrial development were often superior in the GDR and throughout Central Europe. D. D. Erigin, who also had experience in Eastern and Central Europe, suggested a "fundamental rethinking" of the "role of the advising apparatus" in the people's democracies, concluding, "We cannot say that the Soviet Union occupies the leading place in many areas of the economy."[63] Numerous industrial experts and specialists pushed for greater and more rapid communication with the pertinent economic ministries in Moscow, and they expressed intellectual and professional insecurity about the value of their expertise outside of the Soviet Union. The original "fraternal" equation in practice was reversed, and Soviet officials and advisers increasingly seconded what Central Europeans had been long saying to themselves: Soviet engineers and other specialists should go to places like Czechoslovakia and Poland for training to improve their qualifications and knowledge.[64]

The Chinese embassy in Moscow reported to Beijing on 3 January 1956 that Chinese institutions, universities, factories, and so on could now "directly initiate ties with institutions and [their] responsible individuals in the people's democracies." This was no small matter, as the examples above suggest. Reform in intrabloc exchange corresponded to the process of industrial reform in the Soviet Union itself. There was more at stake in the wider bloc, however, especially in the tumultuous year of 1956. The Soviet decree explicitly sought to address the "increasingly complicated relations of friendship and collaboration among the people's democracies."[65] The Chinese viewed the advising program as part of a series of larger issues that deeply concerned the Soviets. The two countries remained distant and "understood very little about each other," maintained Chinese embassy officials a few months later. The advising program and intrabloc exchange were characterized by "shortcomings," and the chief culprit was "great-power hegemonic ideology" in the Soviet Union and Eastern Europe. The Chinese remained hopeful, however, because reform was taking place and the Soviets were now listening to the criticism from the bloc countries. "Great power hegemonic thought and sentiment can be overcome."[66] The notion that the bloc should value Chinese "experience" more highly would become extremely sensitive after 1956.

The intersection of the problems of the advising program with the stability of the bloc itself was especially evident in the fall of 1956, as the rebellion in Hungary took place. The Chinese had specifically raised the problem of Soviet "great-power chauvinism" on numerous occasions, and now the political consequences seemed to be on display. That October, a Chinese delegation including Liu Shaoqi, Deng Xiaoping, and other top leaders went to Moscow, where it contributed to a Central Committee decree of 30 October 1956 titled "Declaration on Further Strengthening of the Foundation of Friendship and Cooperation between the Soviet Union and Other Socialist Countries." Although most historians of international relations and the Cold War have been more interested in the Chinese contribution to the decision to use force in Budapest to maintain the "unity" of the bloc, the original purpose of this visit was to discuss the advising program and intrabloc relations, as the Soviet document maintained. The "principles of national sovereignty, mutual interest, and equality in economic relations," the decree proclaimed, were also pertinent to the advising program. "As is known, in the period of the formation of a new social system, the Soviet Union, at the request of the governments of the countries of people's democracy, sent to these countries collections of their specialists—engineers, agronomists, technicians, military advisers. Recently the Soviet Union has posed before the socialist states the question of the withdrawal of the advisers."[67] The call for at least a reduction in the amount of advisers from certain areas, if not a total withdrawal, initially came from the Far East Department of the Soviet Ministry of Foreign Affairs.[68]

The Chinese state-builder and original architect of the program, Liu Shaoqi, declined this proposal. In a discussion with Iudin the very day the declaration was issued, he conceded that perhaps the time had come to consider "whether or not the advisers should return to the USSR (but not the technical specialists)."[69] In an early public announcement of the advising program soon after the 1949 revolution, he had noted that when "their time of service is no longer important to China, they will return to the Soviet Union."[70] The Soviet declaration similarly declared victory, suggesting the people's democracies had now created their own "qualified national cadres," making the advising program unnecessary.[71] In fact, however, numerous institutions and enterprises, including military ones, continued to remind the Soviets of the Chinese lack of knowledge and experience and need for aid.[72] Liu Shaoqi was aware of frustrations with the program, but he was not in favor of ending it. As a state-builder highly invested in the exchange, he primarily feared the consequences of an abrupt Soviet rethinking of the exchange. He recommended further discussion and "collaboration with the interested countries, refraining from the sudden withdrawal of all the specialists, as was done in Yugoslavia."[73] The Soviets would not forget this Chinese interest in the program. Khrushchev, for example, reminded the Eastern European parties of this earlier Chinese reluctance to part with the advisers in his explanation of the 1960 withdrawal.[74]

Chinese Ministry of Foreign Affairs commentary proclaimed the "Declaration on Further Strengthening" to be "correct" and "highly significant," in particular for its attention to equality and its willingness to address the "mistake of great-power chauvinism."[75] In an important twist, Chinese officials described "great-power chauvinism" as an "error" associated with "bourgeois chauvinism," laying the foundation for Mao's later reasoning that the Soviet Union had become a "revisionist" state reproducing capitalism.[76] This logic was a product of the overall Chinese encounter with the socialist bloc system rather than a purely textual interpretation drawn from Marxist-Leninist tradition.

The break was still several years away, however, and in the meantime liaison representatives from Soviet ministries continued their effort to improve intrabloc coordination and communication. In December 1957 some forty-nine OVS representatives from numerous ministries and institutions gathered to consult with GUES. Many of the issues identified intermittently by concerned officials now surfaced in a more systematic fashion. P. M. Korienko, from the Academy of Construction and Architecture, suggested a simplification of the process of sending Soviet advisers and materials abroad, as well as financial support for cordial activities accompanied by "tea, sandwiches, drinks, souvenirs, etc." V. G. Ermolenko of State Construction (*Gosstroi*) suggested a reorganization and standardization of the payment system for advisers throughout the bloc ("payment for translators, payment of accompanying engineers, transportation expenses, entertainment, souvenirs, etc."), as well as more attention to the formulation of a "work program" for advisers before they embarked on their journey. V. M. Stenaev, an OVS official from Gor'kii, similarly demanded clear plans for all foreign specialists before they left on *komandirovka*, regardless of their destination or country of origin.[77] OVS managers wanted a rational system of exchange between the bloc countries to help them determine the value of goods and services from diverse countries and parts of the bloc (debts were cleared according to the "transfer" ruble, which in practice amounted virtually to a complicated form of barter). Ermolenko and M. S. Pobedonostsev suggested the creation of a new institution to hold and distribute information and technical material developed as a product of the numerous bloc exchanges. Experts and advisers were continually reinventing the wheel, and forgetting the lessons learned in previous exchanges.

Besides the numerous practical problems and issues surrounding intrabloc exchange, the gathered OVS officials identified a broader political dilemma that plagued the overall administrative system known as "socialism." Veterans of bloc affairs knew the weaknesses of the socialist system, in the same way that provincial Soviet managers understood the incentives and practices that limited their productivity. Economic managers, officials, and advisers resisted the centralizing demands of the Soviet state and viewed the SEV (Comecon) as a constant interference in matters best left to local managers of a given exchange. Their criticisms of the SEV extended beyond its inefficiency and failure to store and distribute information. Officials from diverse ministries were frustrated by the SEV's political intrusion into the administrative and economic functioning of the Soviet system. They wanted more political autonomy, expressed above all in the power to select and send experts, equipment, and technical documentation between ministries and bureaucracies without intrusion from above. Their criticisms of the Soviet industrial system were similar to those offered by non-Soviets from the broader bloc. They wanted GUES to serve as a kind of library of blueprints and the history of the exchanges, and they even hoped to eliminate the SEV from the equation.[78]

In spite of this, the lower-level forms of bloc exchange continued to attract the attention of central officials and planners, from ministries in Moscow to embassies throughout the bloc to Ministry of Finance officials demanding control over any expenditure that took place outside of the Soviet Union.[79] P. M. Kornienko worried about the small moments that inhibited cultural exchange and international relations within the socialist world. The Czechs treated the Soviets well in Prague, he pointed out, but "when they travel here, we can't even locate a small sum to offer them some sort of present (an album or a souvenir) that only costs 70–100 rubles; you just try to get that money from the accountant—you'll never see it." A simple translation sometimes required the input of several different ministries. Non-Russians, from the Czechs to the Chinese, reported M. G. Zemskov of Moscow, were often wondering why their basic requests and concerns took so long to address. I. M. Pumpianskii, from Iaroslav, pointed out that the proper selection of cadres and specialists for trips abroad was virtually impossible in the face of an urgent demand from Gosplan.[80] The concerns of the OVS representatives and GUES officials amounted to a basic critique of the centralized and politicized Soviet administrative system, which inhibited or even prevented local factories, managers, and enterprises from developing rational programs and exchanges among themselves. Soviet advisers in China, and the Chinese themselves, quickly came to similar conclusions.

Socialist Bloc Planning and the Dilemma of China

Reforming these institutional practices was difficult because central planning by definition was an attempt to use the resources of the bloc to serve the broader needs of "socialism," which was defined in Moscow and usually pertained to Soviet needs and the prosecution of the Cold War. The emergence of planning in the bloc was inevitably tainted by political concerns. Just as Moscow made plans to control resource and labor allocation in distant provinces, so it did for the broader bloc after 1948–49. Anastas Mikoyan and Viacheslav Molotov chose representatives from Eastern European countries to participate in a select meeting in January 1949 to form a coordinating council for bloc planning, import-export targets, the oversight of plan fulfillment, and technology transfer. Issue number two on the agenda of the newly created SEV (26–28 April 1949) was "relations with Yugoslavia."[81] Yugoslav frustrations over the joint companies, the Soviet advisers, and other bloc practices, of course, contributed to the contentious split in 1948.[82] Bloc planning also possessed this political dimension, and Mikoyan and Molotov wanted to ensure that bilateral economic relations with Moscow took precedence over any regional federation or emerging forms of regional integration.[83]

China maintained only observer rather than membership status within the SEV in the 1950s, and industrial coordination was instead handled by the Scientific-Technical Commission. The two sides' original agreement on scientific-technical collaboration was signed on 12 October 1954. The commission met frequently to draw up plans for its yearly programs of work, generally alternating between Moscow and Beijing. The first session took place in Moscow in December 1954, followed by the second session in Beijing in June 1955. As the Great Leap Forward complicated the Sino-Soviet relationship, the commission actually met more frequently. The eighth session, for example, was in January 1959 in Beijing, followed by the ninth session in Moscow in July 1959 and the tenth session beginning on 12 October 1959 in Beijing.[84] This increasing frequency of meetings was repeated with the Central and Eastern Europeans.[85] The commission evolved in response to changing Chinese concerns. Its early work generally addressed the Chinese effort to establish the foundations of large industries, such as the manufacture of ships, hydroelectric turbines, cars, heavy metallurgical equipment, and so on, while after 1958 the Chinese focused more on developing the academic and research expertise that would allow them to develop and sustain their own industries. The new agreement of 18 January 1958 reflected this transition, as well as emerging tensions in Sino-Soviet affairs.[86]

The socialist bloc and China were learning about each other, and China's reluctance and inability to conform to the planners' expectations and needs caused a dilemma as early as the fall of 1954, when the Chinese complained that socialist bloc goods and equipment were sometimes inappropriate for Chinese needs and often difficult for them to service and repair. While large Czechoslovak diesel motors, for example, might be appropriate in large Chinese ships, smaller ones for other vehicles might just as well be built by the Chinese themselves. Czechoslovak officials such as Ambassador František Komzala worried about this Chinese reluctance to conform to the plan, so to speak, in October 1954. He pushed his colleagues to be more flexible and sensitive to Chinese needs and expectations.[87]

Those concerns, however, were not appreciated by the Chinese, who generally remained uninterested in the impact and consequences of their actions in other parts of the bloc. The Chinese surprised and irritated the Czechoslovaks with their propensity to alter previous trade agreements, such as a 1954 agreement for the Czechoslovak export of an electrical generator in 1955.[88] In April 1955 the East German ambassador to the Soviet Union, Johannes König, similarly complained about "several difficulties for the GDR" created by China's changing plans.[89] König was the GDR ambassador to China from 1953 to 1955 and had been a member of the embassy staff in Beijing since 1950. The much larger 4 July 1956 agreement with Czechoslovakia called for fifteen heavy industrial projects in China, with the Czechoslovak investment at 2,257,000 crowns and the Chinese investment at 1,870,000 crowns.[90] The

Chinese Central Committee met from 10 to 15 November, however, and sent Zhou Enlai to break the news to the Soviet Union and bloc officials about an impending 17–18 percent cut in China's previously promised investment in the projects.[91] Zhou Enlai adopted a contrite tone in a conversation with Iudin, blamed China's own economic planners for the miscalculations, and conceded that "serious economic measures" such as this should not be formulated with only the "interest of one's own country" in mind.[92] Other important planning officials such as Li Fuchun explained to Ambassador Antonin Gregor and Czechoslovak foreign affairs officials that new Chinese needs required a contraction of their previous commitments.[93] The Czechoslovaks claimed the reduced Chinese commitments that continued to unfold through early 1957 meant a 50 percent shortfall from the original 4 July 1956 agreement.[94] Chinese officials were posing increasingly skeptical questions about the suitability of the socialist bloc industrial model for China. In the spring of 1957 Liu Xiao explained to Soviet embassy official Nikolai Fedorenko that the Chinese intended to back out of the joint production of the MiG-17f airplane and the VK-I-F motor by late 1958. They were looking into other airplane models that would better "answer contemporary needs and Chinese conditions."[95] These plans and equipment had been specifically requested by the Chinese in the 15 May 1953 agreement on military cooperation.[96] This was part of the general reduction in the Chinese import of military equipment from the Soviet Union and the bloc that began in 1956. "We realize this will create some difficulties" for the Soviet government, apologized Chen Yun to Nikolai Bulganin.[97]

Frustrated officials throughout the bloc quickly calculated the economic impact of the changes for their countries, again illustrating the financial constraints and limitations of "proletarian internationalism." The Czechoslovak Ministry of Foreign Affairs found itself under pressure from heavy industry ministries at home such as the Ministry of Metallurgy. A whole series of factories in Brno, Prague, and the provinces in Czechoslovakia had put significant funds and effort into preparing equipment, blueprints, and materials for electric generators, enterprises, and factories in China. The Czechoslovaks wanted reimbursement from the Chinese for their losses, and they also were frustrated and insulted by the apparent Chinese obliviousness to the consequences of their abrupt actions. R. Dvořák of the Czechoslovak Ministry of Foreign Affairs recommended bringing a team of Chinese planners and finance officials to Prague to show them the nature of socialist planning and the losses incurred by the Czechoslovaks. Foreign affairs officials composed a detailed chart illustrating the costs incurred by diverse enterprises in Czechoslovakia as a result of China's rethinking of its plan.[58] Czechoslovak officials in Beijing warned their colleagues in Prague in late 1957 that the planning situation was deteriorating, and likely to get worse.[99] The chaos of the Great Leap Forward in 1958 and 1959 meant far greater changes to the character of socialist bloc exchange with China, of course. The Chinese import of tractors from Czechoslovakia decreased from 11,500 to 5,235 between July and November 1958. There were reductions on a similar scale for cars, construction equipment, buses, and other products.[100] As we have seen in the previous examples, however, there was a much earlier history to this problem. Sino-Soviet frustration was "mutual," to borrow a term from the era: bloc industrial advisers were learning from experience about the dilemmas posed by China's incorporation into their economic system, and the Chinese were realizing the extent of the intrusion into their own society required by the practical arrangements of socialism.

Prague over Beijing

For bloc advisers, plan fulfillment was not the only source of frustration with China. They complained about the excessive railway costs charged by the Chinese, the waste of military materiel provided for the Korean War, and even the prospect of the import of Asiatic cholera, smallpox, typhus, and cattle plague with goods from China.[101] More important, however, the socialist bloc advisers began to question the very contribution China's resources and economy might make to the cause of the "camp." What did China offer the bloc? Mao and other leaders referred often to Soviet interest in China's natural resources and other goods, and in frustration numerous Chinese leaders criticized the Soviet Union for not appreciating their many contributions to the "construction of socialism," but many bloc advisers did not see it this way. They instead wondered about the usefulness of the incorporation into the bloc of China's agrarian and undeveloped economy.

Forestry specialist N. A. Koronov, for example, concluded of his fall 1959 exposure to the Chinese logging industry: "In reality I didn't see anything in logging in the PRC that we might adopt in the Soviet Union."[102] Other advisers identified potential areas of collaboration (such as microscopes, seeds, sheep breeds, ceramics, academic exchange, cartography, weather forecasting, termite control, and fishing), but they were not especially hopeful.[103] Sometimes the potential was real (as with cobalt, nickel, platinum, and chromium in Gansu and Yunnan provinces), but the problems of identification, excavation, and production made it likely that the Soviet Union would supply rather than acquire these minerals in the near future.[104] For the Soviets, the prospect was at best one of promise and potential rather than specific gains. After seeking results from a series of experiments on the production of diesel engines, diesel fuel engine expert M. N. Karpov noted that apparently the experiments failed to take place.[105] In 1960, coal industry experts and academics continued to hold conferences, seminars, and discussions with the Chinese to talk about the likely future benefits of their collaboration.[106] Those advisers who were enthusiastic about what China had to offer the bloc were sometimes oblivious to the fact that "Eurasian" technology (Chinese coal-burning stoves, for example) did not represent an ideal future for the numerous more Western-oriented officials in the Soviet bureaucracy.[107]

Even more frustrating for advisers was their inability adequately to track technological developments that they had previously identified as important to their own needs, or that they suspected had evolved beyond their control in the course of the decade. Numerous bloc countries, several ministers, and a wide variety of high officials were involved in the setting up of China's telecommunication networks and postal system.[108] Zhou Enlai, Chen Yun, and Liu Shaoqi directly oversaw the collaborative project to construct Beijing Central Telegraph.[109] Such huge advising projects reflected the interests of China's leaders in national unity and integration, and the new orientation toward the bloc and away from the West and Japan. By 1958 Soviet officials and their counterparts in the bloc had established telegraph connections between Moscow and Ulan Bator, Ulan Bator and Beijing, Moscow and Beijing, Warsaw and Beijing, and Ulan Bator and Vladivostok.[110] A year earlier, Ministry of Communications officials from Moscow and Beijing had completed construction of twenty-four-hour radio and telephone lines from Moscow to Beijing and from Moscow to Shanghai.[111] Later in the decade, however, visitors from the Soviet Ministry of Communications were dismayed to discover that they had been left uninformed of Chinese progress in the construction of a national electrocommunications network. At the Shanghai Telegraph Bureau, communication specialists M. I. Stoianov and N. I. Chistiakov found markedly smaller and less clumsy telegraphs than in the Soviet Union, and at Beijing Central Telegraph they discovered single-wave radio equipment imported from Siemens, the West German company. They immediately requested "full technical documentation" from Liu Jingcheng of the Ministry of Communication.[112]

From the standpoint of previous Soviet practices and assumptions about technology transfer and the needs and agenda of the socialist bloc, the exchange with China was increasingly viewed by many advisers as unsatisfactory. Soviet officials continued to prefer Central Europe for its expertise, education, and access to the West, in dramatic contrast to China's agricultural society, prone to unpredictable political campaigns. The vision of the vast "Eurasian" socialist bloc of cooperation and pooled resources that emerged in the postwar era signified little to the Soviet Union by 1960. Hungary rather than China would help the Soviet Union compete with America. The Hungarians at the Tungsram metal galvanization factory, for example, were aware of metal production practices in America and could produce platinum that was "qualitatively [and] significantly better" than anything "prepared in the fatherland's industry."[113] The method was "analogous" to American methods, A. A. Zakharov wrote to S. I. Stepanenko.[114] Close collaboration with Hungary in machine construction, argued another Soviet official in 1962, would in time produce "an economic effect in the economy of the Soviet Union."[115] Research practices in the gas industry in Czechoslovakia were vastly superior to those of the Soviet Union, argued Russian officials in 1961, and are of "rich interest" to their nation.[116] The most efficient form of pressurizing oxygen for metallurgical work within the bloc was developed at the Klement Gottwald Metallurgical Factory in Prague, based on blueprints originally obtained from Stacey Dresser Engineering in America.[117]

The Soviets looked to Prague for automobiles, tractors, film, and candy; to Budapest for electronic computing devices; to Dresden for materials testing equipment; and to Warsaw for factories, technology, and workers in the coke and coal industry.[118] Polish textile institutes, reported Soviet industrial adviser N. I. Truevtsev, have "more opportunities" for exposure to Western technology and literature than institutes in Leningrad.[119] In 1961 Soviet officials in the gas industry bluntly demanded the full technical documentation for the complete reproduction of a new Czechoslovak device to measure the quantity of water in natural gas.[120] The Soviets relied on the European side of the bloc to fulfill new projects and exchanges contracted with India and other parts of the developing world, or to facilitate progress in oil production in Groznyi.[121] In the wake of the "kitchen debate," the Ministry of Mass Consumption sent its specialists to a factory in Pravice, Czechoslovakia, to study the production of new wooden floors for use in kitchens. The floors have "become more significant in the USA and Europe" and were currently produced in seven American factories, wrote A. Vasenko, a Soviet consumer goods specialist in Czechoslovakia, to ministry official G. G. Gotsirdize.[122] The floors did not exist in the Soviet Union.

The Soviets also stepped beyond Central Europe to court the Americans directly, anticipating Khrushchev's trip there in September 1959. Exhibits, cultural exchanges, and tentative economic and technological relationships with Western Europe and America were one facet of the diverse foreign affairs reforms enacted by Stalin's successors, and an example of the regime's effort to respond to the concerns of its managerial and industrial elite. That interest was not new but a revival of Soviet Russia's long-standing interest in American technology, Ford cars, and the industrial efficiency methods of Winslow Taylor. Anastas Mikoyan, then commissar of trade, declared in 1930: "In the scale of its economy, in the methods of production (mass production, standardization, and so forth), America is the most appropriate for us."[123] Future commissar of industry Sergo Ordzhonikidze told Soviet students in 1928 that he intended to "send hundreds and thousands of our young engineers to America so that they can learn for themselves what to do and how to work."[124] America's primary lure, of course, was its technological expertise, equipment, and factory organization.

The fresh air after the death of Stalin encouraged Soviets to study the technology of ultrasound and radioactive isotopes in the United States, food processing in France, and hydro-machine construction in Italy.[125] The Soviets began courting visitors from American firms and educational institutes. An American delegation of representatives from the Ford Motor Company, Bendix Aviation Corporation, and Westinghouse Electric toured numerous Soviet factories, universities, and technical institutes in December 1955. Economic exchange that highlighted the contrasts between Russia and the West remained difficult for the regime to address. L. Bean of the Ford Motor Company told his hosts that levels of mechanization at the Molotov Automobile Factory in Gor'kii reminded him of the state of American car production in 1935. Predictably, the official version of this exchange published by TASS did not mention this comment.[126] The Soviet opening to the West that so frustrated the Chinese was also evident at this level of economic, industrial, and educational exchange. Far from the world of high-level polemical accusations about "revisionism" and "capitulationism" to the West and numerous other colorful and dramatic notions, we can see the implications for the Sino-Soviet relationship of this broader social transformation and new orientation within the Soviet Union. These changes within the Soviet Union were in turn connected to the world of the broader socialist bloc.

The Central and Eastern European economies and cultures remained central to the Soviet effort to gain access to the West. The purpose of the SEV was to work with this part of the bloc to ensure Soviet access to the latest innovation. Zhou Enlai sent only an observer rather than a delegation to participate in early discussions in Berlin in the spring of 1956 about the reform of the SEV, and that autumn the Chinese decided not to participate at all.[127] They remained suspicious about the potential intrusion of this Muscovite institution into the Chinese economy and institutions. Significantly, the rejuvenation of the SEV came after the Sino-Soviet split, by which time the Sino-Soviet relationship and the general orientation of the bloc were clear. The new Permanent Commission for the Coordination of Scientific and Technical Research (Postoiannaia komissiia po koordinatsii nauchno-tekhnicheskogo isledovaniia), designed to oversee the numerous other institutions previously engaged in the matter, was formed in 1961 and first met 31 July to 2 August 1962. A series of new commissions (banking, railways, metals, finance) were formed to coordinate diverse forms of exchange in the bloc.[128] SEV official I. Ruzhichka wrote on 18 October 1962 to D. M. Gvishiani, the chair of the Permanent Commission, that their work would bring familiarity with both the "leading scientific research among the member countries of the SEV," as well as "the accomplishments of global science and technology on the most important problems."[129] For this objective the Central Europeans had long been useful, as when Poles went to Italy and France in 1957 to learn about European oil production techniques.[130] In time, of course, they would stop looking back, which the Soviets also understood and feared at this early date. With resignation, engineer A. P. Nikanorov described the Bulgarian rejection of Soviet weaving machine-tool models in March 1960 in favor of available Italian and Swiss varieties. This, too, however, was acceptable, as long as the finished product and the plans were shared with the Soviets.[131]

The socialist bloc would conduct its business without the Chinese, the makers of the largest socialist revolution of the twentieth century. The Eastern and Central Europeans had a special role to play for the SEV in Russia's important relationship with the West, which China had proven incapable of fulfilling. The SEV turned its attention and administrative pressure to demanding that Eastern and Central Europeans help the Soviet Union in its desperate quest. This was not always easy. Czechoslovak, Polish, Bulgarian, and German attendees at a metallurgy and precious metals conference in late June 1960 asked the SEV Permanent Commission if its recommendations were to be "obligatory" for the other countries of the bloc. The Poles wanted to process their precious metals in their country. After more discussion and several "explanations," the group accepted the suggestions of the SEV.[132] Throughout the decade the Romanians carefully manipulated the Sino-Soviet relationship to provide themselves with the space to sell their oil, once dear to the Nazis, on the global market. Until the end of the communist era, officials in Moscow struggled to oversee trade among the Eastern and Central Europeans, eliminate "parallelism" in technical exchange, enforce their political concerns on the bloc, and ensure that each relationship fulfilled the needs of the "central planning organs, committees, and other institutions of the USSR."[133] From the Soviet perspective the relationship was far from ideal but preferable to cooperation with China in vast Eurasia. The path to a competitive engagement with the Americans went through Prague rather than Beijing.

Conclusion

Weak, small, and devastated by the experience of World War II, the Central Europeans still remained the "leading people" of the bloc in their levels of education, technological expertise, managerial experience, and ability to make productive use of the even more sophisticated West European economy. This was not the official story, however, as publicly they knew it was best as a small people in the borderland space of Central Europe to proclaim their gratitude to the Soviets, who had "liberated" them from the Nazis and continued to protect them in the Cold War. In return, however, they made the most of the opportunity to develop their economies, trade with the bloc and the wider world, improve their consumer economies, and proudly maintain high culture traditions that were also respected by the Russians.

Much to the relief of the Central Europeans, the bloc and the Soviet Union itself changed significantly between 1950 and 1960. The decade was marked by de-Stalinization, which had important implications for intrabloc exchange and relations. "Reform" in industrial exchange meant an effort to make the bloc more productive and efficient in order to "catch up with and surpass" the West and America in particular, and the Central Europeans were at the forefront of this effort. Soviet industrial managers and advisers on *komandirovka* emphasized to their superiors that Stalin-era isolation was unproductive, and they especially valued the edges of the bloc for the greater exposure there to the outside world. The process of reform again directed the attention of industrial advisers and experts to the Central Europeans.

China, by contrast, was partially a disappointment to bloc industrial and economic advisers. This frustration began early, as advisers and managers quickly learned that China was a large agricultural society with little to offer the Soviets' science, technology, and industry in their effort to compete with the West. To make things worse, the Chinese routinely altered without warning previously made plans, decisions, and production targets. Central Europeans such as the Czechoslovaks and the East Germans wondered how bloc planning and coordination were even possible under such circumstances. This was happening well before the self-destructive and provocative course eventually charted by Mao after 1958. Even Tito's Yugoslavia would ultimately be perceived as more useful to the Soviet Union than Mao's China, an inconceivable notion in 1948–49.

Central and Eastern Europeans had much to fear from Mao's vision for the socialist bloc. They jumped at the opportunity to orient the bloc toward the economies of the West, and they were rewarded with the opportunity to pursue consumer reforms and receive oil and natural gas at prices below international norms. One of the longer-term consequences of the reconstitution of the socialist bloc and the resolution of the China problem was the gradual integration of the socialist world into the trading practices of the West. One of the longer-term unintended consequences of that integration was significant socialist bloc indebtedness to the capitalist world by the 1970s ($62.9 billion by 1980). "Developed socialism" was in crisis.[134] By that time the leaders of the Soviet Union had significant incentives to continue their search for a beneficial engagement with the West and America in particular.[135]

CHAPTER 3

Interpreting the Red Poppy

Practical Learning, Spiritual Pollution

Czechoslovakia and East Germany both are countries with a
high level of industrial mechanization.
—Chinese Ministry of Foreign Affairs official, 31 July 1957

As in most societies, engagement with foreign cultures and influences in China
was often selective and instrumental, especially on the part of its rulers. The
Qing emperors, for example, were especially interested in Western learning
and knowledge that would "reconfirm their legitimacy as rulers of China," as
Joanna Waley-Cohen explains.[1] According to Chinese political scientist You
Ji, Chairman Mao absorbed the tradition of the Hunan School of the late Qing
era in distinguishing between Chinese learning (the "essence" or "fundamental
structure") and foreign learning ("for practical use").[2] China's proponents of
"self-strengthening" believed they could absorb the scientific and technological innovations of the West without the cultural and political contamination
the rulers feared and associated with the outside world.[3] This long-standing
tension in China's relationship to foreign countries shaped the character of
socialist bloc collaboration and exchange. The dilemma, evident throughout
the decade of the 1950s as the Chinese acquired more knowledge about both
Soviet and Eastern European culture and society, was especially pressing to the
leadership in the wake of 1956. This chapter explores the dilemmas posed for
China as a result of its engagement with the industrial norms, cultural attitudes
and values, and even the personal contacts that went along with socialist bloc
exchange. As in the nineteenth century, the consequences of China's interaction with the outside world could not be contained.

Soviet Film Festival in Guangzhou, 1955. (RGAE f. 635, op. 1, d. 307, l. 730b.)

Technology versus Culture:
Czechoslovak and East German Political Orthodoxy

"Learning from the Central Europeans" was especially attractive to the Chinese because peoples such as the Czechoslovaks and the East Germans managed to combine their achievements in industrial technology and managerial expertise with political loyalty. Historically, Slavic peoples in Bohemia and Moravia such as the Czechs had looked to Russia for support against Austrian rule, which Russian pan-Slavists were eager to exploit. Tsar Nicholas II and other imperial Russian officials often referred to Russia's close links to the western Slavs, "in blood and faith," as Europe prepared for the First World War.[4] Soviet minister of foreign affairs Viacheslav Molotov was quite comfortable returning to these themes in his conversations with Czechoslovak president Edvard Beneš and other Czech leaders in the wake of the disaster the Nazis brought to the region.[5] Disappointed in the West, Beneš and many other Czechoslovaks still suffered from a "Munich complex" that compelled them to seek security guarantees from the East.[6] In December 1943, the Czechoslovaks became the first Central Europeans to sign a friendship treaty with the Soviets, the Agreement on Friendship, Mutual Aid, and Postwar Cooperation.[7] After the war Czechs themselves routinely referred to the shared "Slavic blood" spilled in the fight against Hitler.[8]

Czechoslovak stability during the "events" of 1956 greatly comforted the Chinese. The Chinese Ministry of Foreign Affairs assembled a large contingent of their Czechoslovak counterparts in China in late November 1956, and congratulated them warmly, as M. Žemla reported, for the "calm of our country and leadership in the complicated contemporary international situation."[9] At the same time, Peng Zhen and his large Chinese delegation were in Moscow and then Prague, where they similarly rejoiced in the absence of trouble in Czechoslovakia that fall, a contrast to the disturbing "counterrevolutionary putsch in Hungary." The Chinese were impressed by the proper "morality" of the Czechoslovak people and workers in a time of "counterrevolution."[10] The following year featured a month of cultural activities, sponsored by the Friendship Societies and dedicated to this useful Czechoslovak-Chinese relationship. A Czechoslovak cultural delegation in Beijing that March agreed with Mao and other leaders such as Zhou Enlai, Bo Yibo, and Li Fuchun that their opposition to counterrevolutionary forces in Hungary the previous fall was the correct policy, as it stopped an impending "intervention" from the "imperialists."[11] Iudin closed the series of Friendship Society events with a speech about their common interests and solidarity, in his view a continuation of the work accomplished by the communist parties that assembled in Moscow in November 1957. In a similar closing speech on 11 December 1957, Czechoslovak ambassador Ján Bušniak recalled the events of 1956, when "imperialist propaganda" had exerted its disturbing impact on not only Hungary but also Poland and Yugoslavia. "At that time the Czechoslovak Communist Party and the Chinese people together maintained the position of internationalism," he reminded his listeners, a form of solidarity that revealed the "strength of our friendship."[12]

The Chinese felt they had found a perfect ally in Czechoslovakia, economically advanced yet politically safe. Peng Zhen and his delegation, noted their hosts, routinely "emphasized the high standard of living in Czechoslovakia."[13] The Chinese were impressed by Czechoslovak clothes, the accessibility of consumer goods to workers, the vibrancy of student life in Bratislava, and the prosperity of western Bohemia and Karlový Vary. Chairman Mao himself, in a 29 September 1957 conversation with Bušniak, emphasized the importance for China of Czechoslovak experience, productivity, and technology.[14] The Czechoslovaks were comfortable with this relationship, and even proud to illustrate their "high technical level and experience" in distant Asia. European technology and experience in their view could help the Chinese in the competition with America in Asia.[15] Czechoslovak Ministry of Foreign Affairs officials also understood the value of their greater political reliability in the eyes of the Chinese, and they took measures to ensure that visiting experts such as historians would not speak too freely and irritate Chinese sensibilities.[16] The Chinese were interested in some things more than others, determined to identify and address their own weaknesses while attempting to shield their population from other aspects of foreign cultures and ways. This was a familiar part of the history of China's interaction with the outside world, and it was partly a product of weakness and a corresponding temporary expediency. The "political revolution" had been accomplished, Mao noted to Bušniak, while the "economic revolution" still required time and learning from the Czechoslovaks as well as from the Chinese bourgeoisie in places like Shanghai, who possessed education, skills, and a high "cultural level."[17] The conciliatory statement was simultaneously a threat. As soon as the Chinese stopped needing to learn from the bloc, they would go their own way.

The Chinese similarly valued the East Germans for their industrial technology and development. East German political orthodoxy drew on a different history from that of Czechoslovakia, but it served a similar function for the Chinese. Both the GDR and the PRC faced a powerful America determined to deny their efforts at reunification, in part by protecting a highly sensitive piece of territory (West Berlin, Taiwan). The PRC and the GDR throughout the 1950s made much of this common "plight," which was above all about the problem of the national recovery of territory. Early Chinese exhibits and cultural events sponsored by the German-Chinese Friendship Society in the GDR, for example, frequently linked China's struggle against "global imperialism" to the campaign against Hitler and explored the problem of reunification in the two countries.[18] The East Germans thus pushed an issue dear to Mao, as their own struggle for achieving state legitimacy and their ongoing rivalry with West Germany inspired their criticism of a West German "imperialism" and "militarism" that they also associated with America.[19] "Within Germany right now we have a powerful America," complained GDR leaders to Chairman Mao in September 1954. "Our main enemy is American imperialism." The two parties perceived themselves to be holding down the precarious frontiers of the bloc, ensuring a contiguous space of socialism from the heart of Europe to distant East Asia.[20]

China's exposure to the bloc, however, could not be limited to the import of sophisticated turbine steam engines from Czechoslovakia or machine tools from East Germany. The alliance and its forms of socialist collaboration by definition meant other forms of exposure and interaction as well, sometimes to the chagrin of the CCP. The consequences of China's sustained encounter with outsiders were difficult to control.

Interpreting the Red Poppy

European high culture and its historic connection to privilege and colonialism presented a dilemma to many Chinese well before the more radical era of the Great Leap Forward. In commemoration of the Sino-Soviet relationship, the Bol'shoi Theater staged a ballet called *The Red Poppy* (*Krasnyi mak*) in the fall of 1950. The ballet was set in a large port city in 1930s China, presumably Shanghai, inhabited by a desperately poor population and "coolies" hard at work for an abusive American shipping company. Taking its cue from the Cold War struggle, the ballet attempted to represent Sino-Soviet solidarity in the face of European imperialism, with America as the heir to that oppressive history. These would become familiar tropes in the Sino-Soviet relationship, of course. East German musician Karl Heinz Schleinitz, in China for two years on *komandirovka* from the Staatliche Volkskunstensemble der DDR, shared an exchange with a "Chinese worker." He contrasted the world of rickshaws, coolies and the "system of the Han Dynasty and Jiang Jieshi, or 'Made in USA'" with the "Epoch of Mao Zedong and 'Made in USSR.'"[21] Vague references to "American imperialism" were common in both Russian and Chinese discussions in the 1950s, of course. The Chinese term *meidi* (from *meiguo diguozhuyi* [American imperialism]) was a staple of Chinese political discussion. Yet even this common ground was not enough to unite Russian and Chinese viewers of this polemical ballet. Chinese cultural collaborators in Moscow remained uncomfortable with certain aspects of the production of *The Red Poppy*. Even a work of culture specifically designed to celebrate the political relationship could not surmount the cultural stumbling blocks inhibiting the "friendship." The nuances and tensions that were characteristic of the overall exchange were evident in this early effort at Sino-Soviet cultural collaboration.[22]

The clichéd figures of Soviet propaganda appeared on stage: "Chinese rickshaws escort a collection of foreign 'bosses' to a restaurant in the port section of the town: they include American and English officers, accompanied by wealthy and fancily dressed women, businessmen, and owners of concessions and banks." The "coolies" load and unload American cigarettes, supervised by Li Shangfu, a Chinese "reactionary" eager to "fulfill all the instructions of the Boss." "These are the sort of products brought by the American bosses to China, these are the sort of things they bring from their homeland." The laboring class appears calm, but on closer inspection the viewer gets a glimpse of the workers' anger and frustration. All they need is a hero to lead them, and he appears in the form of the brave young laborer Ma Licheng, whose face "expresses not only hatred but a manly preparation for struggle."[23] He lends a hand to a distraught fellow worker recovering from a beating by an American overseer.

The second scene is set in a restaurant, where Li Shangfu dines with the Americans. The scene generally and the table itself illustrates what the "carriers of Western civilization" have to offer: disreputable women, cigarettes, and alcohol. The female lead is the dance teacher Tao Hua, compelled to perform for the patrons of the restaurant. When the American "Boss" declares that he wants "to get to know" Tao Hua, Li Shangfu arranges an introduction. The political message is obvious: the traitorous Chinese "reactionary" is complicit in the rendering of the innocent Chinese female body to the predatory American. Different global forces, however, interrupt the consummation of this international relationship. "Suddenly the commander of the port appears to inform the Boss of the imminent arrival of a Soviet steam ship."[24]

The presence of the Soviet sailors, who perform their own labor without Chinese help, inspires confidence among the Chinese port workers, who are now on strike. Tao Hua performs a dance in honor of the Soviets and receives a red poppy as a present from the ship's captain. The subsequent dance scene expresses "the will of the people to struggle, independence, and freedom." The red poppy endures through the rest of the story, at one point ripped from Tao Hua's hands by Li Shangfu, at another serving as a "symbol of struggle" in a series of scenes from Tao Hua's dreams about the striking coolies and their leader, Ma Licheng, whom Tao Hua loves. The ballet culminates in a full-scale rebellion by the Chinese workers, during which Li Shangfu prepares to shoot Ma Licheng. Tao Hua steps in front of the pistol and is killed. Her sacrifice is not in vain, however, as China moves forward to revolution and its "historic victory, freeing the motherland from the yoke of the foreign and native bourgeoisie."[25]

While the clear political themes of the ballet resonated with the assumptions and expectations that shaped and informed the "Great Friendship," even this story was not entirely suitable for the Chinese stage. Zeng Xiufu, a graduate student in Moscow in the Academy of Sciences, was invited to discuss the translation of the ballet for Chinese audiences. Zeng Xiufu was generally enthusiastic about a prestigious Bol'shoi production exploring the "rebirth" of China, but he argued that it "should be done with Chinese folk music and by means of Chinese folk dance." The content explored the impact of socialist Russia in Chinese history, but the form of the ballet evoked European culture. The music for the Bol'shoi production, by R. M. Glier, M. I. Kurilko, and V. P. Tikhomirov, was in Zeng Xiufu's view designed for Russian visitors to the Bol'shoi. Even the name was inappropriate. *Red Poppy* reminded Chinese viewers of the "remnants of feudal China," in this case the English opium trade and colonialism generally in China. Zeng Xiufu suggested the name be changed to *Red Flower*.[26]

A more subtle problem was the demeanor and general presentation of the Chinese laborers, who appeared too "servile" in their relationship to the American boss. "Chinese dignity," emphasized Zeng Xiufu, could be better expressed and illustrated, in spite of the poverty and the colonial exploitation evoked by the setting. Along these same lines, this critic suggested that the Chinese might be better portrayed as industrial workers. The clichés and traditional propaganda images of socialism informed the ballet, but disturbing to the Chinese was the presence of enduring Russian and European images of all Chinese as coolies and rickshaw drivers. In spite of the revolutionary changes and the collaboration of the "Friendship," Soviet Russians still appeared to be part of the heritage of European colonialism in China. The Chinese suggested that the Russians draw more carefully on the advice of both Russian and Chinese historians, ethnographers, and area specialists. Zeng Xiufu also recommended that the Russians change the name of Ma Licheng, which resonated among Chinese as a Muslim name, tone down the romance between Tao Hua and Ma Licheng, and focus on exploitation and colonialism by Europeans generally rather than just by Americans.[27] The Chinese were frequently frustrated by Russian approaches to the politics of culture throughout the period of the Great Friendship, and even this attempt at revolutionary ballet fell short of Chinese expectations. The misunderstandings and contrasting Soviet and Chinese notions of European culture and its historic relationship to imperialism, a source of significant friction by the end of the decade, were evident from the beginning of the Sino-Soviet alliance.

Classical Culture in Europe and "Originality" in Beijing

As the Chinese discovered in regard to *The Red Poppy*, the socialist bloc world was surprisingly traditional in matters of culture and unsurprisingly competitive about its cultural achievements, which it enjoyed contrasting with the

A Soviet cultural adviser in China.
From *Suzhong youhao*, no. 13 (1959).

supposed materialism and absence of high culture among the Americans. The socialist world was shaped by a series of "developmental hierarchies," notes György Péteri, a "symbolic geography" that grew out of Russia's historic experience in Eurasia.[28] Cultural figures and advisers in China shared a broad cultural vision that gave their own activities a mission and a purpose, connected the western and eastern portions of the socialist world, and illustrated a form of (superior) "socialist" identity that again contrasted to the values and practices of the West.[29] From the eighteenth century on, the eastern frontier (Crimea, the Caucasus, Middle Volga, Turkestan) presented opportunities for imperial educated society to fulfill its civilizing missions in the East and illustrate its special contribution to Western culture.[30] The Soviet state drew on this heritage in its far more ambitious and coercive efforts to transform itself and its multiethnic citizenry.[31] The key terms and notions in the East were *kul'tura* and *kul'turnost'*, or high culture as a form of achievement to be emulated and cultivated by a common people historically distant from these traditions, as well as the *druzhba narodov*, or "friendship of peoples."[32] This latter program was a state-sponsored effort to foster multiethnic cohesion in the Soviet Union, and combined universal notions of (European) culture and progress with the persistent promotion and support of non-Russian nation-building. The first component was even integral to the latter, as Eastern cultures understood to be in need of regeneration and revival were to benefit from their exposure to literacy, a press, an intelligentsia, and a high culture tradition. This was part of the promise of the Soviet experience, led by its "leading people," the Russians.

These notions crossed the borders of the Soviet Union to the Asian areas of the bloc, such as Mongolia, North Korea, and China. Russia thus remained true to its Eastern mission and also remained at the center of proletarian internationalism, with its traditional notion of high culture somehow of value in the construction of "socialism."[33] In the imperial era educated Russians on the frontier drew from Romantic thought to visualize the flowering of small and often "Oriental" peoples historically denied the opportunity to cultivate their own traditions. Russian imperial rule, according to this framework of development, was far preferable to domination by the surrounding Islamic empires. In the Soviet era the "friendship of peoples" was also to offer small peoples and Asian peoples the opportunity to progress culturally, free from the obstructions of traditionally privileged elites, religious figures, or the predatory imperialism of colonial powers. The "extension of domestic policy principles toward the Soviet nationalities" to the broader bloc, argued East German commentator Alexander Martin, was the very definition of "proletarian internationalism."[34]

Russia's traditional respect for the virtues and achievements of high culture naturally directed the attention of its cultural figures and workers to Central Europe, obviously closer to the West and famous for its traditions of classical music, opera, and the arts. In matters of culture, as in technology, trade, consumerism, and other areas, Central Europe again occupied an important place in the diverse socialist bloc. In matters of culture, then, this program seemed to offer something for everyone. Russians and Central Europeans shared similar notions about the value of high culture; they believed they were good at it (and, of course, better than the materialistic Americans); and they had shared experience in Soviet Asia. East Germans, for example, were proud to contribute to the expansion of book production, theater attendance, the use of reading rooms and libraries, and access to education among women in Soviet Central Asia.[35] And the Chinese, too, could comfortably be exposed to a world of classical artistic training, performance, and display without any threat of cultural or political subversion.

The problem for the Chinese was that the bloc relationship to Chinese culture quickly evolved into what seemed like a very traditional way of

Exhibit of Chinese Industry and Agriculture, Moscow, 1953. (RGAE f. 635, op. 1, d. 272, l. 8)

viewing China and its people, culture, and history. The bloc was excited to illustrate its interest in China, which is what the Chinese wanted, but that interest included a colonial feel that reminded the Chinese a bit too much of the nineteenth century. Moscow, Prague, Berlin, Warsaw, and many other cities were routinely host to "cultural days" dedicated to the East, exhibits of traditional Chinese art, displays of painting, examples of music from the East, and readings of traditional Chinese poetry.[36] Czechoslovak mathematicians and physicists in Prague described the glories of "5,000 years of mathematics" in China, the most ancient "arithmetic on our planet."[37] East German travel writer Paul Halpap similarly described with enthusiasm the "oldest culture [*Kulturvölker*] in the world," its ancient temples, opera, canals, porcelain, and architecture, and its historic accomplishments in mathematics, paper production, and astronomy.[38]

China was rendered to socialist bloc publics as a traditional Chinese landscape painting, and painters, graphic artists, and sculptors visiting China were determined to discover such an image. Mountains, trees, and birds, approvingly reported a visiting Soviet group in late 1956, were rendered by their Chinese artistic colleagues "completely the same as in classical works." Chinese artists such as Xian Zhaohe informed the visiting Russians about current debates within the artistic community about Chinese tradition and

European culture, leading them to conclude that the best course of action for China was the "mixing of the national and the global." In their sightseeing the Soviet group was most enchanted by trips to the old sections of cities, and for their own painting they sought out views of what they took to be traditional Chinese scenes: rickshaws, landscapes, peasants carrying water, old winding streets in Shanghai and Guangzhou, tiled roofs in Suzhou, the lakes in Hangzhou, and historic architecture. The group returned home to display their work at an exhibit sponsored by the Union of Artists in Moscow in August 1957.[39]

Soviet and Eastern European audiences were predisposed to the cultural consumption of China in this fashion. In the fall of 1956 *Pravda* and Russian audiences applauded a series of illustrations of the "traditional" and "ancient theater culture of great China" brought to Moscow by the Shanghai Theater of Beijing Musical Drama. For Vladimir Rogov, the artists from Shanghai were an illustration of Chinese "originality [*samobytnost'*, a key term from the Romantic era]," an example of Chinese fidelity to indigenous tradition. The great Chinese actor Zhou Xinfang evoked methods first developed in the Tang Dynasty, a time of "deep originality in scenic and musical form."[40] Chinese traditional culture, "liberated from all that is unnecessary," would serve as a bridge between the "classical heritage and contemporary culture."[41] The classical heritage of Chinese culture, argued A. Vinogradov, which had "accumulated over thousands of years" but had been systematically assaulted by the imperialists, was now infused by a "different content." Russians would help the Chinese recover and maintain the "original [*samobytnyi*]" forms of Chinese culture that had endured in spite of China's colonial era.[42] Organizers of Chinese exhibits in the Soviet Union pushed their colleagues in China to exhibit traditional forms of Chinese culture familiar to Soviet visitors, such as embroidery from Suzhou or silk-making in Hangzhou.[43] When a Soviet cultural delegation that included Minister of Culture N. A. Mikhailov arrived in Beijing to make plans for cultural exchange in 1957, the Chinese announced that the visitors would leave with a gift of some 550 pieces of Qing dynasty porcelain, lacquer, enamel, and embroidery.[44]

Soviet aid sought to help Eastern peoples cultivate their own indigenous traditions, gain access to global (European) high culture and modern (Western) forms of science and technology, and flourish in a way that contrasted with what advisers and administrators viewed as their stagnant past. The revolution, Soviet influence, and the impact of modern forms of science, technology, and culture were to liberate peasants from their timeless traditions and historic helplessness in the face of nature. The Soviet version of scientific enlightenment was particularly important in the historically backward East. A VOKS-sponsored documentary film in Mongolia, for example, illustrated the work of Ukrainian scientists battling crop diseases common in Central Asia.[45] In China Soviet scientists were pleased to collaborate on efforts to transform the Yellow River from a source of devastating floods into a provider of safe forms of electricity to provincial Chinese villages.[46] A timeless and unchanging Chinese geography (as in an eighteenth-century landscape painting) would be preserved and maintained but now coupled with the liberating and progressive potential of modern science and technology.

In humanistic culture, the Russians and Central Europeans also had a special role to play in the East. P. V. Vedenskii, a VOKS official in the Chinese Northeast before 1949, described the "enormous interest" of Mongolians and Chinese in the reading of material provided by VOKS libraries and reading rooms.[47] The best films for the Chinese, noted a contributor to *Russkoe slovo*, were those of a "political and educative [*vospitatel'noe*] significance, that is, those films which will have a good influence on the viewer."[48] The leading lights of Russian cultural and literary tradition were especially suitable for emulation, again in a way similar to the assumptions and practices that were part of the concept of the "friendship of peoples" in the Soviet Union. "Tolstoy and the East," for example, was a theme of scholarly collaboration with China encouraged by VOKS in 1946 with the help of the L. N. Tolstoi State Museum of the Academy of Sciences. As S. A. Tolstaia-Esenina explained, "China occupies an important place" in Tolstoy's writings about the East.[49] Central figures of Russian intellectual history were supposedly keenly interested in the East in a way that distinguished the Russian tradition from a more exploitive and colonial European history.[50] This was a standard Soviet cultural formula in all the borderland regions of the Caucasus and Central Asia, now extended to China. In 1959 the Friendship Society in China prepared memorial conferences devoted to Gogol, Pushkin, Khetagurov, Mussorgsky, Mendeleev, Popov, and Repin.[51]

The presence of Central Europe in the bloc meant the Chinese could also go directly to Europe for exposure to culture. The Czechoslovaks and the Chinese were eager to promote exhibits and various forms of exchange with each other soon after October 1949. Student exchange programs began in 1951, and Czechoslovak films were shown to large audiences in some twenty cities in China already by 1953. The Czechoslovak Film Festival became an annual event, and photography exhibits were frequent. These and other diverse exchanges were supported by a broader cultural agreement signed in Prague by

Ministry of Foreign Affairs officials on 17 July 1954. The exchanges included study opportunities for graduate students, artists, and musicians, exhibits on schooling and children's toys, the screening of Chinese films at the Film Festival in Karlový Vary, and a visit to Prague of a Chinese opera group. The following year included Czechoslovak participation in the huge exhibits in Beijing, Shanghai, and Guangzhou; trips to China by Czechoslovak dance, choral, orchestral, and puppet theater groups; and Chinese participation in the Prague Spring International Festival. Journalists from *Rudé právo* participated in discussions with Chinese journalists, and academic administrators and Academy of Science officials arranged exchanges as well. Czech health professionals, geologists, architects, and graphic designers went to China.[52] The Czechoslovaks sympathized with the Russian notion of the exchange: the best of the European classical tradition went to China, and Prague played host to Chinese renditions of traditional folk music, opera, and dance. To celebrate the tenth anniversary of the Chinese revolution in Prague, the Czechs hosted an arts festival dedicated to traditional Chinese landscape painting, regional variations of Chinese opera, Chinese porcelain and ceramics, and examples of contemporary Chinese literature and film. The Czech Philharmonic played works by Antonín Dvořák, Bedřich Smetana, Alexander Borodin, and other classical composers followed by Chinese folk music, and it sponsored lectures by Czech Orientalists on aspects of traditional Chinese culture.[53]

The East Germans as well were eager to contribute. They were confident of their relationship to European tradition, believed their own policies to be distinct from "the brutal colonial policies of German imperialism in China," and claimed kinship to a German cultural tradition that had not been corrupted by the decadent Americans (as in West Germany). The East Germans presented themselves as the perfect vehicle for the exposure of the Chinese to high culture in a way that respected and encouraged indigenous Chinese cultural development.[54] "As is known, the great European painters such as Rembrandt and Leonardo da Vinci were impressed by the achievements of Chinese artists," noted musician Karl Heinz Schleinitz.[55] Schleinitz saw evidence of success in socialist bloc cultural collaboration everywhere he looked: composer Rolf Gilek enjoyed working with disciplined Chinese musicians in the Chinese Youth Orchestra, who admired Franz Schubert ("a typical German work") and yet altered the tempo slightly to reflect the "rhythm of their own national music"; the new People's University supported the study of traditional Chinese music along with modern departments of industrial planning and statistics; even the architecture at the new Higher Technical School in Shenyang was "modern and yet Chinese."[56] The alternative version of modernity offered by the bloc respected and maintained indigenous Chinese cultural tradition.

The balance in this equation between European and Chinese culture was never equal, however. Schleinitz was most impressed by a German choral concert before 15,000 spectators in Guangzhou that concluded with the presentation of a gift "of a European violin to two young Chinese."[57] The Russians as well never strayed from their views about the importance of traditional forms of expertise in high culture, which they understood to be even more important as the relationship deteriorated. The musicians chosen by the Ministry of Culture to perform and teach in China, for example, were well-trained and accomplished classical musicians. Violinist Vadim S. Chervov, a laureate at the International Festival in Berlin in 1951, graduated from Moscow State Conservatory in 1952, began graduate work in 1955, and taught at Moscow State University from 1953. In 1955 he went to China for a two-year stay to teach violin and cello at the Central Conservatory in Tianjin. Evgenii G. Brusilovskii, a composer and graduate of Leningrad State Conservatory, and Pavel P. Grigorov, a graduate of Moscow State Conservatory and former director of the Pushkin Theatre of Opera and Ballet in Gor'kii, both began their exchanges in Kazan. Grigorov enjoyed a successful stint there as teacher and orchestra director at the Kazan State Conservatory. Musicians with teaching experience in the non-Russian regions of the Soviet Union often qualified for the China trips. Brusilovskii proved to be an effective instructor at several Kazakh musical institutions in Almaty. Nina Konstantinovna Kuklina-Brana, a Russian singer raised in Kazakhstan, previously taught at Almaty State Conservatory and worked in Albania as well. She spent two years in Tianjin. VOKS officials such as B. Belyi sought out the best musicians from diverse Soviet conservatories to travel to China to introduce the Chinese to "Russian classical and Soviet composers."[58] Such musicians as composer G. M. Shneerson pushed officials to devote more resources to producing higher quality versions of the classics of the Russian musical tradition for distribution in China and the bloc.[59]

The bloc preoccupation with high culture gradually led the Chinese to suspect the revolutionary credentials of their "elder brother." The advisers, teachers, and cultural figures remained oblivious to the historical suspicion of urban and high culture in the Chinese countryside, the culture from which the Chinese Communist Party emerged. In spite of their beliefs in a nonimperialistic form of collaboration that would facilitate the cultivation of indigenous Chinese culture, cultural exchange visitors from the bloc struggled to understand the emerging nativist inclination that deepened in response to their work.

Tatar composer Nazib G. Zhiganov, director of Kazan State Conservatory, traveled to Shanghai and Guangzhou supported by VOKS in 1957. While there he became quite disturbed over a common theme of debate among Chinese composers concerning the merits of foreign and indigenous tradition in music composition. Chinese composers, Zhiganov reported, proposed the creation of "*Chinese harmony* (?!) only in Chinese music. This theory will perniciously influence the development of Chinese music. This theory amounts to a 'Global Chinese Wall.' It will 'defend' Chinese music from foreign and global musical culture" (emphasis in original).[60] Zhiganov emphasized as a Tatar that his own culture had gained access and exposure to the culture of the world precisely because of Soviet rule. In his view China too was fortunate to have the opportunities afforded by Russia to the non-Russian borderland cultures.

Similarly, Bashkir musician Ismagilov Vinogradov and the Buriat Aiusheev were hosted by the Union of Musicians in China in December 1957 and January 1958. Their goal was to connect with their historic cousins (Turkic peoples and Mongols) in China, again united by a common musical background and veneration of classical music. The Russians sent Buriats to Mongolia with similar aims, and sponsored Buriat cultural events there in order to remind Mongolians of the successful development of Buriat culture within the Soviet system.[61] The Bashkirs in China contributed to performances of Shostakovich's Eleventh Symphony in Beijing, Wuhan, Shanghai, and Tianjin, and then also in Huh-Hot in Inner Mongolia. They were pleased to find many well-trained classical musicians, such as Ma Sazong, the director of the Tianjin Conservatory, who had studied in Paris. They also noted, however, the need for Soviet institutions and advisers to pay more attention to "younger composers" such as Xi Xinghai, who were "fighters for a new Chinese music" and determined to cultivate the "development of original national characteristics." Vinogradov began to echo some of the new trends in the emerging cultural revolution in China: "I should know how the worker understands [things]; I myself should labor, and then can I write about it." He was impressed by the Chinese instances of "speaking bitterness," or the stories from Chinese musicians about their former poverty. He reminded his Soviet colleagues that they needed to understand more about the Chinese "way of life [*byt*]. We didn't meet with the people. It is necessary to say that we were placed in such a situation where we didn't walk anywhere, we were in a car all the time, and at all times we were accompanied by interpreters."[62] Other officials were receiving a similar message: our delegations should "socialize more with the broader masses of the Chinese population and the workers and peasants, instead of being limited to the intelligentsia," concluded A. N. Kuznetsov in 1958.[63] In 1957, Chinese officials informed Czechs at the Central Conservatory of Music in Beijing (there were twenty-seven Soviets there as well) that from then on their course of musical instruction was "divorced" from both "national tradition" and "practice." The students were better off engaged in manual labor and the instruction of reading to peasants.[64] The Chinese began searching for their own relationship to culture and tradition that was distinct from the ideas of the advisers and teachers from the bloc.

Oldřich Havlíček and Zhen Peilu in Shanghai, 1955–1958

Sometimes the exchange meant more exposure to foreign culture and influence than Chinese officials had in mind, and even at a profoundly personal level. Oldřich Havlíček from Czechoslovakia first came to China in February 1955 to work at the Chapei and Yangshu Electrical Stations in Shanghai. He was in China for some eighteen months on this tour, returning to Czechoslovakia in November 1956. He came back to China in March 1957 as the chief of operations for a series of Czechoslovak power plants in Nanjing, Tangshan, Nanding, and Kunming. The Chinese looked to the Czechoslovaks for help especially in the area of the generation of electricity and the construction and running of power stations. The Czechs, of course, were known for their Kaplan Turbines, and Havlíček was a well-known specialist in their assembly who had worked in the past with East Germans and Soviets, and trained other Czechoslovaks arriving in China.[65] The original agreement for the plant was arranged with the Czechoslovaks on 3 September 1952 and called for its completion by the fall of 1954.[66] The Chapei Electrical Station was one of the more significant components of the third session of the Scientific-Technological Commission for 1953–56.[67] Before Havlíček's arrival, the Chinese had been concerned about inefficiency at the Chapei plant that had resulted in significant cost overruns, which would eventually be an issue reducing the Chinese commitment to components of the exchange a year or so later.[68] From the start the Chinese were very concerned about the capabilities of the plant, and they sent their officials to Prague to clarify timetables and emphasize the importance of the project to Chinese industrial development.[69]

Havlíček was a successful and prominent foreign adviser in China. Already after just six months at Chapei, Haviček reported progress to Czechoslovak ambassador Antonin Gregor in meeting deadlines for turbine work.[70] The Chinese were always impressed by his many accomplishments and fine work record. All accounts confirm that he was committed to his work and eager to serve in China. Even as his personal life became complicated, the Chinese hoped for a sincere self-criticism on his part that would resolve things and allow him to continue to be productive. Chinese officials noted that he always "organized the work well" and effectively led the "labor collective of Czechoslovak experts." He contributed to the improvement of China's "technical level," enjoyed teaching the Chinese, trained some "400 local comrades," and had fine personal relations with a wide variety of Chinese coworkers and colleagues, noted Chinese Ministry of Energy officials.[71] The thirty-three-year-old engineer was "very popular" with the Chinese, added Czechoslovak consular official L. Kubiš.[72] Havlíček crossed a line, however, in a way that became a diplomatic incident within the socialist bloc and quickly opened up a series of sensitive issues in intrabloc relations.

Havlíček fell in love with Zhen Peilu, a thirty-one-year-old accountant in the Shanghai office of the Ministry of Energy. That is not how Chinese and Czechoslovak officials put the matter: in spite of his many accomplishments, there was an "inadequacy" in his "private life." There were walks in the park, afternoons at swimming pools, dates at restaurants and movie theaters, and "people started to comment." In the spring of 1956 the couple attended a dance at the cultural club, and returned afterward to his hotel room. Chinese officials in the Ministry of Energy were aware that Zhen Peilu would "visit there often through the evening." Several more of these episodes led to "more than comradely relations," as Czechoslovak consul general Ján Fierlínger subsequently explained to colleagues, that is, "kissing, and then intimacy."[73] Eventually the matter would find its way into official reports in diplomatic correspondence between the bloc countries: "In the summer of 1956 the Chinese side affirmed that relations between Comrade Havlíček and Ms. Zhen had become intimate," reported Czechoslovak consulate official L. Kubiš.[74]

At this point the Chinese refrained from contacting Czechoslovak officials, hopeful that they could resolve the matter without creating a larger incident or obstructing Havlíček's work. "International" romance in the socialist world was generally discouraged and rare, but not impossible. The East Germans were particularly prohibitive, while the Czechoslovaks and Bulgarians were more lenient. Hungarian Borna Tálas married a Pole while a student at Beida in the 1950s. In all cases, veterans of the era recall, Chinese women found themselves under severe pressure to avoid any such entanglement.[75] Chinese specialists and advisers in the Soviet Union were generally quiet about romance with the Russians. Liu Xiao uncomfortably reminded Iudin in 1959 that

Chinese pregnancies in the Soviet Union only became known to the Chinese government after the birth of the child.[76]

In the case of Zhen Peilu, the Chinese authorities tried to prevent her from visiting Havlíček's hotel room at the Picardie in Shanghai, forced her to participate in a "self-criticism" session, and attempted to transfer her to a new position in Beijing. The two kept seeing each other, however, sometimes in Beijing when work brought them to the capital city. This was not only a romance, however, but an affair. Zhen Peilu had two children and a husband who worked for the Ministry of Energy in Beijing, and Havlíček had a wife and child in Czechoslovakia. Zhen Peilu's husband, Zhu Yaopao, found out about the relationship when she visited Havlíček in Beijing, and he made a formal complaint to the Czechoslovak embassy against Havlíček.[77] The Chinese effort to resolve the matter quietly now came to a close, and Czechoslovak officials found themselves in an uncomfortable position. The angry Zhu Yaopao demanded that Havlíček be sent home to Czechoslovakia immediately, and he said he intended to take the matter to the Higher People's Court in Shanghai.[78]

The confident Oldřich Havlíček, however, was not about to repent. Successful and prominent advisers in the socialist world were not frightened of diplomats, and Havlíček took to the offensive. The relationship was a "normal friendship," he declared. He was outraged by the treatment of Zhen Peilu, who was subject to renewed pressure from the Ministry of Energy on 4 October 1957 and resigned her position. The next day the Chinese talked to the very "irritable" Havlíček, who threatened to quit and return to Czechoslovakia.[79] The Chinese now took a different tack. Yu Kuang of the Ministry of Energy tried to convince Havlíček that he was a victim of Zhen Peilu's manipulative effort to gain money and gifts from the more affluent foreigner. Her family was alarmed by these significant gifts from a "foreign expert." Going further, he informed Havlíček that Zhen Peilu's brother was a member of the GMD, and "from a political point of view" breaking off relations would be the correct thing to do.

Czechoslovak consulate officials had a sense of Havlíček's character and were frustrated and frightened that the matter would inevitably grow to larger proportions. Consul General Fierlínger criticized Havlíček for not being more forthcoming with him about the state and history of the relationship.[80] Fierlínger understood that Havlíček was determined to advocate for his innocence before the Higher People's Court, and the consul general believed he would lose and also severely complicate and compromise the more important political relationship with the Chinese. Officials in Beijing and Prague entirely agreed. Fierlínger's preference was to put Havlíček on a plane to Prague within twenty-four hours.[81] They began assembling research about Chinese family and divorce law since the revolution, which they passed on to their colleagues in Beijing and Prague. They wanted Havlíček to cooperate with the Chinese, but they were also alarmed at his potential fate in the Chinese legal system. They learned about a rape case involving a foreigner in Zhulin, and another case where a "bourgeois" figure landed in prison for two and a half years for adultery with a Chinese woman (who received a one-year sentence). Testing the Chinese legal system could be "dangerous" for him, the Czechoslovak officials told Havlíček.[82]

Fierlínger's fears about the escalation of the matter were confirmed when the Chinese officials from the Ministry of Energy arrived with a thick file for a deposition on 27 November 1957. For several hours, Fierlínger and L. Kubiš from the consulate in Shanghai, along with Volácek from the Ministry of Foreign Affairs in Beijing, sat with Zhen Tuoshan, Tang Xingpo, and another official from the Chinese Ministries of Energy and Foreign Affairs. Both the Chinese and the Czechs wanted Havlíček to leave town quickly, and the Chinese still believed that families could be reconciled and the matter resolved.[83] The Chinese also did not want a major disruption in matters of electrical supply and production. They continued to express their gratitude for Havlíček's fine work history. That was not the issue. By blaming Zhen Peilu with their insinuations and direct accusations about her financial and personal motives, they offered Havlíček and the Czechs a means of resolving the matter and moving forward. The Chinese officials also blamed themselves, looking forward now to improving this area of intrabloc relations. Much to the frustration of the Russians, the Chinese in Shanghai presented their report to the Czechs in English, since this language often endured as the language of global communication within the diplomatic community in China. In broken English the Chinese explained to the Czechs: "First of all during his long stay in China we had not often and in an all-around way informed the Expert the Chinese custom and tradition. When being informed of the abnormal intercourse between the two of them, we not gone one step further and adopted efficient step to stop them. Then the matter went to a bad consequence that Zhen's husband came to charge the Expert at the Czechoslovak Embassy and people's courts. We should draw lesson from this matter."[84] The Chinese offered a resolution to the delicate situation at hand.

The Chinese also drew other "lesson[s] from this matter," however, just as Fierlínger feared. They intended to blame the woman, reconcile the families, and move on to address much larger issues in Sino-Soviet and socialist bloc relations. Zhen Tuoshan wanted Havlíček to undergo a self-criticism session and offer repentance, but he really was more interested in directing the Czechs' attention to the larger issues surrounding the socialist bloc advisers in China. Their "social conditions" were "inadequate," and they needed more opportunities for healthy forms of activity and recreation away from work.[85] Zhen Tuoshan wondered about family life and the possibility of encouraging more support for spousal and family travel to China. The Chinese concern for the social life of the Czechoslovak contingent, however, in part emerged from their fear that in fact the outsiders were becoming too close to their Chinese colleagues and people. Borrowing industrial technology and techniques from the Central Europeans should not necessarily include exposure to their customs and ways, and certainly not romantic relationships. More critically, the Chinese officials described a world of privilege inhabited by the foreign advisers in China that was inappropriate and demoralizing for the Chinese. Their status and high pay negatively influenced Chinese labor morale, Zhen Tuoshan charged. How could "fraternal" socialist countries find themselves in these relationships in the first place, almost a decade after the Chinese revolution and the end to the practices of colonialism that were, of course, most visible in eastern cities such as Shanghai?[86] If Havlíček were to test the Chinese court system, Zhen Tuoshan added, he was obligated to understand and abide by Chinese law and Chinese penalties, which was the least a sovereign state could ask of its visitors.[87]

The Havlíček case threatened to damage Chinese relations with the rest of the socialist bloc in a time already tense because of the prospect of the Great Leap Forward, the numerous related debates about the Chinese model and path to communism, and the general questions about the character of the Soviet-led advising project. Czechoslovak officials in Beijing and Prague carefully followed the situation in Shanghai, hoping for a quick resolution.[88] To the relief of officials from both sides, their pressure on Havlíček encouraged him to return home rather than face an uncertain fate in the Chinese legal system. Sometime that winter of 1957–58 Havlíček returned to Prague and employment with the Ministry of Heavy Industry, in montage work at the I. Brněnská Factory. His work as an adviser in the bloc was finished; he "will not be sent abroad," concluded foreign affairs official Miloš Paris.[89]

Czech diplomats in China continued to struggle with the consequences of the Havlíček affair in 1958. They told the Chinese and themselves that they had learned from their mistakes, and they took measures to address weaknesses identified by the Chinese in the course of the case. They paid more attention to evening activities hosted by hotels for socialist bloc advisers, tried to encourage the experts to find healthy social outlets while abroad, and arranged sporting events, physical activities, and day trips to tourist locations and the countryside. They sent Czech books to the experts and encouraged them to learn more about Chinese history, the revolution, and the Chinese language. Fierlínger hoped the women among the groups might facilitate healthy and responsible social activities. The advisers themselves, ironically, needed more opportunities for access to cultural events. Fierlínger and his colleagues were now on the defensive, protecting the reputations of the Czechoslovak advisers before the suspicious Chinese. The issue of the behavior of the advisers was discussed at the 21st Party Congress in January 1959 in Moscow, and at the 11th Congress of the Czechoslovak Communist Party in March 1959 in Prague.[90] The Chinese notion of industrial, technical, and cultural exchange did not include the exposure of their citizenry to the sort of relationship pursued by Oldřich Havlíček and Zhen Peilu.

The Víta Nejedlého Army Cultural Group

As in industrial and other forms of exchange, in matters of culture the Chinese were exposed to forms of behavior and activity that raised questions about socialism in practice. This was evident in everyday cultural exchange. The Czechoslovak Víta Nejedlého Army Cultural Group (Armádního uměleckého souboru Víta Nejedlého, AUS-VN), for example, visited China in September and October 1952, returned by train through the Soviet Union, and then conducted a series of follow-up educational events about their trip in Czechoslovakia through the spring of 1953. Their work was presented in the press as enormously successful, and the cultural exchange itself was a very public event.[91] The group of more than eighty musicians, made up of ballet, orchestral, and choral members, led some 850 performances, lessons, and group demonstrations in China. More than 136,000 Chinese attended these events. The group visited schools, enterprises, and PLA regiments, and were generally well-received and complimented for their "careful and conscientious" work, as well as their spirit of "proletarian internationalism" that aided the PLA in particular. The experience brought "glory to the Chinese people, Mao Zedong, Klement Gottwald, and J. V. Stalin."[92]

Upon their return to Czechoslovakia, the army cultural group visited enterprises, factories, and military installations and hosted discussions and fielded questions about their experiences in distant China. They led sixty-seven such events in February 1953, reaching 20,361 Czechoslovaks.[93] At these events, sometimes called "An Evening of Questions and Answers about the PRC," group members displayed large maps of China, shared their photographs of the country, and offered their insights into daily life, the economy, conditions in the military, and their impressions of culture and the arts.[94] The political significance of the trip was clear; it was a victory in the "ideological [battle] front against bourgeois and cosmopolitan influence and remnants." The Czechoslovak troupe was motivated by the "spirit of proletarian internationalism, patriotism, national pride, and affection toward the vast Chinese people and the Soviet Union, and fraternal solidarity with all the peoples of the great socialist camp."[95]

Party cadres and security officials were not entirely satisfied, however, and they closely monitored these events in provincial Czechoslovak cities and institutions. While officials described them as generally successful, they noted that the enthusiasm of both the troupe members and their audiences seemed too much confined to a fascination with China as an "'exotic' country." The military musicians and their audiences paid scant attention to the development of Chinese industry, the "attitude of the Chinese people to the war in Korea and global struggle," or their "hatred for the Anglo-American predators."[96] Čestmír Skála complained that the presentations seemed designed to promote tourist trips to China rather than communicate the "heroic enthusiasm of the Chinese people for Mao Zedong and the CCP." The vast geographic dimensions and wonders of the country were a frequent topic of conversation and interest. Troupe members themselves often missed political discussion sessions and openly ignored the "political workers," added security official Václav Podzimek.[97]

By early 1954 security officials were well aware of more serious problems. The archival materials left in Prague surrounding the AUS-VN's visit to China are there only because security officials in the Czechoslovak Ministry of Defense initiated an investigation in response to a series of anonymous letters from various troupe members in 1954.[98] The investigation eventually led to a variety of disciplinary measures and reprimands of several leading group officials, although the Ministry of Defense also concluded that the larger problems identified by the anonymous denunciation writers had been exaggerated. The writing of denunciatory letters was a common method of bringing attention to problems within the Soviet and socialist bloc administrative system, and it was sometimes prompted by less than admirable motives. In this case, the denouncers were perhaps jealous that they had been excluded from access to the fruits of their common experience in China.

The military musical group was plagued by a series of administrative mishaps and ethical lapses that were routine in the Soviet Union and throughout the bloc. Several troupe members described for the Ministry of Defense in 1954 a cultural troupe completely lacking in the necessary prestige and status even to conduct cultural performances in the bloc. The anonymous denunciation letters identified troupe officials as the source of the problem, among them several "evil characters" as well as the notorious "Jarda the Rum Drinker" (Jarda rum), who routinely boasted about his ability to "outdrink anyone anywhere," which he apparently did on numerous occasions in the USSR in particular. The writers described political and administrative cadres such as Ladislav Mazal, Captain Poděšt, and Major Kondrát as especially suspect, disorganized, corrupt, inclined to alcoholism, and lacking the group's confidence.[99] Mazal "enjoyed the bottle (especially rum)," which routinely interfered with his ability to lead the group in performance and other forms of bloc exchange. In the subsequent investigation, cultural officials in the military quickly turned on each other to defend themselves. Josef Machalous associated the administrative disarray with Václav Pichlík, describing Pichlík's work and that of other cadres as a far cry from a contribution to the "realization of Marxism-Leninism in practice."[100]

Drunkenness, incompetence, and disorganization were familiar matters that would elicit a reprimand from the Ministry of Defense. The larger issue that was not addressed, however, was the problem of socialist bloc exchange itself. In China the Czechs procured enough ivory, porcelain, silk, and other valuable consumer goods to fill two train cars on their voyage home. "Socialist" exchange did not stop there, however, as the trip through the Soviet Union was an opportunity not to be wasted. Czech delegations in general in the Soviet Union were well aware of Soviet consumer deprivation that made their own private possessions ("clothes, shoes") surprisingly valuable.[101] A Comrade Ponomarenko of the AUS-VN sold a crate of perfume in Kharkiv; others traded Chinese cigarettes for food and other goods in the Soviet Union.[102] The Ministry of Defense censured a number of officials for incompetence and "insufficient party vigilance," but it also concluded that the complaints about the resale and expropriation of consumer goods from China amounted to an "exaggeration."[103] They were apparently reluctant to learn too much about the forms of exchange and privilege that were, of course, endemic to the socialist system. As in other areas of cultural and industrial exchange, the Chinese were watching closely and coming to their own conclusions about the character of Soviet "socialism."

Conclusion

History was important in the socialist world, shaping the attitudes and ideas of the advisers to China and also the concerns of the Chinese as they went about borrowing and learning from the bloc. As in the nineteenth century, the CCP debated the best way to borrow advanced methods, industrial technology, and cultural expertise from the bloc without disturbing the supposed harmony of Chinese society and culture. For the CCP, this effort predictably included extensive attention to political stability and orthodoxy, especially in the wake of the "events" of 1956. They were most hopeful about the Czechoslovaks and East Germans, but even their influence proved problematic, evident here in culture, industrial planning, personal relationships, and cultural exchange. The traditional notions about China that were common among many of the bloc cultural advisers, teachers, and officials seemed almost colonial, disturbingly reminiscent of an era that the Chinese were determined to overcome. Even bloc cultural figures and teachers profoundly enthusiastic about the "friendship" with China produced images and ideas that the Chinese found offensive. Personal moments of interaction could be even more alarming, especially to the authorities. Highly trained experts such as Oldřich Havlíček, much valued by the Chinese, had other compelling interests that Chinese authorities did not associate with the terms of the "socialist friendship."

PART 2

Mao's Second Visit to Moscow

The November 1957 Conference

CHAPTER 4

China's Conditional Affirmation of
Soviet Leadership, 1956–1957

> We now wait to see what the analysis of the Chinese party will be.
> —Czechoslovak official to Zhen Likang, 6 January 1957

Khrushchev's "Secret Speech" at the 20th Party Congress in February 1956 was a huge event in the history of the Soviet Union and the socialist bloc. "The Soviet regime never fully recovered," writes a biographer of Khrushchev, "and neither did he."[1] The unfolding of de-Stalinization had consequences for the bloc. The accelerating crisis in Poland that summer and fall, which included demonstrations and riots in Poznan on 28–29 June that left fifty-three dead, was resolved when Władysław Gomułka assured Khrushchev that Poland would not abandon the Warsaw Pact. Hungary's Imre Nagy was not considered as trustworthy by the Soviets, who exerted pressure and used force against his country in late October and early November 1956.[2]

Drawing from the memoirs of former participants in the Sino-Soviet relationship as well as newly available archival materials, scholars such as Chen Jian, Lorenz Lüthi, Xu Zehao, Zhihua Shen, Li Danhui, and Yafeng Xia have described the CCP's contribution to the Soviet interpretation of the "events" in Poland and Hungary that fall. Zhihua Shen and Yafeng Xia, for example, confirm a claim initially found in the memoirs of Shi Zhe, Mao's interpreter in Moscow in 1949–50, about the contrast drawn by China's leaders between the events in Poland and Hungary. Liu Shaoqi, Deng Xiaoping, and others were in Moscow in late October, and contributed to the Soviet decision on 31 October to use force to end the innovations promoted by Nagy and his reformist socialism. As these scholars conclude, the Chinese were critical of the Soviets in Poland but worried about the very "survival of socialism" in Hungary.[3]

Rather than offer new evidence about a dramatic Chinese intervention in these leadership debates of late October, this chapter draws instead on Ministry of Foreign Affairs material from Moscow, Beijing, Prague, and Berlin in order to describe the character of the intrabloc discussion of these issues at a level generally below that of the high leadership. The Stalin question and the rebellions in Poland and Hungary were the subject of extensive embassy communications in the wake of 1956 that included direct and important exchange between the Chinese and especially the Central Europeans. East Germany and Czechoslovakia, important sources of industrial technology, equipment, and managerial skill, were also comparatively stable during the precarious summer and fall of 1956. A similar contrast unfolded within the advising community in China itself. As a result of these private intrabloc debates, the Chinese emerged proud and pleased with their increasingly important leadership position as a consequence of their response to the Stalin problem as well as the "events" of 1956. Mao and the CCP, the traditional recipients of advice and guidance in the socialist bloc, now felt that they had much to offer the Soviet Union and the bloc as a whole.

The CCP leaders were not disposed to promote any sort of instability in the bloc, however, even as they voiced their concerns about Soviet policy and "great-power chauvinism." Polish dissenters and even Central Committee (CC) members were proclaiming the likelihood of Chinese support for their special "path" of opposition to the Soviet Union, but this was not to happen.[4] The Chinese were the upholders of bloc "unity" in the larger Cold War struggle against "imperialism." This was expressed in the intrabloc debates about the location of the "center" or "head" of the camp. This remained the Soviet Union, but with important qualifications. China offered conditional support for Soviet leadership of the bloc, in part because the Chinese believed they had made compromises for the sake of bloc "unity." In yet another area, the stage was set for the Chinese to conclude by the end of the decade that they had been misused and betrayed by the Soviet Union and the bloc.

The Stalin Question

New scholarship on the Khrushchev era illustrates the complexities of reform and de-Stalinization among a population accustomed to traditional ideas about rulers and rulership. As Iuri Aksiutin has recently argued, many Soviets with no direct experience of political persecution and the gulag found themselves alarmed by the reformist assault on a powerful leader until recently widely revered.[5] Party officials were engaged in a dangerous and confusing effort to explain and educate the citizenry about the nature of the problem and the significance of the criticism. The reconciliation with the Yugoslavs a year earlier had posed a similar dilemma for party officials long accustomed to describing Yugoslavia as a "fascist dictatorship" and its leaders as "enemies, spies, and murderers."[6] The now accessible Central Committee archive in Moscow illustrates the confused concerns of numerous party members and officials throughout the Soviet Union regarding the treatment of Stalin. City and regional party committees reported numerous questions and confusing discussions in the weeks and months after Khrushchev's Secret Speech. "Can we still use the works of Stalin, and will they still be published?" "What do we do with all the portraits and statues of Stalin?" "Is the grave with the body of Stalin going to remain in the mausoleum?" "To what extent is this document going to be known among non-party members?" "What does it mean that the press did not mention the anniversary of the death of Stalin on 5 March, and how do we answer this question?"[7] Other questions disturbingly explored the responsibility of senior Politburo leaders and officials for the crimes of the Stalin era. "Why didn't presidium and Central Committee members eventually correct Stalin?" "If Stalin created a dictatorship and many comrades died as a result of it, then how do we, as communists, explain this to non-party members?" "Why couldn't the mistakes of Stalin be revealed and stopped when he was alive? Indeed, weren't these same comrades there during his life?"[8] Even the surviving wife of recently executed NKVD chief Lavrenti Beria raised the issue of the complicity of the leadership in a plea for clemency from prison.[9] And finally, echoed by Zhou Enlai, party members wondered about the wisdom of besmirching the name of a leader "long preserved in the hearts of the Soviet people."[10]

Such confusion and sentiment common to the Soviet Union was also evident far from Moscow, as material from Wuhan suggests. Ambassador Pavel Iudin and embassy officials O. B. Rakhmanin and I. A. Efremin heard similar concerns and queries at a meeting there in May 1956. Wang Renzhong, the first secretary of the Hubei Provincial Committee, demanded explanations for the "unexpected" criticism of Stalin. Who of the "other leading cadres was also responsible for these mistakes that have arisen?" Why were foreign newspapers discussing the matter, wondered CP First Secretary Zhang Pinghua, when "we, for example, at this time still knew nothing?" Who else was involved in the Leningrad Affair? How could the heroic name of Stalin, asked Song Kanfu, be associated with the "physical destruction of his potential rivals"? The "victories of the Red Army" were "associated with his name." The evening discussion lasted for six hours.[11] Like many party members in Eastern and Central Europe, many Chinese wondered why the Soviet general secretary would take measures that weakened the legitimacy of their own rule. "Rightist elements" and the "national bourgeoisie" were emboldened by the criticism of Stalin, charged Ministry of Culture official Qian Junrui, and were "using the situation in the country to criticize the leading role of the party" in Chinese life.[12]

Chairman Mao himself, however, did not seem particularly threatened. Ever quick on his feet, Mao used the Secret Speech as an opportunity to raise contemporary issues in the Sino-Soviet relationship. In a lengthy exchange with Pavel Iudin on 31 March 1956, Mao blamed Stalin for his support for the GMD and Wang Ming, the mistaken policies of the Comintern, the expropriation of the Changchun Railway and Port Arthur, the "practical transformation [of Manchuria and Xinjiang] into spheres of influence of the USSR," and his own treatment in Moscow during the negotiation of the Sino-Soviet Treaty.[13] China and Mao personally were apparently also victims of Stalin's policies, and Mao enjoyed using the events surrounding the Secret Speech to remind the Russians of their historically lukewarm support for revolution in China. Iudin attempted to steer the conversation back to themes such as the importance of "self-criticism" and Stalin's "cult of personality, bordering on deification," but Mao instead launched into a discussion of "several philosophical problems."[14] Mao stressed similar themes to a visiting Czechoslovak military delegation in December 1957.[15]

Mao successfully recast the event in Chinese terms and presented himself as a strong supporter of the new policy. He spoke approvingly in March 1957 to I. Kurdiukov of the Ministry of Foreign Affairs Far East Department about the new "spirit of criticism and self-criticism" that was sure to strengthen the party.[16] To prove this, as part of the later polemical exchanges of 1960, Soviet embassy officials themselves compiled mountains of material illustrating Chinese support in 1956 and 1957 for the 20th Party Congress and peaceful coexistence.[17] Chinese public discussion followed Mao's lead and also deftly handled the problem of the "cult of personality [gerenchongbai]." In this case commentators turned the event into a pedagogical lesson about the virtues of Chinese collective leadership, and the importance of close ties between the party and the "masses."[18]

Mao had attempted, to a certain extent successfully, to situate himself as the chief and most useful interpreter of Stalin and his era. The significance of this was huge, of course, as "learning from the Soviet Union" and the experience of the "first socialist revolution" were ideas long embedded in public discourse throughout the bloc. Also implicated was the quite sensitive matter of the very legitimacy of the communist parties in the bloc. They all ruled in Stalin's name, and the very viability of the bloc and the future of socialism was called into question as a result of Khrushchev's extraordinary speech. Among themselves, officials discussed their frustration with the element of surprise at the 20th Party Congress, a strategically foolish approach in the view of Zhou Enlai in particular.[19] A GDR embassy official in Prague, Franz Everhartze, summed up the matter for the Czechoslovaks in April 1957: "We have been informed that the Chinese comrades strongly rebuked the Soviet comrades for their manner of resolving the problem of the cult of personality this past year, and the concrete measures taken to criticize c[omrade] Stalin. All of this led to the development of events that took place last year in Hungary and Poland."[20]

Mao thus acquired, as Chen Jian suggests, a moral high ground in the matter of Marxist-Leninist theory and the supposedly global story of unfolding international revolution.[21] The Secret Speech now appeared somewhat hasty, poorly conceived, and oblivious to its consequences for the Soviet Union, the bloc, and even the broader Cold War. Khrushchev faced similar concerns from his own domestic rivals, such as Foreign Minister Viacheslav Molotov, KGB chairman Aleksandr N. Shelepin, and others who would eventually find themselves removed from their positions.[22] Molotov's traditional vision of the importance of "camp" solidarity and "unity" in opposition to the West had long been comforting to the Chinese.

Immediately after Khrushchev's speech, the Chinese clearly suspected that the question of the interpretation of Stalin was not yet resolved, as the Ministry of Foreign Affairs, the CCP's Liaison Department, and Xinhua immediately began compiling reactions to it in the "fraternal" countries, and they even studied the "reactionary press."[23] This material served as the foundation for Mao's first word on the matter, "On the Historical Experience of the Dictatorship of the Proletariat," which appeared in Renmin ribao and Pravda in early April 1956. The foreign ministries and Liaison Departments of the socialist world thanked and congratulated the Chinese. The enthusiasm from party cadres was genuine, and to the Chinese confirmed the legitimacy of their views and the importance of their own "experience" (learning from Soviet "experience" was, of course, a constant theme within the alliance). Soviet party cadres were asking questions about the "three oppositions movement" in China, reported Liu Xiao from the embassy in Moscow, and suggesting it was time to "look at the system of the Chinese Communist Party."[24] Embassy officials who queried the population heard from teachers and professors that Mao's essay was "a good document; its theoretical and ideological level is very high." Party members told the Chinese it was of "great educational significance."[25] The

Chinese illustrated their insight into the "correct management of the internal contradictions among the people," Hungarian officials in Budapest informed the embassy in May 1956.[26] The Chinese response to the Stalin issue was of "genuinely great significance," Liu Xiao reported from Moscow in June.[27]

The second article ("More on the Historical Experience of the Dictatorship of the Proletariat"), which appeared on 29 December 1956, was even more important to the Eastern and Central Europeans, as it came in the wake of a harrowing fall. This article was a "great help to Hungary" and very important in the "Hungarian ideological struggle."[28] The Chinese again were pleased. They were correct in their "estimation of Stalin and the basic experience of the Soviet Union," Hu Jibang, the *Renmin ribao* correspondent in Budapest, told the Hungarians in January 1957, and he dismissed the Yugoslav insinuation that the Chinese were "Stalinists."[29] Other foreign affairs officials echoed Mao's sentiment that Stalin's "achievements outweigh the mistakes."[30] Czechoslovaks, Poles, East Germans, and other party officials were similarly pleased.[31] Khrushchev's report was an "exaggeration," a Czechoslovak official in Prague told Zhen Likang; how could a "true communist" like Stalin have persecuted so many people in the party?[32] To the Chinese this all seemed to contrast with the consequences of Soviet policy and pronouncements, which brought confusion and instability to intrabloc affairs and even threatened to prove useful to the "imperialists."

Mao and the Chinese thus acquired an increasingly important role as a result of the evolving question of the Stalin problem, and this role was recognized by the bloc parties and the Soviet Union itself. It was at the Chinese embassy in Moscow that Khrushchev himself declared it necessary to curtail some of the more explosive implications of the Secret Speech. At a reception there on 17 January 1957, Khrushchev declared that "the name of Stalin is inseparable from Marxism-Leninism."[33] Molotov later made fun of both this event and the general course of reform, suggesting that the leadership would say one thing with Zhou Enlai in the room and another thing when he left.[34] Chinese ambition and needs were intersecting with the politics of reform in the Soviet Union, as the Chinese seemed to be accomplishing now what conservative critics of Khrushchev counseled before the Speech itself. Presidium discussions on the eve of the 20th Congress, for example, included efforts by Molotov, Lazar Kaganovich, and others to temper and restrain the criticism and anger that went into the Secret Speech. "But Stalin, as a great leader, must be recognized," offered Molotov. "You have to say in the report that Stalin was a great successor to the work of Lenin. I insist on that," he continued at the

1 February 1956 Presidium meeting, where he was supported by Kaganovich and Kliment Voroshilov.[35] Khrushchev did not say this in the Secret Speech, but he did refer to Stalin as a "genius" in front of the Chinese and other bloc representatives at the conclusion of a 1 May 1956 celebration in the Kremlin. At the same time, however, Stalin "ignored the party" and the Central Committee, and absurdly thought Molotov and Voroshilov were foreign spies. Khrushchev went on to defend the historic contributions of Molotov to the Communist Party.[36] In Moscow, Chinese ambassador Liu Xiao maintained close contacts with Molotov after the 20th Party Congress.[37]

China's taking on of a more significant role in bloc affairs centered on stability and order rather than protest, however. This was often misunderstood at the time by both national publics and bloc officials, perhaps because China's evolving position was not yet clear. The trip to Georgia of Politburo member and Marshal Zhu De, after he attended the 20th Party Congress, illustrates this ambiguity. His trip happened to coincide with a series of violent pro-Stalin demonstrations in Tbilisi, where some 120 to 150 students gathered on 5 March 1956 at the Palace of Labor with portraits of Stalin, honoring the third anniversary of his death. The next day a larger group carried portraits of Stalin and laid wreaths at the Stalin monument. At the House of Government some 8,000 to 10,000 people gathered and chanted slogans like "Glory to the Great Stalin" and "Glory to Stalin the Leader." The crowd demanded the return of flags and portraits of Stalin in the city.[38] "Why do we not have hanging on the facade of the State Soviet the panel with the images of Marx-Engels-Lenin-Stalin?" yelled the crowd, reported S. Statnikov, a journalist for *Trud*. A student from Moscow told the crowd that students all over the Soviet Union were supportive and the "revision of Marxism can only be done by enemies of the people!" A Muscovite woman told the crowd, "Moscow supports us. Right now meetings are taking place not only in Georgia but in Stalingrad, Leningrad, and other cities."[39] There were indeed large demonstrations in Gori, Sukhumi, Batumi, and other Georgian cities.

The crowds frustrated with the denunciation of Stalin perceived Zhu De as a potential ally, especially as he had just taken a pilgrimage to Gori, the birthplace of Stalin and home to a museum dedicated to his life. This was a totally misplaced hope, however. Zhu De greeted demonstrators in Krtsanisi, where he was staying at a government-owned dacha, but he was reluctant to visit the Stalin monument in Tbilisi.[40] F. Baazova reported that the demonstrators "demanded insistently that [CC first secretary V. P.] Mzhavanadze support the efforts of Mao to restore the remains and the honor of Stalin."[41] The

Soviet authorities quickly brought the demonstrations under control, and high officials evoked the usual suspects. Nikolai Bulganin referred to "anti-Soviet elements" in the Georgian party that deserved to be "purged," and Khrushchev complained about speculators and "good for nothings [*bezdel'nikov*]."[42] Other observers made reference to "hooliganism," nationalist chauvinism, and outside agitators, and criticized party city committees in Tbilisi, Gori, Kutaisi, Sukhumi, and other cities for their failure to move quickly against "nationalist and hostile elements."[43] Party members, worse than simply "passive observers," "turned out to be mixed up in the disturbances" themselves.[44]

Zhu De was disturbed by the events of the 20th Party Congress, but he did not go to Georgia to promote sympathy for Stalin in opposition to Khrushchev. Promoting opposition and rebellion was still far from the minds of Chinese officials at this point. Just before his attendance at the party congress in Moscow, Zhu De participated in defense consultations in Hungary, Czechoslovakia, and Poland.[45] In Moscow, according to a Chinese Ministry of Foreign Affairs report, Zhu De, Deng Xiaoping, Wang Jiaxiang, and others attended an exhibit dedicated to the peaceful uses of atomic energy. The group also speculated happily about the prospects of the transfer of the bomb to China.[46] They were not interested in antagonizing their hosts in any way.

Poznan and Budapest, 1956

The Chinese were generally sympathetic to the "national coloring" of intrabloc exchange that endured within the world of bloc "internationalism."[47] China's long indigenous preoccupation with Chinese uniqueness raised questions about the socialist tradition decades before the emergence of the postwar socialist world. At the CCP plenum in 1938, Mao warned of the dangers of "abstract Marxism" and the necessity of attention to "concrete conditions prevailing in China."[48] At the initial 1949 meetings with the Soviet advising group led by Ivan Kovalev, according to the memoir of translator Li Yueran, Mao immediately emphasized that China would not "completely and indiscriminately copy Soviet experience."[49] Zhihua Shen describes numerous warnings from diverse figures beyond Mao through the 1950s about the need to achieve the proper balance in the delicate matter of "learning from the Soviet Union." The matter came up in higher education, at the Central Committee Marxist-Leninist School (later the CC Party School), in the military, in debates over industrial and agricultural development, and so on.[50] This tentative language of Chinese nativism generally juxtaposed "self-reliance [*zili gengsheng*]," "independent decision-making [*duli zizhu*]," and socialism "with Chinese characteristics" against "imitation," "blind faith" in the virtues of foreign methods, and the "mechanical" transplanting of foreign experience in China.[51]

Thus the Chinese were well situated to observe the unfolding of the debates about diverse "roads" or "paths" to socialism that emerged around the time of the 20th Party Congress. As in the nineteenth century, the Poles were in the lead in this twentieth-century version of "organic work." "We have paid too little attention to that which is innate in our movement, in our historical road, in our methods of construction," explained a Polish contributor to *Nowe Drogi* in October 1955. Reform-minded Soviets were sympathetic to this discussion. "All nations," declared a *Pravda* editorial of 16 July 1955, "will arrive at socialism, Lenin pointed out; that is inevitable, but not all will arrive there in exactly the same way."[52] Khrushchev affirmed the importance of "separate paths to socialism" at the 20th Party Congress in February 1956.[53] A Chinese Ministry of Foreign Affairs report about the congress favorably noted innovations in Yugoslavia and described China as possessing "special characteristics" and a "unique situation." "Increasingly levels of diversity emerge [*yuelai yueduo yanghua*]" as we get closer to socialism, the Chinese concluded.[54]

Few anticipated the consequences of the Secret Speech in the broader bloc, however. The hierarchical bloc system of control over the transmission of information, like the "nervous system," in the formulation of Elidor Mëhilli, could also spread "shocks" and provoke "seizures."[55] Different kinds of reformers, dissidents, intellectuals, and even workers posed frank and critical questions about the Soviet system throughout the bloc but especially in Poland and Hungary, and the determination of the opposition surprised not just the Soviets and the Chinese but the entire world. As Chinese officials reported with alarm that July, both Poles and Hungarians were suggesting there was "no need to move toward communism together with the Soviet Union."[56] The Chinese were aware, however, that Eastern European frustration with the Soviet Union mirrored their own.

In Poland the Chinese thus honored the concerns and needs of a small people facing potential intrusion by a great and historically imperialist power. Chinese ambassador Wang Bingnan in Warsaw reported to Beijing that the Poles were looking to find their "own path to socialism" and were not in danger of "restoring capitalism to Poland." "Every country and people has its own path to socialism, and Poland also has its own path," Gomułka explained to Wang Bingnan. "We want friendly cooperation with the Soviet Union," other Poles explained to the Chinese, "but we want our own independence to resolve our own affairs."[57] Again indirectly comparing the Polish-Soviet relationship to the Sino-Soviet relationship, Wang Bingnan noted the absence of "equality" as well as the problem of the "mechanical copying of Soviet experience in a doctrinaire fashion."[58] These were issues now familiar to the Chinese, who had experienced six years of close Sino-Soviet collaboration.

If the Chinese were sympathetic to the Poles that fall, however, they also found themselves in dangerous territory in a way that is likely to have affected their thinking about Hungary. As the Polish October was unfolding, Chinese officials were surprised to find themselves increasingly perceived as potential antibloc insurrectionists. "Rightists" in Poland were now looking to China for support, reported the embassy on 23 October, even suggesting Poland might "take the Chinese road."[59] Another rumor pushed things further: "Comrade Mao Zedong supports a Polish independence movement against the Soviet Union."[60] Radical students at Warsaw University were "grateful for China's support."[61] The experience of opposition crossed the borders of the bloc, and many Poles followed with excitement the events simultaneously unfolding in Budapest. Demonstrators at Warsaw University raised the issues of democracy, legality, increasing trade with the capitalist countries, and "support for the Hungarian people."[62] Even Polish party members were under the impression that "from today forward the Polish party plans to take the Chinese path."[63] Poles visualized the Chinese as an ally to the small peoples of Eastern and Central Europe in their effort to end traditional Russian imperialism in the region. Rumors continued to circulate, the Chinese embassy reported on 5 November, that the "Poles and the Chinese are in telephone contact, and China acknowledges that the Soviet Union already is not a socialist country, and openly takes part in invasions."[64] Party members throughout the bloc engaged in open speculation about emerging alliances: the Poles, Yugoslavs, Romanians, and Chinese against the Soviets, Czechoslovaks, and East Germans?[65] A frustrated Polish official that December told Chen Kezhai in Warsaw that events in both Hungary and Poland were "created by the people and a people's revolution."[66] The Chinese were in the thick of a bloc political controversy and crisis that threatened the bloc's very viability, which was not what they intended. And the Poles dangerously had the impression that the Chinese were the opponents of Soviet policy in Hungary in late October and early November.

The Chinese were determined to be the upholders rather than the subverters of the bloc's "unity." Memoir material from Wu Lengxi does not correspond to the flavor and tenor of the discussions explored here. "If the Soviet Union dispatches troops," Mao allegedly told the Politburo on 20 October, "we will support Poland."[67] Mao could often be impulsive and even reckless before certain audiences, but statements such as these are more suggestive of the rumor mill within the socialist world at this time, far from the careful calculations of the CCP leadership and its embassy personnel. The CCP leaders were not disposed to promoting any sort of instability in the bloc, even as they voiced their concerns about Soviet policy and "great-power chauvinism." Wu Lengxi possibly was giving voice to the sort of rumors and speculative statements that were part of intrabloc debate at that time.

The Chinese instead thought of themselves as the "saviors" of the bloc, as they later proudly proclaimed after the split. In both Poland and Hungary, the Chinese felt justified in their conclusions and actions and proud of their contribution to the stability of the bloc. Intervention in Hungary was the wise choice, the Chinese concluded, and the CCP again emerged proud of its insight into the "management" of "contradictions among the people" within a socialist society. "The Hungarian situation [was] complicated," wrote Li He, a foreign affairs official in Budapest, to Deng Tuo that December. The Western countries as well as the "Hungarian reactionary parties" were poised to take advantage of the situation.[68] As with the interpretation of Stalin, the bloc again needed the experience of the Chinese. Liu Xiao was proud to hear, at the 7 November 1956 banquet in Moscow attended by Mikoyan, Molotov, Voroshilov, and other high Soviet officials, that the Hungarian situation had been "resolved," and "our mutual unity and support" had strengthened the camp and kept the Americans, British, and French in check. Liu Xiao was pleased to report to Beijing: "Regarding the problems in Poland and Hungary, Khrushchev's estimation of the support of China is very high, and he said: 'The Chinese party sent a very high-level delegation, and this sort of support was very important. Many useful things came out of all the talks with the Chinese comrades.'"[69]

The Chinese, the traditional recipients of advice, now gave it freely to everyone. Wang Jiaxiang, for example, lectured Iudin on the differences between Gomułka and Tito in December 1956 (Gomułka was "no match" for Tito, i.e., far less of a problem).[70] Liu Shaoqi counseled Hungarian ambassador Ezhef Sall and Czechoslovak ambassador Antonin Gregor that same month about the best means to limit the influence of Soviet "great-power chauvinism" in their countries (focus on practical economic matters rather than politics and culture).[71] When Lüe Saiyang, a trade union delegate, arrived in Budapest for a 24 December 1956 meeting with János Kádár and other Hungarian officials, he immediately presented himself as someone with special insight into the problems of the bloc. How can we facilitate bloc "solidarity"? he inquired.[72] The Chinese managed to appear wise in two seemingly contradictory areas: as maintainers of bloc stability against the American threat, and as instructors on the delicate matter of improving intrabloc relationships.[73]

The Soviets themselves were openly (but not publicly) grateful for Chinese support and insight in wake of 1956, which was precisely what the Chinese wanted to hear. In a late November 1956 exchange between Mikoyan and Liu Xiao, Mikoyan expressed his relief that the crisis had been resolved and his gratitude to the Chinese for their contribution. He assured Liu Xiao that Poland was stable ("Poland is not Yugoslavia"), emphasized the importance of the new Soviet subsidies of oil, meat, and consumer goods that would now improve the stability of the bloc (and "make sure that Germany doesn't purchase goods from the capitalist countries"), and blamed the current difficulties on the Stalin era. "Once Stalin went to the grave, the problems had been resolved," claimed Mikoyan. Most important, he was explicit and clear about China's contribution to what was becoming the joint leadership of the bloc: "Comrade Mikoyan noted China's very useful [contribution] at the time [of the events] in Poland and Hungary, which exerted a very good influence."[74] The Chinese heard this often in the fall and winter of 1956–57.[75]

In Central Europe the Chinese Ministry of Foreign Affairs also received confirmation of China's new role in the bloc. A Hungarian official in their Liaison Department for exchange with the bloc pointedly contrasted China's experience to that of the Soviet Union. China underwent a "ninety-year" revolutionary struggle that produced a strong party and "excellent cadres" who successfully created under difficult conditions a "dictatorship of the proletariat," a "second October revolution." The Soviet era of revolutionary struggle, by contrast, lasted only from March to November 1917. Consequently the "international workers' movement pays significant attention" to the Chinese. Even further, "all the countries of the world pay close attention to China, and when problems arise the world first listens to the views of the Chinese comrades."[76] Other foreign affairs officials in Hungary thanked Chairman Mao in particular for "instruction" on both the Stalin question and "opposition to great-power hegemony and the violation of the interests and sentiments of small peoples and countries."[77] Similarly, a Czechoslovak official in Prague told Zhen Likang that the rest of the bloc now waits "to see what the analysis of the Chinese party will be."[78]

East Germans and Czechoslovaks against
Poles and Hungarians in China

The politically explosive character of intrabloc exchange unfolded within the advising and diplomatic community in China itself, much to the chagrin of both the Soviets and the Chinese. As in Central Europe in the fall of 1956, in China the East Germans and Czechoslovaks were generally more fearful of innovation and the consequences of diverse "paths" to socialism. By contrast, Hungarians throughout the bloc and the world generally were deeply affected by the uprising of 1956. This was a regular topic of conversation among officials in the Soviet International Department of the Central Committee, who generally associated potential Hungarian disloyalty with the Yugoslavs. The son of the Hungarian minister of foreign affairs, Imre Horváth, fled to the West in the fall of 1956, and several deputy ministers in the ministry were supposedly "pro-Yugoslav." Yugoslav diplomats, warned Hungarian foreign affairs officials István Shubik and László Vatsi, had their eye on cultivating ties with "wavering" Hungarian diplomats abroad.[79] On 4 November 1956, Hungarian reformer Imre Nagy sought refuge in the Yugoslav embassy in Budapest, confirming the suspicions of bloc officials about the dangers of links between the Yugoslavs and the Eastern and Central Europeans.[80]

There were quite a few "wavering" Hungarians among the advising and diplomatic community in China. International Department official K. A. Krutikov and the Hungarian ambassador in Beijing, Ezhef Sall, discussed the Hungarian situation and the "mood of the foreign Hungarian colony" in China in December 1956. Sall worried about the impact of letters from home on the Hungarians in China. He was aware that an adviser in North Korea received a letter from a friend in Budapest informing him that "in the street it is impossible to call oneself a communist, as you might get killed." Hungarians on *komandirovka* were confused and understood poorly the "strengthening of order" that took place by November, Sall explained. "A portion of the [Hungarians in China] still maintain the illusion that Hungary might become a neutral country, that some other path is possible in Hungary, and so on. In general ... much is mixed up in the heads of our people."[81] Hungarian officials supportive of the Soviet intervention noted that numerous party members still supported Nagy, objected to the assessment of the "events" as "counterrevolutionary," were generally "oriented to Yugoslavia," and subject to Yugoslav propaganda about the formation of a "free, independent, neutral bloc" consisting of Yugoslavia, Poland, and Hungary.[82] In Sall's view, clearly the Hungarians in China were also overly influenced by the Yugoslavs. Twenty-six of thirty-two Hungarians in one advising group wanted to quit the Communist Party, he complained, many of them were in contact with Yugoslavs in China, and Yugoslav ambassador Koca Popović was utterly unresponsive to bloc efforts to limit the damage in the wake of the fall of 1956.[83]

The Poles in China were also a concern to Chinese Ministry of Foreign Affairs and security officials. After the visit of the large Polish military delegation to Beijing in October 1957, which included long discussions with Mao and other high officials about the Stalin question, the Soviet Union, and the situation in Poland, the group returned to Warsaw to find itself accused of disloyalty. The Soviet ambassador in Poland and GUES officials suggested the Polish military figures had been speaking openly on their return about Chinese "military strategy." Liu Xiao in Moscow worried that the Poles were revealing "our country's most important military-industrial secrets."[84] Several months later, Zhou Enlai complained that the Poles remained weak in their efforts to purge their party and intelligentsia of the "strong influence of revisionism," which in his view extended to the advising and diplomatic community within the bloc. Were Polish ambassador Stanisław Kiryliuk Chinese, Zhou Enlai angrily suggested, "he would have already been purged as a member of the rightist element."[85] The North Korean ambassador in Beijing, Li En Kho, also routinely argued with Kiryliuk, who retorted that the North Korean was a "Stalinist who understands nothing."[86] These debates about "Stalinists" versus those who were presumably reformers or upholders of genuine socialism took place throughout the bloc and were reproduced within the *komandirovka* community in China. The term became a source of contention for Khrushchev himself, in the company of Georgii Malenkov, Nikolai Bulganin, Viacheslav Molotov, and Lazar Kaganovich at the Yugoslav embassy in late 1954. "There is no such thing as 'Stalinism,'" he complained. "Stalin was a Leninist!"[87] The term disappeared from use in the Soviet press, but not from internal bloc discussion.

The East Germans took it upon themselves to play the role of the enforcers of political conformity in the wake of the "events" of 1956. In Sofia, for example, the GDR ambassador in December 1956 anxiously gave Zhou Zhuan, the Chinese representative there, a rundown on the reliability and behavior of the advising community in Bulgaria.[88] In Poland the East Germans were outraged about Poles who had the audacity to use the term "Stalinism" in reference to the GDR in interviews with the West German press.[89] After a 1 January 1957 meeting at the Soviet embassy in Warsaw, Chinese ambassador

Wang Bingnan described the improved situation in the Polish party, and noted that the East Germans in particular were "helping the party proceed along the correct path."[90] In China the East Germans took it upon themselves to monitor the Chinese and the Poles, especially when they were together. The GDR embassy in Beijing reported on a "notably peculiar" meeting between Józef Cyrankiewicz, the visiting Polish premier, and Zhou Enlai in April 1957. Cyrankiewicz pointedly refrained from any reference to "the leading role of the Soviet Union in the socialist camp." Later that day, however, GDR officials were relieved to discover that the Chinese had restored order, and the appropriate declaration was made at a public rally.[91] The Vietnamese, eager for Chinese support, also played the role of watchdog. They informed the Chinese, based on their experience with Polish visiting delegations to Vietnam, that the Poles disagreed with the idea of a socialist camp led by the Soviet Union and China, and even believed that "Poland and other socialist countries can secretly unite together."[92]

The Czechoslovaks were also suspicious of the Poles in China, and the rivalry intersected with Chinese notions about the dangers of "revisionism" in the bloc. The Czechoslovak general consul in Shanghai, Ján Fierlínger, denounced his Polish counterpart, K. Biernácki, to both the Soviets and Chinese for his supposed lack of political orthodoxy. Biernácki responded in kind, describing Fierlínger to the Soviets as "unintelligent" and responsible for the dangerous selection of a series of unreliable Czechoslovak cadres in China. Biernácki portrayed the Czechoslovaks in Shanghai as far too close to the English. British officials, he claimed, had clearly "bought" a particular Czechoslovak couple with gifts obtained from their frequent shopping trips to Hong Kong.[93] This was all designed as a political denunciation over consumerism, an issue sensitive to the Chinese, but the charge was at least believable. That the wife of a Czech diplomat in China would befriend the wife of an English diplomat in order to access consumer goods from Hong Kong was entirely characteristic of the world of "socialism" in the Cold War.

Yugoslavs in China themselves complicated the question of the bloc's "unity" in its commitment to the Soviet Union. As Zhang Wentian noted to Iudin, the Yugoslavs "bow down before American technology," describe Soviet technology as "backward," and were eager to share these views with the advising community in China and the Chinese generally.[94] Yugoslav ambassador Koca Popović and his wife were particularly troublesome characters in China. Previously Yugoslav ambassador to Moscow and subsequently minister of foreign affairs, Popović was always quick to remind Iudin of the "special path of

Yugoslavia," as he liked to say. The couple spent five years in the United States, and in China enjoyed bringing attention to the "good conditions for workers in the USA" and the high standard of living enjoyed by Yugoslav émigrés to the United States. The wife of Popović, as Iudin complained, was very restrained with the Russians but warm with the English and the Indians, and routinely read and tried to share American and English publications with bloc officials and advisers. It was well known among these figures, as the Albanian ambassador told Iudin, that Popović's wife despised the Soviet Union. Educated in France and fluent in French, English, and Italian, she informed the wife of the Polish ambassador that "she speaks Russian poorly and does not like to speak that language." According to Iudin, she always "dresse[d] loudly, in the latest American fashion."[95]

Describing the Bloc

The Chinese thus emerged, from both the Stalin debate and the "events" of 1956, pleased with their new position and level of prestige within bloc affairs. This raised the question among bloc officials of changing the language used to describe the bloc. This matter was far from trivial. In societies shaped by campaigns and pedagogical programs, the content of propaganda slogans is significant. Within the bloc, the slogans reflected a consensus that emerged from intrabloc leadership debate. The matter of finding the proper description for the bloc was brought to the attention of Peng Zhen by Soviet officials themselves during Peng's December 1956 trip to the Soviet Union. Several Soviet cadres, he reported to Beijing, suggested changing the language used to describe the bloc from referring to it as having "the Soviet Union at its head [or at its center] [yi sulian wei shou]" to having "the Soviet Union and China at its head [yi zhongsu wei shou]." The matter was controversial in several ways, of course. Molotov was long sympathetic to such a formulation, especially as he identified the Chinese as important supporters of traditional socialist bloc orthodoxy and "unity" in the face of the insidious "imperialist" threat. His comment in 1954 about the Soviet Union and the Chinese as both leaders of the bloc made an "enormous impression" on Chinese leaders at the time, according to Peng Dehuai.[96] They were hearing other such voices as well. Czechoslovak ambassador Antonin Gregor put the focus on Asia in his discussion with Mao in September 1955. The Chinese revolution had begun a "new era in the history of the national-liberation struggle of the Asian peoples." His formulation was similar to Molotov's. "Our people are happy that at the head of the camp of peace, democracy, and socialism stand two powerful states—the Union of Soviet Socialist Republics and the Chinese People's Republic."[97] And this was before the "events" of 1956 further changed the equation, leading even some Soviet cadres to feel that the Chinese deserved the honor for their contributions in that year. And further, some Soviet officials considered the formulation to be useful in response to bloc expressions of frustration with traditional Russian imperialism. Soviet officials told Peng Zhen, "You can say this ['the socialist camp led by the Soviet Union'] with authority and to good effect, but we say this and everyone says we're imperialists."[98]

The Chinese would thus help the Soviets by everywhere proclaiming that the camp in fact remained "headed by the Soviet Union." Peng Zhen was eager to demonstrate Chinese support for the original slogan and all it symbolized, noting simultaneously that Chinese loyalty might accelerate the transfer of nuclear technology to China. Thus as a reaffirmation of their commitment to the stability of the bloc and the overall cause of international socialism, the Chinese relentlessly affirmed in the wake of 1956 the traditional slogans about "learning from the Soviet Union" and a bloc firmly "led by the Soviet Union at its head [*vozglavliaemyi vo glave sovetskogo soiuza*]." Peng Zhen was public and demonstrative in December 1955 about China's study of the "leading experience" of the Soviet Union, the significance of October 1917 and its importance as the first socialist revolution (eclipsing in significance that of 1949), and "the great significance of the Soviet Union's leadership of the socialist camp."[99]

As with the Stalin question and the rebellions of 1956, the Chinese again adopted a position much appreciated by the Eastern and Central European parties. In the wake of 1956, Eastern European officials faced far too many challenges to their rule and their relationship to the Soviet Union, and they could not afford to see a contentious debate over the leadership of the bloc intersect with the views of their own domestic critics.[100] The Europeans of the bloc were also, of course, closer to the sensitive Yugoslav challenge, and among them the notion of Mao as an "Asian Tito" had long been a topic of conversation. After 1956 they feared that anything hinting at Yugoslav-style innovation and yet another challenge to the Soviet Union would be too much for the bloc to endure. And finally, the Central European vision of consumerism, technological development, and cultural exchange with the West demanded political loyalty to the bloc and Soviet leadership of the bloc. This was part of the compromise made by bloc leaders with the Soviet Union in the wake of 1956, and they were not interested in seeing their own development in this area derailed by the Chinese.[101]

In time Mao and his supporters would come to drastic conclusions concerning this vision of economic development, but for now they were eager to promote bloc cohesion and stability. In January 1957, closely following the trail of Peng Zhen, Zhou Enlai led a delegation to Moscow, Warsaw, and Budapest and proposed a "preliminary discussion with Tito on problems of mutual relations among the communist parties of the socialist camp, and also on other matters of interest."[102] He never got that far, as Tito feared the emerging forum would turn into another bloc denunciation of the Yugoslavs, as in 1948.[103] From Zhou's perspective, however, the matter at hand was the affirmation of Soviet leadership, and the public declaration of China's support for the Soviet Union. Ministry of Foreign Affairs officials in Prague echoed this sentiment in May 1957 and referred to the importance of the "forty years of experience in constructing socialism" in the Soviet Union. "The socialist camp is led by the Soviet Union, and the socialist countries are united around the Soviet Union." They explained away contemporary anti-Soviet sentiment as a product of "previous historical circumstances (the oppression of imperial Russia)."[104] Zhang Wentian, former ambassador to Moscow, similarly communicated to Iudin that fall that China remained distant from Yugoslav insinuations about the merits of a socialist world not led by the Soviet Union.[105] Politburo member Bo Yibo professed China's "genuine" commitment to "learning from the Soviet Union" and apologized for its past inability to understand the "necessity of foreign and domestic policies like the 'criticism of the cult of personality of Stalin.'"[106]

This was the background to Mao's important role at the November 1957 International Conference of Communist Parties in November in Moscow. The most sensitive topic at hand was the question of the Soviet Union's "leading role" in the bloc rather than the famous "east wind" speech that has attracted more attention from scholars.[107] Bloc commentators at the time were more interested, for example, in Mao's reference in a 6 November speech to the "leading role" played by the Soviet Union in the bloc.[108] The Chinese were still proponents of "unity" within the camp, and thus the conference amounted to a sort of psychological recovery for the bloc parties after the trauma of 1956. Mao returned home again to affirm China's solidarity with the camp and Soviet leadership at the fourth session of the Congress of People's Deputies, reported Czechoslovak officials in China.[109]

Bloc diplomats and advisers in China were paying close attention to the matter through 1957, aware that the endurance of the Chinese position could not be taken for granted. It would be unproductive and even dangerous, East

Germans and Czechoslovaks in China warned, if the Chinese proved reluctant to recognize "the leading role of the USSR in the socialist camp."[110] At the Soviet embassy in Beijing, officials noted with trepidation China's growing sense of its own importance in the promotion of "unity" within the bloc.[111] The Chinese took it upon themselves to continue to worry about the Poles, who remained reluctant to recognize Soviet leadership. The "important thing is not whether or not this slogan is used," Wang Bingnan finally conceded in one frustrating exchange, but rather the need to address the problem of enduring anti-Soviet sentiment.[112] Czechoslovaks in East Germany, by contrast, enthusiastically wanted to alter the slogan to the "Soviet Union at the head of the great socialist camp."[113] The "events" of 1956 were finished but still remembered. The East Germans and Czechoslovaks worried about the Poles, Hungarians, and Chinese; the Chinese worried about all the Eastern and Central Europeans; the Vietnamese were dismayed by the Poles and eager to curry favor with the Chinese; the Soviets worried about everyone and especially the Chinese. A Soviet official complained about the Hungarian translation of a Soviet document at the 7th Party Congress there in 1959, because of its apparent ambiguity over whether or not the camp had "the Soviet Union at its head."[114] The language police were busy in the socialist world, and it is a wonder the bloc even survived the decade.

The Ideological Question

The experience of 1956 prompted much thinking in the CCP about the fate of socialism in power, the lack of a commitment to socialism among the younger generation, and the weaknesses of institutions such as schools that fostered and bred the sentiments on display in 1956.[115] All these things became targets in China in the Antirightist Campaign led by Mao in the wake of the Hundred Flowers episode. The Chinese were proud to do what was best for the bloc and the general state of socialism, but they had expectations of their own. With their guidance the bloc was to get busy addressing the important matters that were presumably obvious to everyone in the wake of the "events" of 1956. This was on the minds of officials at Chinese embassies in numerous socialist bloc cities. Liu Xiao in Moscow, for example, was worried about the health of the bloc and believed Chinese experience in eliminating "counterrevolution" and "rightism" was now especially useful to his bloc colleagues. "The Hungarian people's government is not like that of China," Li He explained to Deng Tuo in Budapest, because the Hungarians lacked experience in anticipating and eradicating dissent. This, however, was sure to change. In 1957 all the countries of the bloc would take measures to address the "problem of ideological work."[116]

In the matter of "ideological work," the Chinese considered themselves to be the most qualified. A "repetition of the events in Hungary" would never take place in China, Zhou Enlai assured Iudin in a 22 May 1957 discussion. China's experience with its own intelligentsia, the "rightists," and the Hundred Flowers campaign, he maintained, made its Communist Party adept at renovating and maintaining the revolution. Zhou explained to Iudin that all the bloc parties could benefit from the "use of Chinese experience among the fraternal parties." Mao, too, he emphasized, had concluded that Hungary needed more attention to "work on the ideological reeducation of the intelligentsia."[117] The situation was similar in Poland, Liu Shaoqi told Iudin later that fall, where the "danger exists of the restoration of capitalism." The emergence of numerous right-wing journals illustrated that the "essence of the problem" was a matter of "ideology." "Bourgeois" parties in Poland would simply keep producing their "harmful" journals. The Chinese, however, had significant experience in ideological re-molding. In China "we did not close a single bourgeois newspaper or journal, but we changed their political orientation." The Americans always accuse us of "'brainwashing,'" Liu Shaoqi continued. "There is a good deal of truth in this. The victory of the revolution is strengthened when an ideological change in the masses takes place. The revolution must influence the consciousness of people."[118] The Chinese embassy in Warsaw complained about the influence of propaganda broadcasts from the West about a "free Europe," and especially about the interest of Polish youth in the American "way of life."[119]

Thus the nature of the task at hand after 1956 seemed obvious to the Chinese: ideological remolding, the transformation of consciousness, the promotion of a socialist mentality, and so on, remained necessary and even vital even though the revolution was secure. The experience of the bloc seemed to be producing a transnational disillusionment and rebellion rather than solidarity and "unity," the constant refrain of officials, as many scholars have pointed out.[120] East German youth were interested in trips to Yugoslavia, American movies, dances such as the "boogie-boogie" and the "mambo," and "modernist experimentation in the spirit of several Polish writers."[121] Budapest University professor Nevai László made similar complaints about his students' lack of interest in socialism and politics.[122] Intellectuals at Humboldt University in Berlin and Karl Marx University in Leipzig were eager to join their frustrated kin at places such as the Lenin Institute in Budapest.[123] Even the Soviet Union was producing a youth culture that raised doubts about its revolutionary character. The *stiliagi*, defined by historian Miriam Dobson as "fashion-conscious youth who rejected Soviet styles, adopting and reworking American trends," were viewed by bloc officials as "an infection, coming to us from the West."[124]

From the Chinese perspective, however, bloc officials were for some reason both reluctant to learn from Chinese "experience" and unable to understand it. The Chinese embassy in Budapest, for example, complained of the Hungarian reaction to the Antirightist Campaign. The press inaccurately described the campaign, expressed "doubts," and explained "contradictions" in China as a product of its vast size and peasant population. The Hungarians, complained Chinese officials in Budapest, did not understand "the basic conditions of our country and the character of the consciousness of the masses." The Chinese party in fact was strong, united, and closely connected to the people, all things that the Hungarians were supposed to be learning about from the Chinese. The current Chinese measures, concluded officials, should have been implemented in Hungary "before what happened in October of last year."[125]

The Soviet Union itself, site of the "first socialist revolution," was similarly in need of renewal. This line of reasoning was not foreign to any of the bloc parties, who all recommended the strengthening of the party and the return to Leninist tradition in the face of the crimes attributed to Stalin. The Chinese read the experience of 1956 differently from the Soviets' interpretation, however. Chinese assumptions about raising the "communist consciousness of the people" and strengthening "the communist education of the masses" had a flavor specific to Chinese political culture that remained more or less foreign to the rest of the bloc.[126] The question of attention to the "standard of living," increasingly a topic in the Soviet press, tended to be viewed by the Chinese as more than purely an economic matter.[127] Like the Hungarians, the Soviets appeared oblivious to their many problems and unimaginative about possible remedies. Soviet youth were uninterested in ideology, indifferent about global revolution, divorced from the experience of labor, and excessively preoccupied with "Western fashion" and the "Western culture and way of life."[128] Young people preferred "romantic films" from Poland over Chinese films dedicated to "socialism and class struggle."[129] The Chinese welcomed even the slightest attention from the CPSU to the need "to raise the consciousness of the Soviet people."[130] Instead of listening to the Chinese and addressing these problems, however, the Soviet Union's leaders contributed to the problem by initiating exchange with the West, culminating in Khrushchev's own trip to America in September 1959. He awkwardly arrived in Beijing that October to celebrate the tenth anniversary of the revolution, having spent far more time and effort in a celebrated and internationally reported month-long tour of the United States. The Chinese felt the bloc was desperately in need of what the Chinese had to offer, and yet the Soviets and their loyal Eastern and Central European allies dangerously pushed it in precisely the opposite direction.

Conclusion

China's leaders were pleased with their newfound position in the wake of 1956, gratified that numerous bloc parties, including the CPSU, tended to recognize their important and helpful role in responding to the challenge of the Stalin question and the "events" in Poland and Hungary. The Chinese were simultaneously successful on several different fronts. They offered stability to the bloc parties, they contributed to the "unity" of the bloc against the ever present outside threat of "imperialism," and they served as the champions of "small peoples" struggling with the "great-power chauvinism" of a Soviet Union still shaped by its imperial heritage. Mao expressed little regret about a Chinese intervention in bloc and even Soviet affairs that dangerously intersected with the sensitive political conflicts of the reform era. The Chinese position on Stalin and the question of "unity" was closer to that of Molotov, who along with Voroshilov and others maintained frequent contact with the Chinese. Lower-level officials routinely voiced frustration and bewilderment over the sudden change in the interpretation of Stalin and wondered how to discuss the matter even within the party. The Chinese focus on "achievements" over "shortcomings" was a formulation useful to communist parties still in power and eager to look forward and beyond the Stalin era.[131]

Mao's new position in the bloc corresponded to his sense of China's progress, presumably largely as a product of socialist bloc aid, from 1949 to 1956. His presence in Moscow at the 1957 Conference of Communist Parties illustrated his important position in the bloc. Showing great humility and concern for the overall health and strength of the bloc, the Chinese acceded to the wishes of the Central and Eastern Europeans in particular in recognizing that the Soviet Union remained the "center" or "head" of the bloc. This was important to the overall Cold War struggle against the "imperialism" of the Americans, which demanded a unified bloc undistracted by internal struggle, neutralism, or Yugoslav-style deviation.

The Chinese had strong expectations, however, about what they were now owed by the rest of the bloc and the Soviet Union in particular. They also assumed that the bloc would proceed to take seriously the ideological issue or the question of "consciousness" as a problem in socialist society. That the CCP would purport to offer something to the bloc in this regard bordered on the absurd, however. The unfolding of the Antirightist Campaign included purges, attacks on primary school teachers, and a "witch-hunt-like political campaign" that persecuted and stigmatized as many as half a million people.[132] That this would serve as some sort of model for the Hungarians and Poles hardly seems reasonable and instead hints at the future direction of China toward the catastrophic Great Leap Forward. By that time, largely because of the reports of the advisers and diplomats located in China, the socialist bloc would come to quite different conclusions.

CHAPTER 5

The Socialist Bloc Comes to Its Senses

Responding to the Great Leap Forward

PENG ZHEN: If the main interest of your comrades is to talk, we can
talk all you want, or we can go have a look [at the communes].

A. ANTONOV: Our Soviet comrades have found out quite a bit about
the communes.

—From a discussion about the merits of the people's communes
in China, 23 August 1959

China's affirmation that the Soviet Union was the "head" of the bloc was conditional, and temporary. Numerous aspects of the Great Leap Forward era
that began in the fall of 1958—such as the people's communes, the skepticism
of expertise in favor of reliance on the "masses," and the time frame for the
transition to "communism"—amounted to a direct challenge to the Soviet
Union and its leadership of the bloc.[1] As in 1956–57, the Chinese challenge
sparked internal bloc discussion of leadership, possible "paths" to socialism,
and the merits of the Soviet Union and Soviet model. The exchange between
the Chinese and the Central Europeans was again central to these debates.
This time, however, the Central Europeans recoiled from the implications of
the Chinese criticism of the Soviet Union. China was no longer perceived
as a contributor to bloc stability or a useful balance to Soviet "great-power
chauvinism" in the bloc. The socialist bloc reaction to Mao's radical vision illustrated the series of compromises the Central Europeans were compelled to
make as a result of the bipolar Cold War. The opportunities that accompanied
these compromises were put at risk by the radical course adopted by Mao
and his supporters. Bloc advisers and diplomats watched closely to see if in
fact the compromises of 1956–57 were about to be undone. While Chairman
Mao's pronouncements and challenges were often dramatic and polemical, the
socialist bloc advisers and their Chinese counterparts continued to engage in
a reasonable debate about methods of development, Chinese traditions and

needs, and even the differences between "European" and "Asian" societies and economies. By 1959–60 the two sides were coming to profoundly different conclusions on all these matters.

The Asian Tito

Through the 1950s and beyond, the example of Yugoslavia continued to stand for a more diverse set of possible "roads" to socialism and serve as a reminder of the historic problem of inequality in intrabloc relations.[2] In part this was attractive, as we have seen, to the Poles, Chinese, and others, but it also stoked fears of betrayal in the bipolar Cold War. For the Soviets, fixated on America, potential Titos were everywhere. The Americans liked to remind the Soviets of their brief outreach to the CCP before the revolution, and Secretary of State Dean Acheson routinely referred to the history of Russian imperialism in the Far East, in one case designed to coincide with Mao's talks with Stalin in Moscow in the winter of 1950.[3] America's "wedge" strategy, however tentative and inconsequential, was designed to encourage a form of "Asian Titoism."[4] China's potentially wayward course threatened the alliance structure of the global Cold War, which also threatened the position carved out by the Central Europeans within the socialist "camp." Central European advisers and diplomats in China worried that Mao could become a "Chinese Tito," as Iudin put it.[5] Czechoslovak embassy official Anton Vasek was present for a four-hour speech on 27 February 1957 in which Mao described the virtues of Chinese "experience" in the construction of socialism and, more ominous, China's aptitude for learning from countries beyond the socialist world.[6]

The similarities between Tito and Mao and their relationship to Stalin and the Soviet Union were indeed striking, as yet another Yugoslav publicist, Vladimir Dedijer, recalled in his memoirs published in the West.[7] Both Tito and Mao led successful partisan movements and possessed strong local sources of authority; both found themselves ideologically suspect in the eyes of Stalin; both made assertive requests for Soviet military support; both found Stalin's capacity to compromise with their prerevolutionary rivals disturbing; and in power both engaged in foreign policy initiatives that did not necessarily conform to Soviet wishes and plans. Both countries struggled with the Soviet Union over the terms and nature of the joint companies and the Soviet aid projects, questioned Soviet policies concerning reparations and war "trophies" in the aftermath of World War II, and experienced the abrupt withdrawal of Soviet advisers and diverse forms of Soviet aid and support.[8] Stalin and Molotov were especially sensitive in 1947–48 to the hint of Yugoslav independence in the making of foreign policy, and to the possibility of betrayal from a frontier area of the bloc. Soviet officials told the Yugoslavs on 5 August 1947 that they had conducted "conversations behind the back of the Soviet government," referring to their discussions with the English about their territorial dispute with Austria. The Yugoslavs went on to form their own treaty arrangement with the Bulgarians, dispatch their own advisers to Albania, and even send troops there, "without consultation with the USSR," complained Molotov.[9] Svetozar Rajak argues that many of these transgressions in fact were manufactured by the Soviets after 1948, and we know from other parts of the bloc that the question of independence and innovation from smaller partners was a perpetually sensitive matter for the Soviets.[10] Soviet officials struggled with similar issues regarding Chinese initiatives toward Taiwan and the various crises in the straits that threatened to complicate Soviet-American relations. Regarding yet another frontier, Soviet official A. Antonov in frustration informed the Central Europeans in October 1959 that casualties had taken place along the Indian-Chinese border, and complained that "the Soviet Union was not informed right away."[11] The two problems even directly intersected, as Chinese independence in foreign relations toward the Central Europeans reminded the Soviets of the dangers of Yugoslav independence, "neutrality" in the Cold War, and the potential consequences of an alternative "path" of development.

The Central Europeans in China understood that they, too, were under suspicion for their own forms of innovation and closeness to the West. The matter of Central European innovation was complicated by the fact that the Yugoslavs themselves were, of course, Slavic, close to Central Europe, historically close to the West, and socialist, however suspect. The constant Soviet refrain about the role of "outsiders" in moments of rebellion in the bloc further heightened the anxiety, and security officials throughout the bloc associated most problems with some sort of potential Yugoslav threat. Czech security officials routinely assigned responsibility for any form of local dissent, industrial sabotage, or organized opposition to the Yugoslavs.[12] East German officials denounced the interest among economists at the Institute of Agricultural Economics in the "special Yugoslav path" and the "Polish experiments."[13] Hungarian officials blamed the Yugoslavs for the promotion of dissent and opposition in the summer of 1956.[14] For some bloc officials, Hungarian reformer Imre Nagy's search for refuge in the Yugoslav embassy in Budapest on 4 November 1956 confirmed their worst suspicions about the dangers of links between the Yugoslavs and the Central Europeans.[15]

For the Chinese the Yugoslavs long represented the sort of compromise with "imperialism" that they eventually associated with the bloc, and as the relationship worsened the Chinese began to insinuate, as Wang Jiaxiang did to Iudin in April 1958, that the Central Europeans seemed far too similar to the Yugoslavs.[16] "Camp" solidarity was the only means of opposing "imperialism," emphasized provincial Chinese officials in Fujian in early 1958, "a third road does not exist."[17] Central Europeans had "compromised" themselves in the struggle against Yugoslav revisionism, Liu Xiao told GDR envoy and former ambassador Johannes König in August.[18] Yugoslavia's activities and supposed neutralism only worked "against the socialist camp," fumed Chen Yi to Iudin in November.[19] The suspicions of bloc diplomats about the Chinese themselves as politically suspect thus enraged the Chinese. Both sides associated the other with Yugoslavia, but with different fears and concerns in mind. "We are not Yugoslavia," Chen Yi told Soviet ambassador Stepan Chervonenko on 4 August 1960. "We do not want you to treat us like Yugoslavia."[20] After most of the advisers were withdrawn in the summer of 1960, Hungarian ambassador Ferenc Martin noted the inconsistencies of the Chinese position to Chervonenko. The Chinese correctly perceive the dangers of "Yugoslav revisionism as a right deviation," he told Chervonenko, but incorrectly "criticize the CPSU as if from a leftist position."[21] Bloc advisers and diplomats in China were themselves in a precarious position as they watched the events that began to unfold in China in 1958.

Soviet Realism, Central European Pragmatism

The Soviets in China were alarmed by the Great Leap Forward, but initially they kept their eyes on their broader concerns for alliance stability in the larger Cold War struggle. In part this was a standard reaction to events in China from foreign policy officials shaped by the Cold War. The first thought of Soviet officials in response to news of a famine in a Chinese city, or the bloody suppression of a rebellion in Tibet, for example, was to calculate any potential gains for the "imperialist powers, and above all the USA."[22] In this sense they remained true to their strategic concerns in the Far East, historically evident in the transition from the 1945 treaty with the Guomindang to the 1950 treaty with the CCP. V. Lazarev, at the Soviet embassy in Beijing, admitted that the embassy staff tended to take "less initiative" and "rarely" queried the Chinese about domestic political developments, in contrast to Soviet concerns about foreign policy issues.[23] This sort of strategic calculation often frustrated the increasingly radical CCP, whose leaders believed the Soviet Union was inclined to sacrifice Chinese interests for the sake of some larger global agenda, from defense policy to the border conflict with India to the effort to subdue Taiwan.[24] Ironically, however, this trend initially predisposed the Soviets to at least try to look favorably on the emerging news about the changes in China after 1958.

In part the Chinese intentionally kept the Soviets in the dark. Mao himself referred to the danger of too much Chinese communication with the Soviets in late November 1958, and the Chinese embassy terminated the supply of its internal research reports (*neibu cankao*) to the Soviet embassy in late 1957. Russians were unable to obtain individual briefings from Chinese foreign affairs officials and instead had to rely on groups of socialist bloc officials for information concerning India, Tibet, Taiwan, and Cambodia.[25] Soviet culture itself also inhibited frankness and helpful communication from the lower levels of its own bureaucratic system. Soviet explanations for the deteriorating relationship in 1959–60, for example, were detached and overly analytical ("the Chinese working class is itself very young"; "the level of theoretical preparation on the part of party members is not high"), again a contrast to the raw Central European reporting of Chinese denunciations of Soviet practices in factories and enterprises.[26] And finally, certain key Soviet officials played a negative role. Ambassador Iudin, for example, with his long and meandering conversations about Marxist theory and history, certainly did not encourage the reporting of useful information from the lower levels of the foreign affairs bureaucracy.

There initially was a Soviet reticence to overreact to the alternative vision from China. At the 21st Congress in January 1959, Khrushchev referred to China's "distinctive characteristics" and suggested that the matter of the comparative advance toward communism was "of little significance."[27] Khrushchev did not explicitly criticize the people's communes until a speech before the Poles on 18 July 1959. Once the matter intersected with leadership politics, as it did at the Lüshan Plenum in July 1959, the whole tenor of the discussion changed. Marshal Peng Dehuai raised sensitive questions about famine in the countryside, Chinese defense strategy, and the viability of "self-reliance" in economic affairs, and distributed copies of Khrushchev's critical comments about the people's communes.[28] Mao then vowed to show the world the "superior nature of the communes."[29] The Soviets tried to tone down the debate, perhaps fearful of provoking Mao on what was obviously a sensitive issue. The Chinese Ministry of Foreign Affairs noted that there was very little discussion of the communes in the Soviet press through the fall of 1959.[30] Soviet scholars and advisers with extensive knowledge of China sometimes tried to maintain optimism about an enduring Sino-Soviet shared experience, and optimistically portrayed the communes as echoing earlier experiments in Soviet history.[31]

While the Soviets were inclined to ignore the big problems likely to complicate bloc "unity" in an increasingly fragile relationship, the Central Europeans were busy carefully compiling a picture of the changes under way in China. The Chinese conversation with the Central Europeans about 1956 and the general Chinese respect for Central European industrial achievements, as we have seen, led to the creation of a fairly well developed system of communication among the embassies of these countries. This seemed to be the case even though there were far fewer delegations and advisers from the Central European countries than from the Soviet Union. The former's better network of contacts produced sharper reporting within their Ministries of Foreign Affairs, which included, for example, more vivid descriptions of emotional mass criticism sessions in a metallurgical factory in Beijing, a ceramics factory in Changsha, and a heavy industrial machinery factory in Wuhan.[32] Their consulate officials in Guangzhou and Shanghai were also more active in their travels, observations, and skeptical questions.[33] The Soviets understood this and queried Central European advisers and diplomats to see if they had more information than them, especially relating to global matters. Soviet official A. Antonov, for example, pushed the Czechoslovaks, East Germans, and others for information about casualties on the Sino-Indian border in October 1959.[34] A month later, embassy secretary Zhilkin requested the help of Czechoslovak official Ján Melničak in alleviating the consequences of one of Khrushchev's unfortunate comments during a toast at a banquet marking the anniversary of 1 October 1959. By telephone he pushed Melničak for help, advice, information, and support, well aware that other bloc officials were by now in a better position to communicate with the Chinese.[35]

The Chinese and the Central Europeans had been consciously cultivating lines of communication since the early days of the relationship. As a small people on the edges of one of the two "camps" in the Cold War, the Central Europeans found it easier to communicate more openly with each other, with representatives of "neutral" countries in China, and even with rivals from the capitalist world. They even used China as a location to cultivate relations with countries such as Finland, Norway, and Yugoslavia.[36] Foreign diplomats, in turn, cultivated a relationship with the Central Europeans in order to get information about China and the socialist world. In 1955, for example, the

Finns in China queried the Czechoslovaks about rumors circulating among the Chinese about the possible American launch of twelve atomic bombs against China.[37] The East Germans in China were especially excited about how China might facilitate their broader foreign policy in the undeveloped world. "Beijing is an extraordinarily favorable place for the establishment of contacts with representatives of Asian countries," reported GDR officials in China.[38] The Czechoslovaks and East Germans routinely met with Indians, Indonesians, Pakistanis, and Burmese, eager to enhance their global status but also thinking that Southeast Asian officials were more privy to the meaning of unfolding events in China.[39]

As the Sino-Soviet relationship deteriorated, the record of diplomatic encounters illustrates the Central Europeans' propensity for keeping themselves informed through a variety of very different sources of information. On 11 September 1959, for example, Nikolai Sudarikov and the Soviet embassy hosted bloc diplomats along with ones from Indonesia, India, Ceylon (Sri Lanka), and other Southeast Asian countries. Czechoslovak representatives Ladislav Rejmán and Jaromír Štětina and their wives queried the Southeast Asians about their views on Chinese-Indian relations.[40] The Yugoslavs were there as well, and Miličevič predictably expressed their independence from the Soviet Union by responding in English to the (Russian) toast by S. Antonov for the benefit of the English-speaking Southeast Asians, "although he speaks Russian well," as Štětina noted.[41] The Yugoslavs enjoyed reminding the Soviets of bloc fragmentation, the increasingly important role of the nonaligned or less aligned countries, and their own independence and dissent. The following night other Czechoslovak officials were hosted by the Dutch at a dinner that included Norwegian and Indian officials.[42] On 14 October 1959 the Indian ambassador to China and his wife hosted a dinner for the diplomats of the bloc in China. The Chinese were not invited, and the Indians played Russian, Czech, and German classical music the entire evening, as if to remind the socialist diplomats of their respectful relationship to European culture, in contrast to the current trends in China. The Czechoslovaks were represented by Štětina and his wife, and Rejmán and his wife.[43] On 20 October 1959 Štětina and his wife attended a dinner hosted by the Burmese ambassador, again with Indian and Indonesian officials in attendance as well.[44] Soviet officials were also active in the international diplomatic community in China, but in contrast to the Central Europeans, their primary interests quickly gravitated to the global dimensions of the Cold War rather than daily life in contemporary China.[45]

The Consequences of the Great Leap
for Industrial Collaboration

Better forms of communication with the Chinese, however, did not translate into more sympathy for the changes emerging in China during the Great Leap Forward. Mao's radicalism posed a challenge to the delicate series of compromises that guaranteed the important Central European position in the bloc by the later 1950s. The Central Europeans were thus quick to pose skeptical and disturbing questions about general events and trends in Chinese society. The Czechoslovaks, for example, wondered about the forced pace of development pushed by the Chinese leadership, they were skeptical of Chinese claims about the radical remaking of the family, and they were routinely frustrated by Chinese willingness to dispense with economic planning and material incentives.[46] The East Germans similarly described the losses to industry that resulted from the extraordinary pace of the Great Leap Forward.[47] A GDR official with the International Department penned three bold exclamation points in the margin in response to a Chinese claim that increased productivity because of the Great Leap would allow China to increase its export of goods abroad.[48] Ambassador Ján Bušniak from Czechoslovakia found slogans such as "Every day of socialist construction will accomplish more than twenty years of capitalist construction" to be preposterous.[49] The Chinese were proposing the very "liquidation of the domestic functions of the state."[50] He and his colleagues ignored Chinese propaganda and instead wrote reports about the deteriorating economic situation in China.[51] In November 1959 Czechoslovak officials in China described for Prague an absurdly rapid tempo of development that produced industrial accidents, including a "catastrophe" that killed thirty people.[52] They queried diplomats from around the globe about their knowledge of conditions in the countryside.[53] The overall economy was a "catastrophe," reported Czechoslovak trade official S. Šimek in September 1960, marked by severe shortages of consumer goods and basic construction materials.[54] A January 1961 GDR report described a mass migration of starving peasants from Hebei, Shandong, and Henan provinces in response to a 40 percent decline in the harvest.[55] Recent scholarship on the extent of the famine in China from 1958 to 1961 suggests that 15 to 46 million people may have died.[56]

The Chinese glorification of manual labor for the educated and skilled classes was predictably of little interest to the Central Europeans. A September 1958 GDR embassy report criticized the Chinese program for its disruption of industrial production. Some 1 million cadres important to industry in the cities were instead engaged in pointless labor in the countryside, the East Germans reported.[57] An educational delegation from East Germany in 1960 described the pointlessness of manual labor for teachers and students, the excessive amount of political discussion in the middle schools, and the constant reading of the works of Chairman Mao.[58] "What will be achieved by it?" asked International Department officials earlier in 1958.[59]

The Czechoslovaks were similarly unimpressed. The merits of "sending down" (xiafeng) members of the "old intelligentsia" for manual labor in the countryside was lost on a labor delegation including Evžen Erban, Michal Štancel, and Adolf Kania from Prague.[60] Embassy official Jaromír Štětina similarly described the absurdity of sending to the countryside trained dancers, pianists, and musicians, whose skills required regular training in order to be maintained and developed.[61] Anton Vasek wondered about the merits of persecuting highly trained "bourgeois professors."[62] In all these areas, the Czechoslovaks suggested, quality was routinely sacrificed for the sake of an extreme egalitarianism that hardly served the interests of China or the broader bloc. Chinese officials, however, tried to reeducate their colleagues from distant Europe. China was an agricultural country, they told Štětina, and the primary focus of the party had to be the countryside rather than the city.[63] The revolution itself grew and emerged from the historically "backward" conditions of the Chinese countryside.[64] Chinese journalists publicly defended the unorthodox pace: "These are indeed communist methods," wrote Lin Fang. "This is indeed the communist style."[65]

The Chinese were abandoning the very practices and assumptions held dear by socialist bloc planners and the technical intelligentsia. The notion of expertise was conceptually suspect in general, and the experts or advisers under siege were all from the socialist countries. Their authority in the factories was routinely questioned by 1959, if not completely stymied and even abolished. Enterprises and factories entirely lacked an "organ of technical control." "In many factories the function of the main technical expert was eliminated," reported Bušniak.[66] The Chinese had replaced rational planning with an obsession with speed and rapid advance, unproductive ideological campaigns, attacks on the bourgeoisie and the educated, and a lack of attention to the "material foundation" of economic development. They had abandoned incentives, failed to respect the notion of "to each according to his labor," and refused to recognize the greater Soviet level of development.[67] Czechoslovak general consul Ján Fierlínger sat in on a lecture at a textiles factory in Shanghai about the failures of "one-man management" and its relationship to the "development of bureaucratism," poor work habits, and the "decline of initiative." The Soviet system, the Chinese informed him, put too much authority in hands of managers and experts, "without the participation of the workers."[68]

China as an Unhealthy Society

The Central Europeans also posed broader and penetrating questions about the Great Leap Forward as a consequence of potentially deeply disturbing trends in Chinese culture and society. Bušniak was alarmed by isolationist trends growing within the CCP. Ministry of Foreign Affairs officials, he suggested, needed more exposure to the outside world and even "capitalist countries," as their level of training and expertise in China was "simply insufficient."[69] While Central Europeans generally tried to encourage greater bloc trade and communication with the West, added trade official V. Koubek, the Chinese were busy accusing virtually every West European trade delegation in China of espionage.[70] Ambassador Bušniak described a bizarre meeting at the Chinese Ministry of Foreign Affairs where he listened to officials express their enthusiasm for "permanent revolution" and the ideas of Leon Trotsky.[71]

The Central Europeans were alarmed by the mass campaigns that were part of CCP political culture. Czechoslovak official Anton Vasek, for example, reported with concern to Prague on 26 September 1958 about the capacity of the CCP to inspire the "Chinese people in the spirit of patriotism and the battle against American imperialism."[72] After a three-hour meeting with Liu Shaoqi on 3 February 1959, Czechoslovak and Hungarian officials similarly wondered about the character of Chinese domestic campaigns and their relationship to foreign affairs.[73] Was the population mobilized in an unhealthy way? Ambassador Paul Wandel from the GDR was also alarmed.[74] Contemporary scholars come to similar conclusions. "The Chinese claim of U.S. imperialist aggression against the PRC served as a rhetorical device to mobilize the masses at home," notes Lorenz Lüthi.[75] Mao himself often referred to the usefulness of foreign foes to his efforts to implement transformative domestic policies. "All the same, it's for the best to have Jiang Jieshi [around]," he suggested to a group of Soviet advisers on 2 October 1958. "His existence helps us unite the entire Chinese people and educate the vast masses. Whether he wanted to or not, he accomplished more than the efforts of any single Marxist," he said to laughter from the assembled group. John Foster Dulles played a similar role, Mao claimed.[76] In November 1957, at the gathering of socialist parties in

Moscow, Mao referred to the "good service" provided by Dulles in a conversation with the visiting Czechoslovak delegation.[77] The Czechoslovaks were well-informed as a result of their direct communication with the Chinese and openly wondered about the extraordinary power of Chairman Mao and his willingness to manipulate the population to achieve his political agenda.

Mao's reluctance, at the Politburo conference in Zhengzhou in early November 1958, to recognize the disaster of the Great Leap Forward similarly alarmed the Central Europeans. Dismayed by his inspection tour of Henan and Hubei later that month, he eventually tempered his views.[78] From 21 November to 10 December the Politburo and the Central Committee met in Wuchang to discuss the situation. By that time bloc officials were well informed about tales of horror and famine caused by Chairman Mao's radical course.[79] At the same time Chen Yi informed the Czechoslovaks that Mao would step down as state chairman in order to have more time for "theoretical work in the area of Marxism-Leninism." Chen Yi emphasized the positive: Mao Zedong would "no longer be the state chairman," but his "position would be even better" and his contributions more esteemed by the Chinese people.[80] The Czechoslovaks were disturbed by the course of Chinese politics through the fall of 1958, and they knew of Mao's role and the criticism it inspired.

Instead of retreating from the radically different Chinese version of "communism," Mao appeared to be backing away from his support for the Soviet Union's "leading role" in the bloc. The Chinese bid for leadership continued to threaten the strategic compromise developed by the Central Europeans over the course of the decade. Were the Chinese even going to "catch up with and surpass" the West before the Soviets and be the first bloc country to achieve "communism"?[81] For some time the Central Europeans were busy trying to reeducate the Chinese about the mistakes of their developmental model, the need to lower their production targets for steel, grain, and cotton, and the urgency of paying more attention to the "theses" presented by Khrushchev at the 21st Party Congress in January 1959. You have "misestimated the character of the modern epoch," explained the East Germans and the Poles.[82] The broader problem was a Chinese failure to recognize that the "productive forces" of the USSR in fact exceeded those of the PRC. It was a theoretical question but one tied intimately to the rivalry over the leadership of the bloc and the global communist movement. That Party Congress, Bušniak reported, helped the Chinese understand the "question of the stage in which China is located," which was the "stage of the construction of socialism" rather than communism. The important experience of "competition with the capitalist

Advertisement for the 21st Party Congress of the CPSU in Moscow in January 1959. In *Suzhong youhao*, no. 4 (1959).

world in the economic realm" was to take place within a united bloc under the leadership of the Soviet Union. This "concrete program of development for the construction of communist society" had been clarified at the 21st Party Congress in Moscow in January 1959, noted Central and Eastern European officials. At that event delegates from the entire bloc "in detail engaged with the theses and referendum of comrade Khrushchev," as Bušniak put it, but the Chinese refused to conform.[83] They remained touchy about Soviet and bloc criticism of the communes, which they still viewed as the "current method for the construction of socialism and the future of communism in the Chinese village."[84] A minor Chinese concession was not enough. Anhui provincial party secretary Zeng Xisheng conceded to Iudin in May 1959 that all the bloc countries would "simultaneously transition to a communist society."[85] The bloc diplomats kept up their effort to reeducate the Chinese, however. Prompted by discussions with "several Soviet comrades," reported Bušniak, the Chinese were coming along.[86] The Central Europeans and Russians were in China to help the Chinese advance along the path to a modern industrial society, and the suggestion that they might follow the Chinese rather than lead was in their view ridiculous and even insulting.

Through the early 1960s officials such as Vladimír Koucký and others continued to analyze what he referred to as two "contradictory currents in the leadership of the CP of China."[87] The Maoist radicals were getting the best of the more reasonable figures within the CCP. With alarm the Czechoslovaks analyzed the destructive "nationalist tendency" within China, and the proliferating cult of Mao.[88] After attending a 1 October 1960 reception hosted by Zhou Enlai, the new Czechoslovak ambassador, Josef Šedivý, produced a lengthy analysis of the problem of the "cult of Mao," which "appeared again (in the form of the ideas of Mao, the PRC CP under the leadership and chairmanship of Mao, the teachings and works of Mao, the putting into practice of the ideas of Mao) and was put forth as the general line of the Great Leap and the people's communes."[89] The East German embassy also reported extensively in October 1960 on the Mao cult and its consequences in China, and they shared their concerns with the Bulgarians and the Soviets.[90] As the Cultural Revolution unfolded in 1966, Czechoslovak and East German officials described its early violence as a "further deterioration" of the line initially adopted during the Great Leap Forward. They warned of an impending military dictatorship, described Lin Biao and Jiang Qing as frightening characters, and viewed Zhou Enlai as the only hope for the future of China.[91] A decade later many Chinese would come to similar conclusions.

The Bomb

The Soviets were rethinking their plan to share the atomic bomb with the Chinese at this time as well. Here, too, the bloc's general orientation toward rapprochement with the West played a significant role. In Moscow, as Vladislav Zubok describes, Khrushchev and Georgii Malenkov were quite genuine in their revulsion at the prospect of nuclear war. Conflict in the modern era, emphasized Malenkov in a public speech of 12 March 1954, would "mean the end of world civilization."[92]

The Chinese, by contrast, routinely made provocative statements about imperialism and the prospect of war in the 1950s. Public statements in politics can be part of a larger strategy, of course, as Chen Yi tried to reassure Pavel Iudin on 19 November 1958. The notion of America as a "paper tiger" was also a "propaganda campaign" that usefully "mobilized the strength of the people for the construction of socialism."[93] Mao essentially engaged in hyperbole for political effect, Chen Yi suggested, another tactic in the struggle against the "imperialists." The problem for bloc officials was that Mao and numerous others returned to this theme constantly in private. Chinese historian Pu Guoliang, without referring to archives, claims that Mao pushed the issue of surviving a nuclear war with the Soviet leadership at the November 1957 Conference of Communist Parties in Moscow. Supposedly Khrushchev responded with alarm: "Paper tiger? Kalinin, Mikoyan, did you hear that? He says nuclear weapons are a paper tiger?"[94] Archival material from both Russia and China reveals that this sort of exchange was common. Even if our "enemies conquer the European part of the Soviet Union," Mao explained to Pavel Iudin on 2 May 1956, "then in that case the USSR will still have the vast and rich regions of Siberia and the Far East." A nuclear exchange was survivable for the socialist bloc. "Chinese history," he continued, "provides much support for the fact that even a significant loss of population does not necessarily mean the destruction of the nation."[95] Ambassador Liu Xiao made similar comments to V. A. Zorin in Moscow in early 1955. Mao believed, Liu Xiao conveyed, that China could withstand casualties of "100 million men or more" in a nuclear attack from America, and maintain the strength to "assert its rights until the end."[96] Zhou Enlai cast the matter as one of Chinese self-sacrifice for the greater cause of international socialism: the Chinese would "sacrifice a portion of our population as a method of securing world peace," he told the Algerian ambassador in November 1958.[97] This Chinese approach again intersected with the views of critics of the reformist Soviet leadership. While Molotov supported peaceful coexistence in the wake of the 20th Party Congress, Liu Xiao reported, he also viewed a nuclear exchange as survivable, and engaged in Chinese-style calculations about the likely demographic consequences for the two "camps."[98]

The Chinese also wanted a bomb for themselves. Liu Shaoqi surprised his hosts during his extended visit to the Soviet Union in the summer of 1949 when he insisted on visiting nuclear installations. On 31 January 1954 Khrushchev included the Chinese in his offer of socialist bloc participation in research on the peaceful uses of nuclear power at the new Soviet Joint Institute for Nuclear Studies at Dubna, outside of Moscow, to be founded in 1955.[99] Chairman Mao made the decision to pursue a Chinese atomic bomb on 15 January 1955, and visiting Chinese officials in the Soviet Union routinely took interest in this issue. Zhihua Shen argues that the nuclear development program itself was partially a product of Soviet domestic politics, with Khrushchev eager to use the program to court Mao's support in moments of political weakness (such as 1954–55, and October 1957 during the opposition of the "Anti-Party Group").[100] Chinese officials themselves seemed to see it this way. When Peng Zhen visited a nuclear reactor and missile site in December 1956 in the Soviet Union, he suggested that the recent turmoil in the bloc might actually accelerate the transfer of nuclear technology to China: "In addition, right now they [the Soviet leadership] are in a difficult situation, and they must support China."[101] From 1955 to 1958 the Soviets and Chinese signed six related accords designed to foster China's nuclear science, industry, and weapons program. They collaborated on uranium mining and production, the development of physics, the education of Chinese students in nuclear physics in the Soviet Union, the utilization of atomic energy, and the construction of a heavy-water research reactor, a cyclotron, and a particle accelerator in China.[102]

The proposed transfer of the bomb itself followed these arrangements. Chairman of the Supreme Soviet Kliment Voroshilov visited China in April 1957, and on 15 October 1957 the two sides agreed on the New Defense Technical Accord. Marshal Nie Rongzhen and his deputies Chen Geng and Song Renqiong went to Moscow to clarify the terms of the exchange.[103] The Soviets were to supply a prototype of the atomic bomb, missiles, and related defense technology to the Chinese.[104] A military delegation led by Minister of Defense Marshal Peng Dehuai stayed on in Moscow for one month after the November 1957 Conference. The two sides attempted to coordinate and standardize weapons production and communication systems, establish research institutes, and foster training and education exchanges.[105] Predictably, the Soviet military was not immune to the many inefficiencies endemic to the Soviet system and bloc exchange, complicating even so delicate a defense matter as the nuclear question. The question of payment, invariably complex and contested, was a familiar problem from the very beginning of Sino-Soviet military exchange.[106] "We'll tell you everything in our prices, and then translate it to hard currency," a Comrade Domrachev, a defense official, informed the Chinese. "We will give you the price that the Ministry of Defense itself gives. The S-75 complex costs 13,650,000 rubles, as the rocket itself costs 360,000 rubles. The R-2 [surface-to-surface missile] without the ground equipment, without any construction—533,000 rubles. We don't know the cost of the ground equipment, as this is handled by a different organization. If you are interested in this question, we can make a note of it and tell you." Qian Xuesen, physicist and director of the Academy of Missile Research, replied that the Chinese would indeed like this information.[107]

The Chinese were willing contributors to defense collaboration that frequently crossed the sensitive lines of sovereignty and independence. This contributed to their sense of betrayal by the Soviets when it turned out the bomb would not be forthcoming after all. In the spring of 1956 alone, for example, the Chinese approved Soviet plans to cross Chinese airspace to fly passenger planes to India, Soviet plans to establish radio communication between Soviet cities such as Vladivostok and Khabarovsk and Chinese cities in the Northeast such as Harbin and Hailar, and Soviet plans to fly military planes across the Northeast and build military depots capable of servicing the seventy-one-ton TU-104 airplanes.[108] The border between the "Russian" Far East and the "Chinese" Northeast seemed irrelevant to Soviet officials as they conceived of these projects. On 6 March 1956, Zhou Enlai responded positively to Nikolai Bulganin's request for the beginning of work on a shortwave radio observation station in southeast China. The Soviets sent four military airplanes to begin work in the spring of 1956, as well as some 150 to 165 specialists, who worked "in civilian clothes."[109] Mao later made a big deal of this moment as an example of Soviet imperialism in China, but at the time the Chinese were quite willing to cooperate.[110] And finally, the Chinese acquiesced to a Soviet request that they begin exporting uranium excavated in China to the Soviet Union. The original agreement of 20 January 1955 called for Chinese uranium to stay in the country to use "for the internal needs of the country," but by July 1956 the Soviets were looking for a bigger return on their investment.[111] "We are very grateful to the Soviet government" and the Soviet advisers for their work on uranium ore production, the Chinese replied. "We completely agree to stop observing the 20 January 1955 agreement."[112]

Russian defense workers began work on an intercontinental missile capable of transporting an atomic bomb in 1953, which they finished in 1956 and successfully tested in May 1957 (the R-7, or "Semyorka," the world's first ICBM).[113] Wang Yi, from the PLA General Staff, eventually put the question directly to the Russians at the 11 September 1957 joint meeting of defense officials: the "best alternative," he pointed out, would be if the Soviets simply provided a guided missile capable of delivering an atomic bomb.[114] As in other exchanges, the Chinese were eager to acquire the finished product quickly. The Russians shipped two R-2 missiles to China in January 1958.[115]

The Russians stalled on the delivery of the bomb itself, however, and the subsequent joint defense ministry exchanges became increasingly testy. Chinese officials such as Zhou Enlai attempted to intervene and accelerate the transfer of nuclear technology and the missile development program to China, but Soviet officials began to slow the process down. By March 1958 they reneged on their earlier promise to supply atomic weapons to China.[116] A month later Khrushchev bluntly informed Zhou Enlai, without any interest in discussion, of the Soviet decision to pursue disarmament and arms control agreements with the United States and England.[117] Gromyko, by contrast, relied on support from the Czechoslovaks in his frank and cordial discussions with officials from Eastern and Central Europe about arms control and new agreements between the Warsaw Pact and the North Atlantic Treaty Organization (NATO). The Czechoslovak ambassador in Moscow, Jaromír Vošahlík, helped Gromyko communicate and discuss these developments with other bloc officials in Moscow, and other Czechoslovak officials in Prague helped communicate the Soviet willingness to move in this direction to international officials stationed in Prague.[118] Central Europeans such as the Czechoslovaks clearly had a strong interest in this form of emerging reconciliation with the West.

While the Soviets stalled, however, they reminded the Chinese of the "nuclear umbrella" that protected all the peoples of the bloc and freed them from having to divert their own resources to defense. The Chinese embassy in Moscow was relieved to hear several references to the security guarantee in the fall of 1958. "Invaders of China are also invaders of the Soviet Union," Khrushchev said in a speech in early September in Moscow.[119] "Soviet-Chinese security interests cannot be separated," Politburo member Mikhail Suslov added, at a reception at the Bulgarian embassy.[120] More officially, the CPSU CC informed the Chinese on 27 September 1958: "For ourselves we can say that an attack on China is an attack on the Soviet Union."[121] Minister of Defense Rodion Malinovsky brought the matter up again at the Czechoslovak embassy on 6 October.[122] In part the repeated reminders were intended to alleviate Chinese suspicion of the emerging test ban agreement discussions that were gradually unfolding with America and England, as well as the rethinking of the decision to provide the bomb to the Chinese. The agreement with China on military-technological cooperation was formally abrogated on 20 June 1959.[123] Khrushchev was careful to emphasize these dimensions of Soviet security policy even, or especially, as he made his trip to see U.S. president Dwight Eisenhower in September 1959. He shared with the Chinese correspondence that had accumulated between him and Eisenhower preceding the trip. Those exchanges, Khrushchev wanted Mao to know, included a strong letter of 12 October that emphasized the Soviet Union's support for China and reminded the American president that Taiwan was an "internal Chinese affair."[124]

The Soviet Union, however, had changed considerably since 1950, as the trip of its general secretary to America itself illustrated. By 1959 Soviet embassy officials in Beijing were busy rethinking the implications of the Great Leap Forward and China's increasingly independent foreign policy, wondering about Mao's character, planning further overtures to America, and pondering the prospect of a nuclear-armed neighbor on their vast eastern frontier. They were highly sensitive about what from their point of view would be a betrayal of their effort to conduct the delicate relationship with the Americans. We need the "support of the entire socialist camp," A. Antonov told Chen Yi on 25 August, just days before Khrushchev's departure.[125] Soviet officials continued to emphasize the importance of the "nuclear umbrella." "War against any socialist country," G. M. Pushkin told Chen Yi on 20 August 1960, "is a war against the socialist camp."[126] The security question was related to the consumer question. "Soviet missiles in a time of need will be our missiles," explained Czechoslovak embassy official J. Melničak to Jie Zhusheng of the Chinese International Department, allowing the peoples of the bloc to develop their consumer economies.[127] "Right now a nuclear conflict is impossible," an East German student in Moscow told Chinese embassy officials in the fall of 1960, "because of the existence of the powerful Soviet Union." Instead, "peaceful competition" meant an opportunity and safety for the Central Europeans. "We need ten to fifteen years of peaceful competition, and when our standard of living is higher than the standard of living of the capitalist countries, the people [there] will want their own revolution."[128]

The Chinese, by contrast, were disturbed by Soviet policy over the bomb as well as the apparent rapprochement emerging with the American "imperialists." The Chinese thought of themselves as victims yet again of "great-power chauvinism," another example of the emerging "revisionism" characteristic of the high leadership of the Soviet Communist Party. They had willingly and enthusiastically contributed to the overall defense strategy of the bloc, and even accepted what would be understood in a traditional relationship as violations of their sovereignty, and yet they were abandoned by Khrushchev and his allies, sacrificed because of what the Chinese saw as Soviet willingness to abandon socialism itself.

The Cultural Question Revisited

As in industrial collaboration, in matters of culture the socialist bloc advisers were not impressed by the radical new trends emerging in China. The advisers were not sympathetic to the Chinese efforts to infuse their own "national tradition" and the virtues of Chinese "practice" into what they viewed as technical areas of expertise concerning, notably, music instruction. In part the radical cultural trends that surrounded the Great Leap Forward were present throughout the 1950s and represented the evolution of the continuing Chinese effort to strike a better balance in the effort to foster "mutual" cultural exchange and sources of shared cultural expression distinct from the era of European imperialism and the high culture that presumably accompanied it. Chinese music students, for example, were to combine the "harmony of the European concert system with Chinese folk melody."[129] They were still attempting to reconcile the new cultural concerns of revolutionary China to the impressive but historically colonial heritage of Europe in China. In November 1958, a visiting Smetana Quartet in Beijing performed the works of Bedřich Smetana, Leoš Janáček, Antonín Dvořák, and other figures from the European classical tradition. Visiting Czech composers Julia Kalaše and Bartoloměje Urbanec argued that the "folk" element and the influence of the general populace were indeed significant and evident in the history of classical Central European music.[130] The Chinese, however, wondered about the "reactionary influence of the West" on historic Czech culture, and the impact of the "era of colonialism in culture" for all the peoples of the world.

Associating Smetana and Dvořák with folk culture was about as far as bloc cultural advisers were willing to go, however. As the relationship deteriorated, they became even more convinced of the importance of promoting high-quality classical music and culture in China, and of further exposing the Chinese to the European high culture tradition. A piano performance was now of great political consequence for both sides. The Russians were excited in the fall of 1959 about the arrival in China of orchestras from Prague and Dresden, and a ballet group from the Bol'shoi in Moscow. The Bol'shoi toured Beijing, Shanghai, Guangzhou, Wuhan, and several smaller cities.[131] The Czechs proudly provided material to the Chinese on the history of the Czech Philharmonic, their many concerts abroad, and laudatory reviews and clippings from the Western press. Embassy official Ladislav Rejmán briefed the many visitors about the importance of their work and the delicacy of current relations with China, and embassy officials took great care to secure the participation of only the best soloists from Prague (they included Josef Suk and Jana Panenky). On 19 November 1959 the orchestra performed works of Smetana, Dvořák, Robert Schumann, and Modest Mussorgsky before some 1,400 people in Beijing, followed by Pyotr Ilyich Tchaikovsky, Dvořák, and Ludwig van Beethoven the following day before 8,000 Chinese.[132] Foreign affairs officials were generally pleased by the quality of the concerts and the impact of the events. The concerts "acquainted the Chinese public with Czechoslovak music" and illustrated the "high cultural level of the Czechoslovak People's Republic."[133] The trip was a "great event in the history of the Czech Philharmonic," reported Jaromír

Chairman Mao listens to a Soviet pianis: at the Soviet exhibit in Beijing, 1954.
(RGAE f. 635, op. 1, d. 291, l. 9)

Štětina.[134] The Dresden Philharmonic, which performed in Beijing, Shanghai, Guangzhou, and several provincial towns, one evening presented a "Czech-German Evening of Nineteenth-Century Music" dedicated to the works of Dvořák and Johannes Brahms.[135]

The music of Dvořák, Tchaikovsky, and Brahms was the bloc's response to Chinese efforts to explore the revolutionary politics of culture and pose questions about the politics of European high culture in a global context. Russians and Central Europeans were even unsympathetic to Chinese skepticism about the significance or appeal of a particular genre. Liang Hanguang, deputy director of the Shanghai Experimental Opera Theater, routinely sought out advice and support from Mikhail Chulaki of the Bol'shoi Theater after their meeting in Shanghai in 1956. The group attempted to perform Smetana's *The Bartered Bride* (*Prodaná nevěsta*) after reading in Soviet publications about the performance of this opera at the Bol'shoi in 1948. Next they tackled a Soviet opera by Nikita Vershinii that was based on "the friendship of the Soviet and Chinese peoples," a theme Liang Hanguang felt sure would inspire Chinese audiences. The group struggled with the themes as well as the genre, however, and begged for instruction and advice from Soviet musical circles.[136] Chinese cinematographers were similarly enthusiastic but frustrated by the lack of "concrete forms of cultural exchange" that might benefit the nascent Chinese film industry.[137] When it came to practical matters of translation, some Chinese wondered if their revolutionary enthusiasm for things Soviet had been misplaced. The Chinese Youth Artistic Theater struggled to present the heroine, Nastia Kovshova, from *Story about the MTS Director and the Agronomist*. They wrote to the author, Galina Nikolaeva, for advice and information about costumes, scenes, and architecture in Altai, the setting for the story. The Soviet peasant setting, the collective farms system, and the machine-tractor stations (which were abolished two years later) were unfamiliar and confusing to the Chinese theater group.[138]

The radical interrogation of socialist bloc hierarchy, privilege, and managerial practices was accompanied by the similarly radical politics that anticipated the Cultural Revolution. As Wu Lengxi suggested in retrospect, the methods and tactics of the Soviet side in the course of the relationship and dispute offered the Chinese "a look at their 'civilization.'"[139] The Chinese preferred a different vision. "Dance specialists," argued Zhou Yizhi in 1958, needed to "study the masses." "Revolutionary dance and ballet," for example, was a form of culture that emerged as a product of class struggle itself, shaped by the contributions of workers and peasants.[140] "Village knowledge [*cunke*]" was preferable to that of "scholars" or "men of learning [*xuezhe*]."[141] "Faith in the masses" and "reliance on the masses" was a challenge to the traditions of learning and expertise brought by the bloc advisers.[142] The Chinese were particularly frustrated by the orientation of the Central Europeans to Western Europe and the capitalist world. In the summer of 1958 the Chinese demanded the removal of Zbyšek Hovork, who had been the coordinator of the Czechoslovak Film Laboratory in China since 1956, because of his supposedly suspect political orientation.[143] They complained that the 1958 Czech film of Jiří Sequens, *Bratr ocean*, did not adequately portray the difference between class society in the West and the socialist world.[144] The Chinese were also frustrated by socialist bloc overtures in the film industry to the Yugoslavs, who were invited to attend a bloc-wide conference on film in Prague in 1957. Yugoslavia, the Chinese reminded the Czechs and the rest of the bloc, in their view was not a socialist country.[145]

Even from China, however, the Czechoslovaks cast their eyes well beyond the socialist bloc. The Czech Philharmonic had previously performed in Japan and was headed to Hong Kong and India.[146] The Czechoslovak Ministry of

Foreign Affairs pointedly criticized the Chinese preoccupation with the supposed divide between the capitalist and socialist worlds, and suggested measures the Chinese might take to facilitate greater cultural exchange with the world beyond the bloc. "Information about the cultural life of the leading capitalist countries in the PRC is simply insufficient," argued Ambassador Ján Bušniak.[147] The Chinese would not retreat, however. After the concert by the Czech Philharmonic in Guangzhou in November 1959, the Chinese brought the entire group to perform at a people's commune outside of the city. Zhu Wu and Xia Ren, from the Ministry of Foreign Affairs and the Friendship Society, insinuated that the orchestra had merely "commercial" aims in its trips to the "capitalist lands of East Asia."[148] The rival Indians recognized opportunity in this rift over the politics of culture. At a dinner for socialist bloc officials on 14 October 1959, the Indian ambassador to China provided classical music from Czech, German, and Russian composers to complement the occasion.[149]

There would be no compromise on the cultural question. Like the cultural managers, liaison officials, and VOKS representatives responsible for other parts of the world, the Russians who worked with China also received mountains of radical manuscripts and compositions that they relegated to the trash bin.[150] The deteriorating relationship inspired the Russians to pay even more attention to matters of quality and expertise in the exchanges devoted to documentary film, painting, dance, sculpture, music, and the fine arts generally.[151] Russian musicians, academics, and composers charged ahead with their mission. Professor S. Skrebkov gave lectures to his Chinese colleagues for almost four weeks over the year of 1960–61. His main objective was to provide for Chinese conservatories a series of lectures on musical theory and its instruction that Chinese professors could then reproduce in their conservatories. Skrebkov addressed the "style of Prokofiev," the nature and possibilities of the fugue, polyphony in contemporary music, the history of classical music, composition, and the structure of the Department of Music at the Moscow Conservatory. He listened to Chinese students perform their works and compositions and attended operas and ballets.[152] By contrast, a short time later Lu Zi, the chair of the Union of Musicians in China, was writing to S. Aksiuk of the Union of Composers in the Soviet Union about the artistic value of traditional Chinese instruments and the merits of a new work by composer Xian Xinghai called *Holy War*.[153] Soviet composer A. G. Novikov was similarly subjected to extended efforts in February 1961 from the Chinese Union of Musicians to convince him of the merits of engaging peasants directly about their views on music in order to produce a distinctly Chinese "national opera." Instead, he proceeded to recommend measures to increase the dissemination and popularity of European classical music in China.[154]

Concern for the disintegrating relationship prompted the Russians to send Dmitrii Shostakovich himself to China for a series of concerts in Beijing, Shanghai, and Wuhan in January 1960. Shostakovich felt the Soviet model offered a viable resolution to the current concerns of the Chinese. In conversations with Chinese musicians She Leming and Yang Yiliu, Shostakovich argued that the Chinese might reasonably combine a respect for classical tradition with the nativist impulse in music. In his work he considered himself "faithful to the traditions of the great Russian classical [composers], whose creativity was closely linked to popular culture." There was not necessarily a conflict between tradition and progress in the present. Indeed, creativity in the present, Shostakovich offered, was a product of the successful assimilation of the contemporary and historic works of global culture. Alexander Borodin and Nikolai Rymskii-Korsakov, he suggested, were of value to contemporary Chinese musicians. On his recent trip to America, he continued, he learned much about African American culture and American folk tradition through the work of George Gershwin and Aaron Copland.[155]

Advisers and diplomats expressed little interest in even considering the Chinese position through the early 1960s. They remained confident in their views about the purpose and importance of European high culture in China. The vice consul in Shanghai, Iu. Osadchii, fought to contain his laughter at a staging in Shanghai of a revolutionary opera dedicated to American imperialism, called *The Phoenix Rising from the Fire*.[156] More tactfully, Czechoslovak ambassador Bušniak posed questions about the artistic dilemmas of exploring political revolution in music.[157] Soviet ambassador Stepan Chervonenko, alarmed by the worsening relations and "political obstructions" in December 1961, felt safest only with the arrival in China of the "highest quality" Soviet violinists and ballerinas.[158] Officials and advisers ignored what were by now frank Chinese objections.[159] The Chinese far more forcefully expressed their old reservations about comparative budgetary responsibilities and the value of certain Soviet trips and events.[160] In December 1961 G. Grushetskii of the embassy reported that the Chinese refused to celebrate the 250th birthday of Russian scientist Mikhail Lomonosov. The Friendship Society only provided 150 tables for the viewing of a film on Lomonosov, in *"the dancing hall of the International Club"* (emphasis in original).[161] The arrangement was obviously intended as an insult to the Soviets. To Grushetskii's mind, the relationship between the brilliance of Lomonosov and the promotion of proletarian internationalism needed no explanation. Russian musicians continued a lively correspondence with their Chinese counterparts about the virtues of classical music, and Russia's continuing contributions to that tradition, through the early 1960s.[162]

Chinese cultural radicalism offered little to Central European advisers, teachers, and artists in China, who were proud to offer their expertise in their own historic high culture traditions to the cause of "socialism." The Chinese alternative forced culture workers at home to clarify further the relationship between socialism and culture. "Permanent revolution in the area of culture and ideology" was a mistaken notion, explained the East Germans; the cultural question was already resolved with the formation of the dictatorship of the proletariat. The Chinese claims about "our blind worship of the cultural traditions of the bourgeoisie" were deeply insulting.[163] In the early 1960s East German literary scholars devoted their work to the translation into German of pre-1919 Chinese works of literature, examples of the "great cultural and humanist tradition of the Chinese people."[164] The classics endured in the socialist world, immune to the radical ideas of the Chinese in 1958–60.

Conclusion

The socialist bloc rejection of China's radical path from 1958 was complete—in culture, industry, defense, and other areas. In 1956–57 the Chinese successfully presented themselves as both important to the stability of the bloc in the wake of the rebellions, and as useful critics of Soviet "great-power chauvinism." Their reminders about Stalin's contribution to the making of the bloc were useful to Central European parties at a time when the very viability of the bloc was in question. The many practices and trends that were part of Mao's Great Leap Forward crossed a line, however, and the advisers and diplomats in China were the first to sound the alarm. The Central Europeans now firmly sided with their Soviet partners, worried not just about destructive and unhealthy trends in China but also about association with a potentially dangerous Chinese challenge to Soviet leadership of the bloc. Mao was even worse than a "Chinese Tito," as his vision for the future reminded advisers and diplomats of the distance of agrarian China from their hopes for the future of the socialist world.

CHAPTER 6

China's Outreach to a World Betrayed

The Response to Soviet "Revisionism," 1958–1964

In the struggle against revisionism we can rely directly on the
Soviet people.
—Chinese ambassador Pan Zili, Moscow, 17 December 1965

Chinese views of Soviet "revisionism" were consistently expressed in several different contexts.[1] Above all the Chinese were fixated on the question of betrayal by the CPSU and the high Soviet leadership: of China, of course, but also of the other peoples of the bloc, of the cause of international socialism and "national-liberation" movements in the Third World, and even of their own Soviet citizenry. Much of the socialist world remained revolutionary and sympathetic to the Chinese position, according to this vision, but these nations were betrayed by their soft leaders and their preoccupation with Western-style consumerism. This was the weakness of the GMD as well, Mao reminded Iudin in March 1958, as he prepared the unfolding of the Great Leap Forward.[2] As unlikely as all this seemed, these notions informed a series of important moments and events in the deteriorating relationship from 1958 to 1964, including the withdrawal of the advisers in the summer of 1960, the subsequent overtures to the Central Europeans, and even the response to the ouster of Khrushchev in October 1964. The Chinese were remarkably consistent in their ideas about what they now had to offer the international communist movement and a bloc minus the "revisionist" Soviet leadership. The era of internationalism was over, and the experience of collaboration was an increasingly distant memory.

International Communism

Chinese ambition regarding its potential leadership role in the bloc, as we have seen, was emerging gradually through the 1950s. China's potential revolutionary role in Asia and in the international revolutionary movement, forcefully articulated by the early 1960s, was also emerging gradually during the years of the "Great Friendship." Mao first articulated his ideas about China's special role in the "intermediate zone" of countries emerging from the colonial experience and unaligned with the two blocs in an interview with journalist Anna Louise Strong in 1946. These ideas were reaffirmed by CCP propaganda chief Lu Dingyi in 1947 and then Liu Shaoqi in Moscow in the summer and fall of 1949.[3] The Soviet Union was still in the lead (the "commander in chief" of international communism, supported by China, "one of its military command posts"), but China was increasingly accorded a special role in Asia.[4] Soviet envoy and politburo member Anastas Mikoyan came back from his secret trip to Xibaipo in April 1949 convinced of the significance of the Chinese model for revolution in Asia generally.[5] Central Committee proclamations and press editorials similarly routinely referred to the importance of the Chinese "model."[6] Liu Shaoqi's speech at the Trade Union Conference in November 1949 evoked the "path taken by the Chinese people in defeating imperialism" as a model that should be adopted by the "people of various colonial and semicolonial countries in their fight for national independence and people's democracy." The speech appeared in *Pravda* the following January.[7]

The "Bandung discourse" in Chinese foreign policy connected China's travails to the broader anticolonial and "national liberation" movements of the Third World.[8] After Zhou Enlai visited Delhi in July 1954, his joint statement with Prime Minister Jawaharlal Nehru affirmed that these principles were to apply to "their relations with other countries in Asia as well as in other parts of the world."[9] The Chinese, and not the Soviets, were invited to take part in the nonaligned movement that emerged from the Bandung Conference of 1955 in Indonesia.[10] "Chinese revolutionary theory and experience is especially significant for the Asian fraternal parties," emphasized Wang Jiaxiang at the March 1955 Party Congress in Beijing.[11] The Chinese in 1956–58 routinely confirmed their commitment to "peaceful coexistence," one of the policies articulated at the 20th Party Congress, but their vision of the notion drew more from the Bandung experience than from the Soviet notion.[12] Or to put it another way, the Soviets were above all concerned with their notion of the "coexistence" of the two social systems and the related experience of "peaceful competition" in the meantime, while the Chinese notion more usefully spoke to the problem of imperialism, the American presence in Southeast Asia, and the prospect of American intervention.[13]

The notion was also useful to the Chinese within the bloc itself. The "five principles of peaceful coexistence" adopted at Bandung in April 1955 (noninterference, nonaggression, mutual respect for territorial integrity and sovereignty, equality and mutual benefit, peaceful coexistence) from the Chinese perspective usefully spoke to both superpowers.[14] This language was part of China's contribution to the Soviet "Declaration" on intrabloc relations that was issued on 30 October 1956, the very time as the deliberations on the situation in Hungary were taking place. The two matters were, of course, related. The document referred explicitly to the Bandung notions, and the Chinese discussions surrounding the document used the same language: "Therefore, mutual relations among the socialist countries should be based on the five principles of peaceful coexistence."[15] Other "dissident" communities within the world of intrabloc exchange used the language of Bandung in their own way as well. The principles of "equality, independence, and mutual noninterference" were to be the norm in intrabloc affairs, Polish officials in Prague informed the more obedient Czechoslovaks in May 1957.[16]

China's ambitions in Asia were not discouraged by the Soviets after 1950. Soviet foreign policy, notes Ilya Gaiduk, was predominantly oriented toward the German problem, America, and the West, and its leaders were hopeful that China might be useful in the East and the developing world.[17] On 2 May 1956 Pavel Iudin noticed Mao's continuing interest in what he called the "transitional [*promezhutochnye*]" states, which he hoped would be of great "benefit to the camp of socialism."[18] The Soviets again seemed to need the help and support of the Chinese. As Liu Xiao reported from Moscow during his participation in the 7 November 1956 celebrations, "The Soviet comrades hope China can use Premier Zhou's trip to Sri Lanka and India as an opportunity to strengthen the anti-English and anti-French position of the two countries."[19] As in other areas, if the Soviets needed the Chinese to do things they apparently could not do themselves, at what point would the Chinese find it advantageous simply to take over the business?

Both the Soviets and the Chinese could be counted on in the late 1950s to make strong public proclamations about "imperialism" and U.S. foreign policy. On 18 July 1958, for example, Chen Yi issued a series of declarations condemning the American and British dispatch of troops to Lebanon and Jordan. "Jordan's affairs should be managed by the Jordanian people themselves, and the affairs of the Arab countries should be managed by the Arab people themselves, in which no foreign intervention is allowed."[20] Among themselves, however, as the internal discussions reveal, the Chinese were far more serious about the matter than their alliance partners. They were confident of their ability to convene and lead groups of envoys from the "Asian and African countries" and other "peaceful countries," build on the accomplishments of Bandung and other events such as the Afro-Asian Solidarity Conference in Cairo in December 1957, and simultaneously maintain the full support of the "fraternal countries."[21] Mao could even be a bit menacing on the question of America, as he was during his interview with a visiting Polish military delegation in the fall of 1957. The "enemy" was formidable, conceded Mao, "and our enemy is American imperialism. Who is your enemy?" The interrogated Polish military official knew the Poles were suspect in the wake of 1956, but even his carefully phrased answer—"capitalism, imperialism, and the strongest force in the imperialist camp is America, [and] German militarism"—might have been too complicated.[22] Chinese leaders now viewed the promotion of global communism as the primary purpose of the alliance, which, of course, in the era of the Cold War meant opposing America. The Chinese rendition of the Mao-Khrushchev discussions of 31 July to 3 August 1958, in which Mao notably failed to inform Khrushchev of his impending assault on the islands in the Taiwan Strait, claimed the discussion focused on the need to "decisively support Asian, African, and Latin American countries who are all today engaged in national independence movements." This was the meaning, argued Chen Yi, of Mao's reference to the "east wind prevailing over the west wind."[23]

In 1959 Di Zhaoding informed Soviet officials that most of the delegates to the African-Asian Organization on Economic Cooperation believed that "the interests of the USSR, as an industrialized, developed country, do not coincide with the interests of the backward countries of Asia and Africa."[24] "Internationalism" could not redeem the Soviets, who remained in the Chinese view far too similar to the Europeans and their heritage. By that time Soviet officials were carefully monitoring competitive Chinese efforts to court the Indians, Burmese, Pakistanis, Afghanis, and others.[25] Soviet officials queried the Chinese about their own policies and initiatives: "Does China have any broadcasts that go out to Asia, Africa, or surrounding areas?"[26] After the split they took far greater initiatives. Zhou Enlai and Liu Shaoqi between them visited over thirty Third World nations from 1963 to 1965. China gained recognition from fifteen African nations and offered approximately $296 million in aid to Africa from 1960 to 1965.[27]

Challenging the East Germans

Besides the Soviet Union, China's other rival in guiding the Third World in the struggle against "imperialism" was East Germany. As in industrial exchange, the initial GDR-PRC relationship was cooperative and perceived by the Chinese as useful and beneficial. By the late 1950s, however, a quiet competition over foreign policy had emerged. The Chinese envoy in Berlin, Ambassador Wang Guoquan, carefully reported on increasing GDR efforts to court the United Arab Republic, Burma, Cambodia, Vietnam, India, and Iraq after the coup in 1958.[28] The GDR was especially interested in courting the "neutral countries of Asia and Africa," noted Wang Guoquan, and they were looking for Chinese "help." "Our support in this area is the main request of the German government," wrote the ambassador in January 1957.[29] The Chinese were eager to show they were the worthy beneficiaries of GDR technological support in areas such as machine construction, and here was an area where at least they could reciprocate. Increasingly confident, they wondered if they might even be more effective in this area than the GDR itself. In contrast to the other fraternal nations, including the Soviet Union and the GDR, "China . . . has well-developed ties with these countries," reported Wang Guoquan in June 1958.[30]

The GDR was alarmed by any potential Chinese threat to international stability. The East Germans' primary concern was to solidify their position as a legitimate state and heir to German tradition. The Soviets were committed to the survival of the GDR, and the superpower equilibrium was central to this outcome. The GDR addressed the problem of its porous border by building an "antifascist protective barrier" (the Berlin Wall), and now was eager to continue to implement its domestic and foreign policy visions (within the parameters of the bloc).[31] When Chen Yi suggested the two countries collaborate on the recovery of Taiwan and West Berlin in January 1961, Ambassador Paul Wandel retorted that such an effort would only lead to world war.[32] The central foreign policy concern of the GDR was bloc policy toward West Germany, and its officials wanted a "coordinated policy."[33] GDR officials were proud of their increasing contacts with the "young nation-states" recovering from colonialism, among them Cuba, Burma (Myanmar), Cambodia, Indonesia, Ceylon (Sri Lanka), Mali, Afghanistan, and Pakistan, and they did not appreciate the competition from the upstart Chinese.[34]

China's disappointment with these perceived compromises of bloc foreign policy again left it with an expanded role as leader of the international communist movement.[35] Wang Guoquan in Berlin carefully shared figures illustrating that China gave greater financial support to Cuba than did the East Germans, Hungarians, and Czechoslovaks, in spite of China's own current "difficulties."[36] America and its "invading activity [*qinlue huodong*]" was an "interventionist" power in Vietnam, the Chinese warned, and yet the bloc did little, even in response to urgent Vietnamese pleas.[37] "We have already expressed our great support for the Vietnamese, but the support of the Soviet Union and the Eastern European fraternal countries has been insignificant."[38] Instead, the test ban agreements between the United States, Great Britain, and the Soviet Union revealed the colonial instincts of great powers that included the supposedly socialist USSR, all designed to "isolate us," concluded officials in the Ministry of Foreign Affairs.[39]

A Chinese role originally condoned and even encouraged by the Soviet Union in 1949–50 now came back to haunt the bloc. Officials now accused the Chinese of inappropriately cultivating a racial solidarity with the peoples of the Third World, even though originally they encouraged this very approach. The Chinese, complained GDR officials in Beijing, claimed to have special knowledge of the needs and concerns of the peoples of the East and the formerly colonized world, and thought of themselves as the head of a "united front of 'colored' peoples [*Einheitsfront der 'farbigen' Völker*]."[40] At the 6 July 1963 CC plenum, Soviet ideologist and Politburo member Mikhail Suslov declared the Chinese notion of the "intermediate zone" to be "theoretically unsustainable" and "politically harmful."[41] The Soviets adopted the Chinese's own language to denounce them: the Chinese were guilty of "nationalism," "great-power chauvinism," and even "racism" in their general "opposition to white people."[42] Khrushchev mocked the Chinese efforts to cultivate a revolutionary solidarity with the Africans: "The Chinese leaders point out to the Africans, for example, that, look, the Russians are well-fed and dressed, but we are hungry and without shoes, therefore we are in favor of revolution, and the Russians are not."[43] All the countries of the bloc, including the Soviet Union, by the late 1960s derided Zhou Enlai's overtures to the "so-called 'third world.'"[44]

The Withdrawal, June–August 1960

China's sense of its own revolutionary purity was evident in its treatment of the advisers there, even in the circumstances surrounding the withdrawal in the summer of 1960. The Chinese imagined a socialist people betrayed by its "revisionist" leadership and hence thought they could appeal for support directly to advisers, military personnel, and diplomats in China. The Soviets saw this as yet another example of a nationalist and ungrateful CCP determined to use the alliance to weaken the Soviet Union. These tensions were evident in the formal Soviet announcement of the withdrawal of 18 July 1960. The Soviet embassy in Beijing complained generally of a Chinese effort to "impose their viewpoints upon the Soviet experts and try to lead them into opposition to the CPSU and the Soviet government."[45] Related material from the Ministries of Foreign Affairs in both the Soviet Union and China offers further detail on these contrasting viewpoints.

Soviet reports describe tension between the two sides at a party conference of military specialists in Beijing on 21–22 June 1960, just a month before the dramatic Soviet departure. General Fu Zhong, head of the PLA Propaganda Department, used the occasion to point out that the "final destruction of war requires the destruction of the source of war—the capitalist system."[46] He returned to the "east wind" theme offered by Mao at the November 1957 conference in Moscow, which was presently "overcoming the wind from the west" and providing "unprecedented confidence and courage to all the peace-loving forces in the world" in their struggle against imperialism.[47] This sort of talk should not have been surprising to Soviet officers in China. According to the Soviets, more disturbing was that Chinese officials from the PLA made explicit efforts to convince Soviet military officers and advisers of the virtues of Chinese positions on military strategy, and provoke them into discussions of sensitive topics. The Soviets were prone to exaggeration in matters of security, of course, but the charge is believable as it corresponded to Chinese actions throughout the bloc. The Chinese viewed the population and military of the socialist world as sympathetic to the Chinese position but betrayed by the "revisionist" high leadership. Soviet security officials were especially alarmed by the Chinese willingness to share high-level documents from Sino-Soviet negotiation and exchange with a wide variety of advisers.[48] "The Chinese comrades inappropriately began to acquaint the Soviet specialists with the confidential notes of the government of the USSR and the PRC, suggesting that they share their opinions on these documents," Stepan Chervonenko complained to the Vietnamese ambassador in China, Tran Du Binh.[49]

According to Chinese accounts, Soviet military officials behaved bizarrely and awkwardly, even mysteriously, that summer. A military liaison officer to the advisers, Xiao Xiangrong, reported on the behavior of a contingent of some 100 Soviet military advisers in Beijing led by a military official named Batov. According to his account, in late July the Soviets suddenly and without explanation canceled a planned trip to Qingdao, refused to attend meetings, held other meetings and banquets to which he was pointedly not invited, and behaved in a "cold" and "taciturn" fashion at a 31 July embassy reception. The Soviet military advisers even "drank very little" and never offered alcohol to the Chinese at the event. This perception of Soviet behavior again corresponded to the general Chinese notion of "revisionism." The "anti-Chinese" policy was dictated from above by the misguided Soviet leadership but not shared by the people themselves, and especially not by the officer corps. The military advisers in Xiao Xiangrong's estimation were awkwardly trying to deal with misguided orders from above. They were "internally conflicted [*xinli hen maodun*]," he argued, as they continued to have warm feelings about the Chinese and the alliance. They left, claimed Xiao Xiangrong, with a heavy heart, but ultimately loyal to their government. "I am a Communist Party member, I always take the Soviet position," one adviser told him. "Soviet people are very loyal to their government." But the withdrawal was a policy they did not entirely understand. Another adviser "emphasized decisively that the Soviet government is mistaken," and another extolled the virtues of Chinese communism: "If there were no Marx, Engels, or Marxism-Leninism in the world, they would definitely be born in China."[50]

While the Soviets were behaving strangely during these uncomfortable encounters through the summer of 1960, according to the Chinese, Chervonenko instead described a concerted Chinese effort to make explicit overtures to the Soviet military. A 4 August 1960 discussion with remaining Soviet military advisers featured a Chinese effort to "sow seeds of doubt regarding the withdrawal of specialists from the PRC" and turn them against the Soviet Union, Chervonenko told Chen Yi.[51] Both sides thus again righteously emerged as victims of misuse and betrayal. The Soviets claimed they were victims of a Chinese betrayal of their aid and "selfless internationalism" and subject to a treacherous effort to undermine even their military advisers and officers. The Chinese instead confidently believed themselves again to occupy the moral high ground in the wake of the withdrawal. As victims of a Soviet "revisionism" that did not correspond to the inclinations of the Soviet population, and as victims of Soviet "great-power chauvinism" that continued to disrespect Chinese contributions to the alliance, they confidently courted the Central and Eastern Europeans through the early 1960s.[52] That fall Zhou Enlai continued to hope that the Central European advisers would stay even after the Soviets had gone.[53]

China and the Central Europeans after the Withdrawal

The withdrawal of most of the advisers enabled the Chinese to lose all inhibition in their overtures to the rest of the bloc.[54] Top Chinese leaders made their case about the deleterious impact on the Chinese economy of the rash Soviet actions, a claim still evident in more recent Chinese scholarship. The Soviet "step greatly damaged" the economy of the PRC, Zhou Enlai told Czechoslovak ambassador Josef Šedivý in late September.[55] It was impossible, Chinese officials told the Czechoslovaks, even "to discuss our views with the Soviet Union." The Soviets would not even listen to rational appeals to at least delay the withdrawal until the completion of ongoing projects.[56] The Chinese now demanded full credit for saving the bloc in 1956, for resolving the "tense situation" in Poland that fall and causing the "reactionaries to retreat."[57] No longer needing to defer to Moscow, Wang Guoquan, the ambassador in Berlin, in December 1960 proclaimed Chairman Mao and the CCP the "head" of the bloc and insisted that China would soon illustrate its "superiority" to the capitalist countries.[58] In 1963 Chinese foreign affairs officials explained to the Czechs that the Soviets themselves created a "crisis in the entire international worker's movement" and were only saved from "catastrophe" in Poland because of Chinese intervention.[59]

A procession of top Chinese leaders appealed to the bloc countries after the withdrawal of Soviet advisers. Would the Eastern and Central Europeans stay on and limit the damage? Even the Indians wondered if now the Czechoslovaks and East Germans would "fill the vacuum" left by the abrupt Soviet withdrawal.[60] Liu Shaoqi appealed explicitly to the Hungarians along these lines in August 1960, about the same time as Chen Yi asked foreign affairs official Jaromír Štětina for help in approaching other bloc countries.[61] At a reception at the Bulgarian embassy on 14 September 1960, Chen Yi made his appeal: "The Chinese people have highly valued and [continue to] value the friendship and unity with the Bulgarian people and with the people of the entire socialist camp."[62] In August, PLA officials approached Czechoslovak military officials with an appeal to the sanctity of "internationalism."[63] Ambassador Šedivý met with Zhou Enlai the morning of 27 September 1960 and also had a "very friendly" discussion with Liu Shaoqi the same day. On 29 September Zhou Enlai and Chen Yi were careful ask the East Germans and Czechoslovaks if their advisers in China had any "problems or wishes." Zhu De made his pitch to the Czechoslovaks on 11 October 1960. According to Šedivý's report that fall, the Chinese made direct efforts to turn Czechoslovak and bloc advisers against the Soviet Union, seeking to "influence our experts in the spirit of the Chinese position."[64]

The Chinese continued their appeal to the Central Europeans in 1961 and 1962, looking for areas of "mutual" interest with parties they hoped were still "fraternal," as Chen Yi referred to the Hungarians and Czechoslovaks.[65] The

Chinese were especially unlikely to give up hope on the historically reliable and technologically advanced Czechoslovaks and East Germans. They tried to find common ground on matters such as American imperialism, or the prospect of revolution in Latin America.[66] At a 31 December 1961 reception in Guangzhou, Chinese officials suggested to Šedivý that it was a tragedy that the atom bomb belonged "only to the Soviet Union" within the camp; the bomb "in the hands of more socialist states" would more effectively weaken the imperialists.[67] PLA deputy chief of staff Luo Ruiqing again tried to appeal to the East Germans in March 1961 on the basis of their shared experience at the edges of the socialist bloc, referring to the GDR's holding down of the "west side of the socialist camp."[68] In January 1964 Deng Xiaoping returned to these tactics and ideas, reminding GDR officials of the gains to be had from China's support for East Germany's vulnerable position "in the West on the front line of the battle with imperialism." He flattered the East German officials by favorably comparing their chemical industry to that of the Soviet Union, and for good measure told them he found them far more politically reliable than the Czechoslovaks.[69] By the end of the decade bloc officials would refer to this Chinese tactic as one of "differentiation."[70]

The Chinese were frustrated by the apparent solidarity of the formal "fraternal" parties. The socialist countries "give information to each other," complained Chen Yi to Hungarian ambassador Ferenc Martin in March 1962, which in this very case turned out to be true: the Hungarian ambassador passed on the record of this exchange to the Czechoslovak Ministry of Foreign Affairs.[71] The Czechoslovaks similarly were informed of Deng's efforts to appeal to the East Germans. China's actions probably even encouraged intrabloc communication and solidarity.[72] In other cases the Central Europeans found the Chinese irritating, as when the Chinese routinely compared the quality of the orchestras from Prague, Dresden, and Moscow, as well as the work of various other cultural delegations.[73] Hungarian journalist Ferenc Fabian of *Nepszabadsag* bluntly addressed Chen Yi in a 4 March 1961 interview: "Why was it necessary to reorganize the national economy?" Fabian would not retreat from his line of questioning about the weaknesses of the communes and the Great Leap Forward, and he pushed Chen Yi to explain Indian-Chinese relations, the discussions among socialists at the November 1960 meeting, and the character of America. "Some say America has changed its unrealistic policies toward China," he wondered. Chen Yi dismissed any such speculation, however, as an "illusion."[74]

The peoples of the bloc were not about to choose China over the Soviet

Union, and the Chinese–Central European relationship quickly deteriorated. The Chinese used cultural exchange events such as exhibits and Friendship Society exchanges as a vehicle to confront their former allies. In August 1962, Zhong Xidong complained to K. Kurky about an ostensibly apolitical stamp collecting exhibit sponsored by the Czechoslovaks in China. The exhibit, he said, featured historic Guomindang stamps from the earlier era, and others illustrated and referred to "Tibet." The Czechoslovaks were now guilty of "inadequacies" in their "political character."[75] The Chinese stepped up surveillance on diplomats from the socialist bloc and removed cadres from the 1950s who had long worked with the Friendship Societies and the Ministry of Foreign Affairs.[76] Chinese officials infuriated and insulted the Czechs with their comments about China's "independent" revolution, in contrast to the "European states, where the socialist revolution only occurred thanks to the victory of the Soviet Union [in the Second World War]."[77] They told a visiting technical delegation in Tianjin in October 1963 that they preferred Klement Gottwald's "intelligent policies" regarding Stalin to those of the current Czechoslovak leadership. Stalinists in Czechoslovakia were preferable to the reformers who emerged throughout the bloc after Khrushchev's Secret Speech.[78] When the Chinese canceled exhibits they specifically addressed the consumer issue, claiming that the Czechoslovak consumer goods on display were far less appealing than those available in many other parts of the world.[79]

When Hungarian ambassador Ferenc Martin parted with several top Chinese leaders in late 1963, he faced criticism from Zhu De and Chen Yi, and from Zhou Enlai he heard the "sharpest words against the Hungarian ambassador that c[omrade] Martin has ever experienced in his time in the PRC." Other leaders simply refused to respond to his requests for an audience. Chen Yi refused to plan appropriately for the meeting, left him waiting in the hallway before a sudden announcement that he would be granted a meeting, and left early to visit a delegation from Algeria (who at this time were in an anticolonial struggle against the French). Zhu De warned Martin of Soviet and American aggression, and of the dangers of counterrevolution and revisionism. "The imperialists for many years have attempted counterrevolution in Hungary and have also stuck their nose in the problem of Yugoslav revisionism," he advised. "You have much experience in this which you must take into consideration, and above all you must consider the case of Yugoslavia. Yugoslavia lives off of American money." The Hungarians and other Central Europeans were not to be deluded about the Yugoslav path, or the "third path that does not exist." "There is no third way," Zhu De warned. Chen Yi informed Martin that the

Chinese would soon develop a nuclear bomb. "The Americans have accomplished the production of the atomic bomb," he said, "which is proof of their achievements; however we are not more stupid than the Americans, and our socialist system has far better possibilities." Zhou Enlai attributed the sudden reduction in Chinese trade with Hungary and the bloc to the difficult famine in 1961, but he was careful to add that "there was another reason for the severe situation in the PRC, which no one wants to talk about. This reason was the withdrawal of all the Soviet specialists, which meant a catastrophe for the PRC in industry, and the necessity of stopping production in a series of industrial enterprises." He proceeded to describe the many goods that the bloc and the Soviet Union had received from the Chinese over the years, and he grew angry at Martin when it became clear that the Hungarians would continue to support the bloc and the Soviet Union. The Hungarian embassy concluded that relations were pretty much over, judging from the fact that "we conceded nothing, [and] this led to an angry reaction during the visit on the part of Zhou Enlai."[80]

As in 1956, the East Germans and Czechoslovaks offered more hope. They still, of course, remained in the Chinese view important sources of heavy industrial equipment, technology, and trade generally. In Berlin the Chinese embassy counseled China's remaining foreign exchange students to steel themselves against the "invasive [spread] of bourgeois ideology" while maintaining their focus on their "specialty" and course of study.[81] In traditional fashion it remained especially important to focus on acquiring foreign knowledge without the accompanying cultural and ideological contamination. In April 1964, Zhou Enlai welcomed the new ambassadors from Czechoslovakia and East Germany, Vaclav Křistek and Günter Kohrt, with a reminder that the CCP had long been "concerned about" the construction of socialism in their countries, but he hoped there was still potential for promising relationships with both countries in the future. He also offered condolences to the wife of GDR prime minister Otto Grotewohl after the latter's death in September 1964.[82]

The Hopeful Chinese Embassy in Moscow

The Chinese were still hopeful about the Soviet citizenry itself. The open and public Chinese struggle against Soviet "revisionism" did not deter the Ministry of Foreign Affairs and its embassies in the bloc from their efforts to appeal to the countries' citizens. This effort again was a reflection of the very notion of "revisionism," which in the Chinese view was the product of mistaken policies adopted by the CPSU, the high leadership, and above all, of course, Nikita

Khrushchev. By attempting to maintain a link to the supposedly disaffected citizenry of the Soviet Union, the Chinese also illustrated their fidelity to their version of socialism, which to their mind remained available to all people in the world, and the inhabitants of the bloc in particular.

Chinese embassy officials regularly attempted to discern the views and feelings of the citizenry toward the split. Their primary sources of information came from Moscow and Leningrad, and they often relied on information from the remaining Chinese exchange students. Throughout the cities of the Soviet Union they found numerous people who confirmed their "gratitude to the Chinese Communist Party" for their efforts to disseminate the truth to the people of the Soviet Union.[83] In parks, museums, and other public places they met people who referred to Khrushchev as "cunning" and an "ambitious mover [yexinjia]." Mao, by contrast, was the "Lenin of today."[84] A machine-tool worker in Moscow complained that "Marxists" were no longer in existence in the Soviet Union; instead people were specialists of some sort or another: "scientists," "chemists," and other things.[85] "This is all the doing of Khrushchev," added another citizen. "Regrettably," added a female worker, "the Soviet Union does not have a Mao Zedong."[86] The Chinese found citizens who affirmed that the Soviets could not believe their own press and public culture. "There is no truth in Pravda," exclaimed a technician from an institute in Moscow. "If it says something is white, for sure it is black; if it says black, it is definitely white."[87] A Russian student, also from Moscow, declared, "Khrushchev has led us to oppose the Chinese people, but in fact the Soviet people do not agree. You return home and tell the Chinese people that the Soviet people will forever be together with fraternal China."[88]

Chinese embassy officials similarly discovered Soviet discontent with Khrushchev's effort to reconcile with the Americans. An elderly worker in Moscow felt the Soviet Union had lost a reliable ally in the Chinese. "If the imperialists attack, only China will help us, in contrast to the unreliable Poles and Yugoslavs."[89] Others mocked the ubiquitous slogan of "catch up with and surpass": "There's no bread to eat, but Khrushchev says the production capacity of our population will equal and surpass that of America."[90]

Some Muscovites were sympathetic to bloc criticism of Russian "great-power chauvinism." "After the death of Stalin," suggested a student in Moscow, "domestically the Soviet Union has become like imperial Russia in its great-power chauvinism."[91] Even in Moscow, the Chinese continued to bring this issue to the attention of the Central and Eastern Europeans. As we have seen, the Eastern and Central Europeans were especially perceptive in their linking of "great-power chauvinism" within the bloc to the history of interethnic relations within the Soviet Union. Polish students, claimed an embassy attaché, remained open to such reasoning about Soviet society.[92] By 1963, however, meaningful diplomatic exchange was confined to the Albanians, another source of information for the increasingly isolated Chinese. Russians always say "we" when in fact they mean "Russia," reported an Albanian official to the Chinese, and use "Russian" to refer to the overall Soviet Union. "Right now Soviet people do not say the three characters 'suweiai' [Soviet], but instead use 'eluosi' [Russian]."[93] The Albanians had their own particular concerns in the Balkans, of course. Another Albanian official in Moscow affirmed his country's support for the Chinese position in the Indo-Chinese border conflict with a simultaneous reminder that "Yugoslavia is not a socialist country."[94]

China's intersection with Soviet society under Khrushchev inevitably returned to the Stalin question. "Stalin would not put up with this business," claimed an elderly man and worker. "Please tell the Chinese people, that we workers have not been deceived." Another worker commented, "Mao Zedong and Stalin are real men, while Khrushchev is some sort of charlatan [wanyi]."[95] At the Lenin International Naval Institute in Moscow, perhaps predictably, they found strong support for Stalin and his legacy among especially the officer corps. One officer pulled out a photograph of Stalin to show the Chinese visitor: "'Do you recognize him?' I answer, 'Of course I recognize him.' He says: 'Right now quite a few of the troops carry a picture of Stalin. We miss him very much, [and] we also miss comrade Mao Zedong very much.'"[96] Other naval officers criticized Khrushchev, and foresaw changes after his death.

Yet alternative views also emerged from this Chinese version of opinion polling that embassy officials felt obliged to report. Some of this sentiment was fairly astute politically, even reflecting knowledge of the interconnected history of the two communist parties. In part the sophistication was a product of CPSU instruction at educational institutions that took place on the sensitive topic of Sino-Soviet relations. Chinese students would attend party-sponsored lectures at universities precisely in order to learn about Soviet policy, sentiment on international affairs, and the Sino-Soviet relationship. Leaders such as Gao Gang and Peng Dehuai, they learned, found themselves in trouble only because they cooperated too eagerly with the Soviet Union. Such figures were declared by the CCP to represent an "anti-Party element [fandang fenzi]," accused of setting up "their own separate party." In international affairs, reported the Chinese students, their Soviet counterparts accused them of mere posturing before the imperialists: "Who supported them in 1958–59 when America was active in the [Taiwan] Strait?" Similarly, according to the Soviets the Chinese formerly talked constantly about overtaking Great Britain in fifteen years but now had quietly abandoned this effort because of their own economic collapse.[97] It was the Chinese rather than the Soviets who were prone to incessant border conflicts. What about Korea, Vietnam, and India, in addition to, of course, the Soviet Union? Other Soviet voices, mediated through the reports of the Chinese foreign language students and the Chinese embassy, perceptively addressed the issue of Mao's ambition regarding the international socialist movement. The real meaning of Mao's reference to the "east wind" prevailing over the "west wind" was that "China wants to prevail over the Soviet Union."[98] Another similarly skeptical but discerning voice described Mao as "divorced from the people" and determined to create "two socialist camps."[99]

Perhaps more reflective of popular sentiment were the many examples of frustration with what many Soviets felt was a Chinese betrayal of good Soviet intentions. "We helped the Chinese have a revolution, [we helped them] build their country, and gave them arms and food, and [now] we've done something wrong!"[100] Others described Mao as a traditional Chinese "emperor," or referred to China as a "Stalinist" country.[101] The theoretical level of the Chinese party was "very low," emphasized Soviet students in Moscow. Mao himself was not educated, and the people were prone to the "cult of personality" (or "blind superstition [geren de mixin]" about his infallibility). China rather than the Soviet Union was guilty of excessive nationalism, Soviet students said. "Asians who visit China say China has great-power chauvinism." And further, Chinese defense strategy was likely to provoke a nuclear conflict.[102]

For embassy officials, however, these alternative views could be explained as a product of the relentless propaganda and controlled press endured by the average Soviet citizen. They shared such information with Beijing to help the Ministry of Foreign Affairs understand the true depth of propaganda and misunderstanding common to the Soviet experience, and the betrayal of the people by their "revisionist" and treacherous leadership. People shared such ignorance with embassy officials and Chinese exchange students. "Is China against the cult of personality or not?" "Why does Khrushchev want to send specialists to China if China does not want them?" Or some people were even mean and cruel, hostile to the remaining Chinese foreign exchange students. A Soviet student returned to the sensitive matter of interethnic romance: "After you graduate you won't return to your country, because it's pretty good to stay in the Soviet Union with the Russian Natuosha [Natasha] (a girl's name), eh?"[103]

The Chinese were consistent in their views about the contrast between the population and the leadership in the Soviet Union. Delegations to the PRC, according to this reasoning, by this time were no longer representative of the population in the slightest. Mao himself occasionally took the time to insult the increasingly rare Soviet visitors to China. Just days before Khrushchev's ouster, Mao delighted in interrogating a Soviet delegation chosen to attend the fifteenth anniversary of the revolution on 1 October. To Mao's mind, the meager standing of the delegation (Friendship Society officials, education administrators, a member of the Kirgiz Supreme Soviet, etc.) was itself worthy of comment. "Comrade Grishin," Mao asked, "have we met before? Maybe I saw you in 1957." "We haven't met because I wasn't there," responded V. V. Grishin. "So this is the first time that we have seen each other," Mao pointed out. "I want to unite together to overthrow imperialism." Mao proceeded to toy with the chairman of the delegation, Kirgiz official Turabai Kulatov: "So, you are Chairman, I also am Chairman, the two of us are both Chairman!"[104]

The Ouster of Khrushchev, October 1964

Given these perceptions of the Soviet populace and significant portions of the CPSU itself, the Chinese saw the sudden coup against Khrushchev in October 1964 as potentially an extraordinary opportunity. Embassy officials in Moscow carefully surveyed the Soviet press, the bookstores, and Vietnamese exchange students (there were increasingly fewer Chinese) for any information they might glean about potential changes in the Soviet position.[105] There were a few promising but cryptic signs. *Pravda*, for example, made a reference to "internationalism" and the need to "strengthen equality" in the bloc, which could signal a return to the Molotov-style emphasis on bloc "unity."[106] The embassy passed on a report to Beijing that included hopeful comments from students at the naval academy in Moscow, mediated via a Chinese exchange student. Chinese exchange students also heard, from a child of a Central Committee member, that Khrushchev was criticized by that body for his general running of foreign affairs, and in particular for his use of his son-in-law, Aleksei Adzhubei, as an envoy.[107]

The Chinese were thus confirmed in their view that the general population was ready for a change of course in Sino-Soviet relations. "Now a new person will take office," suggested a Muscovite, "and from now on Chinese-Soviet friendship will be restored."[108] Chinese students in Leningrad reported hearing that the withdrawal of the specialists in 1960 amounted to the illegal breaking of the terms of the 1950 treaty.[109] Foreign affairs officials continued to misread Soviet socialism, or the evolution of a society that was less and less of a dictatorship. To the Chinese ambassador, the absence of an outpouring of grief over Khrushchev's exit was a sign of the leader's unpopularity. People cried in the streets when Stalin died in March 1953, he noted, as if this were a sign of a healthy public life and society. The ambassador offered what amounted to an alternative history of Soviet socialism undergoing reform, instead describing a healthy party in 1953 subsequently under "attack" at the 20th Party Congress, subject to "unjust" expulsions in June 1957 (the Antiparty Group), and even desecration in 1961 (the removal of Stalin's body from the mausoleum). Soviets in 1964, claimed the ambassador, did not trust Suslov or Mikoyan, the wavering and "sly old devil," and instead preferred the leaders of a decade past, such as Malenkov, Dmitri Shepilov, and above all, Molotov. Chinese officials claimed a prominent Soviet scholar recommended to the CPSU Central Committee that the Soviet Union send a delegation to China to repair the relationship.[110]

Russian memoir accounts describe "certain circles of [Soviet] society" in ideological work, foreign affairs, security, communications, TASS and academia as prepared to rethink the finality of the Sino-Soviet split, sentiments also confirmed by the recent research of Sergey Radchenko.[111] Soon after the ouster of Khrushchev, Andrei Aleksandrov-Agentov accompanied Leonid Brezhnev, Aleksei N. Kosygin, Iuri Andropov, K. V. Rusakov, and other top officials by train to the Soviet border with Poland to meet with Communist Party first secretary Władysław Gomułka. The state of the socialist bloc was the topic of discussion. "Everyone agreed that the removal of Khrushchev could be used to normalize to a certain extent the relationship with Beijing," Aleksandrov-Agentov recalls.[112] Kosygin was particularly hopeful. "We are communists," he emphasized, "and they are communists, and it's not possible that we can't look each other in the eyes and come to an agreement!" Andropov recommended caution, however, in the face of a complicated relationship and the "cunning" and "crafty" Chairman Mao.

Mao was tentatively hopeful and sent a delegation that included Zhou Enlai, Marshal He Long, and Kang Sheng to Moscow to explore the possibilities.[113] Zhou Enlai had been making his pitch to both the Soviets and the Eastern and Central Europeans throughout the month. The removal of Khrushchev, he enthusiastically told officials from Poland, Bulgaria, Mongolia, Hungary, and Czechoslovakia, was a "significant change" that was sure to have a "positive influence on China's relations with the Soviet Union and with the fraternal countries." The Chinese fore_gn minister and premier congratulated the new Soviet leadership. "The 16th of October I sent a congratulatory telegram thanking the new Soviet leadership and expressed our hopes" about a visit and the improvement of relations, he informed the group. Again attempting to play off the Europeans against each other, he told Czechoslovak ambassador Vaclav Křistek that Gomułka and the Poles were very interested in this effort to forge anew the spirit of "proletarian internationalism."[114] China again was the promoter of bloc "unity," promising the integration of even the perpetually wavering Poles. The Chinese embassy in Moscow counseled its staff and related personnel to continue its critique of revisionism but refrain from directly criticizing the new Soviet leadership.[115]

The Russian memoir accounts, like their Chinese counterparts, are likely prone to exaggeration and an inadequate sense of the broader Sino-Soviet relationship. The official Soviet line was not about to change. There was certainly no hint of this in the Central Committee discussions before 1964, and even the 14 October 1964 communication announcing Khrushchev's ouster illustrated the enduring depth of suspicion toward the Chinese.[116] The Soviet invitation to Zhou Enlai to attend the anniversary of the revolution in Moscow on 7 November 1964 was thus designed without a substantial Soviet concession in mind. The Chinese embassy in Moscow was exposed to evidence about enduring bloc hostility to the CCP. "China has a personality cult of Mao Zedong," a party instructor proclaimed at the Moscow Air Force Academy, "and those who oppose it like Peng Dehuai end up doing hard labor. . . . Soviet relations to China cannot change."[117] Chinese embassy officials also hopefully surveyed the Eastern and Central European diplomats in Moscow for any signs of change in their attitudes toward China, but they were disappointed.[118] They could still maintain a fanciful optimism about the inclinations of the populace, but the bloc parties were not about to budge. To Czechoslovak officials, the notion that the Poles might differ in their position from the bloc on such a fundamental matter was absurd. Ministry of Foreign Affairs officials highlighted these claims in amazement as they read these telegraphs from Beijing.[119] Walter Ulbricht emphasized his commitment to the Soviet Union, whose recognition of the GDR was the "foundation of Soviet German policy."[120] The Soviet population, however, supposedly saw things differently. Through November Chinese embassy officials reported hearing from Soviet citizens who remained hopeful about the results of Zhou Enlai's visit, and the "resolution" of the Sino-Soviet split.[121]

Zhou Enlai went to Moscow, but the Chinese also were well past the point of compromise. They would not tolerate the continuation of the relationship in anything close to its original form, and traces of any sort of diplomatic or any other sort of exchange disappears from the archives of all the countries of the bloc. The era of "internationalism" was over. The "bizarre incident" of 7 November, as Radchenko puts it, between Zhou Enlai and Soviet defense minister Rodion Malinovskii was perhaps a fitting conclusion to these efforts to renew the relationship. Malinovskii clumsily insulted the Chinese delegation and apparently advocated the overthrow of Chairman Mao.[122] The episode has been described in both Russian and Chinese memoir accounts, in some cases written by former officials who might have had privileged access to Chinese archival materials. While possibly an exaggeration, the account is consistent with other depictions of Malinovskii and Sino-Soviet exchange by 1963–64. Malinovskii routinely attempted to emphasize the enduring common ground between the bloc and the Chinese in a way that suggested the polemics were a temporary product of leadership conflict.[123] This could have been interpreted by the Chinese as threatening, as the idea that the Soviets were contemplating some sort of leadership intervention was increasingly the norm in Chinese circles. In January 1963 the embassy reported: "There are Soviets who fiercely say: China should replace its leadership, and only then will Sino-Soviet relations return to their former positive state."[124]

In February 1965 Kosygin and Andropov stopped briefly at the airport in Beijing on a trip to Vietnam, and that April Kosygin replaced Stepan Chervonenko with Sergei Lapin as the chief Soviet envoy, possibly in an effort to cultivate a better relationship.[125] Lapin tried to initiate conversations with top Chinese leaders in Beijing. On 11 May 1965, he met with Liu Xiao, the former ambassador to the Soviet Union during the earlier period of collaboration and now deputy premier, but both sides recognized that compromise was unlikely. Lapin referred to their common goals (the construction of a "new society"), but Liu Xiao quickly interjected: "And the most important problem is the question of our relationship to the system of imperialism." Lapin could not see any common ground. "In this area, we do not have any similar views."[126] The February–March 1965 Chinese attacks on the U.S. embassy in Moscow communicated a similar idea, if in a rather different format.[127]

The Cultural Revolution that would soon engulf all of China allowed little space for cultivating a relationship with anyone in the bloc. "Revisionism" at home was the principal target of Mao and his allies, who had long given up on foreign socialists. Chairman Mao returned often to the question of the training of a future generation of "millions of successors who will carry on the cause of proletarian revolution," and he possessed important allies in this struggle by 1966.[128] "After many decades Stalin had still not resolved this [ideological class] struggle," claimed Lin Biao at the Central Work Conference of 25 October 1966. "The Soviet Union has existed for fifty years, but it is now ruled by revisionists. Unless we constantly and persistently grasp the Cultural Revolution, that will also be the outcome here."[129] The few remaining cultural exchange events with the countries of the bloc were canceled in the summer of 1966.[130] By the winter of 1967 the Central Europeans in China were caught up in the increasingly violent days of the early Cultural Revolution, which included attacks on the Soviet embassy in Beijing. Diplomats from the other socialist countries brought food and provisions to the besieged Soviet diplomats.[131] Czechoslovaks Josef Přibyl and Bořivoj Čuda, for example, were detained by crowds on 26 January 1967, and the Chinese government informed the Czechoslovak embassy that it could not "in the current situation ensure the safety of Czechoslovak [diplomatic] workers."[132] The Chinese had lost hope in the possibility of salvaging their relationship with the Czechoslovaks, who now proved to be guilty of "anti-Chinese acts" and "following in the tracks of the Soviet revisionists."[133] The Czechoslovakian "revisionist clique" had "devotedly served the Soviet revisionists and helped imperialism."[134] The evacuated families of Soviet diplomatic personnel took their children to Prague to finish the school year in Russian international schools there.[135] Their future, and the general future of the bloc, lay to the West rather than the East.

Conclusion

The Chinese were persistent and consistent in their beliefs about the "revisionism" of the bloc that betrayed China and left it as the principal bastion of support for the international communist movement. Intent on subverting completely the Sino-Soviet relationship and the premises of the original alliance, the Chinese were determined to lead the Central and Eastern Europeans and even the Soviet people against the Soviet leadership. The Chinese believed they had been betrayed and misused by a Soviet leadership hopeful but deluded about the benefits of reconciliation with the Americans. Globally, the increasingly assertive Chinese challenge to not just the Soviets but also the East Germans was evident well before the split. Within the bloc, the Chinese appeal to the Central and Eastern Europeans was an effort to continue the conversation and forms of exchange that were well developed from especially the crisis year of 1956. They were on shakier ground in their effort to make a direct appeal to the citizens of the Soviet Union. The Chinese were consistent and serious, however, in their efforts to court military officers in China in the summer of 1960, use their embassy in the Soviet Union as a means to appeal to sympathetic citizens in the wake of the split, and benefit in their hopes for a new Sino-Soviet relationship after the ouster of Khrushchev.

These hopes were in part wishful delusions and in part a product of continuing Chinese confusion and misunderstanding about the evolution of the Soviet political system and culture. "Dissent" in the Soviet Union was not monolithic and was not by definition sympathetic to the West or the United States. The Chinese were intersecting with a cynical Soviet population weary of political campaigns and its own leadership. That there might be "capitalist elements" within the CPSU leadership, for example, as the Chinese charged, was something everyday Soviet citizens might relate to as an example of the utter bankruptcy of Soviet socialism.[136] Other Soviets were alarmed by the changes and instability of the post-Stalin era and hoped for a return to "order." Other "dissenters" enjoyed using the slogans of the propaganda state and the pedagogical leadership against the leadership itself. They were amused by the idea that the Chinese might actually "catch up with and surpass" the outside world at a faster pace than the Soviets, and enjoyed pointing this out. "CHINA HAS SURPASSED THE U.S.A. IN WHEAT OUTPUT," screamed a frustrated resident of Kyiv in 1959. He mocked Khrushchev's effort to compete with America, suggested the country had abandoned socialism, and described China as a land ruled by "genuine Soviet power."[137] This mixed picture, however, offered no reason to believe that Soviet citizens were prepared to consider seriously the CCP as some sort of alternative to their own party. The Chinese were similarly misinformed about the Central Europeans, whose careful strategic compromise with the Soviet Union and cultivation of a special role for themselves within the bloc could not possibly be served by an alliance with the Chinese against the Soviet Union. Chairman Mao and his supporters were still overestimating the importance of their supposed role as the much appreciated saviors of the bloc in 1956.

CHAPTER 7

Friends, Neighbors, Enemies

The Chinese Transformation of the Friendship Society

Friends are divided into genuine and false ones. Genuine friends are
sympathetic to us, support and assist us, and demonstrate sincere
and honest friendship. False friends are friendly on the surface.
They tell you one thing but do another, or even devise some evil
designs; they fool the people and afterward take joy in the people's
disasters. We should be alert on this point.
—Chairman Mao to Anastas Mikoyan, February 1949

China's transformation of the alliance was complete by 1964. This last chapter describes an institution common throughout the bloc, the Friendship Society, to explore China's fascinating ability to transform and remake foreign institutions to serve Chinese needs and concerns. The many branches of the Friendship Society, part of VOKS, were generally designed to encourage goodwill toward the Soviet Union, educate the population about the virtues of Soviet experience, and promote the study of the Russian language and Soviet culture. They sponsored photo exhibits, language instruction, and lectures and seminars on history and culture and generally facilitated cultural exchange. By the early 1960s the Chinese were using them, by contrast, to sponsor the dissemination of "correct" information about Chinese positions in the Sino-Soviet split.

The evolution of VOKS in the Soviet Union was again indicative of the important changes taking place in Soviet society and the foreign policy establishment through the 1950s. Friendship Societies, like the notion of "friendship" itself, were generally reserved for collaborative relationships with socialist societies. As the interests of Soviet foreign policy moved beyond the bloc, diplomatic officials struggled to adapt their own practices and notions, even their language, to emerging exchange with the "enemy." What was the purpose of a Friendship Society in a rival or even hostile land? After the death of

Stalin numerous Soviet organizations (among them the press agency TASS, the Foreign Language Literature Publishing House, the Ministry of Culture, the Union of Writers, the Ministry of Foreign Affairs, the Soviet embassy in the United States, the International Department of the Central Committee, trade representatives, exhibit organizers, and so on) developed outreach programs for the cultivation of more or less "friendly" people in America. The Soviets targeted presumably sympathetic people in an otherwise hostile land. In practice these initiatives often led to relatively pointless discussions with obscure American leftists, an inefficiency that in the era of reform more trained and savvy Soviet officials recognized and addressed.[1] These efforts drew on the Stalin-era strategy of inspiring prominent Western intellectuals to contribute to a positive narrative about the achievements of the Soviet Union.

A more coordinated and realistic attempt to communicate globally, from America to Africa, emerged in tandem with the reorganization of VOKS in the late 1950s. The SSOD (Soiuz sovetskikh obshchestv druzhby [Union of Soviet Friendship Societies]) was created specifically to facilitate new forms of global cultural exchange.[2] This evolution was significant: instead of attempting to court such groups as disaffected leftists, alienated intellectuals, and African Americans in U.S. society, the practices of the SSOD reflected an effort to conduct "normal" international relations with the broader society. This transformation and outreach to the Americans deeply disturbed the Chinese, as did Khrushchev's dramatic trip to America in September 1959. Interestingly, the VOKS and SSOD discussions with the Americans were actually more cordial and warm, especially in the months preceding Khrushchev's trip, than were those with the Chinese at that time. The nature and purpose of the exchange with the capitalist enemy were more easily defined and understood by Soviet officials than the confusing relationship with the Chinese. Soviet Friendship Society officials struggled to find the terminology appropriate to the evolving Sino-Soviet relationship, and even to clarify the purpose of the exchange and activity. Were the Soviets and Chinese once "friends" but now respectful but distant neighbors? Was this a "normal" state-to-state relationship within the international system but outside of the socialist world? Or were Friendship Society officials and participants actually in hostile territory? By 1963–64, as we shall see, both sides had come to the latter conclusion.

The Friendship Societies in China

The Friendship Societies played an early and important role in the expansion of the Soviet Union into eastern locales such as Korea, Mongolia, and China. VOKS initially supported the Chinese-Soviet Cultural Society, which sponsored exhibits and cultural events in both countries, served as a patron and source of influence among the Chinese intelligentsia, and attempted to counter the appeal of the West among the Chinese.[3] The Chinese-Soviet Cultural Society routinely sent books and other materials to diverse Chinese groups and institutions, such as the Guanxi Library in Guilin, Zhongshan University in Guangzhou, and the Ministry of Agriculture. The society's January 1944 exhibit in Changchun, previously the seat of Japanese-occupied Manchuria, was attended by 15,000 people. The society gave musical scores to Chinese composers, conductors, and musicians; literature to Chinese writers; and financial support to the Chinese Theater Society.[4] It created a radio station that featured daily programs in Chinese on Soviet music, theater, literature, and the arts.[5]

The Friendship Societies grew out of these exchanges. They served as a model for the overall cultural exchange that continued throughout the whole period of the "great friendship," with the Northeast again serving as a "laboratory for the setting up of the socialist state," as Odd Arne Westad explains.[6] While the earliest local Friendship Societies dated to the 1930s in Nanjing and Shanghai, generally it was the Northeast that provided an early trial run for the alliance. In 1945, the Society for Chinese-Soviet Friendship (Obshchestvo kitaisko-sovetskoi druzhby, OKSD) was established in Lüshun (Port Arthur) on 3 September and in Dalian on 27 September.[7] On 24 October, Chinese in Harbin met at a local film theater to discuss the opening of a branch there. With a significant Russian population since 1898, Harbin was a logical location for the activities of VOKS. Harbin's history of shared Russian and Chinese life, suggested *Russkoe slovo*, made it a "symbol of friendship between the Chinese and Soviet peoples."[8] The founding committee worked to offer material support to "various circles" sympathetic to the Soviet Union in Harbin; increase membership enough to create a local branch; and sponsor publications, musical events, and a theater. The Harbin branch first met on 5 November and quickly grew to 3,000 members. Smaller branches were established in smaller cities in the Northeast, such as Peiyang, Hulan, Zhaodong, Shuangcheng, and Tunan. There were forty-five Friendship Societies by 1946.

The characterization of Harbin as a "symbol of friendship" between the Russians and the Chinese was somewhat optimistic. Historiography and memoir-

"Transform Railway Transportation; Work to Serve the Industrialization of the Nation."
Agitation and propaganda car on the Chinese Changchun Railway, 1953. (RGAE f. 1184,
op. 31b, d. 136, l. 360b.)

writing on the history of Harbin is sharply contested among Russians and
Chinese. Russian accounts of the history of Harbin, charges Chinese historian
Shu Li, incorrectly describe the area as "utter wilderness before the building of
the Chinese [Changchun] Eastern Railway."[9] In 1898 the Russians acquired not
only the railway concession but also the two ports on the Liaodong Peninsula,
and in 1900 they occupied Manchuria.[10] The Russian population of Harbin
grew rapidly, but the Chinese remained largely segregated in Fujiadian and unable to settle in the Russian sections of the city. Educated society and privilege
was reproduced in the manner of imperial Russia, tied to the officials of the
Chinese Changchun Railway. In 1925, A. N. Ivanov established the Russian-
Chinese Railroad Library to accompany a movie theater, a ballet school, and
other cultural institutions, largely for the growing Russian population.[11] The
frontier town featured prostitution and poverty, only a single Russian-Chinese
marriage before 1917, and "very few truly Russianized Chinese."[12]

The defeat of the Japanese by August 1945 brought the Soviets back to Manchuria, which evolved into an opportunity for the expansion of the CCP in
the Northeast. Harbin and the region became a base and testing ground for

CCP programs in the ongoing civil war. Li Zhaolin, a former commander of the Third United Anti-Japanese Army in Manchuria, became the first chair of the Harbin Friendship Society but was assassinated by Guomindang agents on 9 March 1946. The society's city committee and the CCP were forced to abandon Harbin, but CCP forces retook the city the following year and the Friendship Society began commemorating the anniversary of Li Zhaolin's death.[13] By early 1947 the Harbin branch had developed extensive connections and cooperative relationships with branches in Dalian, Lüshun, Fushun, and Mudanjiang. The Harbin branch featured photo exhibits, libraries, reading rooms, a store selling periodicals, choirs, an orchestra, and evening language programs in both Russian and Chinese.[14] Photo exhibits about the Soviet Union in 1947 were attended by more than 25,000 people.[15] By June 1949 there were 202,244 OKSD members in the Lüshun-Dalian region, some 25 percent of the population.[16]

The early branches in the Northeast understood their purpose to be the dissemination of accurate information about the Soviet Union. The photo exhibits sought to acquaint the Chinese "with achievements in various regions of the life of the peoples of the USSR."[17] The impact and influence of America and Europe again loomed in the background of this effort, as Friendship Society activists were keenly aware that many Chinese held positive views of the wealth and power of the West and negative impressions of Soviet communism. As Qian Junrui, the general secretary of the OKSD's central administration, put it, many Chinese were influenced by "anti-Soviet ideology and mistaken conceptions of the Soviet Union."[18] Thus the society branches emphasized Soviet achievements and Soviet aid and support to the Chinese. On 6 February 1947, the Harbin branch sponsored a protest in a public park against the trade agreement signed between Jiang Jieshi and the United States.[19] Branch members were active in 1947 in the celebration of the twenty-ninth anniversary of the Soviet Army and the thirtieth anniversary of the October Revolution and, in 1948, in commemorations of the third anniversary of the liberation of Northern Manchuria from the Japanese. The Shenyang branch sponsored lecture and discussion sessions with such titles as "How Great Is the Soviet Union?" "What Kind of Help Is the Soviet Union Providing to China?" and "Why Does the Soviet Union Help the Chinese People?" Worker Hu Shouzhun said at one of the lectures: "In the past I believed reactionary Guomindang propaganda. My mood was hostile to the Soviet Union. I was suspicious of my friend. This was my mistake. Now I understand that the Soviet Union is our best friend."[20]

The political dimension of the Friendship Society was explicit and remained crucial from its inception to the Sino-Soviet split. VOKS officials were often suspicious of even their bloc allies. In April 1949, a certain Savinich was charged with attempting to determine the orientation and inclinations of each member of the large Chinese delegation (led by Guo Moruo) of artists, educators, and cultural figures.[21] Ding Ling was "one of the more sincerely oriented to the Soviet Union," reported the Soviet handlers, while Gong Pusheng, "it seems, has been significantly influenced by England and America. She speaks English well. She behaved in a very restrained fashion."[22] Officials encouraged the use of only Russian and Chinese during future exchanges; indeed, one of the purposes of the society was to promote the study of Russian. Visitors to the Soviet Union, from whatever country, were to return with a positive impression of Soviet life, standards of living, and the consumer economy. A VOKS official with an April 1949 Chinese group was dismayed when several members of the delegation went on a shopping trip and were unable to find a cigarette lighter, detergent to remove a clothing stain, or a sleeping cap.[23]

The early Friendship Society exchanges also illustrated the series of tensions that characterized Sino-Soviet relations generally. The Chinese at the society branch in Harbin, for example, requested that the Soviets reduce their rental fees for films by 10 percent and arrange for a more efficient and timely distribution of the films. Frustrated by the slowness of VOKS, they tried unsuccessfully to negotiate directly with Soviet Eksportfilm. They raised questions about the Soviet desire for financial profit in the rental of films. Soviet officials countered that the films belonged to them and defended their rights of sale, profit, and distribution.[24] There were numerous practical cultural problems in addition to the economic issues. Officials were critical of the slow pace of language learning in Dalian in the fall of 1950, and noted that "the Russian teachers and the Chinese teachers very rarely socialize together." Chinese Friendship Society members in the Northeast also raised questions about the privileges and advantages that accrued to the Russians in the Northeast, an early Chinese introduction to the hierarchies of the Soviet Communist Party and its administrative system.[25] Visitors to the Soviet Union in the early exchanges were also often disappointed by the secrecy and paranoia of Russian life that inhibited their ability to learn about the Soviet Union. E Weiming, who wanted to learn about Soviet trade unions, pay levels, the length of the working day, and vacation opportunities, exclaimed, "I would like to visit the home of a typical worker."[26] He was asking for more than the Soviet Union was prepared to deliver.

Contesting the Gift

The archaic language of debt, responsibility, and the notion of the gift infused and shaped the world of Friendship Society exchanges. Li Junfu, the chair of the Harbin branch, gave a speech at the 1948 anniversary of the defeat of the Japanese in Manchuria in which he noted that "the Chinese people are in debt to the Soviet Army for the liberation of North Manchuria from the Japanese yoke."[27] Li reproduced a standard trope of Soviet political language as identified by Jeffrey Brooks, that is, the notion of the obligated populace in debt to the benevolent leader and his actions.[28] Stalin, of course, stood at the center of this political world. Stalin, Li Junfu proclaimed, "brought independence, democracy, and freedom to the population. This historic event can never be forgotten by the Chinese people, and today we welcome the Soviet Army and its leader Generalissimo I. V. Stalin."[29] The Chinese of the Northeast, and by extension presumably the entire mainland, were fortunate to have received what the Friendship Society presented as crucial and decisive Soviet support in the defeat of the Japanese. At a meeting of the Shenyang Friendship Society branch in December 1949, Gao Gang, chair of the All-Manchurian Friendship Society among his other responsibilities, emphasized the importance of the numerous presents that had been sent to Stalin from diverse sections of the Chinese population. The Ming dynasty jewelry, engraved woodwork, and ancient Chinese vases seemed to express all of Chinese tradition and history in gratitude to the Soviet Union. Coal workers in Fushun sent Stalin a red lantern engraved with their signatures.[30] Precarious and distant frontier regions were especially grateful for support from the patron at the center. The Koreans, too, noted a contributor to *Suiyan ribao,* shared a "deep expression of gratitude" to the Soviet military for its "liberation of Korea."[31]

The institution was yet another example of "internationalism," distinct from the previous practices of the imperialists and the contemporary practices of the capitalists. The society was part of the "gift" of Soviet aid that supposedly inspired a sense of Chinese gratitude but actually required "nothing in return," as Liu Shaoqi emphasized in his speech at the founding session of the OKSD as a countrywide organization on 5 October 1949.[32] The Friendship Society became the focal point for the general contesting and reworking of the ideas at the heart of the Sino-Soviet relationship and the advising program generally. If the relationship in fact was "mutually beneficial [*pingdeng huhui*]," for example, as the Chinese frequently pointed out, they wanted this fact to be reflected in the work and activities of the Friendship Society.

In this spirit the Chinese demanded the creation of a Chinese-Soviet Friendship Society in the Soviet Union. Chinese visitors to the Soviet Union were frustrated by the Soviet population's lack of knowledge and interest in Chinese history, culture, and society, and they pushed for the creation of a companion institution in the Soviet Union to remedy this.[33] Sensitive Soviet advisers on *komandirovka* were similarly struck by this need for reciprocity, and many of them strongly urged the creation of such a companion society. The matter had previously come up in a similar way among Poles, Bulgarians, Romanians, and others.[34] "Often in conversations," lamented the writer Boris Polevoi, who advised the International Department, "or during reports prepared for us we were given inspired questions about whether or not we have a similar society in the USSR, how many members does it have, and so on. Our responses to the effect that cultural ties with all governments are handled by VOKS, and that we have several million friends in China, did not sound particularly convincing. The answer that we do not have such a society creates [the impression] of an unjust inequality in the mutual popularization of achievements, and it seems to us that this has already come to the attention of Chinese public opinion." Polevoi also suggested publishing more material from the Soviet press and Soviet literature in China in Chinese.[35] The Society for Soviet-Chinese Friendship (Obshchestvo sovetsko-kitaiskoi druzhby) was founded in 1957 as the Soviet branch of the OKSD, although Chinese visitors routinely faulted it for its failures to educate better the local Soviet population about China.[36] Along the same lines, in 1957 Liu Xiao suggested to Nikolai Fedorenko that a Chinese publication in the Soviet Union would be a useful counterpart to Russian publications in China.[37]

The Failure of *Suzhong youhao*

One response from the Soviet Union to the accelerating cultural misunderstandings of the late 1950s was the collaborative production of the journal *Sovetsko-kitaiskaia druzhba* (*Soviet-Chinese Friendship*). The journal was published in Russian in the Soviet Union beginning in October 1957 and translated into Chinese and distributed in China as *Suzhong youhao*. The Soviets also distributed the Chinese version among Chinese students and exchange participants in the Soviet Union. The short-lived publication was intended to serve as a forum for Sino-Soviet discussion and exchange, educate the Chinese about the nature of Soviet aid and broader developments within the bloc, and address these Chinese concerns about equality. The deteriorating Sino-Soviet relationship alarmed experts and scholars from both sides, and the journal emerged as a product of the assumptions of party officials, Russian Sinologists, and propaganda experts about the need to correct and counter mistaken and negative trends within Chinese political life that were deleterious to the alliance. This endeavor was yet another example of the Soviet "propaganda state" at work, as one scholar put it, a term useful for the young Chinese state as well.[38] If something was remiss, it was likely to be a product of the misconceptions of an uneducated people again in need of tutelage from above. The Chinese, however, brought their concerns to the editorial discussions surrounding the production of the journal. *Suzhong youhao* could not endure these contrasting pressures, and became another casualty of the deteriorating alliance.

The Friendship Society and its networks of communication were central to the journal's production. The society provided several editorial board members as well as regular oversight and advice. It also received financial support from VOKS and logistical help from Sovinformburo in China.[39] To complement the work of the thirty-five Soviet contributors and cover the crucial issues of translation, local production, and distribution, the journal engaged fourteen Chinese as literary editors, advisers, translators, and production workers, including Li Zhuang and Ding Haode from *Renmin ribao* and Fang Xian from Xinhua.[40] By April 1950 the staff of the journal had grown to seventy people, consisting of fifty-seven Soviets and thirteen Chinese. Fourteen of the fifty-seven Russians spoke Chinese. Soviet officials proclaimed their customary enthusiasm for the potential and possibilities of the relationship, and those with a scholarly and literary bent even imagined the journal as a significant intellectual contribution and form of engagement with the Chinese intelligentsia, in the tradition of Vissarion Belinskii and other social critics of the nineteenth century.

The Chinese, however, quickly raised numerous concerns to the editorial board, which experienced Russian hands in China such as scholar and diplomat S. L. Tikhvinskii tried to address. Li Zhuang, the adviser from *Renmin ribao*, engaged Tikhvinskii in a series of discussions designed to communicate these Chinese concerns to the Russians. Many of these issues were practical problems familiar to workers in the world of socialist bloc propaganda. For instance, Li Zhuang felt that the journal needed more colored photographs, clearer captions to images, catchier titles, and more material that addressed matters beyond the Soviet Union itself. More worrisome, however, especially to Soviet China watchers who were by 1958 long concerned about the state of

Sino-Soviet relations, was Li Zhuang's view that the journal was unable to connect with the interests and concerns of the Chinese reader. Li Zhuang was frustrated with articles and titles that "say nothing to the Chinese reader," or those that failed to be "concrete" and "lively." Even thought-provoking articles often "do not correspond to issues of life in China."[41] *Renmin ribao*, he explained, was much better. Tikhvinskii got the point and raised further with his Soviet colleagues the more serious matter of the overall transferability of the Soviet experience. How do we identify and convey, he wondered, the "specific topics that will help systematically express the experience of socialist construction in the USSR?" Our Chinese colleagues, he warned, expect and await useful help in the resolution of "pressing tasks in the construction of socialism in China."[42]

The chorus of Chinese complaints came to the attention of Ambassador Iudin, who pushed M. V. Zimianin of the Far East Department of the Ministry of Foreign Affairs, A. A. Andreev from the Friendship Society, and G. A. Zhukov from VOKS to devote their energy to improving the quality and effectiveness of the journal.[43] These were important officials within the Soviet diplomatic establishment. The quality of Soviet work was always a concern for Russians in China, as they knew the Chinese were watching carefully. "Poor articles will only embarrass us before our Chinese friends," explained Friendship Society chairman A. A. Andreev.[44] Fashioning himself a significant theoretician, Iudin characteristically suggested more "solid, theoretical, summarizing, articles and essays with a specific problematic."[45] The editorial board of the journal—headed by V. N. Rogov and also including N. M. Potanov, P. S. Kapitsa, S. L. Tikhvinskii, B. G. Kokashvili, Iu. I. Balanenko, and I. S. Shcherbakov—sponsored a series of discussions from 1958 to 1960 that drew on the expertise of these institutions, with substantial Chinese contributions as well. The Friendship Society played host to these "Readers' Conferences" in numerous Chinese cities, among them Beijing, Shanghai, Tianjin, Wuhan, Chengdu, and smaller provincial cities. They also invited further Soviet attendance at these events by officials associated with the Central Committee, the Academy of Sciences, Soviet publishing houses, and numerous other institutions and enterprises. Rogov and his editorial board read unsolicited letters to the journal from the Chinese public and pushed for effective and regular "Readers' Conferences" in Beijing and throughout China to respond to the concerns of the Chinese and improve the deteriorating relationship.

In response to the overwhelming Chinese criticism, the Soviets quickly dropped their initial pretensions about Belinskii and the traditions of the intelligentsia from the nineteenth century. The Soviets could not direct their message, said P. V. Zakharov, at "one category of people," by which he meant the educated; instead, the specific concerns of Chinese peasants and workers needed to be expressed in the journal if it were to be successful.[46] In a similar vein, a Comrade Popenko at a October 1958 discussion noted that connecting with the Chinese reader meant addressing the concerns of peasants and the "simple Chinese man."[47] Another contributor suggested a section called "On the Street," which would provide information about "any street in any city, and show who lives on this street, how they live, and the theaters, clubs, stores, and schools there."[48] Managing to insult these imagined readers even as he attempted to recognize their needs, Popenko noted that the concession to the reader's interests was a particular challenge because the "simple Chinese reader is insufficiently educated compared to our average reader." Numerous Chinese letter-writers to the journal made clear their concerns, forcing the scholars, advisers, and officials to question the very notion of "friendship" between the Soviets and the Chinese. How might they address the everyday needs and "small details" of relationships between individuals that raised issues far different from matters of collaboration between large enterprises and institutions? Soviets such as Popenko and his colleagues were made aware that they had failed to produce material that spoke to the "situation in China."[49]

Yet the worried Russian contributors to this discussion could only visualize a traditional resolution to the problem of improving the relationship. This was especially the case in the Soviet Union. At a meeting sponsored by the Society for Soviet-Chinese Friendship in Moscow in July 1958, with only one Chinese present, Russians from a wide variety of institutions proclaimed their affection for Chinese culture, tradition, and architecture. Officials more distant from recent developments and tensions in the Sino-Soviet relationship especially tended to return to traditional Russian notions about the purpose and potential of the Russian mission in Asia. Officials from ministries as unrelated as construction and culture all suggested more attention to stories about Chinese traditional literature and architecture and the history of Chinese opposition to Western imperialism. A representative from the Library of Foreign Literature wanted to read more about "national customs, mores, and so on." Others proclaimed their respect for ancient Chinese history. At a June 1958 discussion in Irkutsk, P. P. Khoroshikh from Irkutsk State University explained that many works of Chinese architecture "were created close to 5,000 years ago" and "attest to the creative value of the Chinese people."[50] This Russian preoccupation with antiquity, as we have seen, was common in the borderland regions of both the Russian and Soviet empires, and numerous Russians oblivious to concerns and trends in China continued to visualize the proper cultivation of the national past as one of the virtues brought by the umbrella of the socialist bloc alliance.

In the *Suzhong youhao* discussions, the Russians remained oblivious to the Maoist preoccupation with the importance of peasant culture and the problem of the accessibility and significance of high culture. A Comrade Severin of the Ministry of Culture suggested more attention to the writings, birthdays, and biographies of famous Russian writers, composers, and theater directors, as well as more material on violin and piano competitions in which Soviet musicians excelled. "In China the piano schools have not attained the accomplishments of our own," he proclaimed. Severin continued to frustrate the Chinese by suggesting that the journal focus more on the example of the Uzbek adoption and use of aspects of Russian and European high culture. Russians often criticize the paucity of cultural talent among the Central Asians, he offered, but instead they should proudly celebrate it wherever it appears in Central Asia and the East.[51] China was to his mind a related example. This perpetual reference to the extension of culture to the Soviet Asian frontier insulted a nation comfortable with its own civilizing missions toward its frontier peoples and was oblivious to the contemporary Chinese exploration of the virtues of peasant culture.

The Chinese press heralded the appearance and potential of *Suzhong youhao* in China, but in a characteristic manner that reflected and served Chinese visions of future development and the alliance. The discussions surrounding the journal illustrated the two sides' inability to communicate. Contributors to *Jiefang ribao*, *Renmin ribao*, *Guangming ribao*, and numerous other publications drew on the typical notions about proletarian internationalism, socialist solidarity, the Friendship, and the Soviet Union as "China's tomorrow," but in a way that recast the Soviet experience and visualized future goals in Chinese terms.[52] Chinese letter-writers to the journal and contributors to the numerous Readers' Conferences throughout China similarly visualized Chinese experiences in the Soviet Union. At a Readers' Conference in Tianjin in July 1959, Chinese contributors professed excitement about the "high speed" and "grandiose extent" of industrial accomplishments in the USSR.[53] It sounded as if the supposed struggles and victories of the Great Leap Forward were unfolding in the Soviet Union. Li Yi similarly imagined Soviet production growth in steel as a Soviet version of a "great leap."[54] In Shanghai in March 1958 Chinese attendees at the Readers' Conference also referred to the great upsurge in productivity currently taking place in the Soviet Union.[55] In the everyday moments of cultural exchange, foreign terms, notions, and practices were inevitably recast in a language and format comprehensible to local society and experience.

By visualizing the Soviet Union in Chinese terms, the Chinese could convince themselves that the Great Leap Forward and the increasingly radical Maoist themes in Chinese culture and politics did not necessarily challenge the Soviet model. In this view, the Soviets and the Chinese were together making rapid strides forward. "The Chinese people under the leadership of the Communist Party," stated Weng Yunsheng of the Dagongbao Publishing House, "utilizing the achievements of Soviet science and technology, will be able to make a leap in its development even faster."[56] Long Yunqing, a rural schoolteacher from Sichuan province, wanted to learn about the role of "physical and intellectual labor" in overcoming the divide between the city and the countryside. Li Haijiong described a "cultural revolution" in the world of Chinese education, which was "quickly educating a red, proletarian intelligentsia," and he suggested that the Soviets offer material to further such a development.[57] Other Chinese letter-writers expressed their interest in heroic and utopian Soviet activities, such as the experiences of settlers in the Virgin Lands.[58] Maksim Gorky was worth reading, argued Zhang Yuquan from Beijing Pedagogical Institute, because he persuasively linked "education with labor."[59]

For the Chinese, the USSR's efforts to "catch up with and surpass" the advanced West were at the forefront of the general Soviet program and purpose. Chinese writers made grandiose claims about the journal as a "bridge" between Soviet and Chinese societies and as an illustration of the "glorious victories of the USSR" in every imaginable area. "The Soviet Union in several important areas of science and technology," wrote He Bizhang in *Fuxian ribao*, "has already by far overtaken the leading capitalist countries."[60] A contributor to *Zhongguo gongren* directed readers to *Suzhong youhao* precisely because it provided evidence from Soviet economists about matching the United States in iron production by 1968, and steel the following year.[61] Chinese letter-writers and those queried in the Readers' Conferences routinely requested more material in the journal about the heroic efforts to construct Soviet socialism in the past, as well as the future achievements that would catapult the socialist world past the world of the advanced West. Song Ji told Rogov in October 1958 that Chinese readers wanted to learn more about the "work and struggles of the Soviet people—for example, about the acquired strengths of the Soviet people that will enable them to surpass the USA in the course of seven years."[62]

The most significant recasting of the Soviet model thus concerned the United States. Yao Zhen, a journalist and a Central Committee official in international propaganda, bluntly told Rogov and his colleagues: "If you want to have more subscribers, regularly print in each number material about how the USSR is overtaking the USA. In China right now everyone is interested in one question: how the PRC is overtaking England and how the USSR is overtaking the USA." Avoid generalities and vagueness, he continued, and stick to the "concrete: facts and figures."[63] Xiong Fu, an official from the Committee for Cultural Ties with Foreign Countries, hoped to see all discussions of Soviet achievements in comparative context, and, of course, the comparison that mattered concerned the United States. Tell us "concretely in what areas the USSR will surpass America," he demanded of the editorial board at a Readers' Conference. Lu Xiangxiang also suggested "Chinese workers" wanted specific information about Soviet measures to overtake America.[64] The Chinese also pushed the Soviets to clarify their vague claims about the glorious transition to communism. Cheng Guangrui of *Renmin ribao* argued that the journal needed to provide "concrete examples of how the USSR will exceed the United States in per capita production."[65] Deng Tuo, the *Renmin ribao* editor-in-chief who took his own life as the Cultural Revolution unfolded in 1966, similarly advised, "In the area of economic information it would be best to make comparisons with the capitalist countries. In such a way the material will be the most pertinent, and will inspire enthusiasm and strengthen the faith of the reader that we will overtake the capitalist countries."[66] With different interests but along the same lines, Wen Zijie, a young man from Shanghai, wanted to know how the Soviet volleyball team fared against the Americans in its recent trip to the United States.[67]

Chinese interest in the moral and ethical dimensions of daily life and the struggles involved in constructing a new utopian society illustrated some of the basic dilemmas of the Sino-Soviet relationship. In early 1958, Yang Hansheng, associated with the Ministry of Culture as well as the Committee for Cultural Ties with Foreign Countries, focused on personal matters: "We are very interested in the family life of Soviet people, such as the relations between spouses, parents and children, and so on."[68] What were the Chinese looking for as an alternative to a distant Soviet Union that seemed too "abstract and imprecise," as Shen Zheng of the PLA suggested?[69] We have a "great interest in the daily life of Soviet people, in their habits and customs," emphasized

Qi Ke, a poet and editor of the newspaper *Yangze*. In the fall of 1958 Rogov and his colleagues solicited contributions from a collection of literary and newspaper figures. Li Erzhuang, a writer, Friendship Society administrator, and Wuhan City party secretary, similarly pushed the Soviets for more poems, songs, and pictures of Soviet daily life, requesting more "material about the way of life of Soviet people."[70] At a similar discussion in Shanghai, *Xingwan* editor Liu Shimo looked for basic human moments of camaraderie and care: he appreciated a story about Soviet doctors taking a personal interest in Chinese patients in Heilongjiang.[71] Yu Changfu from Harbin offered his own story about personal help from a Soviet border guard after he broke his leg near the Sino-Soviet border.[72]

However, the world of daily life and personal relationships was a contradictory problem for the Soviets. How could this enormous governmental relationship, signed into law by the agreement between Mao and Stalin in 1950, address and cultivate these moments of cultural exchange from daily life? How could the "Friendship," which after all meant a series of socialist bloc exchanges in industrial and economic development, address the personal matters of affection and sociability suggested by the term itself? And what could the Soviet Union in the wake of Stalinist dictatorship and the tragic degradation of public life possibly offer to anyone in this area? Indeed, the surliness of Russian public life had been a well-known constant throughout the entire twentieth century. Ironically, it was precisely the "empathetic" character of American consumerism, as Victoria De Grazia puts it, that specifically addressed these matters.[73] The Soviet notion of "friendship" entailed a series of demands that included exclusive loyalty to Moscow. And romance, as we have seen from the example of Oldřich Havlíček and Zhen Peilu in Shanghai, was decidedly not part of the Chinese political vision. *Suzhong youhao* contributors attempted to address this issue with articles on topics such as the positive experiences of Chinese students in the Soviet Union, the affectionate family life of a typical Russian worker, the fine relationships cultivated by a Soviet music teacher in China, and various other connections between Russians and Chinese as examples of "friendship."[74]

The expectations, demands, and needs of socialist bloc allies such as the Chinese pushed the Soviets to recast their own history and experience in a way they knew would conform better to current Chinese concerns, however divorced this was from Soviet reality and history. In June 1958, V. D. Kudriavtsev enthusiastically welcomed Mao's speech about the arrival of the "east wind" in international politics. He addressed Chinese efforts to overtake Great Britain in steel and iron production and professed that Soviets were "genuinely happy about the successes of the workers of China in the industrial area."[75] P. V. Zakharov recognized the Chinese desire to see Soviet readers more respectful of and interested in Chinese conditions and contributions, and suggested stories about traditions and practices foreign to Soviet readers, such as the big character posters (*dazibao*) then common in China, the glorification of physical labor, and the experience of agricultural labor in the countryside for urban cadres and intellectuals.[76] Radical trends characteristic of the interests of Chairman Mao were depicted by the Soviets as familiar and part of their experience. Current Chinese artists depicting peasants were behaving as good socialist realists, painting the "life of the village."[77] Soviet history itself needed to be more effectively recast in current Chinese terms. As a means to connect with Chinese readers, Rogov suggested that the journal return to the earlier stages of the construction of socialism in the Soviet Union and describe the difficulties and dramatic struggles of the 1929–33 era.[78] The Soviet Union as well had its youthful experience with revolutionary change, cultural revolution, and utopian idealism. The Chinese were interested in labor history, historic Russian efforts to construct socialism, and communist education methods, but instead Soviet publications focused on theater, art, music, and film, complained longtime embassy official Nikolai Sudarikov.[79] He pushed for more attention to the "advantages of the Soviet system," the "economic strength of the USSR," Soviet accomplishments in industry and agriculture, Soviet aid to the countries of the bloc, and Soviet support for developing countries. Provide "portraits of simple Soviet people, who labor without losing their strength," advised another board member.[80] Soviet officials in foreign affairs, culture, and propaganda worked together with Chinese colleagues in Moscow and China to craft these stories and a general vision that is evident in the pages of *Suzhong youhao*. Soviet contributors themselves thus contributed to the "sinicization" of the journal, optimistically assuming that Russians and Chinese shared much in common in 1958–60.[81]

The language of the journal came from Chinese political history and culture, even when describing events in the USSR. The collaborative nature of the journal's production and the need to address the assumptions of the Chinese audience encouraged the use of slogans and terms taken from contemporary Chinese politics. As a result of the "good path [*meihao de daolu*]" articulated in the new Seven-Year Plan, the Soviet Union was daily "striding toward communism [*xiang gongzhanzhuyi maijin*]."[82] Soviet industrial development was marked by its "speed."[83] Khrushchev's competitive notion of peaceful coexistence and "catch up with and surpass" was a "campaign" and a "movement." "This movement has the support of the party and the entire people," wrote the editors in early 1959.[84] Russian slogans, notions, and names were inevitably sinicized. "The party's plan is the Soviet people's plan [*dang de jihua shi sulian renmin de jihua*]," wrote one Karasev (Kalaxiefu). Or sometimes the language about the Soviet experience was drawn entirely from China. "The Soviet people's path is glorious [*sulian renmin de daolu shi guangrong de*]," concluded Karasev. "Communism definitely will be constructed!"[85]

In other areas, however, the journal made no concession to Chinese concerns. Its purpose was to educate the Chinese about the stages of socialism, the nature of the development of the bloc, and, of course, the importance of Soviet leadership of the bloc. Soviets with experience in China saw the party program unveiled at the 21st Party Congress as useful in Sino-Soviet relations, for these were the official events where the nature of the transition from socialism to communism and its meaning were clarified. "Let's publicize in full the party program," argued editorial board member B. G. Kokashvili to his colleagues.[86] N. G. Sudarikov similarly picked up on this issue, suggesting inclusion of information on "problems relating to the transition from socialism to communism in the USSR."[87] The Soviet embassy in Beijing in 1958 regularly brought attention to the issue of the stages of socialist development and the "theoretical" matter of the "gradual transition from socialism to communism."[88] Soviet plans and recent events, suggested Karasev, illustrated that "we are decisively moving toward the next stage of advanced communism."[89] The journal was designed to reeducate Chinese who thought otherwise or who thought the Chinese might get there first.

Soviet observers who were aware and also fearful of the direction of Chinese politics advised caution in this complicated effort to address simultaneously two very different reading audiences. At the height of the Great Leap Forward in June 1959, B. Gurevich and Iu. Lysenko argued for the necessity of "tact" in the presentation of sensitive political matters. For Chinese readers, the Russian editors suggested, the journal should refrain from discussing the prevalence of "material incentives" in Soviet industry.[90] They were aware of the pointed concerns from many radical Chinese readers about the apparently suspect "class structure" still in existence in the Soviet Union. "Are there in your cities and countryside classes, like landlords, kulaks, and capitalists?" asked Zao Dengwan of the PLA.[91] But there were Soviet readers of the journal as well, and they were likely to be confused by too much knowledge about what was really happening in China. For Soviet readers, Gurevich and Lysenko suggested that the journal shy away from articles on the people's communes in China, "even though the organization of the communes throughout the country on a massive scale had already been completed."[92] Certain basic trends and practices in both societies were best left unexplored at present.

Acceptable to everyone, however, was the inclusion of more information on how the Chinese were going "to catch up with and surpass England" in the next fifteen years.[93] The Chinese thus played a fascinating role in pushing the Soviets to take seriously their own claims about the making of a communist society. Publish the speech from Lenin at the 3rd Komsomol Congress, suggested an editorial board member in October 1958, because in it Lenin claimed that "communism will soon be built."[94] "Show in the journal the country in 1965," urged a Chinese contributor queried at a November 1958 session, a picture of a factory, a collective farm, industrial productivity, a television station, and so on, as they will be in this future.[95] An article appeared the following year on precisely this topic.[96] Chinese contributors to the journal could offer personal testimonies about the seriousness of the Soviet commitment to tackle the "construction of communism as a great objective and task."[97] Vague claims about the distant future were perhaps the easiest to make, but what was helpful in one context did not necessarily work in another. Closer to the West and more informed about its prosperity, Czechoslovaks found Khrushchev ineffective because he was ultimately "unrealistic" in his numerous plans and grandiose claims, especially regarding this matter of catching up with the West.[98]

The Soviets continued to have difficulty absorbing Chinese concerns, even as Rogov and his colleagues tried to listen. The continuing Chinese complaint about the absence of a "mutual" exchange baffled Soviets who took their pedagogic mission for granted. Still in May 1960, Li Zhuang continued to remind Nikolai Sudarikov that "in the Soviet Union there is less printed and discussed about China in the newspapers and journals than about the Soviet Union in China."[99] Why were the Russians not more interested in the Chinese and their culture? The journal sought out stories and experiences that illustrated Russians learning from the Chinese, and published articles about Russian students engaged in Chinese-language lessons, Russian enthusiasts of Chinese traditional medicine, the study of Chinese literature in the Soviet Union, and the positive experiences of Chinese workers, specialists, and graduate students in the Soviet Union.[100] The Society for Soviet-Chinese Friendship in the Soviet Union, founded in 1957, was conceived with this problem in mind as well.

Even the progress of Central Asia under Soviet rule, a matter of pride for the Soviets and visualized by them as directly pertinent to the experience of

China, was interpreted differently by the Chinese. *Suzhong youhao* often visualized 1965 in places like Kazakhstan and Uzbekistan, when Central Asia was to be a central contributor to the socialist bloc community in machine tool production, precious metals, the chemical industry, and other areas. Steel factories in Kazakhstan were "better and then some than America's best factories."[101] Between 1959 and 1965, Kazakhstan planned to build some thirty new electric power stations, again bringing the region "near to the American level" in the quantity of electric power produced per person.[102] The Kazakhs routinely sent their ballet and other cultural groups to Moscow, where they were greatly appreciated by sophisticated audiences in the capital.[103] This vision, however, was not necessarily appealing to the Chinese, who did not imagine themselves as beneficiaries of Russia's traditional civilizing mission in Asia.

The discussions surrounding the production of *Suzhong youhao* illustrate the complicated dialogue and diverse interests that influenced the making of the Soviet notion of "catch up with and surpass." In many ways, communication and collaboration between the Russians and Chinese was difficult. Each side misunderstood the other, but both tried to recast the very different foreign society as something familiar and comprehensible. Soviets aware of the radical trends shaping Chinese politics in 1958–60 focused not on the challenges they posed for the bloc but on their likely contribution to the common effort to "catch up with" and even "surpass" America. This greater goal was still shared by the two sides, and proved to be a more acceptable topic for conversation than the contrasting practices in industry and culture that divided them. The Chinese deluded themselves into thinking that the Soviet Seven-Year Plan and 21st Party Congress amounted to a mobilization "campaign" of the sort that was familiar in Chinese political history. As the socialist societies sparred with each other about competition with the United States, they overlooked the fact that competing with America was an impossible proposition for anyone in 1959, and a dangerous one for ruling communist parties that based their rule on unending public discussions and pronouncements about the nature and timing of a future "communist" society.

The fate of *Suzhong youhao* serves as another example of the diverse needs and expectations shaping socialist bloc collaboration and Sino-Soviet relations that all parties found impossible to accommodate. Chinese contributors to the many Readers' Conferences expressed their desire to become closer to Soviet society, engage in deeper forms of communication, and to learn more about the Soviet people and their everyday lives. The paternalist Soviet vision of "cultured" communism, however, was only capable of perpetually offering the safe and pedagogic models of proper personal and social behavior for emulation drawn from Soviet experience and history. Khrushchev himself complained to Peng Zhen, while the two of them were in Romania on 26 June 1960, that the Chinese were inserting material into the journal that the Soviet Union did not want to see in print in either country.[104] The journal was shut down in September 1960. Chinese interpreters and journalists such as Wang Yiying departed Moscow on 12 September, still hopeful that the journal, a "small link in our great and eternal friendship," would someday make a comeback.[105] That would never happen.

The Subversion of the Friendship Society

The Friendship Society itself, the very institution designed to celebrate and promote Sino-Soviet Friendship and the alliance, was gradually subverted and taken over by the Chinese. Soviet embassy workers in the spring of 1959 were dismayed to realize that OKSD branches in China were selectively responding to the material they were receiving from the Soviet Union, reproducing in the Chinese press only 389 articles of the 1,290 they received from the embassy.[106] The Friendship Societies were burying reports and information about Khrushchev's September 1959 trip to America, which Soviet officials noticed with frustration. What they understood to be a major event in international relations and Soviet policy in 1959, they discovered, had been relegated in Harbin to a brief lecture by a lower-level official in propaganda and agitation of the party city committee.[107] A film was made about Khrushchev in America, but the Friendship Societies were not showing it. "In the province of Sichuan in 1959," complained the Soviet embassy, "the OKSD branch did not produce a single poster or brochure propagandizing Chinese-Soviet friendship and the achievements of the USSR, although last year there were many publications." Indeed, Soviet officials noted far fewer events about Soviet life in late 1959 among numerous branches of the Friendship Society. "The administrators of the local branches of the OKSD do not listen to our radio broadcasts in Chinese and do not know when they are available."[108]

The Russians were disturbed to discover they possessed waning influence within their own Friendship Societies. In December 1958, curious about the chain of authority over the local Chinese branches, the Soviets initiated a series of discussions to determine their relationship to official policy and the Communist Party. "All of our work," emphasized Xiang Yan, the deputy secretary of the Shanghai Friendship Society branch, "is administered by the city committee of the party."[109] Chinese Friendship Society officials were reminding their Soviet counterparts that, whatever the history of the Friendship Society as a vehicle of Sovietization and a conduit for information about the Soviet Union and Soviet policies, the local branches were controlled by the Chinese Communist Party, whose policies were changing. This was the purpose of another discussion on 24 December 1958 between embassy officials N. G. Sudarikov, Iu. I. Razdukhov, V. I. Voshchankin, and Ge Baoquan, deputy general secretary of the society's central administration in Beijing. Ge Baoquan was a well-known scholar of Russian language and literature, and he had accompanied Liu Shaoqi to Moscow in the summer of 1949. He had remained there to help set up the new embassy of the PRC.[110] Now, however, he could only try to help his Soviet colleagues understand the relationship between the Friendship Society and the Communist Party and its hierarchy. The Central Committee communicated with lower party organizations in cities and provinces, who administered the daily work of the local Friendship Society branches. This discussion should not have been surprising to Soviet officials like Sudarikov and his colleagues, but in fact what they were witnessing was the loss of an administrative structure that historically had been a vehicle of Soviet control and Soviet policy.[111]

Sudarikov continued his discussions through 1959, attempting to connect with still cordial Chinese officials who might offer advice about resolving practical difficulties, such as Zhang Zhixiang, a VOKS liaison official and member of the state soviet, and Lu Ming and Gao Diewei, state soviet experts on socialist affairs. Even the sympathetic Zhang Zhixiang, however, identified practical matters about which he felt the Soviets had very little understanding. The Soviet desire for equality (evident in the 1957 founding of OKSD branches in the Soviet Union), he explained, was "mechanically observed" and put into practice in a pointless way. Soviet paint restoration workers traveled to China, and hence Chinese specialists were sent on a return trip to the USSR. But Chinese oil paint restoration was far behind Soviet knowledge in this area, and the trip was a waste of money. Cinematic collaboration was in principle a fine notion, Zhang continued, but differences "in customs and traditions of our peoples" and cultural differences over how to express a political issue artistically made collaboration difficult. "In the joint production of a film it is difficult to satisfy both Soviet and Chinese viewers."[112] Chinese delegations to the Soviet Union by 1959 were extremely sensitive about any issue pertaining to Russia's lack of knowledge or appreciation of Chinese accomplishments. Liu Shuzhou, the deputy chairman of the People's Committee in Shanghai, was pleased that his hosts in Leningrad "warmly congratulated the Chinese comrades for their own successes in their Homeland." A. Elizavetin, the general consul in Shanghai in touch with Liu Shuzhou and the group from Shanghai as well as officials from the Shanghai City Committee, reminded Friendship Society officials that it was imperative for them "to study as deeply as possible the economic and political processes currently under way in the PRC."[113] Russian ignorance of Chinese ideas and developments was an extremely sensitive matter to Chinese visitors.

High-level officials as well could do little to stop the progressive deterioration. The ten-year anniversary celebration of the founding of the Friendship Society in January 1960 was attended by Zhou Enlai, Peng Zhen, Chen Yi, Guo Moruo, and other important political and cultural figures. Song Qingling, chair of the OKSD's central administration, hoped the strong relationship could overcome the recent difficulties: "Our friendship has endured many experiences, and both in difficult times and victorious ones we are always together."[114] Chinese figures suspicious of Maoist radicalism and extreme nativism, and conservative supporters of the socialist camp in the Soviet Union, could do no more to halt the slide. A Chinese delegation that included Li Zhuchen of the Ministry of Light Industry, Central Committee member Liu Changsheng, and other officials in culture and the arts received an audience with Mikhail Suslov and Frol Kozlov in February 1960 but subsequently felt slighted by even a leading figure in conservative ideology such as Suslov. "Yesterday your delegation was received by Comrades Zhu De and Chen Yi," complained Liu Changsheng. "Zhu De is among the top five leaders in our country, and Chen Yi ranks among the top ten."[115] The group felt they had insufficient time in the Soviet Union, and its members wondered about the lack of attention in the national press to their visit.

The deteriorating relationship demanded new conceptions of the purpose of the Friendship Society. On 29 April 1960 a new agreement was signed that instead regulated exchanges of "tourist-activists." The Soviet agency Inturist was now involved, with visiting Chinese delegations now curtailing their traditional cooperative moments of "international" solidarity at the Friendship Houses as well as their public appearances, on the grounds that they were only in the Soviet Union as "tourists." The change in terminology was a fascinating example of the confusion over what communist cooperation entailed between two nation-states. The Russians and Chinese were apparently no longer "friends." But the visitor as simply "tourist" posed difficulties, too, because both sides understood that visitors from capitalist countries, increasing in number in the Soviet Union, were also called tourists. Consequently the Chinese visitors were "tourists" with a commitment to socialism, however contested or ambiguous this might be, or "tourist-activists." Iu. V. Novgorodskii at one point referred to the Chinese as "foreign guests" in his written report on the exchange, which he then crossed out and replaced with "Chinese group."[116] The new terminology reflected the enduring ambiguity about the internal borders of the socialist world, as well as the deteriorating state of the relationship. Were Russians and Chinese now "foreigners" to each other? The Chinese wavered between continuing overtures to the bloc and accusations of outright Russian betrayal of the socialist movement.

To make matters worse, the Chinese were introduced to yet another set of absurdities characteristic of Soviet life. Inturist workers failed to meet the delegation at the airport, the Inturist hotel in Kyiv was filthy, and the food throughout the trip was bad. This made a particular impression on visiting delegation member Zhuai Huansan, the deputy general director of the Chinese tourist agency.[117] The relationship was far from over, but in Soviet eyes the Chinese no longer possessed a privileged status within the bloc. And "tourists" were from a different world, far less valuable to the "construction of socialism" and often even threatening. A Chinese group of "tourists" in the Soviet Union in the spring of 1960 (already simply "tourists" and not "tourist-activists") found themselves prohibited from observing a factory in Leningrad because, as the manager informed them, "in general foreigners are not allowed here." "Tourists" were "bothersome," he added, and an obstacle to the work of the factory.[118] The Chinese reciprocated. Soviet visitors in November 1962 complained of the formal and vague nature of the exchange, in which they too were treated as inconsequential tourists. G. Grushetskii, a first secretary of the Soviet embassy in Beijing, complained that the entire relationship was increasingly handled at the "deputy" level. The group met the deputy rectors at universities, deputy chairmen of provincial People's Committees, and deputy factory directors.[119]

Abrupt Chinese administrative change stunned the Russians. Oleg Rakhmanin and G. Grushetskii of the Soviet embassy subsequently complained that the "experienced workers" who "knew Russian, were connected to the Soviet Union and related to it well" suddenly disappeared, replaced by people from the "party-propaganda apparatus of the CCP."[120] Czechoslovak officials made similar complaints against actions taken by the Ministry of Foreign Affairs.[121] Qian Junrui, the general secretary of the central administration, was replaced by the "anti-Soviet chauvinistic" Zhang Zhixiang. Deputy Secretary Ge Baoquan was replaced by the totally inexperienced Li Xigeng, the deputy editor of *Chinese People's Liberation Army Daily*. Soviet officials tried to embarrass Zhang Zhixiang by pointedly posing questions about the present location and activities of Ge Baoquan.[122] The new deputy general secretary was Bian Cheng, who "did not possess even an elementary knowledge of the USSR." He "used to work in construction at an electric power station," reported V. Feoktistov.[123] The new administration transformed the House of Friendship into a "Potemkin village" and tried to "hide the almost complete inactivity of the organization," complained Rakhmanin and Grushetskii.[124] The ambiguity that demanded analysis and deciphering by the Soviet China experts was an example of the assumptions and attitudes that clouded and complicated the relationship. The two sides were now barely communicating, but were they not still "friends"? Soviet officials concluded among themselves that the Chinese were in fact pretending to be "friends" and were dissimulating and feigning an outward acceptance of the relationship.[125] In a "communist" world shaped by the customs of the mutually beneficial connection (*blat/guanxi*) and relationship, it was indeed conceivable from the Soviet perspective that the Chinese had become manipulative and ungrateful receivers of the gift, and were determined to maintain appearances and continue to benefit from the relationship. They were surely contemplating, the Soviets feared, an open split and a complete betrayal of the generous history of "selfless" Soviet aid.

Soviet suspicions that the Chinese were cynically manipulating Soviet aid now clouded the Friendship Society exchanges. P. A. Zagrebel'nyi complained in his October 1962 trip to Wuhan that in spite of the obvious signs of Soviet aid such as the massive Wuhan bridge, he found it "insulting" that the group "heard not one word about the great help that China had received from the Soviet Union." At a people's commune south of Wuhan, there was "no reference in any form" to "Soviet experience in agriculture."[126] A moment of personal duplicity in gift-giving for the Soviets was the case of Huang Lifu, who traveled to Irkutsk and Baikal. The Russians decided to present him with a fine watch as a gift and souvenir of his trip. "But when the conversation ended, comrade Huang Lifu went to his friends and began to pull other valuable things from his pockets to give to his friends, cunningly laughing."[127] The perpetually manipulative Chinese were unworthy of Soviet generosity. This Russian perception of Chinese ulterior motives came up on several occasions. The Poles and Hungarians in particular also complained about the system of payment for specialists and honorariums for cultural figures. The Poles and Hungarians felt underpaid in China, in contrast to what Chinese figures received for travel to

Eastern Europe. The Chinese abroad "are well-paid, return home with several suitcases full of purchased goods, are not interested in travel excursions or cultural events, and only pay attention to money," reported Soviet officials in March 1959.[128] Greedy and self-interested, the Chinese increasingly illustrated some of the traditional characteristics familiar from European colonial representation.

Signs of change had been obvious for some time, but the Soviets were still left off balance by how their Chinese colleagues and hosts treated them. A Soviet group led by F. V. Konstantinov found themselves invited to attend only several of numerous Friendship Society meetings scheduled in February 1961.[129] The evenings were obviously dedicated to a very different sort of discussion about the Sino-Soviet relationship. The November 1961 Soviet delegation, headed by education official M. A. Prokof'iev, found their references to Khrushchev, the 22nd Congress, and CPSU programs greeted with absolute silence at a large auditorium meeting, with the only positive public response reserved for references to Soviet support for Cuba. When Prokof'iev and his colleagues met lower-level officials, they were made aware of better treatment afforded the Koreans and Vietnamese, and of a meeting of officials from the Albanian-Chinese Friendship Society with Mao Zedong, Zhou Enlai, and Chen Yi. They were shown a film on tsarist imperialism and informed by a translator that the "idea of the film is that it is impossible to make agreements and live peacefully with an enemy; [instead] he must be destroyed."

The Chinese used the exchanges to emphasize their support for Cuba and criticism of America, presenting a song with the words "the one is worse than the other—Kennedy is worse than Eisenhower."[130] Li Xigeng, a deputy in the OKSD general secretariat active with Prokof'iev's group, which returned in November 1962, informed its members and embassy officials that "genuine communists should behave like Fidel Castro. The USSR has removed its rockets from Cuba. That is its affair, and regarding this it is difficult to present one's own opinion. But we think that before the military threats of the imperialists we should not retreat or yield. We must fight, not sacrifice our sovereignty, and conduct a ceaseless struggle—only then can we defend Cuba." The American inspection of Soviet cargo ships in the Cuban Missile Crisis was for Li Xigeng a low point for the Soviet Union and the entire socialist camp. "The Soviet people is a heroic people, which has spilled much blood," he offered. "The USA has scattered its bases throughout the whole world, and do they allow anyone to conduct inspections?"[131]

The Friendship Society exchanges were increasingly viewed by the Chinese as opportunities to confront visiting Soviets about Soviet foreign policy, the nature of Soviet socialism, and the practices of the socialist bloc. A. N. Kuznetsov, leader of a Soviet delegation in China in October 1961 to celebrate the forty-fourth anniversary of the Russian revolution, had the microphone ripped from his hand when he tried to talk to students gathered at Beijing University.[132] Or the exchanges became opportunities for the Chinese to recruit potentially sympathetic figures at odds with their "revisionist" leadership. During the November 1961 visit Li Xigeng privately approached V. F. Feoktistov after a visit to a diesel factory in Shanghai to query him about his personal views on the Cuban missile crisis.[133] The Chinese adopted a similar approach to their ongoing Friendship Society trips to the Soviet Union.

Chinese Propaganda Trips to the Soviet Union

Similar to the assumptions and efforts of Chinese Ministry of Foreign Affairs officials in the Soviet Union, Chinese Friendship Society delegations used the remaining exchanges as an opportunity to communicate with a presumably socialist populace that had been betrayed by its "revisionist" leadership. The party and state leadership of the Soviet Union rather than the Soviet people had revealed themselves to be an "enemy" to China. Chinese officials pushed for more exchanges and trips in order to engage the Soviet citizenry more effectively. Cultural exchange meant an opportunity to encourage social change in the Soviet Union, giving the Chinese branches of the Friendship Society something in common with the U.S. Information Agency and other branches of the American cultural effort directed at the Soviet Union. Chinese groups in 1962, noted T. Skvortsov-Tokarin, "tried to use every opportunity to establish contacts with Soviet citizens." In Kyiv, Zhang Yunqi attempted to address veterans at the Tomb of the Unknown Soldier and challenge Soviet policies on "peaceful coexistence." A group in Tbilisi, Georgia (Stalin's native republic), in May 1962 "joyfully met the city residents, hugging them and kissing them, greeting them on the streets and buses as they did in no other city." Gao Zhendong dramatically informed a group of workers: "We were with you in good times, and now, in this difficult time, we are still with you."[134] The group that arrived for a 28 August–19 September 1963 visit ignored Soviet tourist sites at the Kremlin and instead began distributing literature in Russian to visitors to the Lenin History Museum and asking Soviet visitors if they followed Beijing radio broadcasts. Inside the museum they fought with the guides and contested their presentation of Lenin and his views on war and peace and the personality cult.[135] A group in Irkutsk in the fall of 1963 arrived with three suitcases of anti-Soviet material, which its members promptly began distributing to Soviet citizens. Zhang Jiangwuzhi from Wuhan posed questions such as, "Whose home is this? Is it private? Whose car is this? Also private? If a person has his own home and car and dacha, what distinguishes him from a bourgeois?"[136]

Georgia began to assume special significance for the Friendship Society groups from China, who always pushed Soviet officials to include Tbilisi as part of their itinerary. In 1962 the signs of this interest were somewhat muted, and some Soviet officials were even unaware of Chinese intentions. A group in Moscow from Jiangxi province in the summer of 1962, for example, spent an inordinate amount of time at the Georgian pavilion at the Exhibit of Achievements of the National Economy (VDNKh). Zhou Zhenyuan, reported Soviet observers, "behaved rather strangely," approaching Georgians and engaging them in conversation with phrases in Russian such as "We are China, Mao Zedong. . . . Georgia is good!" The Chinese group in the Soviet Union in the spring of 1961 accused coordinator P. Bazarov of delaying the trip so that it would not coincide with a celebration of the fortieth anniversary of the Georgian republic.[137] In addition to being Stalin's birthplace, Georgia had been the site of demonstrations in March 1956 protesting the denunciation of him at the 20th Party Congress. Subsequent Chinese Friendship Society delegations expressed sympathy with an imagined popular resistance movement against the "revisionist" betrayal of Marxism-Leninism and the heritage of Stalin.

Through the early 1960s Chinese Friendship Society exchange groups continued to push the Soviet side to include trips to Georgia as part of their itineraries. A group in Tbilisi in September 1963 visited the Park of Culture and Rest only to discover an empty pedestal where a Stalin statue once stood. They began a public demonstration, attempted to engage Georgians in conversations about Stalin, and demonstratively photographed the empty pedestal. The group congratulated passing Georgians as a "heroic nation," and Yang Tingti said: "The monument can be removed but the name of Stalin will never disappear from history."[138] A Georgian suggested they visit the Stalin museum in Gori (the town where Stalin was born), but Zong Kewen countered that Soviet organizers in the Friendship Society refused to schedule such a trip.

The Chinese assumed they had supporters among the populace and also in the Communist Party of the Soviet Union. The Friendship Society branches in China attempted to capitalize on the split within the Soviet leadership in a way already explicit by January 1959, as N. G. Sudarikov made clear to

Moscow: "In the Shanghai Friendship House and OKSD branch there are numerous brochures and photographs that feature members of the antiparty group: Molotov, Malenkov, Bulganin. Their portraits are widely distributed and sold in Shanghai bookstores."[139] The Chinese used the Friendship Society to attempt to engage Soviet citizens in dialogue about Stalin and the question of reform. "We have always felt that the mistakes of Stalin were detrimental to the Soviet Union," wrote Cheng Yunshan to S. Andreeva in February 1961, "but all the same the socialist Soviet Union underwent enormous development." Another writer suggested that the real mistakes of leadership in the Soviet Union dated from Khrushchev, who damaged China by "ending all agreed-upon scientific and technical aid."[140] A Soviet delegation in November 1961 visited a photo exhibit in Nanjing that featured Stalin-era imagery, such as photographs accompanied by material that dramatized Stalin's role in the October Revolution.[141] A Chinese group in Irkutsk in 1963 claimed that Soviet citizens were asking them things like, "Is it true that Stalin's son lives in Beijing?" and "Is it true that Molotov now lives in Beijing?"[142]

The visiting Chinese were convinced that their Friendship Society hosts were in fact the chief impediments to a meaningful encounter with the unfortunate Soviet citizens whose leaders had betrayed them. They claimed the Soviet branches had long been determined to derail meaningful exchange, such as when Friendship Society officials in Moscow in December 1960 invited Chinese students to an evening party and then demonstratively gave the available tickets to African, Indian, and Vietnamese students instead.[143] In Sochi, Mu Jiafan launched into a speech in front of a Lenin statue, claiming that peaceful coexistence was a "betrayal of the socialist camp," and in Kyiv the group persistently requested of their Soviet guides fewer excursions and more free time. At "every opportunity" the Chinese group "would continue to query Soviet citizens about whether or not they listened to Radio Beijing and whether they liked it or not." The group sought out evidence of "revisionist" practices everywhere. At a collective farm outside of Kyiv, as the Soviets complained, the Chinese spent the whole time trying to determine "whether or not the state collective farm was profitable, and convinced themselves that the workers of the state collective farm spent more time interested in their private plots than the state property." Later in the trip, at the Hermitage in Leningrad, the visitors ignored their tour guides and wandered around the museum seeking out conversation with Soviet citizens about standards of living, wage scales, agricultural problems, and the shortage of goods in shops. At another collective farm, Zhao Zhen, from the Friendship Society branch in Zhengzhou, wondered why there were "not that many workers visible on the collective farm. Probably you have everything so mechanized that workers are unnecessary."[144]

By this time it was clear to Soviet Friendship Society guides and officials that the purpose of these exchange trips was to engage the Soviet population in ideological discussion about socialism. Officials T. Skvortsov-Tokarin of the Friendship Society and Iu. Ushakov of Inturist recommended ending the exchange trips entirely, or at the very least removing Georgia from the schedule. Georgia offered the Chinese "fertile soil for their views," they complained. The Chinese visitors were "essentially uninterested in everything they saw in the USSR," they noted, "and did not say a single positive thing about what they saw here." Eventually, instead of refusing the Chinese entry, Soviet officials tried to deter them from visiting Tbilisi by fabricating various excuses about the difficulties of travel there.[145] The effort to promote positive impressions of the USSR among people of influence in China was increasingly pointless. More seriously, the trips bordered on espionage. Soviet officials warned each other to "pay attention" to Cui Yunchang, a journalist who "directly queried" Soviet people about droughts and floods in their regions, Soviet relations with Albania, "the views of our people about Tito," the "pay level of our workers, the prices of goods, and what is for sale in our stores in the USSR."[146] G. Kungurov, the Friendship Society chair from the Irkutsk branch, also argued in September 1963 for an end to the exchanges, on the grounds that the whole experience was embarrassing and even demoralizing.[147] Soviet ambassador Stepan Chervonenko, however, fearful of a potential Chinese propaganda victory, in November urged continuing the exchange. Just as the Chinese assumed sympathetic Soviets existed in the Soviet Communist Party, so the Soviets assumed "reasonable" Chinese could still be engaged in the Chinese Communist Party. Chervonenko wanted to continue the debate and provide effective Soviet responses for Chinese audiences.[148] This was a goal that his country was unable to achieve.

Conclusion

The curious fate of the Friendship Society illustrates the diverse tensions that surrounded the Sino-Soviet relationship from even before the formation of the alliance. The institution founded to educate the Chinese about the Soviet Union and the character of the bloc was gradually subverted and transformed by the Chinese. Like previous outsiders in China, the socialist bloc visitors found themselves subject to Chinese expectations and traditions, ultimately complying with them. For the Soviets there were limits to their flexibility, however, evident in the efforts of party officials and Sinologists in *Suzhong youhao* to clarify for Chinese readers key questions about the character of the bloc, the path to communism, and Soviet leadership. The journal could not withstand the different demands of Russian and Chinese readers and was disbanded along with so many other forms of Sino-Soviet exchange in 1960.

Friendship Society exchanges limped on through 1963 and 1964, as hopeful officials from both sides wondered if sympathetic and reasonable figures from the other side might come to their senses and restore the relationship. Mao's critics might prevail, and China might come to see the wisdom of the Soviet developmental model and its practices and priorities; or Khrushchev's rivals might return to prevent the lapse of the Soviet Union into a revisionist betrayal of Marxism-Leninism. Either scenario illustrated the explosive intersection of the two highly unstable political systems. Chinese Friendship Society visitors arrived with an appeal to the populace and a challenge to the leadership of the Communist Party of the Soviet Union. Chen Yuanzhi, from Heilongjiang, told his Friendship Society hosts in Moscow in the summer of 1963 that the "Chinese are grateful to the Soviet people for the help they have given them in the construction of socialism. But the greatest gift for us has been Marxism-Leninism, which was brought to China by the October Revolution."[149] The gratitude for the gift of Marxism-Leninism contained a threat, however. Faithful to the spirit of the original gift, the Chinese vowed to continue to honor and develop a tradition that apparently was no longer that important to the Soviets, even if such fidelity brought them into conflict with the Soviet Union.

The Sino-Soviet alliance, from its formation to its collapse, remained shaped by the strange and archaic language of gift-giving, loyalty, and personal and filial relationships. Hubei Communist Party first secretary Zhang Pinghua returned to the metaphor of the brotherly relationship in the family to discuss the state of affairs at a reception in October 1961. The elder brother had betrayed his responsibilities, he explained, and China was compelled to make difficult decisions to maintain the character and integrity of the family.[150] The early language of Mao himself contained a hint of this possible turn of events. For Stalin's seventieth birthday in December 1949, he reissued a speech from Stalin's sixtieth birthday in 1939 titled "Stalin: The Friend of the Chinese People." "But who are our friends?" he asked. "Several of our so-called friends refer to themselves as our friends." But they can turn out to be like Li

Lingfu, the treacherous minister who "had a tongue of gold, but a dagger for a heart."[151]

Like many other visitors to China, the Friendship Societies sponsored by VOKS found themselves gradually transformed as a result of their intersection with the culture and ways of the Middle Kingdom. By the early 1960s the Chinese were using the institution to attempt to promote dissent within the Soviet Union, with far greater experience and knowledge of the Soviet Union than the U.S. Information Agency. The Soviet Union faced simultaneous cultural challenges from both the Americans and the Chinese, directed at its domestic society and designed to subvert its claims to authority. A decade later Russia's two rivals would find common strategic ground as well.

Frustration and Betrayal

Russian Imperialism, Chinese Ambition, Central European Pragmatism

In China every factory and every bridge [is a result] of the sweat and toil of Soviet engineers.
—Soviet deputy chair of the OKSD, 2 September 1960

We helped the Chinese have a revolution, [we helped them] build their country, and gave them arms and food, and [now] we've done something wrong!
—Soviet citizen to Chinese embassy official, Moscow, summer 1963

The Marxist-Leninist tradition evolved into a politically useful vision for undeveloped, poor, and largely agrarian societies struggling to compete with far more affluent societies. Lenin himself explicitly appealed to the "peoples of the East" in this fashion.[1] The Sino-Soviet alliance, presumably a product of a mutually shared relationship to that tradition, saw its numerous claims about novelty and the future instead shaped by tensions and trends familiar to historians of the region. That region was enormous, of course, demanding an international history that includes attention even to the role of the Central Europeans. The very term "Sino-Soviet relations," an important field in international relations history, inadequately describes the dimensions and complexities of the "Great Friendship."

The relationship between the Soviets and the Chinese through the 1950s was familiar to both sides from the past. The Soviets were largely the givers of advice and instruction—to schools, factories, cities, ministries, enterprises, engineers, teachers, technicians, party members, and so on. This was a familiar and comfortable role for Russians on their Asian frontier and also historically for educated Russians in their relationship to the peasantry and lower classes. The Chinese were largely the recipients of advice, which also put them in a

208

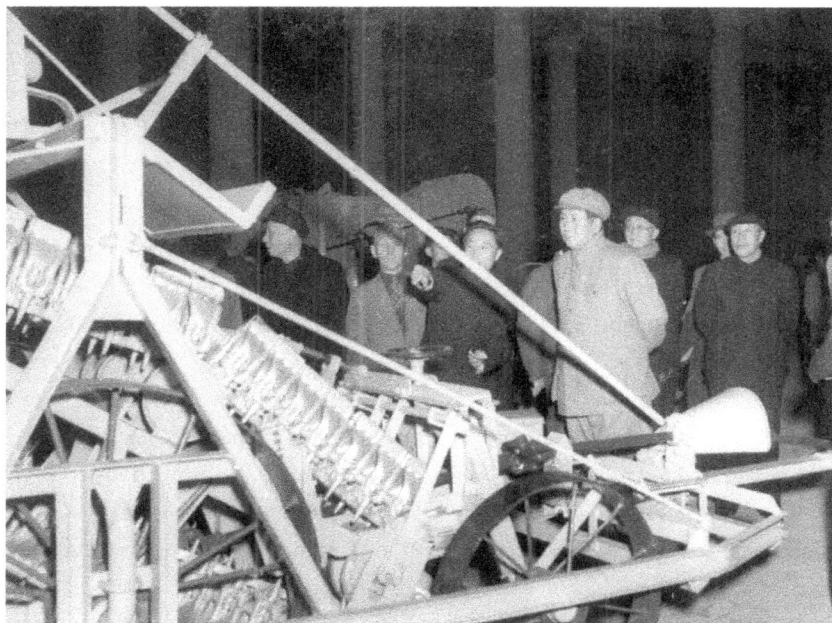

Chairman Mao, Liu Shaoqi, and other officials inspect agricultural equipment at the Soviet exhibit in Beijing, 1954. (RGAE f. 635, op. 1, d. 291, l. 80b.)

familiar position vis-à-vis more powerful and affluent foreigners. The familiar binary oppositions between tradition and modernity, between Asian backwardness and the European present, endured in the socialist world. Czechoslovak officials and advisers took it for granted that their purpose in China was to construct "modern factories," eliminate China's "technological backwardness," and raise the level of the Chinese economy to "global standards."[2] Soviet architectural advisers and urban planners were pleased to bring "the most modern" methods and technology to the reconstruction of Beijing.[3] The socialist bloc advising project followed a long history of Western instruction of the Chinese, a relationship long characterized by confidence, disappointment, and a sense of superiority.[4]

The *komandirovka* system, part of Soviet experience and in use in Eastern and Central Europe, was the key vehicle that sustained the alliance. Russians were proud to share their own advisers and experts, and help in the indigenous development of a technically trained and managerial elite throughout the bloc, "one of the concrete forms of [their] multifaceted and selfless aid."[5] Many specialists from Eastern Europe and the Soviet Union were eager to travel to China and work there. Liu Shaoqi and other Chinese leaders often pushed for more specialists and were not shy about admitting to the "low cultural level of [our] cadres" in discussions over Soviet aid.[6] The advising program itself was the very definition of "internationalism," a form of Soviet aid designed to facilitate the spread and development of socialism, especially in less fortunate countries such as China. There were countless efforts to justify and explain the overall aid program, the work of the advisers, the collaborative projects, and the practices of *komandirovka*. This was part of the general notion of socialist bloc exceptionalism, a world supposedly offering a sharp contrast to the decadent, threatening, and exploitive capitalist world beyond. The contrast was routinely explored in housing, employment, culture, leisure, trade, and even personal forms of interaction. Countless exhibits and discussions sponsored by the Friendship Society sought to clarify the meaning of the relationship and the nature and purpose of the Soviet aid programs.[7] Guo Moruo was one of many Chinese leaders who argued that the Soviet Union could be trusted as "faithful" and reliable, China's "most intimate friend," who generously shared its own resources and expected nothing in return.[8]

In numerous ways the Chinese were victimized by this hierarchical relationship and the many imperial practices that made up the socialist system of intrabloc collaboration. Like the other peoples of the bloc, they were exposed to misbehavior, inefficiency, colonial practices and attitudes, and the many other dimensions of "proletarian internationalism" that seemed neither "friendly" nor "socialist." And there were bills to pay. Chinese workers were criticized by Soviet managers and visiting advisers, who frequently complained of their incompetence and lack of preparation.[9] For the Chinese, much of this reminded them of the history of foreign privilege and imperialism. Chinese "learning" about the Soviet Union meant exposure to "great-power chauvinism" and "great-power hegemony," new terms to address an old dilemma, the problem of empire in Russian history. The promise of "internationalism" was not enough to overcome the heritage of empire. Moscow was the center of the bloc, and the Russians were supposedly its "leading people," yet another Soviet formulation extended to the broader socialist world. Intrabloc exchange and development efforts in practice were shaped by Russia's history of empire in Eurasia. Border crossing meant more often a return to the imperial community than a leap forward into a new world of "internationalism." The Chinese Northeast, in the conception of Soviet officials, was little different from the Russian Far East, both recently subject to "foreign intervention" and in need of "liberation."[10] The socialist advisers on *komandirovka* sometimes seemed more like officials on the distant eastern frontier of the nineteenth-century empire, reporting back to Moscow (rather than St. Petersburg) about potential dilemmas and outside threats that might complicate the cohesion of the political community. In both centuries, Russians enjoyed their role and demanded to be at the center of a vast transnational community whose borders would become inconsequential. Today this history continues to complicate Russian foreign policy toward its "near abroad," yet another linguistic formulation that reminds us of this complicated history.

Russia's cultural mission in the East was similarly shaped by the heritage of empire. In matters of culture as well, the Soviets considered the Chinese fortunate to be exposed to the cultural world of the bloc, marked by its ability simultaneously to cultivate and even rejuvenate the high culture of the West and promote and support the indigenous development of the cultures of the East. This was culture as *kul'turnost'*, or something to be mastered or acquired, a traditional form of achievement promoted by specialists among backward populations historically without access to this world of education and enlightenment. This was the mission of the "friendship of peoples" within the Soviet Union, which the Soviets were proud to extend to the broader socialist "camp" after the war. The Central Europeans had a prominent role to play in this cultural mission, and they too were eager to share their traditions of classical music, literature, and the arts with the Chinese. Socialist "internationalism" was by definition distinct from the imperialism of the West, which left the bloc advisers in China oblivious to historic Chinese sensitivities about this issue. Thus *The Red Poppy*, a ballet performed at the Bol'shoi Theater in the fall of 1950 and designed to celebrate the relationship, raised uncomfortable questions among Chinese in Moscow about Russia's relationship to European colonialism. A decade later bloc advisers were far more sensitive to Chinese concerns about "great-power chauvinism" and "equality," but they remained oblivious and unsympathetic to Chinese ideas about "revolution" in culture, the virtues of "village knowledge," and the limitations of expertise, "scholars," and "men of learning."[11] The advisers were still the "experts," and quite comfortable in that role. They pushed forward with the promotion of Brahms, Beethoven, and Dvořák in China and were bemused by and frustrated with the Chinese insistence that highly trained bloc musicians visit people's communes in the countryside. They never really understood the nature of the problem at hand—their response to the emerging breakup was to emphasize further and more forcefully their own achievements in cultivating the European high culture tradition. The Czechoslovak Ministry of Foreign Affairs was uninterested in Chinese criticism of their successful global marketing of the Czech

Philharmonic and instead recommended greater exposure of the Chinese to the "cultural life of the leading capitalist countries."[12] Advisers were proud to present violins as gifts to young Chinese musicians.

The strength of Marxism-Leninism as a global developmental model exacerbated this hierarchical relationship and the broader problem of empire. For the advisers, whatever served their effort to "catch up with and surpass" the West could be called "internationalism." The advisers considered the Chinese fortunate to be part of the bloc, and they were not inclined to apologize about resource exploitation, the joint companies, or their comparatively better pay rates, travel benefits, and living conditions. The socialist bloc advisers adamantly defended adviser privileges and pay and suggested that the Chinese were insufficiently grateful, callous, and even ignorant about what the absence of such educated specialists meant to the other national economies of the bloc. The criticisms of the visiting advisers by Chinese intellectuals and specialists were discounted by both the Soviet and Chinese authorities as characteristic of a prerevolutionary mentality, misguided in its admiration of American affluence and accomplishments.

Chinese enterprises and factories were incorporated into the production plans of the bloc, and Soviet ministries devised blueprints and procured orders for them as if they were within the Soviet Union. Like enterprises and factories in provincial Russia, the Chinese found themselves subject to the unwieldy and inefficient system of Soviet industry, whose distant ministries were incapable of coordinating and responding to the many demands and needs created by this vast transnational system of exchange and collaboration. Ministries in Moscow and factories in Russia seemed barely capable of opening their mail. Soviet blueprints were costly and not always up to global standards. Projects were defined by (Russian) planners in the hierarchical Soviet system, and advisers on *komandirovka* in distant China often seemed to be without a purpose or plan.[13] At times their advice seemed "devoid of content," or drawn from outdated materials.[14] Sometimes they proved to be less than ideal models of socialist virtue, or any kind of virtue. Too often they drank too much, and they seemed excessively interested in Chinese women. Intoxicated Soviet sailors committed crimes in Chinese ports.[15] Even the vast Soviet exhibits in the major cities of China reminded Chinese viewers of the distance of Soviet conditions from their own. Would the Soviet combine on display in Guangzhou, wondered Chinese agricultural specialists, be "suitable for the way we do our planting?"[16] When Chinese specialists had an opportunity to see the real thing, they were also frequently disappointed. Chinese communication officials, for example, were dismayed in 1955 to discover that Leningrad Central Telegraph "needed a major renovation."[17] Visitors in 1957 found the buildings and equipment in Moscow to be "old" and the cars "ancient."[18]

Far from being apologetic, bloc advisers and industrial officials in China were frequently frustrated with the Chinese. Chinese industrial managers, complained the Soviets, routinely disregarded the importance of qualifications, expertise, pay scales, and uniform factory standards in a given industry. Soviet advisers complained that they could not even initiate reasonable discussions on these topics, so different were the cultural assumptions about egalitarianism and the value of manual labor.[19] The Czechoslovaks and the East Germans complained about a lack of respect among their Chinese counterparts for the planning process, and the Chinese tendency to break previous commitments and alter production and trade targets. This was already happening in the "honeymoon" of the relationship, as early as 1954 and 1955.[20] By 1957, much to the chagrin of economic planners in other parts of the bloc, China was altering previously agreed-upon plans and coming to its own conclusions about priorities and the allocation of resources and advisers.[21] As Peng Zhen put it in a discussion with Soviet officials at Lüshun in October 1957, China would continue to "study the Soviet Union, but critically."[22] The Soviets did not want to hear anything about this. Collaboration created interdependence, and the bloc industrial advisers wanted to know that they could count on the Chinese to keep their end of the bargain. Soviet advisers increasingly began to depict the Chinese as ungrateful for the "selfless aid" and munificent "gift" offered by the Soviet Union. The Chinese, by contrast, continued to emphasize China's contribution to the exchange, in terms both large (space, people, strategic minerals) and small (tea, silk, handicrafts, agricultural products, foodstuffs). They blamed, and sometimes continue to blame, the Soviets for the lean years of the early 1960s.[23] These contrasting perceptions of the relationship have complicated Russian-Chinese relations to the present day.

China was inspiring to many advisers, at once exotic and intriguing, as in the past, and a potential market and source of wealth in the future. In time, however, China's agrarian and undeveloped society looked more like a liability than an asset in the effort to catch up with the Americans, especially in comparison to the more developed societies of Central Europe. The advisers as well "learned" about China. Economic managers, engineers, geologists, and industry experts were intensely interested in production techniques and knowledge in China that remained from the European colonial era.[24] They were eager to secure resources and promote forms of production that would be useful to the broader socialist world, as they did in the European portions of the bloc. As these advisers became increasingly disappointed, the Sino-Soviet alliance began to appear a relic of the Stalin era, when autarky and self-sufficiency were to be produced by a contiguous empire destined to remain separate from the West. The Treaty of Friendship, Alliance, and Mutual Assistance itself, of course, was arranged and signed by Stalin and Mao. After 1953 autarky and isolation was increasingly a vision from the past, "Europe" was more accessible, and Central Europe possessed the skills, history, and knowledge to facilitate the socialist bloc's access to that world. The participants in socialist bloc exchange traveled widely throughout the bloc, and they were coming to new conclusions about its needs in a changing international environment. Bloc advisers reevaluated the promise and potential of China. "In reality I didn't see anything in logging in the PRC that we might adopt in the Soviet Union," reported N. A. Kononov of his survey of the Chinese timber industry in 1959.[25]

The Chinese were far from blameless in this relationship, which they after all eagerly courted. The civil war and the anti-Japanese struggle left a devastated China eager for Soviet aid, and the Soviets and the Chinese found themselves in agreement on numerous challenges as they extended the boundaries of the socialist empire farther into Asia. The Chinese perceived themselves as survivors, like the Soviets, of devastating warfare and social dislocation that complicated their efforts to modernize archaic social institutions and "catch up" with the wealthy West. The shared Marxist-Leninist tradition was a highly useful developmental model. China was about to "jump from feudalism to the forefront of the international community," writes Michael Hunt.[26] Having lost some 90 percent of its railways, 50 percent of its heavy industry, and 50–70 percent of its overall economy in the Northeast, as Zhihua Shen explains, China had significant incentives to "lean to one side."[27] Chinese and Soviet state-builders were pleased to cooperate in securing their borders, educating and forming a new technical intelligentsia, and promoting everything from fossil fuel development to a new five-year plan for the transformation of the university curriculum. They shared similar values about the role of centralized planning, socialist industry, and their own leadership as a means of avoiding a return to the dislocations of capitalism and the devastation of the recent war. Their security officials collaborated on common problems (the administration of camps, purges, and the "destruction" of "hostile elements") and perceived themselves to face common challenges and enemies.[28]

The Chinese were eager to acquire and copy as quickly as possible the industrial and technological achievements of the socialist world. They were especially interested in the accomplishments of the Czechoslovaks and East Germans, who also desirably combined their technological prowess with political allegiance to bloc cohesion and solidarity. Ironically, in spite of the many Chinese declarations about the importance of "self-reliance" and indigenous development, it was the bloc advisers themselves who at times would push their Chinese colleagues to pay more attention to the establishment of a local Chinese foundation for future industrial, technological, and cultural development.[29] The Chinese, by contrast, were sometimes eager to acquire the finished product and run. This included even their approach to the ultimate "gift" to be dispensed by the Soviets: the atomic bomb and its delivery system. While critical of the lack of socialist bloc attention to the special "characteristics" of China, when push came to shove the Chinese preferred to rely on the continuing advice, skills, and resources of the visitors from the bloc. Lower-level officials especially continued to value and request Soviet expertise in numerous areas of the economy, from railways to industrial technology to defense.[30] The Soviets responded to Chinese criticism by calling their bluff in 1956, offering to reduce substantially the socialist bloc advising program. Liu Shaoqi was quick to decline this offer, however, and instead emphasized the importance of its continuation. Thus the advisers subsequently posed the question of their betrayal by the Chinese, who in their view misused the "selfless aid" of the bloc to further nationalist Chinese aims. The advisers communicated among themselves their fears about the direction of the Chinese political system after 1958, and they anticipated the dangerous trends of the following decade. The only things truly "mutual," a recurring term in public discussion (generally followed by "aid," "benefit," and "support"), were frustration and a sense of betrayal.

The alliance formed under Stalin and Mao changed significantly during the 1950s. Over the course of the decade the Chinese subverted and transformed the premises of the original relationship. Chinese "learning" from the Soviet Union was especially significant in 1956, again in ways far different from what the makers of the original relationship intended. In the wake of 1956 China's commitment to the Soviet Union and the bloc was already conditional, predicated on the bloc's ability to address the unprecedented problems of a mature socialist society in power. A March 1960 conversation between Stepan Chernonenko and Lu Dingyi illustrated the transformed nature of the alliance. When Lu Dingyi referred to the old slogan about "learning from the Soviet Union," Chernonenko took the initiative to correct him: "That sort of learning was in the past. Now we learn from each other." Lu Dingyi wondered if Chernonenko actually meant this: "You are being polite." "This is not politeness," Chernonenko responded. "The CCP has become very powerful," he said, and has "enriched [Marxist-Leninist] theory." The many industrial successes and achievements of the bloc belonged to everyone, including the Chinese: "This is our common achievement. This victory belongs to the Soviet Union, China, and the socialist camp in common."[31] This was a nod to the prospect of shared Sino-Soviet leadership of the bloc, one of the sensitive matters to emerge in 1956–57. The two figures went on to discuss tensions surrounding the advisers, hopeful that the vast program could endure at the center of the Sino-Soviet relationship. That was wishful thinking, of course, and the circumstances surrounding the withdrawal of the advisers were again shaped by the transformed relationship. Each side was convinced that it had been betrayed by the other.

The tensions during the summer of 1960 that contributed to the withdrawal of the advisers were thus predictable, as they reflected this transformation of the Sino-Soviet relationship. The Soviets accused the Chinese of betraying their privileged access to the military secrets of the alliance, and even of attempting to subvert the integrity of their own officer corps.[32] A 4 August 1960 discussion with remaining Soviet advisers featured a Chinese effort to "sow seeds of doubt regarding the withdrawal of specialists from the PRC" and turn them against the Soviet Union, Chervonenko told Chen Yi.[33] China's overtures to the advisers were in the spirit of its general effort to court the Central and Eastern Europeans through the early 1960s and, through the Friendship Society exchanges, the Soviet population itself in the wake of Khrushchev's ouster in October 1964. The Soviet leaders, the Chinese consistently believed, were hopelessly "revisionist" betrayers of the alliance as well as of their own people. From the Soviet perspective, by contrast, it was the Chinese who had misused the generosity of the advising program, and were attempting to subvert the bloc's primary tasks and goals in the new era of peaceful competition with the West. The Chinese were perceived by the Soviets as "arrogant," Qing Chenrui, a student in Moscow and former translator for advisers in China, reported to the Chinese embassy. Soviets complained that the Chinese "by nature assume they can do everything themselves."[34]

In the 1950s, the Soviet Union was not just changing but proud of its evolution. Soviet officials and the Soviet elite were eager to participate in international society in a new way and to benefit from their new status as a great power in the postwar era. They were even eager to use their position to help the PRC, which they assumed would be much appreciated. They pushed for membership status for China in the United Nations as part of their aid to the

Chinese, and as part of an effort to encourage the PRC to value such international legitimacy as well. Describing their efforts on behalf of China, the Soviets as a matter of course shared a list of international organizations to which they belonged in the fall of 1956. The list was long: the United Nations; the International Labour Organization; the United Nations Educational, Scientific, and Cultural Organization; as well as organizations focusing on medicine, railways, archives, wine, bridges, geophysics, mathematics, bicycles, gymnastics, table tennis, chess, lawn tennis, hockey, and grass hockey.[35] Such participation confirmed the new postwar great-power status of the Soviet state, an extraordinary achievement considering the position of tsarist Russia before the revolution, as officials frequently noted. By the late 1950s the Soviets had far more to lose from a radical challenge to the international system than the ambitious and frustrated Chinese. As a Moscow State University professor told his foreign exchange students from China in October 1959, "The world is going through some big changes."[36] They needed to start paying attention to new trends in international politics, he warned. The matter again lent itself to a sense of betrayal on both sides: the Chinese viewed the Soviet quest for international legitimacy as a betrayal of their efforts to unify their country and oppose "imperialism," and the Soviets wondered why the Chinese could be so callous about their effort to share a status and position they had fought hard to achieve.

The ultimate betrayal from the Chinese perspective was the Soviet turn west that compromised China's own domestic struggle against "revisionism" and its efforts to consolidate control over frontier regions supported by the Americans (Tibet and Taiwan). Khrushchev himself went to America in September 1959, a trip that revealed broader trends in the Soviet bureaucracy concerning trade and exchange with the capitalist world. The Soviets believed they could compete and win in the economic competition that was part of "peaceful coexistence," which in the meantime required "learning" from that very world. The primary agenda for the Soviet Union was improving its consumer economy, raising its standard of living, and thus competing more effectively with the capitalist world. "In this regard we can study the experience of the capitalist countries," G. M. Pushkin suggested to Chinese officials in Moscow in December 1959.[37] He had been excitedly sharing details of Khrushchev's trip to America with Liu Xiao the preceding summer.[38] The Chinese were initially eager for advice, eager to "learn" from the Soviet Union, and the Soviets proceeded to declare their interest and need to "learn" from the capitalist world. On his way home from Beijing in October 1959, Khrushchev stopped off in Vladivostok, where he addressed the needs of the local maritime economy. His mind was still in America rather than in China. Vladivostok's goal, Khrushchev told local party officials, was to make itself "more beautiful than San Francisco."[39]

Like the Soviet Union, China had evolved over the course of the decade. This was the opinion of Chinese Ministry of Foreign Affairs officials, as they summarized in April 1956 their country's growth since the revolution. The painful "Secret Speech" had been delivered just a few months before, and the Chinese were at the center of a bloc-wide debate about Stalin, Soviet leadership of the socialist "camp," intrabloc exchange, and the advising program. Officials emphasized the positive: there was much to celebrate in rising levels of Sino-Soviet trade, various forms of cultural exchange, an active and successful advising program, and numerous other dimensions of bloc collaboration. "All of this is genuinely of great significance," concluded foreign affairs officials.[40] Things needed to be summed up because the CCP was preparing itself for a new stage in the history of the alliance. With Soviet help, the Chinese had become stronger and were closer to having "stood up," as Mao famously put it in October 1949. They now looked forward to a different future with a greater degree of equality with the Soviet Union, and with greater input into the reconstruction of the advising program and their general relationship. They resented the lectures of advisers about the stages of socialist development that left backward China well behind advanced Europe. They were put off by the traditional language (the "gratis" return of the naval base at Lüshun, the "gratis" supply of blueprints) used to describe the advising program and alliance.[41]

The rebellions that summer and fall in Poland and Hungary further increased the growing confidence of the Chinese. They proved sympathetic to the Central Europeans' complaints about Soviet "interference" in their internal affairs, and the Chinese knew from their own experience the dilemmas of the "doctrinaire" or "mechanical" copying of the Soviet model. The Chinese voice raised against the problem of "great-power chauvinism" added significant weight to the complaints coming from the Central and Eastern Europeans.[42] The Chinese emerged proud and pleased with their growing role in the resolution of the "events" of 1956, and their determination to preserve bloc "unity" through their affirmation of Soviet leadership at the "head" or "center" of the bloc. The affirmation of Soviet leadership was also conditional, however, on the bloc's ability to address the deterioration of socialism that had somehow emerged from within mature socialist societies. Here was an area where the Chinese considered themselves to have special insight and experience. A "repetition of the events in Hungary" would never happen in China, Zhou Enlai assured Iudin, and to help the Soviets he recommended the greater "use of Chinese experience among the fraternal countries."[43]

Some Soviet advisers were listening. Aleksandr Stozhenko, Boris Polevoi, and others took seriously the need for more equality in the Sino-Soviet relationship, and VOKS eventually established a society in the Soviet Union for the dissemination of information about China and Chinese culture. Other advisers brought attention to the diversity of the bloc as well. Soviet visitors to the Changchun Railway hospital in Harbin were pleased to see sick workers exposed to the best of both worlds: "Western" medicine (the "leading methods of treatment") and Chinese acupuncture.[44] Officials publicly proclaimed the possibility of diverse "paths" or "roads" to socialism, which was the response of high-level officials to the concerns of the advising community that emerged from the experience of intrabloc exchange. The "Declaration" on intrabloc relations emerged, with Chinese input, as a response to the tensions of 1956. In part this was "reform," a reaction against some of the practices and weaknesses of the Stalin era and system, and a Soviet effort to be more sensitive to the concerns of Czechoslovaks, Hungarians, Poles, Chinese, and others about the limitations of the Soviet model. The purpose of "reform," however, was to improve the ability of the bloc to compete more effectively with the West. This was perceived by numerous advisers and bloc officials as more important than the criticism of Stalin and the "cult of personality." Khrushchev's denunciation of Stalin was even confusing, as the advising program itself in China was associated with the name of Stalin. "*Women shi Sidalin pailaide*," the advisers described themselves, "We have been sent by Stalin."[45] China seemed to have found a way forward for the bloc and possessed special experience in the supposed management of its own "contradictions." In the rich world of intrabloc exchange and discussion that accelerated in the wake of the trauma of 1956, CCP officials routinely emphasized their special virtues and the merits of Chinese "experience."

The full scope of China's ambition after 1956 profoundly transformed the alliance. This Chinese ambition existed from the very start of the relationship, of course. This was, after all, the "Great Friendship," or the "greatest" of all the other socialist bloc "friendships." Symbolizing this, Chairman Mao occupied the honored seat next to Stalin at his seventieth birthday party in December 1949. Bo Yibo recalled that the "entire audience rose three times" to applaud Mao's recognition of Stalin's birthday.[46] Stalin attended a reception hosted by the Chinese ambassador Wang Jiaxiang at the Beijing Hotel in Moscow, which according to security official Li Kenong illustrated the "special friendship and attention of Comrade Stalin to China and the Chinese people."[47] China usually occupied the first place in the listing of visiting communist parties to Moscow for conferences and party congresses.[48] Molotov himself declared in 1954 that the Chinese and the Soviets shared space at the "head" of the "socialist camp." The comment, as Peng Dehuai informed Iudin the following year, made an "enormous impression" on the Chinese.[49] The Chinese increasingly brought attention to the importance of "equality" and the "mutually beneficial" character of diverse forms of exchange. They had reasons to be proud of what they offered the bloc, and they challenged the traditional assumptions that left Asians as the students of Europeans. Chinese philosophy, explained Lu Dingyi to Iudin in December 1955, was "not worse than that of ancient Greece."[50]

Most advisers were not convinced, however, and the Soviet turn west had important consequences for the Central Europeans, who were eager to carve out an important role for themselves in the bloc. Poles, Hungarians, Czechoslovaks, and East Germans were central to the evolution of the Sino-Soviet relationship. Their important and lively dialogue with and relationship to the Chinese in the 1950s reminds one of the bloc's transnational character and complicates the very notion of "Soviet" foreign policy. In spite of the rhetoric, both the Soviets and the Chinese knew that in terms of technological expertise, industrial efficiency, and consumer development, the Central Europeans were far more advanced than the "leading people" of the bloc. The Central Europeans knew this too, but their position was delicate and compromise was a necessity. The Chinese and the Central Europeans had the confidence and the ability to maintain fairly autonomous relations through the 1950s and even the early 1960s. They communicated frankly with each other, evident in the fascinating intrabloc debate and exchange that covered the Soviet model, the Russians as the "leading people," the question of bloc leadership, and the relationship of the bloc to the West. The Soviet desire to participate internationally in "peaceful competition" increased for the Soviets the importance of the Central European economies. The embargo from the "capitalist states" of "so-called 'strategic goods,'" as foreign policy officials complained, increased the Soviets' need to acquire numerous defense-related, industrial, and consumer forms of technology, expertise, and equipment from their "friends" in the bloc.[51] The Soviets needed the Central Europeans, who were eager to take on this special role in the bloc. The Central Europeans confidently and routinely emphasized what their industrial and technological superiority might offer the rest of the bloc.[52]

The Soviets encouraged these developments, in part because of the pressures of the Cold War competition that increasingly directed attention to this issue. European visitors flocked to the "Praha" café at the Brussels World's Fair in 1958, a "consumer magnet for visitors."[53] This was the global stage that mattered more to the Soviets than agrarian China. Khrushchev publicly praised the "contribution of Czechoslovakia to the development of commerce between the East and the West."[54] Walter Ulbricht confidently explained to Chairman Mao in September 1956 that the GDR would overtake West German standards of living by 1960.[55] The 21st Party Congress in Moscow in January 1959, which took place as Sino-Soviet relations deteriorated, featured extended discussions about daily life, living standards, and the prospects of economic growth in the bloc. Soviet interests coincided with the aspirations of Central Europeans, who took the initiative to develop their consumer economies, raise their standards of living, and even carefully but assuredly cultivate the foundations of independent statehood within the bloc. The Czechoslovak Central Committee established a commission on the "problem of the standard of living" in 1963.[56] Mao, by contrast, as he prepared to launch the Great Leap Forward in 1958, complained to Iudin about the continuing interest of Chinese workers in the "so-called 'five good things'" (consumer goods, especially bicycles, sewing machines, watches, radios, and fountain pens).[57]

The internal transformation of the bloc had implications for international politics and foreign policy. The Soviets became engaged in emerging arms control negotiations with the West, which complicated their collaborative efforts to develop a nuclear industry in China. The Chinese had long wanted the bomb, but the Soviets had doubts about the transfer of the atomic bomb to the Chinese as early as March 1958, and on 20 June 1959 they formally abrogated the agreement on military-technological cooperation.[58] The change in policy gave the Soviets more room to pursue arms control projects with the United Nations that put them on a path toward the test ban agreements with the United States and Great Britain of 1963.[59] Early tentative moves in this direction were denounced by the Chinese.[60] Throughout the decade the Chinese pursued a different strategy toward bloc security, one that included dramatic proclamations about the ability and willingness of the Chinese people to retreat to the interior and reproduce for the longer struggle against the "imperialists." Officials high and low routinely reminded their bloc counterparts about the implications of Chinese demographic superiority and China's ability to withstand catastrophes deemed unacceptable by other peoples.[61] The Chinese viewed the new Soviet orientation as yet another example of Soviet "imperialism," and they were reminded of the history of Soviet strategic realism in the Far East that sacrificed the interests of China for the sake of larger global goals and needs.

In fact it was the initial defense arrangements that were more reminiscent of the heritage of empire in Russian history. In the early 1950s, military advisers visualized the communal defense of contiguous space in Eurasia, coupled with suspicion of what lay beyond its edges. They collaborated with the Chinese to locate defense-related industries in the Chinese interior, distant from the less defensible eastern coastline, historically the entry point for the "imperialist" powers. As Chinese industry official Tan Xilin explained to his counterparts in Prague in June 1952, a defense-related ammonium nitrate factory constructed with Czechoslovak support "will be in the interior of the country and not on the coast."[62] On another occasion the Soviets dissuaded Chinese officials in the automobile industry from constructing another car plant in Harbin, because of the "comparatively close location of both factories to the military-naval bases of the adversary."[63] A cosmopolitan city such as Hangzhou on the southeast coast was not host to a single one of the 156 projects, or even one of the 697 projected major enterprises in the First Five-Year Plan of 1953.[64] In the Khrushchev era of reform and peaceful coexistence, however, the Soviets adopted new policies toward ensuring their security that did not coincide with the consistent Chinese concern about an "imperialist" threat, above all to its efforts to consolidate control over regions such as Taiwan.

The break with China was closely related to the evolution of the bloc in numerous areas of policy and development after 1960. The Central Europeans built up their strategic forces at the expense of conventional forces, preferring quality, training, and expertise over the promises associated with Chinese demography and Eurasian space suggested by Chairman Mao. The armed forces of the Warsaw Pact underwent a military modernization program in the early 1960s.[65] The rejuvenation and strengthening of the SEV (Comecon) also took place around the time of the deterioration of the Sino-Soviet relationship, and the two processes were related. Sino-Soviet relations and the evolution of the bloc as a transnational community deserve more attention as a factor in numerous areas of Soviet history. Soviets still committed to the exchange emphasized numerous Chinese contributions to the bloc economy, but their views were ignored.[66] In industrial and technical exchange the SEV hoped for greater coordination with the Central European countries, and "with the capitalist countries as well," as officials suggested in May 1957.[67] A series of new commissions were set up to coordinate diverse forms of exchange within the bloc in 1961–62. The purpose of the reconstructed SEV was to acquaint the rest of the bloc with the "leading scientific research among member countries of the SEV," which, of course, frequently took place in Central Europe, and also the "accomplishments of global science and technology on the most important problems."[68] The Central Europeans occupied both the leading position in the bloc and the best pathway to the even more advanced West.

The Chinese model after 1958 was a challenge to the socialist bloc notion of an "alternative modernity," itself designed to rival the capitalist world. The Central Europeans recognized and feared the nature and consequences of the Chinese challenge. Chinese radicalism threatened the careful compromises delicately pursued in the wake of the Central Europeans' abandonment at Yalta. The Central Europeans successfully carved out a space for themselves as loyal bloc contributors in return for the opportunity to innovate in the economy, cultivate ties and connections to the West, take the lead in the development of "socialist consumerism," and enjoy Soviet subsidies in certain key resources. The Central and Eastern European advisers and diplomats in China in the 1950s were well aware of the sensitive nature of this special path. They were determined to avoid association with the Yugoslavs, steer clear of rebellion in 1956, and resist Mao's vision of transformation for the bloc unveiled after 1958. The Hungarians and Poles in China were especially careful after the "events" of 1956. Collaboration was a difficult compromise for Central Europeans long proud of their location in the heart of Europe. Extraordinary moments of revolution and rebellion tend to attract the attention of historians, but equally important is the history of collaboration and compromise that allows societies and alliances such as the socialist bloc to function. "Internationalism" would not include the Chinese but came to mean a Soviet-led bloc engaged with the West and offering opportunities to its most Western-oriented members. The Chinese declared "internationalism" dead and the "friendship" betrayed; the Soviets reminded them of an "imperialist power." The Central Europeans in China carefully navigated the treacherous path between Tito and Mao, and toward America.

The reconstructed bloc minus the Chinese took shape. The clarification of the vision and purpose of socialism in the early 1960s continued the polemical debate with the Chinese, an outgrowth of the Sino-Soviet split. China's presence loomed over these discussions even when never explicitly identified. Moscow's paternalistic vision of "socialist consumerism" was formally enshrined in the 1961 CPSU program.[69] The Czechoslovak exploration of the "problem of the standard of living" in 1963 drew on discussions percolating in the 1950s about incentives, living standards, the quality of consumer goods, and the development of retail trade and advertising. Central Committee member Michal Sabolčík identified these issues as crucial for the "entire socialist bloc," and other officials referred to practices and standards in places like France. This was still not to be what "bourgeois" scholars called "convergence," of course; socialist bloc exceptionalism endured. Attention would simultaneously be devoted to improving the "ideological level of people" and educating them in the "spirit of the Marxist-Leninist worldview."[70]

The East Germans stabilized their border and concentrated their efforts on improving standards of living in order to compete with their primary rival and concern, the increasingly affluent West Germans. The matter of competition with the West was long an issue, for both GDR and Soviet officials. It was crucial, explained Soviet officials in the wake of the rebellion in East Germany of June 1953, that "in a short period of time the level of well-being of the working and laboring classes of the GDR not be lower than that of these sections of the population in West Germany."[71] By 1960 this sort of discussion was again part of a running debate with the Chinese. The bloc would avoid a "thermonuclear catastrophe" and make new gains in improving "material standards of living," which had nothing to do with the "restoration of capitalism."[72] Improving the standard of living was the party's primary role and purpose, suggested a 1965 program of the Central Committee of the Sozialistische Einheitspartei Deutschlands (SED, Socialist Unity Party of Germany). The GDR would benefit from "international trends in the scientific-technical revolution" to become a bloc and even global leader in industrial automation, labor productivity, machine building, chemicals, and technology. This was not what the Chinese called "revisionism," however; the bloc still supposedly offered a contrast to the values and norms of the West. "Our party is not only an 'economic party' [Wirtschaftspartei]," the SED told itself; it also addressed broad communal needs in culture, politics, and ideology.[73]

The era of "internationalism" was over, and the socialist bloc states found it far easier to communicate with an America in search of detente than with China. Bloc officials were frustrated by the Chinese challenge in Vietnam, Algeria, Egypt, Mali, and other locations now increasingly central to the Cold War, and the memory of the "Great Friendship" was the background to the evolving struggle.[74] The Chinese reminded potential allies in the Third World of their special knowledge of colonialism, inequality, resource exploitation, cultural chauvinism, and a Soviet reconciliation with the West sure to mean the betrayal of their interests. They sent their own advisers to Vietnam and

Guinea-Conakry, among other places, advisers supposedly far more egalitarian and culturally sensitive than the socialist bloc experts in China.[75] There were lessons learned from the alliance, for both sides. We would never "mechanically transmit Chinese experience" to Vietnam, Zhou Enlai told Iudin several years before the split.[76] The Soviets, by contrast, were more comfortable setting up Friendship Society exchanges and commercial relationships with India, a rival to China and a society, of course, never enmeshed in the relationships characteristic of the bloc.[77]

By the late 1960s, the mutual frustration and betrayal felt by the former alliance partners pushed the Sino-Soviet relationship to unprecedented forms of hostility and conflict, including border conflicts, disputes over territory, arguments about history, personal insults, and the fear of foreign intervention.[78] Scholars generally explore high-level political struggle, different interpretations of ideology, conflicting national interests, and the role of personality as explanations of the Sino-Soviet split. They are especially impressed by the commanding role of Chairman Mao in Chinese domestic politics, and his willingness and ability to make foreign policy serve his domestic agenda. This study, however, has illustrated the significance of profound dilemmas at the lower levels of exchange, exacerbated by the very nature of the socialist bloc system, which made sustained collaboration unlikely over the longer term. "Friendship" meant China's incorporation into a vast system of exchange, collaboration, resource management, advising, and many other things, and the tensions endemic to the relationship were not likely to have been overcome by greater levels of cooperation and compatibility concerning other matters, or by the absence of Chairman Mao. Mao cannot be ignored, of course, but the impediments to a productive alliance were vast and cannot be reduced to the role of a single character.

A half century later, the former subordinate members of the bloc subject to Soviet "internationalism" have created far more productive places for themselves in the global economy and international system than the Russians. The Central Europeans, of course, enjoy independent statehood, membership in newly expanded political and strategic communities such as the European Union and NATO, and the benefits of economic exchanges and development enhanced by their comparatively educated and trained work force. These are extraordinary developments, of course, but not at all surprising given the history of this region within the old Soviet world. China's long road included an era of self-destructive isolationism during the tragic Cultural Revolution (supposedly threatened by both American "imperialism" and Soviet "great-power chauvinism"), which its own leaders subsequently recognized as a mistake. General Secretary Hu Yaobang explained to GDR ambassador Gerhard Schürer in 1985 that China's new policy was to learn from all the countries of the world, regardless of their social system. By the 100th birthday of the PRC in 2049, Hu Yaobang vowed, the CCP would make "our country one of the strongest and most economically developed countries in the world."[79] The consequences of China's progress along this path is the topic of constant public debate throughout the world today. China's leaders created a state-directed export economy that collaborates with international capital at the expense of disenfranchised Chinese workers.[80] This too is an extraordinary change shaped by surprising continuities: the ambitious and enduring ruling party continues to seek out a special niche for itself within the international system, at the expense of its most needy.

The contemporary Russian Federation has turned out to be the least fortunate of the successor states to the old socialist world. The home of "proletarian internationalism" and state-sponsored high culture is now a petro-state, with its new elite a product of Soviet-era privilege mixed with the suspicious circumstances surrounding the "privatization" of Russia's natural resources and other assets in the early years after the collapse of the Soviet Union. Substantially improved Russian-Chinese relations now cover the "normal" areas of modern states engaged in traditional international relations, but the most important matter for both sides is the Russian sale of oil and natural gas to the Chinese.[81] The world of socialist bloc advising and *komandirovka* is a distant memory. Who can imagine today a public campaign to "learn from the Russians" in any area of expertise or industry? The past continues to shape the present, however, as the problem of empire and the heritage of the Cold War endures in contemporary Russia. In public discussion, borderland neighbors no longer part of Russia's world (but still the "near abroad") remain especially sensitive, fragile, and dangerous regions prone to the intrusion of American special forces, Israeli weapons, and NATO designs.[82] Russian officials fear that their nation is at risk of becoming a "satellite" of the United States, with NATO determined to exercise "military-political control over the former spheres of influence of our country."[83] The era of "internationalism" is long gone, but Moscow has yet to prove capable of imagining and developing a relationship truly "mutually beneficial" for the former borderland regions of the historic Russian empire.

Abbreviations

The abbreviations of archives used throughout the notes are listed below. Archival citations identify the date; the title of the conversation, meeting, or event, if available; the compiler or participants in the conversation; and the archive. National citation traditions of course vary, but generally I follow local practices. For Russia, for example this means the numerical identification of the collection (*fond*, or f.), the inventory (*opis'*, or op.), the file (*delo*, or d.), and the page (*list* or l.). The foreign policy archive (AVPRF) in Moscow includes a folder number (*papka* or p.); the Central Committee archive (RGANI) identifies the "roller" (*rolik* or r.). In the Czech Republic generally the box (*krabice*) and the folder (*obal*) are identified. Chinese archives provide a collection number and page number. The names of the collections are identified in the bibliography. The abbreviations of the names of archives appear as they do currently in their own languages. SAPMO, for example, is the abbreviation German scholars use for Stiftung Archiv der Parteien und Massenorganisationen der DDR im Bundesarchiv. This use of original-language names is especially significant for the archives in the Russian Federation, where all the names have recently been changed. In China, the Ministry of Foreign Affairs Archive is referred to as WJBDAG, from Waijiaobu danganguan, rather than MFA or PRCMFA or the other versions currently circulating in English-language scholarship on China. The Beijing Municipal Archive (Beijing shi danganguan), however, is identified as BMA, as this is the norm among China scholars writing in English.

The date of a report listed in the notes generally refers to the day when it was composed or filed, which in many cases is the only date available. A description of a Friendship Society exchange, for example, generally refers to a trip preceding the date of the report by a few weeks or so. If the actual date of a conversation or event is available and pertinent to the discussion, this is likely to appear in the text itself. Scholars familiar with foreign affairs transcripts and the day-to-day activities of high-level leaders should not be confused by the references to reports rather than the dates of actual meetings or conversations. Chairman Mao and Soviet ambassador Pavel Iudin met on 2 May 1956, for example, while the report in the Russian Ministry of Foreign Affairs archive that describes that meeting, and the reference provided here, is dated 25 May 1956. The date of the report rather than the date of the meeting itself is necessary to future researchers in search of this transcript. My thanks to Sergey Radchenko for bringing this to my attention.

AN-II   Antonín Novotný II, Část
AVPRF   Arkhiv vneshnei politiki rossiiskoi federadtsii (Archive of Foreign Policy
         of the Russian Federation, Moscow)
BMA   Beijing shi danganguan (Beijing Municipal Archive, Beijing)

ČLR   Čínská Lidová Republika
ČSOK   Československá obchodní komora (Kancelář gen. komisaře EXPO 58)
GAPK   Gosudarstvennyi arkhiv Primorskogo kraia (State Archive of Primorsk
             Region, Vladivostok)
GARF   Gosudarstvennyi arkhiv rossiiskoi federatsii (State Archive of the Russian
             Federation, Moscow)
KSČ   Ústřední výbor komunistické strany československa
MNO   Ministerstvo národní obrany
MZV   Archiv Ministerstva zahraničních věcí České republiky (Archive of the
             Ministry of Foreign Affairs of the Czech Republic, Prague)
NA   Národní archiv (National Archive, Prague)
RGAE   Rossiiskii gosudarstvennyi arkhiv ekonomiki (Russian State Archive
             of the Economy, Moscow)
RGALI   Rossiiskii gosudarstvennyi arkhiv literatury i iskusstvo (Russian State
             Archive of Literature and Culture, Moscow)
RGANI   Rossiiskii gosudarstvennyi arkhiv noveishii istorii (Russian State Archive
             of Contemporary History, Moscow)
RGASPI   Rossiiskii gosudarstvennyi arkhiv sotsial'no-politicheskoi istorii
             (Russian State Archive of Social-Political History, Moscow)
RGIA   Rossiiskii gosudarstvennyi istoricheskii arkhiv (Russian State Historical
             Archive, St. Petersburg)
SAPMO   Stiftung Archiv der Parteien und Massenorganisationen der DDR im
             Bundesarchiv (Archive of Parties and Mass Organizations of the GDR
             in the German Federal Archive, Berlin)
TO—O   Teritoriální odbory—Obyčejne
TO—T   Teritoriální odbory—Tajné
VÚA   Vojenský ústřední archiv (Central Military Archive, Prague)
WJBDAG   Zhonghua renmin gongheguo waijiaobu danganguan (Archive of the
             Ministry of Foreign Affairs of the PRC, Beijing)

Preface

1. Deng, "Remolding Great Power Politics"; Menon, "The Limits of Chinese-Russian Partnership"; Kuchins, "Limits of the Sino-Russian Strategic Partnership"; Bellacqua, *The Future of China-Russia Relations*.

2. Mancall, *Russia and China*; Paine, *Imperial Rivals*.

Introduction

1. Boterbloem, *The Life and Times of Andrei Zhdanov*, 188; Mastny, *The Cold War and Soviet Insecurity*, 53–54; Dedijer, *The Battle Stalin Lost*, 27.

2. 5 April 1956, "Zapis' besedy," P. F. Iudin and Mao Zedong, AVPRF f. 0100, op. 49, p. 410, d. 9, l. 91.

3. October 1950, "Guanyu Youjin da gedi jiangxue wenti," Liu Shaoqi to Mao Zedong,

Zhou Enlai and Ren Qiangshi, *Jianguo yilai Liu Shaoqi wengao*, 2:405; Quan Yanchi, *Mao Zedong yu Heluxiaofu*, 3.

4. 4 January 1956, "Zapis' besedy," P. F. Iudin and Mao Zedong, AVPRF f. 0100, op. 49, p. 410, d. 9, l. 13–17; 29 December 1956, "Warum wird der Idealismus in der Propaganda zugelessen?," Pavel Iudin, SAPMO DY 30-IV 2/20/119/136-140.

5. Fedotov, *Polveka vmeste s Kitaem*, 14–15. A. Brezhnev is more sympathetic to the work of Iudin but concedes that he was "a man of his time, the epoch of Stalin." See Brezhnev, *Kitai*, 27–36.

6. Spence, *The Gate of Heavenly Peace*, 1–7.

7. Joseph W. Esherick, "Making Revolution in Twentieth-Century China," in Cheek, ed., *A Critical Introduction to Mao*, 33.

8. Chou Tse-tung, *The May Fourth Movement*.

9. Fitzgerald, *Awakening China*; Spence, *The Gate of Heavenly Peace*, 108; Taylor, *The Generalissimo*, 14–34.

10. Spence, *To Change China*.

11. 5 April 1955, "Zapis' besedy," P. F. Iudin and Zhou Enlai, AVPRF f. c100, op. 48, p. 397, d. 39, l. 50.

12. Shu Guang Zhang, *Economic Cold War*, 115–23.

13. 6 January 1953, "Zapis' besedy," Peng Zhen and A. S. Paniushkin, AVPRF f. 0100, op. 46, p. 362, d. 12, l. 17.

14. 14 September 1949, "Obzor o politicheskoi obstanovke i deiatel'nosti inostrannykh diplomaticheskikh predstavitel'stv v Nankine," P. Shibaev, ibid., op. 42, p. 285, d. 6, l. 185.

15. Plokhy, *Yalta*, 56. His study of Yalta and its consequences unfolds with consistent attention to the negotiations' imperial background and setting: the Yusupov Palace (once the playground of Prince Felix Yusupov, the spouse of a niece of the tsar and one of the assassins of Rasputin), the Livadia Palace (built by Alexander II), and the remarkable Vorontsov mansion (once home to Mikhail S. Vorontsov, the tsar's special viceroy in the Caucasus). See ibid., 36–52, 56, 61–63, 134.

16. 1 December 1946, "Politicheskii doklad o polozhenii v Kitae," AVPRF f. 0100, op. 40, p. 212, d. 11, l. 31–32; 20 December 1946, "Zapis' besedy," A. A. Petrov and Gan Haiguang, ibid., op. 40a, p. 264, d. 21, l. 8; 21 January 1946, "Zapis' besedy," A. A. Petrov and Jiang Jieshi, ibid., op. 34, p. 253, d. 20, l. 41; 13 April 1946, "Zapis' besedy," A. A. Petrov and Wang Shijie, ibid., d. 21, l. 32.

17. 30 May 1947, "Zapis' besedy," A. A. Petrov and Wang Shijie, ibid., op. 40a, p. 264, d. 21, l. 113, 132.

18. Tooze, *The Wages of Destruction*, 385–422; Mark Harrison, "The Economics of World War II: An Overview," in Harrison, *The Economics of World War II*, 36–39; Knyshevskii, *Dobycha*, 18.

19. 1947, Khideo Moriguchi, "Eksport man'chzhurskikh soevykh bobov," RGAE f. 8002, op. 3, d. 8, l. 1.

20. 3 September 1945, "Samozásobování příslušníků RA," 25.916/45, MZV TO—O 1945–59, SSSR, krabice 30, obal 26.

21. 14 June 1945, "Uvolnenie spisového materiálu," 382/45, ibid., krabice 30, obal 19.

22. Borhi, "Empire by Coercion," 64; Zauberman, *Economic Imperialism*, 17; Hacker,

Der Ostblock, 497; Spulber, "Soviet Undertakings and Soviet Mixed Companies in Eastern Europe"; Zubok, *A Failed Empire*, 69; 26 March 1958, Rau to Ulbricht, SAPMO DY 30/3726/23.

23. 12 June 1954, "Otchet o rabote sovetskikh spetsialistov-sovetnikov," I. Arkhipov, RGANI f. 5, op. 28, r. 5113, d. 187, l. 81. There is little scholarship on these enterprises. In English the term is often somewhat confusingly rendered as "joint-stock" companies.

24. 18 January 1955, "Otnosheniia mezhhdu SSSR i KNR s 1950g.," N. Fedorenko and M. Kapitsa, AVPRF f. 0100, op. 48, p. 397, d. 39, l. 6–12.

25. 2 January 1950, "Liu Shaoqi guanyu zhongsu liangguo zai xinjiang sheli jinshu he shiyou gufen gongsi wenti zhi Mao Zedong dianbao," *Zhongguo yu sulian guanxi wenxian huibian*, 86–87; Hacker, *Der Ostblock*, 501; Kraus, "Creating a Soviet 'Semi-Colony'?

26. 9 March 1950, "Shibaifu guanyu yu Mao Zedong tanhua qingkuang de baogao," *Zhongguo yu sulian guanxi wenxian huibian*, 164–65.

27. 3 April 1950, "Zapis' besedy," P. A. Shibaev and Mao Zedong, AVPRF f. 0100, op. 43, p. 302, d. 10, l. 84.

28. Li Yueran, *Zhongsu waijiao qinliji*, 103.

29. 16 March 1950, "Priem," A. A. Gromyko and Wang Jiaxiang, AVPRF f. 0100, op. 43, p. 302, d. 8, l. 44. For a translation of conversations from 1952 concerning the Soviet interest in Chinese resources, see Chen Jian et al., "Stalin's Conversations with Chinese Leaders," 10–11, 16.

30. Zauberman, *Economic Imperialism*, 28–32; Hacker, *Der Ostblock*, 429.

31. Hasegawa, *Racing the Enemy*, 300; Goncharov, Lewis, and Xue Litai, *Uncertain Partners*, 1; Zubok, *A Failed Empire*, 19–21; Gorodetsky, *Grand Delusion*, 48; Dimitrov, *Stalin's Cold War*, 44; Vykoukal, Litera, and Tejchman, *Východ*, 26–28; Jordan Baev, "Die politischen Krisen in Osteuropa in der Mitte der fünfziger Jahre und die bulgarische Staatsführung," in Heinemann and Wiggershaus, eds., *Das international Krisenjahr 1956*, 298–300.

32. Xue Xiantian, "Zhanhou dongbei wenti yu zhongsu guanxi zouxiang," and Yang Yulin, "Lun sulian chubing dongbei de lishi houke," in Xue Xiantian, ed., *Zhanhou zhongsu guanxi zouxiang (1945–1960)*, 2, 121; Pu Guoliang, *Zhongsu dalunzhan de qiyuan*, 111–21; Chen Jian, *Mao's China and the Cold War*, 28; Li Jie, "Cong jiemeng dao polie: zhongsu lunzhan de qiyuan," in Li Danhui, *Beijing yu Mosike*, 439; Shen Zhihua, *Sulian zhuanjia zai zhongguo*, 23–35; Niu Jun, *From Yan'an to the World*, 202; Shen Zhihua, *Mao, Stalin and the Korean War*, 17–21; Heinzig, *The Soviet Union and Communist China*, 51–57; Simei Qing, *From Allies to Enemies*, 71. For suggestive comments from an elderly Viacheslav Molotov about Stalin and the heritage of Russian imperial policy, mediated through a Russian journalist, see *Molotov Remembers*, 8.

33. Xue Xiantian, "Zhanhou dongbei wenti yu zhongsu guanxi zouxiang," in Li Danhui, *Beijing yu Mosike*, 5.

34. 1937, "Kraikomkhoz DVK," GAPK f. 25, op. 6, d. 9, l. 4–19.

35. 8 December 1956, "Renda daibiaotuan fangsu fanying," WJBDAG 109-01101-01, 51.

36. Beissinger, "Soviet Empire as 'Family Resemblance,'" 295.

37. Cited in Pryor, *The Communist Foreign Trade System*, 224.

38. M. S. Dzhunusov, "O sovetskoi avtonomii i perezhitkakh natsionalizma," *Istoriia SSSR*, no. 1 (January–February 1963): 13.

39. Martin, *The Affirmative Action Empire*, 452, 432, 430. See also Slezkine, "The USSR as a Communal Apartment."

40. See, for example, 1 February 1956, "Zapis' besedy," P. F. Iudin and Xu Jixing, AVPRF f. 0100, op. 49, p. 410, d. 9, l. 42–57; and 15 February 1956, "Zapis' besedy," P. F. Iudin and Liao Lu Yang, ibid., l. 60–73.

41. 23 February 1954 and 13 February 1954, "Zapis' besedy," P. F. Iudin, Liu Shaoqi, and Zhou Enlai, ibid., op. 47, p. 379, d. 7, l. 25–29, 37; Teiwes, *Politics at Mao's Court*, 35, 254–76.

42. 17 July 1955, "Zapis' besedy," P. F. Iudin and Mao Zedong, AVPRF f. 0100, op. 48, p. 393, d. 9, l. 109.

43. 25 May 1956, "Zapis' besedy," P. F. Iudin and Zhou Enlai, ibid., op. 49, p. 410, d. 9, l. 121.

44. 18 July 1949, "Doklad o vnutripoliticheskom i vneshnepoliticheskom polozhenii gomin'danovskogo Kitaia za 1948," V. Vas'kov, ibid., op. 42, p. 285, d. 6, l. 100–46.

45. Westad, *The Global Cold War*, 39.

46. Nation, *Black Earth, Red Star*, 37.

47. See 1 January 1950, "Zapis' besedy," N. V. Roshchin and Mao Zedong, 31 January 1950, "Zapis' besedy," P. A. Shibaev and Li Kenong; 31 January 1950, "Zapis' besedy," P. A. Shibaev and Zhou Enlai; 7 March 1950, "Zapis' besedy," P. A. Shibaev and Li Kenong, all AVPRF f. 0100, op. 43, p. 302, d. 10, l. 2–4, 40–69; Chen Jian et al., "Stalin's Conversations with Chinese Leaders"; and Radchenko and Wolff, "To the Summit via Proxy-Summits." See also Shen Zhihua and Li Danhui, *Zhanhou zhongsu guanxi ruogan wenti yanjiu*, 5–22; Shen Zhihua et al., *Zhongsu guanxi shigang*, 111–23; Shen Zhihua, *Mao, Stalin and the Korean War*, 88–105; Simei Qing, *From Allies to Enemies*, 113; and Westad, "Fighting for Friendship." For a translation into English of the treaty, see Goncharov, Lewis, and Xue Litai, *Uncertain Partners*, 260–61.

48. 4 July 1949, "Daibiao zhonggong zhongyang lianxi gong (bu) zhongyang Sidalin de baogao," Liu Shaoqi to Stalin, *Jianguo yilai Liu Shaoqi wengao*, 1:15.

49. 21 September 1949, "Zai zhongguo renmin zhengzhi xieshang huiyi diyi jie quanti huiyi shangde jianghua," ibid., 55.

50. 5 October 1949, "Zai zhongsu youhao xiehui zonghui chengli dahui shangde baogao," ibid., 69–70; Shi Zhe, *Zai lishi juren shenbian*, 22.

51. September–October 1950, "Doklad severno-vostochnogo otdela," GARF f. 5283, op. 18, d. 91, l. 231.

52. Guo Moruo, "Guanyu wenhua jiaoyu gongzuo de baogao," *Renmin ribao* (20 June 1950): 1.

53. On the bloc as an alternative version of modernity, see György Péteri, "The Oblique Coordinate Systems of Modern Identity," in Péteri, *Imagining the West in Eastern Europe and the Soviet Union*, 1–12; and Péteri, "The Occident Within."

54. 23 June 1950, "Anotatsiia," GARF f. 5283, op. 18, d. 19, l. 20. See also Hacker, *Der Ostblock*, 446.

55. 8 December 1959, "Zapis' besedy," S. V. Chervonenko and Deng Xiaoping, AVPRF f. 0100, op. 51, p. 435, d. 25, l. 105.

56. 6 February 1958, N. Sudarikov to N. T. Fedorenko, Iu. V. Andropov, and M. V. Zimianin, ibid., op. 45, p. 181, d. 16, l. 10.

57. "Socialist internationalism" subsequently came to define moments of military in-

tervention in places like Czechoslovakia in 1968. See Ouimet, *The Rise and Fall of the Brezhnev Doctrine in Soviet Foreign Policy*; and Dedijer, *The Battle Stalin Lost*, 90. For an official Soviet discussion of the "new type of international relations" characteristic of socialist states, see Adamishin et al., *Istoriia vneshnei politiki SSSR*, 60.

58. 5 October 1949, "Liu Shaoqi zai zhongsu youhao xiehui zonghui chengli dahui shangde baogao," *Zhongguo yu sulian guanxi wenxian huibian*, 19.

59. 31 October 1949, "Wang Jiaxiang zai Mosike chezhan yanjiang ci," ibid., 40.

60. 1 November 1949, "Geluomike guanyu yu Wang Jiaxiang tanhua qingkuang de baogao," ibid., 47.

61. Kong Hanbing, *Zouchu sulian*, 76.

62. 22 December 1949, "Liu Shaoqi jiu qing sulian zhuanjia xiuli xiao fengman shui dianzhan wenti zhi sidalin de dianbao," *Zhongguo yu sulian guanxi wenxian huibian*, 72.

63. See Westad, "Struggles for Modernity."

64. 27 November 1956, "Shi yue qu," 27; 24 December 1956, "Beijingshi renmin zhengfu daibiaotuan fangwen Mosikeshi xuexi jihua gongzuo de baogao," 53–56; 24 December 1956, "Beijingshi renmin zhengfu daibiaotuan fangwen Mosikeshi xuexi gongshui pai shui de baogao," 113–21; 1956, "Beijingshi renmin zhengfu daibiaotuan fangwen Mosikeshi xuexi jiaoyu gongzuo de baogao," 158–206; 1956, "Beijing shi renmin zhengfu daibiaotuan fangwen Mosikeshi xuexi yiliao baojian gongzuo de baogao," 208–13, all BMA 002-008-00066; Chang-tai Hung, *Mao's New World*.

65. Wettig, *Stalin and the Cold War in Europe*, 223.

66. 20 January 1965, "Polozhenie o zemliachestvakh," GARF f. 9518, op. 1, d. 69, l. 5.

67. A. Mizerov, "Sovetskaia nauka v bor'be za rastsvet nashei rodiny," *Krasnoe znamia*, no. 9 (11 January 1951): 2.

68. Arnol'dov, *Sotsializm i kul'tura*, 28.

69. Shen Zhihua, *Sulian zhuanjia zai zhongguo*, 105–9.

70. 7 November 1949, "Zapis' besedy," N. V. Roshchin and Liu Shaoqi, AVPRF f. 0100, op. 42, p. 288, d. 19, l. 39.

71. 22 February 1951, "Priem," V. A. Zorin and Burkhan; 10 January 1951, "Zapis' besedy," A. Ia. Vyshinskii and He Zhangguang, ibid., op. 44, p. 322, d. 11, l. 6, 1; 16 February 1955, "Abschrift," König and Zhou Enlai, SAPMO DY30/3603/64; 29 May 1952, "Zhonggong zhongyang wei malie xuexiao pingqing jiaoshou," *Jianguo yilai Liu Shaoqi wengao*, 4:221.

72. 16 January 1946, "Zapis' besedy," A. A. Petrov and Zhou Enlai, AVPRF f. 0100, op. 34, p. 253, d. 20, l. 7.

73. 7 November 1949, "Zapis' besedy," N. V. Roshchin and Chen Yun, ibid., op. 42, p. 288, d. 19, l. 61.

74. 14 September 1949, "Obzor o politicheskoi obstanovke v deiatel'nosti inostrannykh diplomaticheskikh predstavitel'stv v Nankine," P. Shibaev, ibid., op. 42, p. 285, d. 6, l. 186.

75. 7 November 1949, "Zapis' besedy," N. V. Roshchin and Liu Shaoqi, ibid., p. 288, d. 19, l. 39–41.

76. 14 September 1949, "Obzor o politicheskoi obstanovke v deiatel'nosti inostrannykh diplomaticheskikh predstavitel'stv v Nankine," P. Shibaev, ibid., p. 285, d. 6, l. 189; 4 November 1949, "Priem," A. A. Gromyko and Wang Xiaxiang, ibid., d. 17, l. 22; 7 November 1949, "Zapis' besedy," N. V. Roshchin and Zhang Zhizhong, ibid., d. 19, l. 79; 24 May 1951, "Zapis' besedy," N. V. Roshchin and Feng Wenbing, ibid., op. 44, p. 322, d. 13, l. 14.

77. 22 February 1951, "Priem," V. A. Zorin and Burkhan, ibid., op. 44, p. 322, d. 11, l. 6; Li Danhui (Li Dan'khuei), "Nekotorye voprosy kitaisko-sovetskikh otnoshenii v 1960-e godu," *Problemy dal'nego vostoka*, no 1 (2005): 108.

78. 10 January 1951, "Zapis' besedy," A. Ia. Vyshinskii and He Zhangguang; 5 February 1951, "Obed v chest' kitaiskoi pravitel'stvennoi komissii," A. Ia. Vyshinskii, AVPRF f. 0100, op. 44, p. 322, d. 11, l. 1, 4.

79. 21 April 1953, "Zapis' besedy," V. V. Kuznetsov and Zhu De, ibid., op. 46, p. 362, d. 12, l. 49.

80. 7 November 1949, "Zapis' besedy," N. V. Roshchin and Zhang Zhizhong, ibid., op. 42, p. 288, d. 19, l. 79.

81. February 1957, PLA to N. A. Bulganin, WJBDAG 109-00794-01, 3.

82. 4 March 1952, "Zapis' besedy," N. V. Roshchin and Guo Muruo, AVPRF f. 0100, op. 45, p. 343, d. 12, l. 15.

83. 7 November 1949, "Zapis' besedy," N. V. Roshchin and Chen Yun, ibid., op. 42, p. 288, d. 19, l. 60–61.

84. 24 July 1957, L. Kutakov to N. S. Patolichev, ibid., op. 50, p. 426, d. 29, l. 58.

85. 3 March 1954, "Zapis' besedy," P. F. Iudin and Peng Zhen, ibid., op. 47, p. 379, d. 7, l. 49.

86. 2 February 1953, "Zapis' besedy," A. S. Paniushkin and Peng Zhen, ibid., op. 46, p. 362, d. 12, l. 17.

87. Westad, *Decisive Encounters*, 266–69; Heinzig, *The Soviet Union and Communist China*, 222; Shen Zhihua, *Sulian zhuanjia zai zhongguo*, 39; He Ming, *Zhongsu guanxi zhongda shijian shushi*, 33–35.

88. Dittmer, *Sino-Soviet Normalization and Its International Implications*, 18; "Moguchii potok v nashei zhizni," *Narodnyi Kitai*, no. 1 (1 January 1957): 6; Kong Hanbing, "The Transplantation and Entrenchment of the Soviet Economic Model in China," in Bernstein and Hua-yu Li, *China Learns from the Soviet Union*, 153–66; Kong Hanbing, *Zouchu sulian*, 35–38.

89. Mirovitskaya and Semyonov, *The Soviet Union and China*, 47.

90. Dittmer, *Sino-Soviet Normalization and Its International Implications*, 19.

91. "Obzor ekonomiki KNP za 1955 god," RGANI f. 5, r. 5082, op. 28, d. 38, l. 81.

92. 12 April 1956, K. Koval to D. T. Shepilov, ibid., op. 30, d. 164, l. 96–107; 13 April 1956, "Woguo tong sulian he dongzhou renmin minzhu guojia youhao hezuo de jiben qingkuang, cunzai de wenti he jintian yijian," WJBDAG 109-00736-01, 2–7.

93. Shen Zhihua, *Sulian zhuanjia zai zhongguo*, 4; Zhihua Shen and Danhui Li, *After Leaning to One Side*, 118. See also Deborah A. Kaple, "Soviet Advisors in China in the 1950s," in Westad, *Brothers in Arms*, 120.

94. Lüthi, *The Sino-Soviet Split*; Radchenko, *Two Suns in the Heavens*; Chen Jian, *Mao's China and the Cold War*; Zhihua Shen and Yafeng Xia, "Hidden Currents during the Honeymoon"; Zhihua Shen and Danhui Li, *After Leaning to One Side*. For earlier studies, see Zagoria, *The Sino-Soviet Conflict*, viii; Chu-Yuan Cheng, *Economic Relations between Peking and Moscow*; and Ginsburgs and Pinkele, *The Sino-Soviet Territorial Dispute*.

95. Shen Zhihua, *Sulian zhuanjia zai zhongguo*; Zhihua Shen and Danhui Li, *After Leaning to One Side*; Zazerskaia, *Sovetskie spetsialisty i formirovanie voenno-promyshlennogo kompleksa Kitaia*; Westad, "Struggles for Modernity"; Stiffler, "Building Socialism at Chi-

nese People's University"; Douglas A. Stiffler, "Creating 'New China's First New-Style Regular University,' 1949–50," and Christian A. Hess, "Big Brother Is Watching: Local Sino-Soviet Relations and the Building of New Dalian, 1945–55," both in Brown and Pickowicz, *Dilemmas of Victory*, 288–308, 160–83; Izabella Goikhman, "Soviet-Chinese Academic Interactions in the 1950s: Questioning the 'Impact-Response' Approach," and Douglas Stiffler, "'Three Blows of the Shoulder Pole': Soviet Experts at Chinese People's University, 1950–1957," in Bernstein and Hua-yu Li, *China Learns from the Soviet Union*, 275–302, 303–25; Kirby, "China's Internationalization in the Early People's Republic"; Tina Mai Chen, "Internationalism and Culture Experience"; Julian Chang, "The Mechanics of State Propaganda." Without access to archives but still valuable are Kaple, *Dream of a Red Factory*; and Hua-yu Li, *Mao and the Economic Stalinization of China*. For a personal memoir shaped by the history of Sino-Soviet relations, see Sin-Lin, *Shattered Families, Broken Dreams*.

96. For a survey of the traditional interpretations, see Lüthi, *The Sino-Soviet Split*, 1–17; and Mingjiang Li, "Ideological Dilemma," 387–89.

97. See Jersild, "The Soviet State as Imperial Scavenger."

98. See Rupprecht, "Die sowjetische Gesellschaft in der Welt des Kalten Kriegs."

99. 5 January 1955, "Koncept porady," *Expo 58: Zápisy z porad*, 21. Long before the opening of the archives, scholars explored Central and Eastern Europe as a potential "bridge" between Russia and the West, and a source of exposure for the more isolated Soviet world to new forms of cultural experimentation and modernism. See Zvi Y. Gitelman, "The Diffusion of Political Innovation: From East Europe to the Soviet Union"; Leon Smolinski, "East European Influences on Soviet Economic Thought and Reforms"; Zygmunt Bauman, "East European and Soviet Social Science: A Case Study in Stimulus Diffusion"; and Deming Brown, "Czechoslovak and Polish Influences on Soviet Literature," all in Szporluk, *The Influence of East Europe and the Soviet West on the USSR*, 11–146. For a suggestion from Polish sociologists that their colleagues in the Soviet Union best come to Poland to remedy their "mistakes" and expose themselves to the "sociologists of the West," see 31 October 1961, "Zapis' besedy," F. I. Konstantinov and A. Shaff, GARF f. 9518, op. 1, d. 133, l. 195–96.

100. 20 September 1957, "Peng Dehuai buzhang jiejian bolan junshi daibiaotuan tuanzhang," WJBDAG 109-01129-09, 100.

101. New scholarship on the international history of the Cold War includes new insight into the capacity of smaller states within the bloc to influence and manipulate Soviet policy, and the transnational character to both rebellion and the official response to rebellion in 1956. See Hope Harrison, *Driving the Soviets up the Wall*; Cheng, "Sino-Cuban Relations during the Early Years of the Castro Regime"; Gaiduk, *Confronting Vietnam*; Szalontai, *Kim Il Sung in the Khrushchev Era*; Westad, *Decisive Encounters*; Granville, *The First Domino*; Granville, "Blame the Messenger?"; Shen Zhihua, "Sino–North Korean Conflict and Its Resolution during the Vietnam War"; and Westad, *The Global Cold War*. For efforts to clarify and sum up this research agenda, see I. V. Gaiduk, "K voprosu o sozdanii 'novoi istorii' kholodnoi voiny," 213–22, and "Kruglyi stol: O 'novoi istorii' kholodnoi voiny," 223–47, in Chubar'ian, *Stalinskoe desiatiletie kholodnoi voiny*; as well as Smith, "New Bottles for New Wine."

102. For early and general histories of the socialist bloc, see Brzezinski, *The Soviet Bloc*;

Hacker, *Der Ostblock*; and Fejtö, *A History of the People's Democracies*. More recently, see Vykoukal, Litera, and Tejchman, *Východ*; Volokitina et al., *Moskva i vostochnaia evropa*; and Naimark, "Post-Soviet Russian Historiography on the Emergence of the Soviet Bloc."

103. Boris Meissner, "Sowjetische Hegemonie und osteuropäische Föderation," in Ziebura, *Nationale Souveränität oder übernationale Integration?*, 74; 1 March 1961, "Ansprache . . . des Rates für Gegenseitige Wirtschaftshilfe," Walter Ulbricht, SAPMO DY 30/3405/3.

104. The Russian term for advisers is *sovetniki*, or sometimes *spetsialisty* (specialists). The English is often rendered as "experts," closer to the Chinese term, *zhuanjia*. Scholarly work on the advisers in China is growing, in part inspired by the contributions of Chinese historian Zhihua Shen. See Shen Zhihua, *Sulian zhuanjia zai zhongguo*; and Zhihua Shen and Danhui Li, *After Leaning to One Side*, 117–34. See also Zazerskaia, *Sovetskie spetsialisty i formirovanie voenno-promyshlennogo kompleksa Kitaia*. On the advisers in Eastern Europe, see Noskova, "Moskovskie sovetniki v stranakh Vostochnoi Evropy."

105. Tyrrell, "American Exceptionalism in an Age of International History." For diverse perspectives on international, transnational, and comparative history, see Cohen and O'Connor, *Comparison and History*.

106. Chen Jian, *China's Road to the Korean War*, 215; Chen Jian, *Mao's China and the Cold War*, 7. See also Christensen, *Useful Adversaries*; Mingjiang Li, *Mao's China and the Sino-Soviet Split*; and Lüthi, *The Sino-Soviet Split*, 10. The issue was well understood by a previous generation of scholars, well before any sort of archival access was possible. See MacFarquhar, *Origins of the Cultural Revolution*, 3 vols.

107. Dandan Zhu, "The Hungarian Revolution and the Origins of China's Great Leap Policies"; 11 December 1956, "Guanyu to qingnian zucheng wenti," WJBDAG 109-00762-03, 114–15; Chen Jian, "Mao's China and 1956 as a Turning Point in Cold War and Chinese History."

108. Bayly et al., "AHR Conversation," 1444.

109. David-Fox, "The Implications of Transnationalism."

110. 6 January 1957, "Dui 'Zai wuchanjieji zhuanzheng de lishi jingyan' de fanying," WJBDAG 109-01120-01, 2–5.

111. On the interconnected character of the Sino-Soviet relationship and bloc politics generally, see Zubok, "'Look What Chaos in the Beautiful Socialist Camp!,'" 155; Kramer, "The USSR Foreign Ministry's Appraisal of Sino-Soviet Relations on the Eve of the Split," 180 (n. 4); and Kramer, "The Early Post-Stalin Succession Struggle and Upheavals in East Central Europe," parts 1–3. On the "China factor" in Soviet politics, see Arbatov, *The System*, 93–94. Arbatov used the term negatively in his later memoirs to describe the dilemma for Soviet reformers of a former ally presenting a "militant Stalinist platform justifying the most nefarious and repulsive aspects of Stalin's policy as historically legitimate." For explorations of the uses of China, sometimes as a "mirror" for the discussion of domestic problems, see Lukin, *The Bear Watches the Dragon*; and Rozman, *A Mirror for Socialism*.

112. Radchenko, *Two Suns in the Heavens*, 51–56, 175. See also Wu Lengxi, *Shinian lunzhan*, 562.

113. Péteri, *Imagining the West in Eastern Europe and the Soviet Union*; Péteri, "The Oc-

cident Within"; Connelly, *Captive University*; Gorsuch and Koenker, *Turizm*; Dragomir, "The Formation of the Soviet Bloc's Council for Mutual Economic Assistance"; Mëhilli, "Defying De-Stalinization"; Kemp-Welch, "Khrushchev's 'Secret Speech' and Polish Politics"; Kircheisen, *Tauwetter ohne Frühling*; English, *Russia and the Idea of the West*, 109–11; David-Fox, *Showcasing the Great Experiment*.

114. Yang Kuisong, *Mao Zedong yu Mosike de enen yuanyuan*, 401, 416–17; Zhihua Shen and Danhui Li, *After Leaning to One Side*, 156.

115. 26 December 1957, "Meitong tongbao," WJBDAG 109-01100-02, 26–27.

116. 28 January 1956, P. Judin to CC, NA KSČ–AN-II, krabice 84, folder "Čína: Ruzné materiály, 1956–1967."

117. Bassin, *Imperial Visions*.

118. The report sent to the East Germans is 17 January 1956, W. Akschinski to P. Judin, SAPMO DY 30/3603/76.

Chapter One

1. Hessler, *A Social History of Soviet Trade*; Gregory, *Behind the Facade of Stalin's Command Economy*; Randall Stone, *Satellites and Commissars*.

2. The translation of *komandirovka* as "business trip" is misleading, as this does not communicate the level of ministerial coordination and enterprise integration that was part of the socialist world. Some of these trips lasted for as long as two years.

3. Kappeler, *La Russie*, 41, 105–28, 155–56, 213.

4. Freeze, "The *Soslovie* (Estate) Paradigm and Russian Social History"; Jane Burbank, "Thinking Like an Empire: Estate, Law, and Rights in the Early Twentieth Century," in Burbank, Von Hagen, and Remnev, *Russian Empire*.

5. 1870, "Vsepoddanneishii otchet ... po voenno-narodnomu upravleniiu za 1863–1869 gg.," RGIA f. 1268, op. 15, d. 56, l. 11.

6. Connelly, *Captive University*, 55; Al'bina Noskova, "Vozniknovenie sistemy sovetskikh sovetnikov v strankakh vostochnoi evropy (1949–1953 gg.)," in Toshkova et al., *Bolgariia v sverata na sovetskite interesi*, 39–52.

7. For example, 16 February 1945, "Telegramma," A. P. Pavlov and G. Tamaresku, from AVPRF f. 07, op. 10, p. 24, d. 335, l. 5–7; 14 April 1945, "Iz dnevnika V. A. Zorina," from AVPRF f. 0138, op. 26, p. 132, d. 8, l. 71–74; 16 July 1946, "Informatsiia," R. Slanskii, from RGANI f. 17, op. 128, d. 903, l. 36–40, all in Volokitina et al., *Vostochnaia evropa v dokumentakh rossiiskikh arkhivov*, 156, 203, 483; and Frommer, *National Cleansing*, 124. See also Abrams, *The Struggle for the Soul of the Nation*.

8. Volokitina et al., *Moskva i vostochnaia evropa*, 228.

9. Ibid., 229.

10. 16 April 1953, "Otchet o prebyvanii v SSSR delegatsii," P. Korobova and Z. Korchagina, RGANI f. 5, op. 28, r. 5098, d. 11, l. 7.

11. 24 February 1958, "Vopros mezhdunarodnogo otdela," RGANI f. 11, r. 3808, op. 1 d. 4, l. 9–14.

12. 28 October 1950, V. Grigor'ian to Stalin, RGASPI f. 82, op. 2, d. 1354, l. 113.

13. 2 January 1956, M. Khomutov to A. I. Gorchakov, GARF f. 5283, op. 17, d. 525, l. 5a.

14. 26 May 1954, Günter Simon to V. S. Semenov, RGANI f. 5, r. 5119, op. 28, d. 212, l. 16.

15. 23 October 1953, I. Vinogradov, ibid., r. 5082, op. 28, d. 40, l. 38.

16. 18 April 1955, "Zapis' besedy," V. Pisarev and Zhambaldorzh, ibid., r. 5142, op. 28, d. 310, l. 144–45.

17. 24 January 1958, "Postanovlenie"; 4 February 1958, "Postanovlenie," RGANI f. 11, r. 3808, op. 1, d. 3, l. 131–32, 165.

18. 3 November 1966, S. I. Allilueva to L. I. Brezhnev, from APRF f. 45, op. 1, d. 1562, l. 12, in Murin, *Iosif Stalin v ob'iatiiakh sem'i*, 147.

19. 18 April 1956, "Odvolání návrhu vládního usnesení o pozvání deseti vyznačnych čínských politickych pracovníku na léčení do ČSR," 011544/56, MZV TO—T 1955–59, ČLR, krabice 1, obal 4.

20. 16 January 1956, "Usnesení," 26/5/5, VÚA MNO, krabice 459.

21. 28 December 1952, "Gei Mao Zedong de xin," Liu Shaoqi to Mao Zedong, *Jianguo yilai Liu Shaoqi wengao*, 4:542; 24 April 1955, "Zapis' besedy," P. F. Iudin and Deng Tuo, AVPRF f. 0100, op. 48, p. 397, d. 39, l. 78.

22. 1 December 1954, V. Kuznetsov to M. A. Suslov, RGANI f. 5, r. 5112, op. 28, d. 185, l. 122.

23. 9 July 1955, M. S. Fedotova to N. S. Khrushchev; 15 August 1955, I. Vinogradov and I. Shcherbakov, ibid., r. 5142, op. 28, d. 307, l. 241–44.

24. 20 August 1955, I. Vinogradov, ibid., l. 240. Liu Shaoqi also had a daughter in the Soviet Union, who married a Spaniard. She too returned to China, but without her husband. See Elizabeth McGuire, "Between Revolutions: Chinese Students in Soviet Institutes, 1948–1966," in Bernstein and Hua-yu Li, *China Learns from the Soviet Union*, 363.

25. Sin-Lin, *Shattered Families, Broken Dreams*, 60; Chen Jian, *China's Road to the Korean War*, 197.

26. 14 August 1952, "Guanyu zhongguo tongzhi chu sulian zhibing," Liu Shaoqi to Yang Shangkun, *Jianguo yilai Liu Shaoqi wengao*, 4:289.

27. 12 September 1956, A. Markov to M. A. Suslov, RGANI f. 5, r. 5333, op. 14, d. 17, l. 75. Special medical treatment for important CCP leaders long predated the "Great Friendship." Jiang Jieshi flew Zhou Enlai and his wife, Deng Yingchao, on a private plane to Urumchi in 1939, where a Soviet plane took them to Moscow to treat Zhou's broken arm. Taylor, *The Generalissimo*, 167.

28. Shen Zhihua, *Sulian zhuanjia zai zhongguo*, 232–34.

29. 2 June 1953, WJBDAG 109-0055-01, 46.

30. 24 March 1954, CC CCP to CC CPSU; 2 June 1954, V. Stepanov and I. Shcherbakov to CC CPSU; 2 October 1954, "Kharakteristika," L. Uspenskii, all RGANI f. 5, op. 28, r. 5112, d. 185, l. 36–40, 110.

31. Hacker, *Der Ostblock*, 439–42, 407, 467; Adamishin et al., *Istoriia vneshnei politiki SSSR*, 51.

32. For exchanges among conservatories and musical institutes, see 20 January 1961, S. Skrebkov, RGALI f. 2077, op. 1, d. 1953, l. 8–9; among newspapers, journals, and filmmakers, see 12 December 1953, D. T. Shepilov, RGANI f. 5, op. 28, d. 38, l. 67; and 4 July 1958, A. Kuznetsov to I. I. Shcheglov, RGALI f. 2936, op. 1, d. 1245, l. 4; in higher education, see Stiffler, "Building Socialism at Chinese People's University"; Shen Zhihua,

Sulian zhuanjia zai zhongguo, 111–12; Zazerskaia, *Sovetskie spetsialisty i formirovanie voenno-promyshlennogo kompleksa Kitaia*, 67–73; and Dittmer, *Sino-Soviet Normalization and Its International Implications*, 21.

33. 20 December 1948, "Stav a doplnění statně bezpečnostní služby," Jíndřich Veselý, 34/1–34/3, in Dvořáková, *Státní bezpečnost v letech*.

34. 5 January 1953, A. Romanov, RGANI f. 5, op. 14, r. 5331, d. 7, l. 93.

35. 2 June 1955, B. Khomiakov, RGAE f. 9493, op. 1, d. 210, l. 18.

36. 2 June 1951, "Kontrakt no. 00602," ibid., d. 186, l. 19; also 1952, "Kontrakt no. 00995"; June 1951, "Kontrakt no. 00614"; 21 January 1953, "Kontrakt no. 081700," ibid., d. 183, l. 72, 46, 26–27.

37. 19 June 1953, "Kontrakt no. 111937," ibid., d. 439, l. 9.

38. 16 July 1955, Zhang Wentian, ibid., op. 13, d. 2537, l. 21–22; 27 March 1950, "Soglashenie," A. Vyshinskii and Wang Jiaxiang, GARF f. 9396, op. 19, d. 4, l. 1–3; 2 March 1950, "Priem," A. A. Gromyko and Wang Jiaxiang, AVPRF f. 0100, op. 43, p. 302, d. 8, l. 52.

39. 19 April 1950, "Kontrakt," RGAE f. 8123, op. 3, d. 1137, l. 234–36; 20 March 1958, E. Levin, ibid., op. 13, d. 2728, l. 200.

40. He Ming, *Zhongsu guanxi zhongda shijian shushi*, 36.

41. Shen Zhihua, *Sulian zhuanjia zai zhongguo*, 84–86.

42. 9 February 1950, "Zapis' besedy," A. Gromyko and General Liu Yaolou, AVPRF f. 0100, op. 43, p. 302, d. 8, l. 10–12.

43. Shen Zhihua, *Sulian zhuanjia zai zhongguo*, 83.

44. 5 October 1949, "Liu Shaoqi zai zhongsu youhao xiehui zonghui chengli dahui shangde baogao," *Zhongguo yu sulian guanxi wenxian huibian*, 18.

45. 19 July 1961, S. Stepanenko to K. N. Rudnev, RGAE f. 9493, op. 1 d. 383, l. 21.

46. 3 March 1950, "Priem," A. A. Gromyko and Wang Jiaxiang, AVPRF f. 0100, op. 43, p. 302, d. 8, l. 32.

47. 11 July 1956, Soviet Ministry of Finance, WJBDAG 109-00983-01, 3; 7 April 1952, Soviet embassy to PRC MFA, WJBDAG 109-00562-01, 43.

48. 1952, "Smeta," RGAE f. 8848, op. 19, d. 7, l. 2; see also McGuire, "Between Revolutions," in Bernstein and Hua-yu Li, *China Learns from the Soviet Union*, 364.

49. 22 September 1952, "Smeta," RGAE f. 8848, op. 19, d. 7, l. 4.

50. 19 January 1956, N. Emel'ianov to M. Zemskov, ibid.

51. 9 February 1957, "Kontrakt no. 2248," ibid., op. 13, d. 2624, l. 261.

52. 17 February 1955, S. Kalugin to M. G. Zemskov; 11 March 1955, M. Zemskov to A. A. Dobriakov; 5 January 1957, Gerasimov, all RGAE f. 8848, op. 19, d. 12, l. 106, 109, 199.

53. 23 May 1956, Kurpel to M. G. Zemskov, ibid., 189.

54. 29 March 1957, "Sovetsko-kitaiskoe otnosheniia," I. Kurdiukov, AVPRF f. 0100, op. 50, p. 426, d. 29, l. 33.

55. Shen Zhihua, *Sulian zhuanjia zai zhongguo*, 81–83.

56. Zazerskaia, *Sovetskie spetsialisty i formirovanie voenno-promyshlennogo kompleksa Kitaia*, 49.

57. Stiffler, "Building Socialism at Chinese People's University," 232–33.

58. Shen Zhihua, *Sulian zhuanjia zai zhongguo*, 91.

59. 8 April 1958, J. Kožešník to Pei Lisheng, 020.806/58, MZV, TO—T 1955–59, ČLR, krabice 2, obal 5.

60. 1958, "Soglashenie," RGANI f. 11, op. 1, r. 3808, d. 1, l. 70.

61. 23 March 1958, "Guanyu sulian he dong'ou renmin minzhu guojia zhuanjia zai woguo jingnei chuchai fei biaozhun i. zhifu banfa de tongzhi," BMA 017-001-00659, 26.

62. 1 June 1957, I. Vinogradov, V. Kirillin, B. Riurikov, V. Zolotukhin, RGANI f. 5, op. 28, r. 5200, d. 506, l. 103.

63. Shen Zhihua, *Sulian zhuanjia zai zhongguo*, 219.

64. 30 July 1959, F. Kleimenov to G. V. Aleksenko, RGAE f. 9493, op. 1, d. 1003, l. 55.

65. Westad, *Restless Empire*, 305. For an early effort to identify comparative advantages in the trade of diverse products, see Mah, "The Terms of Sino-Soviet Trade."

66. 1 July 1955, P. Dem'ianenko to A. N. Lavrishchev, ibid., d. 210, l. 63.

67. Shen Zhihua, *Sulian zhuanjia zai zhongguo*, 118–30.

68. Riabchenko, *KNR-SSSR*, 21.

69. 1954, "Spravka," I. Shiriaev, RGANI f. 5, op. 28, r. 5113, d. 187, l. 211–29.

70. 1956, Aleksei V. Stozhenko to Andrei M. Chekashillo, RGANI f. 5, op. 28, r. 5200, d. 506, l. 94–95.

71. Ibid.

72. Ibid., l. 96–97.

73. 26 November 1956, B. Polevoi, ibid., l. 91.

74. Werth, *Russia under Khrushchev*, 235.

75. B. Galanov, "Boris Polevoi i ego geroi," in Polevoi, *Izbrannye proizvedeniia v dvukh tomakh*, 1:5. For a translation of *Povest' o nastoiashchem cheloveke*, see Polevoi, *A Story about a Real Man*.

76. Werth, *Russia under Khrushchev*, 239.

77. June 1957, Ivan M. Korotin to P. V. Nikitin, RGAE f. 9493, op. 1, d. 20, l. 14, 7.

78. 26 November 1956, B. Polevoi, RGANI f. 5, op. 28, r. 5200, l. 92–93.

79. October 1954, "Sulian zhuanjia Andeluoanfu tongzhi zai beshi diyi fu xiao deng sange xiaoxue de tanhua jilu," BMA 153-004-2166, 12.

80. Shen Zhihua, *Sulian zhuanjia zai zhongguo*, 262.

81. Ibid., 305.

82. 6 December 1956, Peng Zhen, "Fangsu qingkuang huibao," WJBDAG 109-01101-01, 47.

83. November 1956, N. Smeliakov RGAE f. 8123, op. 3, d. 1198, l. 230. See also 1956, F. T. Shtan' to Bulgakov, ibid., l. 214.

84. 5 February 1951, Colonel Shadrov to Nosov, RGANI f. 5, op. 14, r. 6184, d. 3, l. 30–33.

85. June 1952, S. R. Savchenko to L. P. Beria, ibid., r. 5331, d. 6, l. 118–20.

86. 12 January 1953, "Spravka," A. Luk'ianov, ibid., r. 5333, d. 15, l. 8–12.

87. 4 December 1956, P. G. Zhecheria, I. M. Akimov, and N. G. Peregudov, RGAE f. 8123, op. 3, d. 1198, l. 113–16.

88. For such an event in North Korea, see 1955, E. V. Viktorov, ibid., d. 1163, l. 31–32.

89. 5 February 1951, Colonel Shadrov to Nosov, RGANI f. 5, op. 14, r. 6181, d. 3, l. 33. On TASS officials in Austria, see 23 March 1950, "Doklad," Petr S. Raznikov, ibid., d. 2, l. 45. Andrei Lankov reports a joke from among the Soviets in North Korea in the 1950s: "Chicken is not a bird, Pyongyang is not abroad." Lankov, *Crisis in North Korea*, 21.

90. 18 August 1957, "Kratkaia zapis' besedy s Genkonsulom Pol'shi v Shankhae Berlatskom," NA KSČ–AN-II, krabice 84, folder "Čína: Ruzné materiály, 1956–1967."

91. 1960, "Spravka o sostoianii raboty s kadrami," Rusalenko, GAPK f. P-68, op. 30, d. 359, l. 65.

92. 31 October 1960, "Spravka," Rusalenko, ibid., l. 72–77.

93. 1 December 1949, "Zapis' besedy," N. V. Roshchin and Li Kenong, AVPRF f. 0100, op. 42, p. 288, d. 19, l. 100.

94. 5 February 1951, Colonel Shadrov to Sedliarevich, RGANI f. 5, op. 14, r. 5330, d. 3, l. 34–35.

95. 8 July 1954, "Otchet o rabote sovetskikh spetsialistov-sovetnikov," ibid., op. 28, r. 5113, d. 187, l. 94.

96. 5 February 1951, Colonel Shadrov to Sedliarevich, ibid., op. 14, r. 5330, d. 3, l. 36.

97. 26 January 1951, Colonel Rogov, ibid., op. 14, r. 5330, d. 3, l. 38–39.

98. 1953, "Godovoi otchet," ibid., r. 5331, d. 6, l. 141.

99. 11 February 1951, "Ob'iasnitel'naia zapiska," ibid., r. 5330, d. 3, l. 67.

100. Shen Zhihua, *Sulian zhuanjia zai zhongguo*, 219–36. For a discussion of alcoholism in the Central Committee's International Department in the 1970s from a former Soviet diplomat, see Brutents, *Tridtsat' let na staroi ploshchadi*, 33–34.

101. 1 December 1954, P. Zamogil'naia to V. F. Garbuzov, RGAE f. 8115, op. 3, d. 985, l. 24; 23 April 1954, V. Zaitsev to A. I. Kostousov, ibid., l. 54; 9 June 1956, "Akt," RGAE f. 8123, op. 3, d. 1191, l. 57.

102. Filatov, *Ekonomicheskaia otsenka nauchno-tekhnicheskoi pomoshchi sovetskogo soiuza kitaiu*, 110, 54. See also Mirovitskaia and Semyonov, *The Soviet Union and China*, 50. A 1959 report from RGAE lists 8,985 blueprint packages sent from the Soviet Union to China from 1954 to 1959, including 1,169 for construction, 3,704 for equipment and machinery, 1,018 for diverse technological processes, and 3,094 other miscellaneous blueprints. The Chinese sent on to the Soviet Union, according to this report, 587 blueprint packages. 31 October 1959, N. Siluianov and F. Kleimenov, RGAE f. 9493, op. 1, d. 1003, l. 5.

103. 1959, F. Kleimenov to A. S. Kakunin, RGAE f. 3527, op. 13, d. 2782, l. 175.

104. 1962, "Spravka," F. Kleimenov, RGAE f. 9493, op. 5, d. 60, l. 55–56.

105. 21 January 1959, N. Siluianov and G. Maliavin to A. I. Shakhurin, ibid., op. 1, d. 1003, l. 23.

106. 25 January 1962, S. Stepanenko, ibid., op. 5, d. 60, l. 14–15.

107. I. Dudinskii, "Nekotorye cherty razvitiia mirovogo sotsialisticheskogo rynka," *Voprosy ekonomiki*, no. 2 (February 1961): 45.

108. Kang Chao and Feng-hwa Mah, "A Study of the Rouble-Yuan Exchange Rate," 193.

109. 1962, "Spravka," F. Kleimenov, RGAE f. 9493, op. 5, d. 60, l. 59.

110. 1963, "Otchet," ibid., d. 61, l. 15–16.

111. Lüthi, *The Sino-Soviet Split*, 178.

112. 20 January 1960, "Záznam," Štětina, 022.189/60, NA KSČ–AN-II, krabice 84, folder "Čína: Ruzné materiály, 1956–1967."

113. 7 March 1963, "Spravka," S. Stepanenko, RGAE f. 9493, op. 5, d. 61, l. 30.

114. 1960, "Perechen'," RGAE f. 9493, op. 5, d. 59, l. 55–82; 1962, "Perechen'"; 23 January 1962, "Vypolnenie"; 14 February 1962, "Spravka," all ibid., d. 60, l. 1–3, 16–17.

115. 28 January 1964, V. Orlov, ibid., d. 62, l. 1–3.

116. 17 February 1954, "Informatsiia o prebyvanii v Kitae gruppy sovetskikh profsoiuznykh rabotnikov," V. Berezin, RGANI f. 5, op. 28, r. 7960, d. 255, l. 4–14.

117. 1952, V. Khoroshev to P. S. Bulgakov, RGAE f. 8123, op. 3, d. 1137, l. 177.

118. Nepomniashchii, *Druzhba, kotoroi vechno zhit'*, 6–23.

119. Hessler, *A Social History of Soviet Trade*.

120. Paul R. Gregory, "The Dictator's Orders," in Gregory, *Behind the Facade of Stalin's Command Economy*, 11–33.

121. Evgenia Belova, "Economic Crime and Punishment," in Gregory, *Behind the Facade of Stalin's Command Economy*, 136.

122. 13 December 1950, I. Sharshakov to P. R. Stepanov, RGAE f. 8123, op. 3, d. 1132, l. 91.

123. 19 April 1950, "Kontrakt," ibid., d. 1137, l. 234.

124. 1956, "Doklad," ibid., d. 1182, l. 39.

125. 2 September 1956, "Otchet," Cheng Gongzheng and Liu Dingzhu, ibid., d. 1181, l. 6.

126. Ibid., l. 3–5.

127. 1956, "Prilozhenie no. 3," Sun Huafeng and Dian Guochen, ibid., d. 1182, l. 76–77.

128. September 1956, "Finansovyi doklad," ibid., d. 1181, l. 83.

129. 15 January 1955, "Doklad . . . o poezdke v KNR," O. Bulgakov and Ignatov, ibid., d. 1167, l. 1–12.

130. 20 April 1956, "Tekhnicheskii otchet," B. Gusev, ibid., d. 1163, l. 49.

131. 19 October 1955, "Dopolnenie," Pavlov and Ding Yi; 28 April 1953, "Dopolnenie No. 1, kontrakt 04024," ibid., d. 1137, l. 58–117, 156–58.

132. September 1956, "Otchet," ibid., d. 1181, l. 113; 12 June 1954, "Otchet o rabote sovetskikh spetsialistov-sovetnikov," I. Arkhipov, RGANI f. 5, op. 28, r. 5113, d. 187, l. 80.

133. September 1956, "Otchet," RGAE f. 8123, op. 3, d. 1181, l. 91–93. The high accident and death rate in Chinese industry came to the attention of the Chinese Labor Union Federation and their Soviet experts. From May 1950 to late 1952, 332,080 people were involved in industrial accidents, resulting in 9,009 deaths and leaving 22,065 severely wounded. The first quarter of 1953 saw another 60,406 injuries, including 718 deaths and 1,294 severely injured. See 17 February 1954, "Informatsiia o prebyvanii v Kitae gruppy sovetskikh profsoiuznykh rabotnikov," V. Berezin, RGANI f. 5, op. 28, r. 7960, d. 255, l. 19–24.

134. 2 September 1956, "Otchet," Cheng Gongzheng and Liu Dingzhu, RGAE f. 8123, op. 3, d. 1181, l. 6.

135. September 1956, "Otchet," ibid., l. 117–18.

136. 2 September 1956, "Otchet," Cheng Gongzheng and Liu Dingzhu, ibid., l. 4.

137. 1955, "Opisanie k plany komandirovki praktikantov v SSSR," RGAE f. 8115, op. 3, d. 1008, l. 38–39.

138. 1954, "Svedeniia o plane," ibid. d. 980, l. 6.

139. 21 August 1954, I. Gusev; August 1954, I. Gusev, ibid., l. 39, 47; 1954, A. Boiko, ibid., d. 994, l. 5–7.

140. 1954, "Kratkie svedeniia," ibid., d. 980, l. 23–31.

141. Zazerskaia, *Sovetskie spetsialisty i formirovanie voenno-promyshlennogo kompleksa Kitaia*, 49.

142. 11 January 1955, "Zapis' besedy," I. P. Gusev and Zhao Bing, RGAE f. 8115, op. 3, d. 1003, l. 14–15.

143. October 1954, "Sulian zhuanjia Andeluoanfu tongzhi zai beshi diyi fu xiao deng sange xiaoxue de tanhua jilu," BMA 153-004-2166, 5.

144. Charles Armstrong, "'Fraternal Socialism.'"

145. 12 January 1955, "Zapis' besedy," K. V. Vlasov, I. P. Gusev, Liu Fang, Zhao Bing, RGAE f. 8115, op. 3, d. 1003, l. 13.

146. 11 January 1955, "Zapis' besedy," I. P. Gusev and Zhao Bing, ibid., l. 15.

147. 8 July 1955, "Zapis' besedy," Xu Ze and I. P. Gusev, ibid., l. 3.

148. 16 February 1955, "Abschrift," König and Zhou Enlai, SAPMO DY 30/3603/65.

149. Jersild, "The Great Betrayal."

Chapter Two

1. I. Dudinskii, "Uspekhi sotsialisticheskoi industrializatsii evropeiskikh stran narodnoi demokratii," Bol'shevik, no. 19 (October 1950): 44.

2. 26 September 1954, "Mao zhuxi jiejian xiongyali zhengfu daibiaotuan tanhua jilu," WJBDAG 204-00005-23, 119.

3. 20 September 1957, "Peng Dehuai buzhang jiejian bolan junshi daibiaotuan tuanzhang," WJBDAG 109-01129-09, 100.

4. 31 July 1957, "Jiekesiluofake dui waimao jiben qingkuang," WJBDAG 109-01124-02, 25.

5. 21 March 1957, "Zhongjie lianhe gongbao," WJBDAG 204-00242-02, 16; 29 January 1957, "Zhude shiguan 1956 nian gongzuo zongjie baogao," WJBDAG 109-00755-01, 2–3.

6. 3 October 1957, "Mao zhuxi jiejian bolan junshi daibiaotuan tanhua jilu," WJBDAG 109-01129-07, 73.

7. June 1957, Ivan M. Korotin to P. V. Nikitin, RGAE f. 9493, op. 1, d. 20, l. 3–13.

8. Kaplan, Československo v RVHP, 63.

9. 20 September 1954, "Otchet," A. Fedorov, RGANI f. 5, op. 28, r. 5108, d. 158, l. 24, 21.

10. 22 December 1955, S. Lopin, ibid., r. 5136, d. 286, l. 73–74.

11. 17 February 1950, "Odjezd obchodní delegace," 182/50, MZV TO—O 1945–59, Čína, krabice 14, obal 3.

12. 21 June 1949; 16 July 1949, "Zapis' besedy," A. A. Gromyko and B. Laštovička, RGASPI f. 82, op. 2, d. 1358, l. 10, 73; 4 July 1949, "Zhongyang guanyu tongyi jieyi qiye gongsi," Zhou Enlai to Liu Shaoqi, Gao Gang, Wang Jiaxiang, Jianguo yilai Zhou Enlai wengao, 62.

13. 1 October 1949, "Priem," A. A. Gromyko and E. Štefan, AVPRF f. 0100, op. 42, p. 288, d. 17, l. 18; 1 October 1949, "Iz dnevnika A. A. Gromyko," RGASPI f. 82, op. 2, d. 1358, l. 85–86.

14. 5 October 1949, WJBDAG 109-00009-01, 1.

15. 16 August 1950, "Vneshniaia politika tsentral'nogo narodnogo pravitel'stva KNR," A. Malukhin, AVPRF f. 0100, op. 43, p. 312, d. 126, l. 94.

16. 21 September 1950, "Zapis' besedy," N. V. Roshchin and Burdinyi, ibid., p. 302, d. 10, l. 150; "Kenixi xiang Mao zhuxi chengdi guoshu," Renmin ribao (25 June 1950): 1; Lian Zhengbao et al., Jiemi waijiao wenxian, 57–70, 111.

17. 22 December 1949, "Mao Zedong jin zhunbei dui su maoyi tiaoyue wenti zhi zhonggong zhongyang de dianbao," Zhongguo yu sulian guanxi wenxian huibian, 71.

18. 24 January 1950, "Záznam," 103.309/50, MZV TO—O 1945–59, Čína, krabice 14, obal 3.

19. 3 February 1959, "Postup jednání s ČLR o dlouhodobé hospodářské spolupráci," O. Šimůnek, 030.106/59, NA KSČ–AN-II, krabice 85, folder "Čína," 1959–61; 20 June 1959, "Problematika rozvoje hospodářských styků s ČLR v letech, 1961–65," 0.12.574/59, MZV TO—T 1955–59, ČLR, krabice 3, obal 6.

20. 25 May 195, "Řadná pololetní hospodářská zpráva," Jan Bušniak, 023.844/59, MZV TO—T 1955–59, Čína, krabice 7, obal 1; 21 April 1953, "Zapis' besedy," V. V. Kuznetsov and F. Komzal, AVPRF f. 0100, op. 46, p. 362, d. 12, l. 42.

21. 21 April 1953, "Zapis' besedy," V. V. Kuznetsov and E. Shafranko; 21 April 1953, "Zapis' besedy," V. V. Kuznetsov and Ia. K. Petkov; 21 April 1953, "Zapis' besedy," V. V. Kuznetsov and I. König, all AVPRF f. 0100, op. 46, p. 362, d. 12, l. 39–44; Jeschonnek, "Freundschaft und Zusammenarbeit mit China—einzig mögliche Politik für ganz Deutschland," 374–78.

22. Skřivan, "Vývoj československého vývozu do číny po druhé světové válce (1945–1959)," 267–74.

23. 16 February 1954, V. I. Loskutov, RGAE f. 8115, op. 3, d. 993, l. 76; 1954, V. I. Loskutov, l. 77.

24. 17 September 1951, "Zadanie," RGAE f. 9493, op. 1, d. 183, l. 9.

25. 18 May 1960, "Otchet," M. I. Birinberg, ibid., d. 717, l. 225.

26. 22 December 1959, "Otchet," V. V. Gushchinn, ibid., d. 717, l. 62.

27. 10 September 1956, "Stenograma," ibid., op. 13, d. 2577, l. 196.

28. 29 April 1960, P. Lysov to K. D. Petukhov; 2 September 1959, D. V. Zheltukhin, ibid., op. 1, d. 1103, l. 49, 63.

29. 19 January 1961, S. F. Laptev to Pronin, ibid., op. 5, d. 66, l. 3–4.

30. 1960, "Chto zhelatel'no poluchi·' iz KNR," ibid., op. 1, d. 1103, l. 65.

31. 5 June 1959, "O peredache," P. Ia Kartashevskii, ibid., l. 67.

32. 22 April 1961, "Tekhnicheskoe obosnovanie," M. Grechin and N. Tarasov, ibid., op. 5, d. 66, l. 27.

33. 19 February 1952, "Poznámky k celkovej činnosti generálneho konzulázu v Šanhaj," 106.09/52; 6 June 1953, 128.883/53, MZV TO—T 1945–55, ČLR, krabice 1, obal 2.

34. 30 May 1955, BMA 125-001-01207, 6.

35. 22 August 1953, "Zhongyang guanyu jiaqiang yu sulian zhuanjia hezuo wenti de zhishi," *Jianguo yilai Liu Shaoqi wengao*, 5:261.

36. 9 November 1953, "Zapis' besedy," V. V. Kuznetsov and Zhao Erlu, AVPRF f. 0100, op. 46, p. 362, d. 12, l. 154; see also 24 March 1953, "Zapis' besedy," A. S. Paniushkin and Gao Gang, ibid., l. 30.

37. 10 September 1956, "Stenograma," RGAE f. 3527, op. 13, d. 2577, l. 191–96.

38. 14 March 1957, M. Mikhailov, ibid., d. 2624, l. 182.

39. 10 May 1957, A. S. Smirnov to D. D. Erigin, ibid., l. 104–5.

40. 20 September 1954, "Dopolnenie k otchetu," A. Fedorov, RGANI f. 5, op. 28, r. 5108, d. 158, l. 33.

41. 14 July 1955, S. Perevertkin, GARF f. 9401, op. 2, d. 465, l. 216.

42. 18 April 1950, M. Pantsev to T. E. Kugler, RGAE f. 9493, op. 1, d. 183, l. 19; 11 May 1956, G. Petrov to A. N. Lavrishchev ibid., d. 212, l. 15; 9 March 1956, K. Vinogradov to A. N. Lavrishchev, ibid., l. 50.

43. 21 August 1950, "Kontrakt no. 00029," ibid., op. 3, d. 1112, l. 89–90.

44. 2 April 1956, P. Sokolov to A. N. Lavrishchev, l 23; 9 March 1956, V. Maiborotsa to V. I. Zaitsev, l. 72; 22 March 1956, S. Evstafeev to N. I. Egorov, l. 126; 24 May 1956, P. Fokin to A. N. Lavrishchev, l. 39, all RGAE f. 9493, op. 1, d. 212.

45. 8 March 1956, A. Panin to V. I. Zaitsev, ibid., l. 82.

46. 3 September 1955, "O nekotorykh nedostatkakh," S. Rumiantsev, RGANI f. 5, op. 28, r. 5136, d. 286, l. 174–82.

47. 17 May 1952, K. Meshkan to Bulgakov, RGAE f. 8123, op. 3, d. 1134, l. 6–10.

48. 1952, "Plan seminarskogo zaniatiia," ibid., l. 116–18.

49. 16 February 1956, F. Novák to Zakharov, RGAE f. 9493, op. 1, d. 212, l. 3.

50. 29 July 1956, WJBDAG 109-00984-10, 39.

51. 30 June 1955, S. G. Kraelov, RGAE f. 3527, op. 13, d. 2537, l. 10–11.

52. 14 November 1955, "Otchet o poezdke sovetskoi molodezhi v KNR," RGANI f. 5, op. 28, r. 5142, d. 308, l. 126.

53. 12 April 1957, A. P. Sorenzon to I. F. Kurdiukov, RGAE f. 3527, op. 13, d. 2624, l. 88.

54. 6 April 1956, "N," RGAE f. 8115, op. 3, d. 1024, l. 86.

55. 1955, F. Pogrebenko to N. A. Smelov, RGAE f. 8123, op. 3, d. 1158, l. 36.

56. 21 January 1956, P. Parshin to A. N. Lavrishchev, ibid., d. 1191, l. 3.

57. 6 December 1956, Tan Wai to P. S. Bulgakov, ibid., d. 1192, l. 26–27.

58. 1 March 1958, Akulenok to Ling Xueqing, RGAE f. 3527, op. 13, d. 2729, l. 6.

59. 19 January 1954, Ding Dang, RGAE f. 8115, op. 3, d. 984, l. 126.

60. 14 June 1955, Udarov to P. I. Parshin, RGAE f. 8123, op. 3, d. 1170, l. 100.

61. Brus, "1957 to 1965," 102–9.

62. 27 September 1955, Iu. S. Muntian, RGAE f. 8123, op. 3, d. 1198, l. 48.

63. 10 September 1956, "Stenogramma," RGAE f. 3527, op. 13, d. 2577, l. 198–200.

64. 27 September 1955, Iu. S. Muntian, RGAE f. 8123, op. 3, d. 1198, l. 49; 20 June 1961, G. Zhukov, GARF f. 9518, op. 1, d. 133, l. 91.

65. 3 January 1956, "Zhu sulian shiguan daibiao Wenning baihui suwaijiaobu Gudefu tanhua jiyao," WJBDAG 109-00983-01, 3.

66. 17 April 1956, "Wo he de, bo, jie, xiong, luo, bu, a qiguo liunian lai wenhua jiaoliu qing," WJBDAG 109-00977-01, 9–11.

67. 30 October 1956, "Deklaratsiia," WJBDAG 109-00744-01, 14.

68. 29 March 1957, "Sovetsko-kitaiskie otnosheniia," I. Kurdiukov, AVPRF f. 0100, op. 50, p. 426, d. 29, l. 32.

69. 22 November 1956, "Zapis' besedy," P. F. Iudin and Liu Shaoqi, ibid., op. 49, p. 410, d. 9, l. 202.

70. 5 October 1949, "Liu Shaoqi zai zhongsu youhao xiehui zonghui chengli dahui shangde baogao," *Zhongguo yu sulian guanxi wenxian huibian*, 18.

71. 30 October 1956, "Deklaratsiia," WJBDAG 109-00744-01, 14.

72. 25 June 1957, Huang Kecheng to Zhou Enlai, WJBDAG 109-00794-01, 14; February 1957, PLA to N. A. Bulganin, ibid., 3.

73. 22 November 1956, "Zapis' besedy," P. F. Iudin and Liu Shaoqi, AVPRF f. 0100, op. 49, p. 410, d. 9, l. 202.

74. 18 July 1960, N. Khrushchev to SED CC, SAPMO DY 30/3605/26.

75. 1 November 1956, "Sulian zhengfu xuanyan de shengming," WJBDAG 109-00744-01, 1–3.

76. 30 October 1956, "Zhonghua renmin gongheguo zhengfu guanyu sulian zhengfu yijiuwuliu nian shiyue sanshi ri xuanyan de shengming," ibid., 7.

77. 26 December 1957, "Spravka," RGAE f. 9493, op. 1, d. 21, l. 7–10.

78. 26 December 1957, "Spravka," ibid., l. 8–9.

79. Ibid; 13 December 1957, "Stenogram," ibid., l. 14.

80. Ibid., l. 14–23.

81. Kaplan, *Československo v RVHP*, 30–33; 23 December 1948, "Reshenie . . . ob ekonomicheskikh otnosheniiakh mezhdu SSSR i stranami narodnoi demokratii," RGANI f. 17, op. 162, d. 39, 149, 199–200, in Volokitina et al., *Vostochnaia evropa v dokumentakh rossiiskikh arkhivov*, 944–45; Volokitina et al., *Moskva i vostochnaia evropa*, 361.

82. Dedijer, *The Battle Stalin Lost*, 82; Spulber, "Soviet Undertakings and Soviet Mixed Companies in Eastern Europe," 165–67; Edemskii, *Ot konflikta k normalizatsii*, 14.

83. Fallenbuchl, "East European Integration," 80–81.

84. 22 September 1959, N. Siluianov and A. Polozhenkov, RGAE f. 9493, op. 1, d. 1003, l. 38.

85. 31 March 1959, "Zpráva ministra zahraničního obchodu k návrhu na konání VII. Zasedání československo-čínské komise pro vědecko-technickou spolupráci," 020.05/59, MZV TO—T 1955–59, ČLR, krabice 3, obal 6.

86. 31 October 1959, N. Siluianov and F. Kleimenov, l. 1–6; 31 July 1959, N. Siluianov and F. Kleimenov, l. 11–12; 22 September 1959, N. Siluianov and A. Polozhenkov, l. 26–28, all RGAE f. 9493, op. 1, d. 1003.

87. 14 October 1954, Komzala, 49.474/54, NA KSČ–AN-II, krabice 84, folder "Telegramy, sífry, depresè, zpravy," 3–10. The total value of Czechoslovak-Chinese trade, however, steadily increased from 1950 to 1960. See 18 May 1962, "Přehled o dosavadním celkovém vývoji hospodářských styků ČSSR s ČLR a Albanskou lidovou republikou," 00199/62, NA KSČ–AN-II, krabice 85, folder "Čína," 1961.

88. 12 November 1954, Komzala, NA KSČ–AN-II, krabice 84, folder "Telegramy, sífry, depresè, zpravy."

89. 7 April 1955, "Zapis' besedy," E. F. Iudin and König, AVPRF f. 0100, op. 48, p. 393, d. 9, l. 66.

90. 5 June 1957, "Jednání s ČLR," R. Dvořák, 0/24.058/57, MZV TO—T 1955–59, ČLR, krabice 1, obal 5.

91. 19 November 1956, 0464/56, MZV TO—T 1955–59, ČLR, krabice 4, obal 2; Skřivan, "Vývoj československého vývozu do číny po druhé světové válce (1945–1959)," 271.

92. 23 November 1956, "Zapis' besedy," P. F. Iudin and Zhou Enlai, AVPRF f. 0100, op. 49, p. 410, d. 9, l. 212–14.

93. 6 February 1957, "Záznam z jednání s es. Li-Fu-Čunem," Humpolec, 057/57, MZV TO—T 1955–59, ČLR, krabice 2, obal 10. Also 26 August 1957, Otakar Šimůnek, ibid., krabice 3, obal 4. For a translation of Chen Yun's 12 December 1956 explanation, which blames the impact of flooding in China, see Zhang Shu Guang and Chen Jian, "The Emerging Disputes between Beijing and Moscow," 159.

94. 5 June 1957, "Jednání s ČLR," R. Dvořák, 0/24.058/57, MZV TO—T 1955–59, ČLR, krabice 1, obal 5. For figures from the Soviet Ministry of Foreign Affairs, see 27 September 1957, "Sovetsko-kitaiskoe ekonomicheskoe i kul'turnoe sotrudnichestvo," AVPRF f. 0100, op. 50, p. 426, d. 29, l. 62.

95. 15 March 1957, "Priem," N. Fedorenko and Liu Xiao, ibid., p. 423, d. 3, l. 20.

96. 21 April 1955, "Pamiatnaia zapiska," ibid., op. 48, p. 393, d. 6, l. 22.

97. 12 December 1956, Chen Yun to N. A. Bulganin, WJBDAG 109-00751-02, 12.

98. 5 June 1957, "Jednání s ČLR," R. Dvořák, 0/24.058/57, MZV TO—T 1955–59, ČLR, krabice 1, obal 5.

99. 26 August 1957, Otakar Šimůmek, ibid., krabice 2, obal 4.

100. 3 February 1959, "Postup jednání s ČLR o dlouhodobé hospodářské spolupráci," O. Šimůnek, 030.106/59, NA KSČ–AN-II, krabice 85, folder "Čína," 1959–61; 3 July 1959, Rejmán, "Telegram z Pekingu," ibid., krabice 84, folder "Telegramy, sífry, depresè, zpravy."

101. 28 February 1952; 21 January 1952, 101.702/52, MZV TO—T 1945–55, Čína, krabice 1, obal 2.

102. 18 October 1959, "Otchet," N. A. Kononov, RGAE f. 9493, op. 1, d. 1098, l. 62.

103. 8 December 1958, G. F. Mukhin; 14 April 1959, V. Iushin; 28 November 1959, P. A. Il'in; 23 February 1960, M. N. Stoianov and N. I. Chistiakov; 6 December 1959, A. Sh. Tatevian; 22 April 1960, A. I. Samoilov, all ibid., l. 70, 73, 86, 117, 150–64; 14 June 1961, V. Ivanov, ibid., op. 5, d. 66, l. 46; 4 March 1960, P. Moiseev to D. Pronin, ibid., d. 67, l. 4.

104. 21 January 1960, M. I. Agoshkov to A. G. Polozhenkov, ibid., op. 1, d. 1063, l. 5–6.

105. 9 January 1960, M. N. Karpov to General Consul, ibid., d. 1103, l. 1.

106. 1960, "Kratkii otchet"; 14 January 1960, A. S. Stugarev, et al., ibid., d. 1063, l. 87–101.

107. February 1960, "Tema no. 12-04," I. M. Lemni-Makedon, ibid., d. 1103, l. 12.

108. 9 December 1955, RGAE f. 3527, op. 13, d. 2537, l. 88–93; 10 September 1955, "Programma," ibid., d. 2522, l. 221–23.

109. 29 July 1956, S. Martsenitsen, ibid., d. 2577, l. 70.

110. 4 January 1959, M. A. Studilin, ibid., d. 2783, l. 25.

111. 15 April 1957, ibid., d. 2578, l. 79.

112. 1960, M. I. Stoianov and N. I. Chistiakov, ibid., d. 2798, l. 5–6.

113. 15 August 1963, A. Gladkov, RGAE f. 9493, op. 5, d. 184, l. 63.

114. 1 August 1963, A. Zakharov to S. I. Stepanenko, ibid., l. 69.

115. 22 March 1962, Zherebtsov, ibid., l. 33.

116. 1961, A. Uskov and S. Stepanenko to K. N. Rudnev, ibid., d. 383, l. 35.

117. 12 March 1953, "Vyžádání sovětské technické pomoci," 4.100/53, MZV, Teritoriální odbory—Obyčejně, 1945–59, SSSR, krabice 27, obal 11.

118. 29 April 1963, N. Smetnev to N. Tarasov, RGAE 9493, op. 5 d. 185, l. 13; August 1955, "Protokol," ibid., op. 1, d. 203; 17 August 1961, V. Zaitsev to K. N. Rudnev, ibid., d. 383, l. 45; 29 August 1963, "Zaiavka no. 53"; 1963, "Tekhnicheskoe obosnovanie," I. Komlev, ibid., op. 5, d. 184, l. 84, 117; September 1964, "Vorprogramin des Kongresses über Materialprüfung," ibid., l. 153–59; 29 June 1962, S. Orudzhev to I. V. Arkhipov, ibid., d. 185, l. 23.

119. 1955, "Otchet," N. I. Truevtsev, GARF f. 9396, op. 19, d. 7, l. 32.

120. 15 July 1961, S. Stepanenko to K. N. Rudnev, RGAE f. 9493, op. 1, d. 383, l. 304.

121. March 1962, A. Babukov, ibid., op. 5, d. 185, l. 49.

122. 1961, A. Vasenko to G. G. Gotsirdize, ibid., l. 105.

123. Ball, *Imagining America*, 24–30, citation from 24. See also Schultz, "Building the 'Soviet Detroit.'"

124. Ball, *Imagining America*, 120.

125. 1955, V. P. Lukin, l. 13; 29 October 1955, P. Selekhov and B. Blinov, l. 19; 4 October 1955, N. Arofikin and I. Anisov, l. 34, all RGAE f. 8123, op. 3, d. 1170.

126. 1955, "Doklad," M. Perelivchenko, ibid., d. 1154, l. 13–16.

127. 25 May 1956, "Zapis' besedy," P. F. Iudin and Zhou Enlai; 25 May 1956, "Zapis' besedy," P. F. Iudin and Zhang Wentiang, AVPRF f. 0100, op. 49, p. 410, d. 9, l. 147, 150; 23 November 1956, "Predlozheniia," ibid., p. 414, d. 37, l. 8.

128. July 1962, "Orienturovochnyi spisok," RGAE f. 9493, op. 5, d. 183, l. 89–91; 28 June 1962, D. Novikov to D. M. Gvishiani, ibid., l. 148; Brus, "1957 to 1965," 114–16; V. Garbuzov, "20 let postoiannoi komissii SEV po valiutno-finansovym voprosam."

129. 18 October 1962, I. Ruzhichka to D. M. Gvishiani, RGAE f. 9493, op. 5, d. 183, l. 122.

130. 1957, "Otchet," ibid., d. 21, l. 93.

131. 2 March 1960, "Otchet," A. P. Nikanorov, ibid., op. 1, d. 717, l. 59.

132. 2 July 1960, "Otchet," I. S. Stepanov, et al., ibid., l. 374.

133. Quotation from 27 September 1962, A. Goregliad, ibid., d. 183, l. 138. See also 29 September 1962, N. Ptichkin to S. I. Stepanenko; 25 September 1962, D. Pronin to A. N. Zademidko; and 24 August 1962, V. Novikov, all ibid., l. 12, 41–42, 137.

134. John M. Echols III, "Developed Socialism and Consumption Policies in the Soviet Bloc: An Empirical Evaluation," in Seroka and Simon, *Developed Socialism in the Soviet Bloc*, 165; David Stone, "CMEA's International Investment Bank and the Crisis of Developed Socialism."

135. For an interesting interpretation of the domestic security dilemmas shared by the Americans and the Russians, see Suri, *Power and Protest*.

Chapter Three

1. Waley-Cohen, *The Sextants of Beijing*, 106.

2. You Ji, "The Soviet Model and the Breakdown of the Military Alliance," in Bernstein and Hua-yu Li, *China Learns from the Soviet Union*, 156. For Mao's views, see Leung and Kau, *The Writings of Mao Zedong*, 94–98.

3. Fairbank and Goldman, *China*, 217–21; Spence, *To Change China*, 284; Westad, *Restless Empire*, 54, 71–91, 301; David Wright, *Translating Science*, xxiii, 22, 176–77.

4. V. A. D'iakov, "Slavianskii vopros v russkoi obshchestvennoi mysli, 1914–1917 godov," *Voprosy istorii*, nos. 4–5 (1991): 3–11.

5. Bystrova, *SSSR i formirovanie voenno-blokovogo protivostoianiia v evrope*, 29–30.

6. 6 August 1941, Edvard Beneš to V. M. Molotov, RGASPI f. 82, op. 2, d. 1356, l. 25; Knapík, *Kdo spoutal naši kulturu*, 17; Kalinová, *Společenské proměny v čase socialistického experimentu*, 28–44.

7. I. I. Pop and M. I. Rossovskaia, "Tiazhelaia ten' vostochnogo soseda: nekotorye aspekty otnoshenii mezhdu Chekhoslovakiei i sovetskim soiuzom," 92–109, and V. K. Volkov, "U istokov kontseptsii 'sotsialisticheskogo lageria,'" 17, both in L. Ia. Gibianskii, *U istokov 'sotsialisticheskogo sodruzhestva.'* The next agreements were with Yugoslavia (11 April 1945), and then Poland (21 April 1945). Hitler's former allies signed agreements later: Romania (4 February 1948), Hungary (18 February 1948), and Bulgaria (18 March 1948). See Hacker, *Der Ostblock*, 440–42.

8. 3 March 1946, "Protokol," GARF f. 5283, op. 17, d. 426, l. 82.

9. 26 November 1956, "Záznam o návštěvě," M. Žemla, 0480/56, MZV TO—T 1955–59, ČLR, krabice 2, obal 10.

10. 11 January 1957, "Zpráva o pobytu," 650.214/57, ibid., krabice 1, obal 6. On Czech willingness to conform to Habsburg rule in contrast to the more rebellious Hungarians and Poles, see Johnson, *Central Europe*, 92; and Jan Rychlík, "Československo a Polsko před rokem 1968," in Blažek, Kamiński, and Vévoda, *Polsko a Československo v roce 1968*, 21–32.

11. 27 March 1957, "Zhonghua renmin gongheguo zhengfu he jiekesiluofake gongheguo zhengfu lianhe shengming," WJBDAG 204-00242-02, 27.

12. 13 December 1957, "Obsah projevu sovětského velvyslance s. Judina—zaslání," Jan Bušniak, 022.103/57, MZV TO—T 1955–59, ČLR, krabice 1, obal 2.

13. 11 January 1957, "Zpráva o pobytu," 650.214/57, ibid., obal 6.

14. 9 November 1957, "Záznam z besedy čs. parlamentní delegace u předsedy ČLR Mao Ce-tunga," J. Busňiak, 0423/57, ibid., krabice 2, obal 10.

15. 31 December 1957, "Telegram z Pekingu," 016.921/56, ibid., krabice 1, obal 4.

16. 5 November 1956, "Zápis č. 80," Klofáč, 0452/56, and 26 November 1956, "Zápis č. 43," Klofáč, 0481/56, ibid., krabice 2, obal 10.

17. 9 November 1957, "Záznam z besedy čs. parlamentní delegace u předsedy ČLR Mao Ce-tunga," J. Busňiak, 0423/57, ibid., krabice 2, obal 10.

18. 30 April 1951, "SED Abteilung Propaganda"; 11 May 1951, "Entwurf," SAPMO DY30-IV 2/20/116/4-11.

19. Horst Gründer, "Kolonialismus und Marxismus: Der deutsche Kolonialismus in der Geschichtsschreibung der DDR," in Fischer and Heydemann, *Geschichtwissenschaft in der DDR*, 671–709.

20. 26 September 1954, "Mao zhuxi jiejian deguo zhengfu daibiaotuan tanhua jilu," WJBDAG 204-00005-23, 123–26.

21. Schleinitz, *Reisebilder aus China*, 189. For some of these themes in new Chinese film, see Paul G. Pickowicz, "Acting Like Revolutionaries: Shi Hui, the Wenhua Studio, and Private-Sector Filmmaking, 1949–52," in Brown and Pickowicz, *Dilemmas of Victory*, 256–87. On the CCP portrayal of Shanghai and its history, see Braester, "'A Big Dying Vat.'"

22. On similar tensions in the film industry, see Tina Mai Chen, "Socialism, Aestheticized Bodies, and International Circuits of Gender."

23. 1954, "Krasnyi mak," RGALI f. 648, op. 7, d. 254, l. 30–31.

24. Ibid., l. 31.

25. Ibid., l. 31, 35.

26. 20 March 1957, V. Golov to N. A. Mikhailov, ibid., l. 26.

27. Ibid., l. 26–27.

28. György Péteri, "The Oblique Coordinate Systems of Modern Identity," in Péteri, *Imagining the West in Eastern Europe and the Soviet Union*, 1–12.

29. "Seen from an Eastern bloc perspective," writes Greg Castillo, "communism was to be not simply the capitalist West's executioner but also its cultural savior." Greg Castillo, "East as True West: Redeeming Bourgeois Culture, from Socialist Realism to *Ostalgie*,"

in Péteri, *Imagining the West in Eastern Europe and the Soviet Union*, 89. On the bloc as a "*rival model of global pretensions*," see Péteri, "Nylon Curtain."

30. Bassin, *Imperial Visions*; Brower and Lazzerini, *Russia's Orient*.

31. Northrup, *Veiled Empire*.

32. Vadim Vokov, "The Concept of *Kul'turnost'*: Notes on the Stalinist Civilizing Process," in Fitzpatrick, *Stalinism: New Directions*, 210–30. For a Soviet explanation, see T. Kudrina, "K voprosu o kul'turno-vospitatel'noi funktsii sovetskogo gosudarstva v usloviiakh razvitogo sotsializma," in Kudrina, *Aktual'nye voprosy kul'turnogo stroitel'stva v period razvitogo sotsializma*, 6–22.

33. Martin, *The Affirmative Action Empire*; also see Slezkine, *The Jewish Century*, 274–75; and David Brandenberger and Kevin M. F. Platt, "Introduction: Tsarist-Era Heroes in Stalinist Mass Culture and Propaganda," in Platt and Brandenberger, *Epic Revisionism*, 3–14.

34. Alexander Martin, "Der sozialistische Internationalismus als Grundprinzip der völkerreichtlichen Beziehungen zwischen dem sozialistischen Staaten," *Deutsche Aussenpolitik* 3 (March 1958): 274.

35. "Ist die Sowjetunion eine Kolonialmacht? Die Entwicklung der zentralasiatischen Sowjetrepubliken auf dem Gebiete des Gesundheits—und Bildungswesens," *Deutsche Aussenpolitik* 4 (April 1958): 416–22.

36. 18 November 1961, "Informatsiia," F. Konstantinov, GARF f. 9518, op. 1, d. 133, l. 218–19; Karl Heinz Hagen, "Die kulturellen Beziehungen der DDR zu den Ländern des sozialistischen Lagers," *Deutsche Aussenpolitik* 11 (1957): 955; Tikhomirov, *Iskusstvo sotsialisticheskikh stran*; S. V. Gerasimov, "Iskusstvo stran sotsializma," *Tvorchestvo*, no. 12 (1958): 1–2.

37. 30 March 1951, "Večer umění lidových démokracií," 1233/51; March 1951, České akademii věd a umění, 1249/51, MZV TO—O 1945–59, ČLR, krabice 8, obal 18.

38. Halpap, *China*, 21, 35–39.

39. Bogatkin et al., *Sto dnei v Kitae*, 9–10, 17–26.

40. "Uspekh kitaiskikh artistov," *Pravda* (11 November 1956): 2; Evgenii Mar, "Kitaiskie artisty v moskve," *Vechernaia moskva* (14 November 1956): 3; Vladimir Rogov, "Gumanizm i mastersvo," *Pravda* (18 November 1956): 4; all RGALI f. 2732, op. 1, d. 1286.

41. "Dragotsennyi tsvetok, vyrashchennyi kitaiskim narodom," *Sovetskaia kul'tura* (November 1956): 5, ibid.

42. Vinogradov, *V strane velikoi iantszy*, 7.

43. 13 August 1957, Ge Baoquan to N. G. Erofeev, GARF f. 5283, op. 18, d. 207, l. 36.

44. 11 May 1957, "O poezdke sovetskoi delegatsii v KNR," N. Mikhailov, RGANI f. 5, op. 28, r. 5200, d. 506, l. 69.

45. 1958, "Spravka," A. Nekhoroshev, GARF f. 9518, op. 1, d. 124, l. 1.

46. V. Ovchinnikov, "Pokorenie drakona," *Zvezda*, no. 10 (1959): 163–71; Zaichikov, *Bluzhdaiushchaia reka khuankhe*; Muranov, *Reka khuankhe*.

47. 7 May 1948, "Materialy o rabote otdeleni obshchestva Kitaisko-Sovetskoi druzhby," P. V. Vedenskii, GARF f. 5283, op. 18, d. 62, l. 18.

48. V. U., "Po puti druzhby mezhdu narodami Kitaia i SSSR," *Russkoe slovo* (15 August 1948): 3, ibid., l. 19.

49. 9 March 1946, "Perepiska s Kitaiskimi pisiateliami," S. A. Tolstaia-Esenina, ibid., d. 50, l. 2.

50. A. Babakhanov, "Istoki bratskoi druzhby," *Zvezda vostoka*, no. 3 (1959): 102–22.

51. 8 April 1960, "Vypiska," GARF f. 9576, op. 18, d. 26, l. 334.

52. 3 January 1952, "Kulturní styky mezi ČSR a ČLR," 101.258/52, MZV TO—O 1945–59, ČLR, krabice 8, obal 18; 18 May 1953, "Mimořadná zpráva o festivalu," 1191/53, ibid., obal 5; 29 July 1955, "Zpráva," 53.202/55, ibid., obal 17; 23 August 1958, "Českovenští stipendisté a lektoři v ČLR," J. Štětina, 020.455/58, MZV TO—T 1955–59, ČLR, krabice 8, obal 1; 12 June 1956, 27 September 1954, "Informace," 418.462; 19 November 1954, "Přehledná zpráva o čínské lidové republice," 421.306, ibid., krabice 1, obal 4; 12 June 1956, "Zdravotnická úmluva," 12.427/57, ibid., krabice 5, obal 7; 17 April 1959, "Výstava čs. loutkového filmu," Ján Bušniak, 022.538/59, ibid., krabice 8, obal 1; 21 June 1956, "Přehled československo-činských styku za II. Čtvrtletí 1956," 014.075/56, and 3 July 1957, "Přehled styků s ČLR, 016.221/57, ibid., krabice 2, obal 1; 25 February 1955, "Koncept," 41/4/1/1, VÚA MNO, krabice 69.

53. 17 December 1959, "O účasti čínských umělců a vědců na oslavách 10. Výročí ČLR," Jaromír Štětina, 033.857/59, MZV TO—T 1955–59, ČLR, krabice 8, obal 1; 25 September 1959, "Záznam pro I náměstka s. Dr. Gregora," 028.351/59, ibid., krabice 1, obal 1.

54. Wolfgang Kiesewetter and Paul Markowski, "Zur Reise Otto Grotewohls durch den Nahen und Fernen Osten," *Deutsche Aussenpolitik* 4 (April 1959): 359; Karl Heinz Hagen, "Die kulturellen Beziehungen der DDR zu den Ländern des sozialistischen Lagers," *Deutsche Aussenpolitik* 11 (November 1957): 949–52; Elaine Kelly, "Imagining Richard Wagner: The Janus Head of a Divided Nation," in Péteri, *Imagining the West in Eastern Europe and the Soviet Union*, 131–52.

55. Schleinitz, *Reisebilder aus China*, 156.

56. Ibid., 163, 119, 144.

57. Ibid., 185.

58. 31 December 1954, "Perepiska s deiateliami kul'tury i iskusstva Kitaia," B. Belyi, RGALI f. 2077, op. 1, d. 1121, l. 13.

59. 6 December 1957, "Zasedaniia biuro inostrannoi komissii soiuza kompozitorov SSSR," ibid., d. 1432, l. 3.

60. 24 November 1957, "Perepiska s OKSD," N. T. Zhiganov, GARF f. 5283, op. 18, d. 207, l. 13.

61. 23 March 1959, "Plan," S. Tikhvinskii, GARF f. 9518, op. 1, d. 124, l. 88.

62. 16 January 1958, "Protokoly i stenogrammy otchetov o poezdkhakh kompozitorov," RGALI f. 2077, op. 1, d. 1432, l. 32, 34, 38.

63. 4 July 1958, "Materialy o kul'turnom sotrudnichestve," A. Kuznetsov to I. I. Shcheglov, RGALI f. 2936, op. 1, d. 1245, l. 4.

64. 14 December 1959, "O návštěvě ústřední konservatoře hudby v Pekingu," Jaromír Štětina, 033.355/59, MZV TO—T 1955–59, ČLR, krabice 8, obal 1.

65. 19 October 1956, "Zpráva o pruběhu vědecko-technicke spolupráce," 017.261/56, ibid., krabice 3, obal 6.

66. 4 December 1953, Jiráska, 147.848/53, ibid., krabice 4, obal 1.

67. 19 October 1956, "Zpráva o pruběhu vědecko-technicke spolupráce," 017.261/56, ibid., krabice 3, obal 6.

68. 2 November 1955, "Závedy při montážích v ČLR," 424.200/55, ibid., krabice 4, obal 1.

69. 7 July 1952, Viliam Široký, 722/52; 30 June 1952, "Záznam o rozhovore," 122.254/52, Viliam Široký and Tan Si-lin, ibid., krabice 4, obal 1.

70. 6 August 1955, O. Havlíček, 422.801/55, ibid.

71. 29 November 1957, J. Fierlínger, 060/57, ibid., krabice 3, obal 3; 29 April 1957, "Zpráva o práci a politickem životě skupin čs. techniků a montérů v ČLR," 0208/57, ibid., krabice 9, obal 3.

72. 6 January 1958, "Opis," L. Kubiš, ibid., krabice 3, obal 3.

73. 23 December 1957, J. Fierlínger, 010.556/58, ibid.

74. 6 January 1958, "Opis," L. Kubiš, ibid.

75. Näth, *Communist China in Retrospect*, 40, 121, 142.

76. 20 May 1959, "Zapis' besedy," P. F. Iudin and Liu Xiao, AVPRF f. 0100, op. 51, p. 435, d. 25, l. 30.

77. 22 November 1957, "Opis," Ču Jao-pao, MZV TO—T 1955–59, ČLR, krabice 3, obal 3.

78. 27 November 1957, J. Fierlínger, 059/57, ibid.

79. 6 January 1958, "Opis," L. Kubiš, ibid.

80. 23 December 1957, J. Fierlínger, 010.556/58, ibid.

81. 27 November 1957, J. Fierlínger, 059/57, ibid.

82. 22 December 1957, "Opis," 061/57, ibid.

83. 30 November 1957, J. Fierlínger, 060/57, ibid.

84. 21 December 1957, "Výnatek ze zápisu," L. Kubiš and J. Fierlínger, 024/58, ibid.

85. For earlier attention to the matter of promoting healthy activity for the advisers, see 28 June 1956, "Guowuyuan waigao zhuanjia ju guanyu zucheng zai woguo gongzuo de sulian zhuanjia," BMA 002-008-00066, 236–37.

86. 29 November 1957, J. Fierlínger, 060/57, MZV TO—T 1955–59, ČLR, krabice 3, obal 3.

87. 6 January 1958, J. Fierlínger, ibid.

88. 31 January 1958, Richard Dvořák, 010.556/58, ibid.

89. 29 May 1958, Miloš Paris, 1933/58, ibid.

90. 22 September 1958, "Zpráva," 0339/58; 22 November 1958, "Zpráva o politickém a společenském životě čs. občanů v ČLR za III. čtvrtleti 1958," F. Vomáček, 0511/58; 23 April 1959, "Zpráva o politickém a společénském životě čs. občanů v ČLR za I. čtvrtleti 1959," Ján Bušniak, 022.498/59, all ibid., krabice 9, obal 3.

91. 8 January 1953, "Zpráva o zájezdu AUS do číný," Josef Strašil, 18/4/5, VÚA MNO, krabice 510.

92. 1953, "Hodnocení přednášek o čině," 18/4/5, ibid.

93. 28 March 1953, "Besedy o čině-hlášení za měsíc únor 1953," 18/4/5, ibid.

94. 24 January 1953, "Besedy o čínské lidové republice," František Navrati, 18/4/5, ibid.

95. 1953, "Hodnocení přednášek o čině," 18/4/5, ibid.

96. 1953, "Vyhodnocení besed s příslušníky AUS-VN," 18/4/5, and 28 January 1953, "Vyhodnotenie besed s príslušníkm AUS," Čestmír Skála, 18/4/5, ibid.

97. March 1953, "Zhodnocení besed o Čínské lidové republice s příslušníky AUS-VN," Václav Podzimek, 18/4/5, ibid.

98. 1 March 1955, "Vyjádření k dopisu o zájezdu AUSVN do číny," František Ohnsong, 18/4/3, ibid., krabice 33.

99. 27 March 1954, "Vyjádření k dopisu o zájezdu AUSVN do číny," 18/4/3, ibid.

100. 2 June 1954, "Vyjádření k dopisu o zájezdu AUSVN do číny," Josef Machalous, 18/4/3, ibid.

101. 8 August 1957, V. Lapitskii, GARF f. 5283, op. 17, d. 528, l. 104.

102. 2 April 1954, "Vyjádření k dopisu o zájezdu AUSVN do číny," Ladislav Mazal, 18/4/3, VÚA MNO, krabice 33; 24 March 1954, "Zpráva," Vladimír Bouša, 18/4/3, ibid.

103. 1 March 1955, "Vyjádření k dopisu o zájezdu AUSVN do číny," František Ohnsong, 18/4/3, ibid; March 1954, "Zpráva o šetření okolností uvedených v dopise darech AUSVN z číny," 18/4/9, ibid.

Chapter Four

1. Taubman, *Khrushchev*, 274.

2. Kramer, "The Soviet Union and the 1956 Crises in Hungary and Poland"; Kramer, "New Evidence on Soviet Decision-Making and the 1956 Polish and Hungarian Crises."

3. Zhihua Shen and Yafeng Xia, "New Evidence for China's Role in the Hungarian Crisis of October 1956"; Shen Zhihua, "Mao and the 1956 Soviet Military Intervention in Hungary," in Rainer and Somla, *The 1956 Hungarian Revolution and the Soviet Bloc Countries*. See also Chen Jian, *Mao's China and the Cold War*, 145–62; Lüthi, *The Sino-Soviet Split*, 46–79; and Xu Zehao, *Wang Jiaxiang zhuan*, 515–35.

4. 23 October 1956, "Bo youpai zai yefang juxing gongzuo de qingkuang," WJBDAG 109-00762-03, 36.

5. Iurii Aksiutin, "Popular Responses to Khrushchev," in Taubman, Khrushchev, and Gleason, *Nikita Khrushchev*, 177–208; Iu. V. Aksiutin, "Novye dokumenty byvshego arkhiva TsK," in Loginov, *XX s'ezd*, 119–29; Aksiutin, *Khrushchevskaia 'ottepel' i obshchestvennye nastroeniia v SSSR v 1953–1964 gg.*, 172–75. On de-Stalinization as a "highly unstable, and de-stabilizing, force in the Soviet public sphere," see Polly Jones, "Introduction: the Dilemmas of De-Stalinization," in Jones, *The Dilemmas of De-Stalinization*, 17.

6. Edemskii, *Ot konflikta k normilizatsii*, 356, 425 (n. 165).

7. 20 March 1956, RGANI f. 5, op. 31, d. 54, l. 43–47; 24 March 1956, RGANI f. 5, op. 31, d. 53, l. 51–52; 19 March 1956, RGANI f. 5, op. 32, d. 43, l. 5; 25 May 1956, RGANI f. 5, op. 30, d. 139, l. 5–27, all from Aimermakher et al., *Kul'tura i vlast'*, 412–13, 422, 425, 528.

8. 21 March 1956, RGANI f. 5, op. 31, d. 52, l. 65, 70–73, from ibid., 418–19.

9. 1 July 1954, Nina Teimurazovna Beria to N. S. Khrushchev, RGANI f. 5, op. 30, d. 78, l. 15.

10. Zhang Shu Guang and Chen Jian, "The Emerging Disputes between Beijing and Moscow," 153–54. Speaking to urban and provincial Party leaders on 15 November 1956, Mao described Lenin and Stalin as two "swords [*daozi*]" for use in battle and complained that the bloc had just been deprived of the latter as a weapon. See Li Danhui, "Mao Zedong dui su renshi yu zhongsu guanxi de yanbian," in Li Danhui, *Beijing yu Mosike*, 320–21; Pu Guoliang, *Zouxiang bingdian*, 26–28; and Lüthi, *The Sino-Soviet Split*, 62–63. On similar issues in Poland, see Kemp-Welch, "Khrushchev's 'Secret Speech' and Polish Politics."

11. 25 May 1956, "Zapis' besedy," P. F. Iudin and party workers in Hubei Province, AVPRF f. 0100, op. 49, p. 410, d. 9, l. 131–35.

12. 25 November 1957, D. Godunov and Qian Junrui, RGANI f. 5, op. 30, d. 228, l. 198–202. See also Chen Jian, *Mao's China and the Cold War*, 64–67; and Quan Yanchi, *Mao Zedong yu Heluxiaofu*, 10–16.

13. 31 March 1956, "Zapis' besedy," P. F. Iudin and Mao Zedong, RGANI f. 5, op. 30, d. 163, l. 89–92; the same transcript is also available as 5 April 1956, "Zapis' besedy," P. F. Iudin and Mao Zedong, AVPRF f. 0100, op. 49, p. 410, d. 9, l. 87–94. Matyas Rakosi in Hungary before his death that year adopted the same tactic. 19 May 1956, "Referat Matyas Rakosi," SAPMO DY 30/3403/53. For excerpts of the Iudin-Mao exchanges in English, see Westad, "Mao on Sino-Soviet Relations." See also Pu Guoliang, *Zouxiang bingdian*, 23; and Quan Yanchi, *Mao Zedong yu Heluxiaofu*, 26–33.

14. 31 March 1956, "Zapis' besedy," P. F. Iudin and Mao Zedong, RGANI f. 5, op. 30, d. 163, l. 97–98. On tactics against the Guomindang in the civil war, see Kim, "The Crucial Issues of the Early Cold War." Dedijer recalls Stalin's admitting to the Yugoslavs in February 1948 that he gave poor advice to the CCP in the civil war. Dedijer, *The Battle Stalin Lost*, 183.

15. 17 July 1958, "Záznam rozhovoru předsedy ČLR Mao Ce-tung s československou vojenskou delegacy," 50/4/2, VÚA MNO, krabice 25.

16. 29 March 1957, "Sovetsko-kitaiskie otnosheniia," I. Kurdiukov, AVPRF f. 0100, op. 50, p. 426, d. 29, l. 24.

17. 22 September 1960, "Nekotorye materialy," N. Sudarikov, ibid., op. 53, p. 457, d. 24, l. 134–87.

18. Zhang Xiangshan, *Weishenme yao fandui gerenchongbai*, 4–31.

19. 12 October 1956, "Telegramma I.V. Andropova . . . o besede s E. Gerö," from APRF f. 3, op. 64, d. 484, l. 64–75, in Orekhova et al., *Sovetskii soiuz i vengerskii krizis 1956 goda*, 303; 8 January 1957, "Zapis' besedy," N. Palolichev, AVPRF f. 0100, op. 50, p. 423, d. 3, l. 1.

20. 15 April 1957, "Záznam o návštěvě rady velvyslanectví Německé demokratické republiky s. Fr. Everhartze," 014.498/7, MZV TO—T 1955–59, ČLR, krabice 2, obal 10.

21. Chen Jian, *Mao's China and the Cold War*, 67. See also Yang Kuisong, *Mao Zedong yu Mosike de enen yuanyuan*, 383.

22. For memoir accounts, see Aleksandrov-Agentov, *Ot Kollontai do Gorbacheva*, 93, 254; and Troianovskii, *Cherez gody i rasstoianiia*, 222, 349. See also "Plenum Transcripts, 1955–1957," *CWIHPB*, no. 10 (March 1998): 58, 51.

23. 3 March 1956, "Qing souji geguo baokan dui sugong ershici daibiao dahui he Heluxiaofu piping Sidalin de fanying," WJBDAG 109-00971-02, 7.

24. 9 April 1956, "Sugong jiceng zuzhuang fandui gerenchongbai baogao fudahou de fanying," WJBDAG 109-01615-01, 2.

25. 11 April 1956, "Si yue wu ri renmin ribao fulun zai su fanying," WJBDAG 109-01615-03, 19.

26. 24 May 1956, "Xiong du zhuxi jianghua de qingkuang," WJBDAG 109-01154-03, 22.

27. 15 June 1956, "Su xuanfu he sixiang gongzuo zhongde ruogan wenti," WJBDAG 109-01617-16, 122.

28. 4 January 1957, "Guanyu 'Zai lun wuchan jieji zhuanzheng de lishi jingyan' fanying huibao," WJBDAG 109-01154-01, 7–8

29. 3 January 1957, "Xiongzhong xuanbu tongzhi tanhua neirong," WJBDAG 109-01154-01, 5–6.

30. 8 January 1957, "Dui 'Zai lun wuchan jieji zhuanzheng de lishi jingyan' fanying huibao," ibid., 10.

31. 1 July 1957, "Mao zhuxi jiangyan fanying," WJBDAG 109-01154-03, 29.

32. 6 January 1957, "Dui 'Zai wuchanjieji zhuanzheng de lishi jingyan' de fanying," WJBDAG 109-01120-01, 3.

33. M.Iu. Prozumenshchikov, "'Sekretnyi' doklad N. S. Khrushcheva na XX s'ezde KPSS i mezhdunarodnoe kommunisticheskoe dvizhenie," in Aimermakher et al., *Kul'tura i vlast'*, 35–36; Taubman, *Khrushchev*, 301; Firsov, *Raznomyslie v SSSR, 1940–1960-e gody*, 260.

34. Prozumenshchikov, "'Sekretnyi' doklad," in Aimermakher et al., *Kul'tura i vlast'*, 40.

35. 1 February 1956, from RGANI f. 3, op. 8, d. 389, l. 52–54, in ibid., 175; also "Zasedanie," 1 February 1956, in Fursenko, *Prezidium TsK KPSS*, 96; Aksiutin, *Khrushchevskaia 'ottepel' i obshchestvennye nastroeniia v SSSR v 1953–1964 gg.*, 157–58.

36. 3 May 1956, "Heluxiaofu tongzhi zai wuyi yanhui shangde jianghua," WJBDAG 109-01615-04, 22–23.

37. 31 April 1956, "Priem," V. M. Molotov and Liu Xiao, AVPRF f. 0100, op. 49, p. 410, d. 6, l. 45–52; 27 March 1956, Liu Xiao, "Moluotuofu tongzhi jiejian suoyou renmin minzhu guojia zhu sulian dashiguan suo shuoming wenti," WJBDAG 109-01617-03, 18–19.

38. 12 March 1956, S. Statnikov to B. S. Burkov, RGANI f. 5, op. 30, d. 140, l. 53–68, in Aimermakher et al., *Kul'tura i vlast'*, 258–59. See also Aksiutin, "Popular Responses to Khrushchev," in Taubman, Khrushchev, and Gleason, *Nikita Khrushchev*, 183; and Taubman, *Khrushchev*, 286, which offers a figure of some 60,000 participants at these events.

39. 12 March 1956, S. Statnikov, in Aimermakher, et al., *Kul'tura i vlast'*, 259–61.

40. Kozlov, *Mass Uprisings in the USSR*, 118; 12 March 1956, S. Statnikov, in Aimermakher et al., *Kul'tura i vlast'*, 259.

41. Kozlov, *Mass Uprisings in the USSR*, 117.

42. 23 May 1956, "Zasedanie," in Fursenko, *Prezidium TsK KPSS*, 134.

43. 12 March 1956, S. Statnikov, in Aimermakher et al., *Kul'tura i vlast'*, 264.

44. 10 July 1956, RGANI f. 3, op. 14, d. 41, l. 26, 52–53, from ibid., 370–72.

45. 16 January 1956, "Usnesení," 26/5/5, VÚA MNO, krabice 459.

46. 16 May 1956, "Zai sulian," WJBDAG 109-00985-01, 28–33.

47. Christoph Boyer, "Der Beitrag der Sozialgeschichte zur Erforschung Kommunistischer Systeme," in Brenner and Heumos, *Sozialgeschichtliche Kommunismusforschung*, 19.

48. October 1938, Sixth Plenum of the Sixth CC, in Schram, *The Political Thought of Mao Tse-tung*, 114.

49. Li Yueran, *Zhongsu waijiao qinliji*, 40. For reports from the Soviet embassy outlining Mao's views, including the translation of essays that illustrated his "adaptation of Marxism-Leninism to the conditions of China," see 5 October 1950, "Prilozhenie" (CCP CC Seventh Plenum, 20 April 1945), AVPRF f. 0100, op. 43, p. 302, d. 10, l. 180–239, citation from l. 181.

50. Shen Zhihua, *Sulian zhuanjia zai zhongguo*, 253–60, 291, 340, 367.

51. 25 May 1956, "Zapis' besedy," P. F. Iudin and Zhou Enlai, AVPRF f. 0100, op. 49, p. 410, d. 9, l. 121; 15 October 1957, "Informatsiia," N. Pridybailo, ibid., op. 44, p. 176, d. 17, l. 28. See Leung and Kau, *The Writings of Mao Zedong*, 95–96; *Mao Zedong waijiao wenxuan*, 254–60; *Selected Works of Mao Tsetung*, 339, 364–65; Zhang Shu Guang and

Chen Jian, "The Emerging Disputes between Beijing and Moscow," 152; and Hinton, *The People's Republic of China*, 655–71. For scholarly treatments of this issue, see Li Jie, *Mao Zedong yu xin zhongguo de neizheng waijiao*, 5, 98; Li Danhui, "Mao Zedong dui su renshi yu zhongsu guanxi de yanbian," in Li Danhui, *Beijing yu Mosike*, 320–21; and Simei Qing, *From Allies to Enemies*, 260.

52. Zinner, *National Communism and Popular Revolt in Eastern Europe*, 8; see also 59.

53. Hacker, *Der Ostblock*, 532–43.

54. 16 May 1956, "Zai sulian," WJBDAG 109-00985-01, 42.

55. Mëhilli, "Defying De-Stalinization," 14.

56. 16 July 1956, "Muqian sulian baozhi xuanfu zhongde yizhen zhongyao renwu," WJBDAG 109-01617-16, 119.

57. 22 October 1956, "Bolan zhengqing," WJBDAG 109-00762-03, 33–34. According to Teresa Toranska, Edward Ochab told Chinese leaders the same thing when he attended the 8th Party Congress in Beijing in September 1956. "The only thing we wanted was for the Poles to manage their own affairs at home within the general socialist framework, just as you, I added, want to manage yours." Toranska, *"Them,"* 67–68. See also Kuo, *Contending with Contradictions*, 73–74.

58. 8 December 1956, "Dui bolan shijian de chubu guji," WJBDAG 109-00762-01, 6.

59. 23 October 1956, "Bo youpai zai yefang juxing gongzuo de qingkuang," WJBDAG 109-00762-03, 36.

60. 20 October 1956, "Jibao bo bazhong quanhui qingkuang," WJBDAG 109-00762-03, 27.

61. 24 October 1956, "Bo ge baodao ji fanying qingkuang," ibid., 42.

62. 31 October 1956, "Bo guofangbu ganbu biandong qingkuang," ibid., 56.

63. 31 October 1956, "Bodang jiang zai mingnian sanyue zhaokai daibiao dahui," ibid., 59.

64. 5 November 1956, "Bo xuesheng toulu bodang mimi huitan jingshen," ibid., 61.

65. 8 November 1956, "Bolan jindi baogao," ibid., 85.

66. 11 December 1956, "Jiechu bo fangren yuande yixie fanying," ibid., 117.

67. Cited in Lüthi, *The Sino-Soviet Split*, 55.

68. 7 December 1956, "Li He tongzhi gei Deng Tuo tongzhi de dianbao," WJBDAG 109-01617-08, 50.

69. 8 November 1956, "Zai su guoqing yanhui zhong Heluxiaofu deng jianghua yaodian," WJBDAG 109-01615-05, 27.

70. 17 December 1956, "Zapis' besedy," P. Iudin and Wang Jiaxiang, AVPRF f. 0100, op. 50, p. 423, d. 5, l. 10.

71. 26 December 1956, "Telegram z Pekingu," Gregor, 019.236/56, MZV, TO—T 1955–59, ČLR, krabice 2, obal 10.

72. 5 January 1957, "Doklad delegatsii vsemirnoi federatsii profsoiuzov o poezdke v Vengriiu," RGANI f. 5, op. 28, r. 5195, d. 479, l. 43.

73. 6 November 1956, "Priem," N. T. Fedorenko and Liu Xiao, AVPRF f. 0100, op. 49, p. 410, d. 6, l. 68; 4 January 1957, "Guanyu 'Zai lun wuchan jieji zhuanzheng de lishi jingyan' fanying huibao," WJBDAG 109-01154-01, 8.

74. 28 November 1956, "Migaoyang tanhua neirong," Liu Xiao, WJBDAG 109-01617-07, 41–43.

75. 21 February 1957, "Zapis' besedy," P. Iudin and Sall, AVPRF f. 0100, op. 50, p. 423, d. 5, l. 18.

76. 11 June 1957, "Xiongdang zhonglianbu chen xiong wo da tanhua neirong," WJB-DAG 109-01154-03, 50–51.

77. 4 January 1957, "Guanyu 'Zai lun wuchan jieji zhuanzheng de lishi jingyan' fanying huibao," WJBDAG 109-01154-01, 7–8.

78. 6 January 1957, "Dui 'Zai wuchanjieji zhuanzheng de lishi jingyan' de fanying," WJBDAG 109-01120-01, 2.

79. 15 March 1957, "Zapis' besedy," V. A. Chernikov, István Shubik, and László Vatsi, RGANI f. 5, op. 28, r. 5795, d. 480, l. 158–9.

80. Gati, *Failed Illusions*, 117; Lampe, *Yugoslavia as History*, 268; Gibianskii, "Soviet-Yugoslav Relations and the Hungarian Revolution of 1956." On Tito's effort to reassure the Soviets, see 8 November 1956, "Pis'mo . . . na sobytiia v Vengrii," from APRF f. 3, op. 64, d. 486, l. 61–67, in Orekhova et al., *Sovetskii soiuz i vengerskii krizis 1956 goda*, 622–25.

81. 17 December 1956, "Zapis' besedy," K. A. Krutikov and [Ezhef] Sall, RGANI f. 5, op. 28, r. 5195, d. 479, l. 79.

82. 27 December 1956, "Zapis' besedy," M. I. Petunin and Ferenc Gödör, ibid., l. 94–95.

83. 17 December 1956, "Zapis' besedy," K. A. Krutikov and [Ezhef] Sall, ibid., l. 79–81.

84. 27 December 1957, "Bojun daibiaotuan jingchang tanlun wo junshi jimi," WJB-DAG 109-01129-08, 93; 6 January 1958, "Qing zhuyi bo fanghua junshi daibiaotuan tan wo junshi jimishi," ibid., 95.

85. 15 March 1958, "Zapis' besedy," P. Iudin and Zhou Enlai, AVPRF f. 0100, op. 51, p. 432, d. 6, l. 79.

86. 1 November 1957, "Zapis besedy," P. Iudin and Li En Kho, ibid., op. 50, p. 423, d. 5, l. 51.

87. Edemskii, *Ot konflikta k normalizatsii*, 349.

88. 5 December 1956, Oskar Fischer to Kundermann; 19 December 1957, Bayer to Grünstein, SAPMO DY 30-IV 2/20/112/2, 40.

89. 1 February 1957, "Zapis' besedy," S. T. Astavin and K. Khager, RGANI f. 5, op. 28, r. 5198, d. 492, l. 50.

90. 2 January 1957, "Dui zailun wuchan jieji zhuanzheng de lishi jingyan de fanying," WJBDAG 109-01130-01, 1.

91. 16 April 1957, "Bericht über den Aufenthalt der polnischen Regierungsdelegation in der VRCh," SAPMO DY 30-IV 2/20/120/29.

92. 6 April 1957, "Yuenan tongzhi tan yuebo huitan de yitie qingkuang," WJBDAG 109-01138-03, 25.

93. 18 August 1957, "Kratkaia zapis' besedy s Genkonsulom Pol'shi v Shangae Berlatskii," NA KSČ–AN-II, krabice 84, folder "Čína: Ruzné materiály, 1956–1967."

94. 7 October 1957, "Zapis' besedy," P. Iudin and Zhang Wentian, AVPRF f. 0100, op. 50, p. 423, d. 5, l. 43.

95. 9 December 1955, "Zapis' besedy," P. F. Iudin and Popović, ibid., op. 48, p. 393, d. 9, l. 182–85; 20 December 1955, "Zapis' besedy," P. F. Iudin and Nase, ibid., l. 221.

96. 7 April 1955, "Zapis' besedy," P. F. Iudin and Peng Dehuai, ibid., op. 18, p. 393, d. 9, l. 33.

97. 30 September 1955, A. Gregor to Mao Zedong, WJBDAG 117-00471-04, 65.

98. 6 December 1956, Peng Zhen, WJBDAG 109-01101-01, 47.

99. 8 December 1956, "Renda diabiaotuan fangsu fanying," ibid., 50.

100. 10 January 1957, "Zapis' besedy," G. K. Ivanov and K. Naumokl,' RGANI f. 5, op. 28, r. 5198, d. 492, l. 37.

101. 27 December 1956, "Zapis' besedy," V. N. Odinokov and Vladyslav Galanzovskii, ibid., r. 5795, d. 481, l. 33; 14 December 1956, "Vystuplenie pervogo sekretaria TsK PORP t. Gomulki," P. Ponomarenko, ibid., l. 55–75.

102. 21 January 1957, "Zapis' besedy," N. Fedorenko and Zhou Enlai, AVPRF f. 0100, op. 50, p. 423, d. 3, l. 4. On their exchange with the Hungarians, see Békés, Byrne, and Rainer, *The 1956 Hungarian Revolution*, 496–503.

103. Rajak, *Yugoslavia and the Soviet Union in the Early Cold War*, 194.

104. 15 May 1957, "1957 nian 5 yue juebo tanpan qingkuang," WJBDAG 109-01138-03, 30.

105. 7 October 1957, "Zapis' besedy," P. Iudin and Zhang Wentian, AVPRF f. 0100, op. 50, p. 423, d. 5, l. 42.

106. 23 January 1958, "Zapis' besedy," P. Iudin and Bo Yibo, ibid., op. 51, p. 432, d. 6, l. 36.

107. Zhihua Shen and Yafeng Xia, "The Whirlwind of China," 517; Zhihua Shen and Yafeng Xia, "Hidden Currents during the Honeymoon," 74–117; Mikhail Reiman, "N. S. Khrushchev i evropeiskie strany 'sotsializma': zametki na vazhnuiu temu (1953–1957 gg.)," in Nosov, *Slavianksie narody*, 424.

108. Emil Jeschonnek, "Buchbesprechungen: Lily Abegg, *Im neuen China*," *Deutsche Aussenpolitik* 2 (February 1958): 177.

109. 4 February 1958, "Rádná politická zpráva za II. pololetí 1957," 011.817/58, Ján Bušniak, MZV TO—T 1955–59, ČLR, krabice 6, obal 2.

110. 15 April 1957, "Záznam o návštěvě," 014.498/57, ibid., krabice 2, obal 10.

111. 24 June 1957, "Osveshenie v KNR poezdki delegatsii," V. Lazarev, AVPRF f. 0100, op. 50, p. 426, d. 32, l. 29.

112. 18 September 1957, "Aohabu tan daibiaotan fang nan qingkuang," Wang Bingnan, WJBDAG 109-01138-04, 39.

113. 11 July 1957, "Debo huitan," WJBDAG 109-01138-03, 21.

114. 7 December 1959, "Su Gebaoyuefu fabiao wodang daibiao zai xiong qida," WJB-DAG 109-01010-02, 43.

115. 11 December 1956, "Guanyu bo qingnian zucheng wenti," WJBDAG 109-00762-03, 114–15; Dandan Zhu, "The Hungarian Revolution and the Origins of China's Great Leap Policies, 1956–57." For an early effort to make this connection by a former Hungarian foreign affairs official, see Rádvanyi, "The Hungarian Revolution and the Hundred Flowers Campaign."

116. 7 December 1956, "Li He tongzhi gei Deng Tuo tongzhi de dianbao," WJBDAG 109-01617-08, 51.

117. 14 June 1957, "Zapis' besedy," P. Iudin and Zhou Enlai, AVPRF f. 0100, op. 50, p. 423, d. 5, l. 31–33.

118. 1 November 1957, "Zapis' besedy," P. Iudin and Liu Shaoqi, AVPRF f. 0100, op. 50, p. 423, d. 5, l. 48–49.

119. 2 January 1957, "Bolan jin xiong de fanying," WJBDAG 109-01138-05, 64–65.

120. See Małgorzata Mazurek, "'Besser, Billiger Schneller': Die Politik der Mobilisierung der Arbeiter im Warschauer Glühlampenwek 'Rosa Luxemburg' nach 1956," 82, and

Boyer, "Der Beitrag der Sozialgeschichte zur Erforschung kommunistischer Systeme," 29, in Brenner and Heumos, *Sozialgeschichtliche Kommunismusforschung*.

121. 14 February 1957, "Zapis' besedy," V. I. Kochemasov and Hans Rodenberg, RGANI f. 5, op. 28, r. 5198, d. 492, l. 73.

122. 19 February 1957, "Zapis' besedy," V. A. Kriuchkov and Nevai László, ibid., r. 5795, d. 480, l. 104.

123. Rüdiger Beetz, "Die 'Rebellion der Intellektuellen' in der DDR 1956/58," in Kircheisen, *Tauwetter ohne Frühling*, 126–41; 3 January 1957, "Zapis' besedy," N. S. Osipov and Pechi Ianoshne, RGANI f. 5, op. 28, r. 5195, d. 479, l. 101; Zinner, *National Communism and Popular Revolt in Eastern Europe*, 403.

124. 14 February 1957, "Zapis' besedy," V. I. Kochemasov and Hans Rodenberg; 8 March 1957, "Zapis' besedy," V. I. Kochemasov and M. Zimmering; 30 March 1957, "Zapis' besedy," G. K. Ivanov and Hans Modrow, all RGANI f. 5, op. 28, r. 5198, d. 492, l. 73–74, 103, 133. On the *stiliagi*, see Dobson, *Khrushchev's Cold Summer*, 122.

125. 9 September 1957, "Guanyu xiong baokan baoling wo fanyoupai douzheng de qingkuang," WJBDAG 109-01154-03, 41–42.

126. 16 May 1956, "Zai sulian," WJBDAG 109-00985-01, 51.

127. 7 December 1956, "Li He tongzhi gei Deng Tuo tongzhi de dianbao," WJBDAG 109-01617-08, 51.

128. 27 November 1960, "Zhenli bao toulu su daxuesheng sixiang xuexi shangde wenti," WJBDAG 109-02077-03, 31.

129. 2 April 1959, "Wo guo dianying zai sulian shangying de qingkuang"; 6 November 1959, "Sulian tongzhi tan woguo dianying yishu de fazhan," WJBDAG 109-01919-05, 67–69, 74–76.

130. 20 February 1960, "Sugong zhongyang fabu guanyu xuan fu gongzuo de jueyi," WJBDAG 109-02078-01, 1.

131. 3 October 1957, "Mao zhuxi jiejian bolan junshi daibiaotuan tanhuo jilu," WJBDAG 109-01129-07, 74; 28 June 1956, "Liu Shaoqi tongzhi jiejian sulian qingnian daibiaotuan tanhua jilu," WJBDAG 109-00743-05, 26.

132. Yen-lin Chung, "The Witch-Hunting Vanguard."

Chapter Five

1. See Zhihua Shen and Yafeng Xia, "The Great Leap Forward, the People's Commune and the Sino-Soviet Split"; Danhui Li and Yafeng Xia, "Competing for Leadership"; Barnouin and Yu Changgen, *Zhou Enlai*, 180; Christensen, *Worse than a Monolith*, 104–57; and Dikötter, *Mao's Great Famine*, 13–57.

2. Václav Kotyk, "Výzkum vztahů mezi socialistickymi státy v ústavu pro mezinárodní politiku a ekonomii," in Drulák and Kratochvíl et al., *50 let českého výzkumu mezinárodních vztahu*, 41.

3. See Chang, *Friends and Enemies*, 65; also see Goncharov, Lewis, and Xue Litai, *Uncertain Partners*, 104, 151. For American commentary on the eventual impact of Russian imperialism upon the fate of the alliance, see Report to President by President's Committee on International Information Activities, 30 June 1953, in *FRUS, 1952–1954*, 2:1808. For reference to the speech in subsequent conversation among Molotov, Vyshinsky, and

Mao in Moscow, see Westad, "Fighting for Friendship," 232–33. For Acheson's account, see Acheson, *Present at the Creation*, 356.

4. On American policy toward Tito, see Lees, *Keeping Tito Afloat*.

5. 5 April 1956, "Zapis' besedy," P. F. Iudin and Mao Zedong, AVPRF f. 0100, op. 49, p. 410, d. 9, l. 91.

6. 1 April 1957, "Poznámky z projevu s. Mao Ce-tunga dne 27. Unora 1957," A. Vasek, 073.286/57, MZV TO—T 1955–59, ČLR, krabice 6, obal 3.

7. Dedijer, *The Battle Stalin Lost*, 183.

8. For the Yugoslavs, this is drawn from 24 October 1946, "Priem," V. G. Dekanozov and Grulovich, AVPRF f. 0100, op. 34, p. 253, d. 18, l. 7–10; Gibianskii, "The Soviet Bloc and the Initial Stage of the Cold War," Banac, *With Stalin against Tito*; Girenko, *Stalin—Tito*; Hacker, *Der Ostblock*, 395–410; Bass and Marbury, *The Soviet-Yugoslav Controversy, 1948–58*; and Yang Kuisong, *Mao Zedong yu Mosike de enen yuanyuan*, 257–68.

9. Girenko, *Stalin—Tito*, 318, 336.

10. Tito's innovations and initiatives in both domestic and foreign policy, emphasizes Rajak, came after the break in 1948. Rajak, *Yugoslavia and the Soviet Union in the Early Cold War*, 9–19.

11. 13 October 1959, "Záznam o rozhovoru," Antonov and Jan Bušniak, 00410/59, NA KSČ–AN-II, krabice 84, folder "Čína: Ruzné materiály, 1956–1967."

12. 28 March 1956, "Tajný rozkaz ministra vnitra," Rudolf Barák, 37/1956, in Tomek, *Dvě studie o československém vězeňství*, 36–43.

13. 14 February 1957, "Zapis' besedy," S. T. Astavin and E. Mückenberger, RGANI f. 5, op. 28, r. 5198, d. 492, l. 57.

14. 2 August 1956, "Zapis' besedy," Iu. V. Andropov and E. Gerö, from TsKhSD (RGANI) f. 5, op. 28, d. 394, l. 208–12, in Orekhova et al., *Sovetskii soiuz i vengerskii krizis 1956 goda*, 212.

15. Gati, *Failed Illusions*, 117; Lampe, *Yugoslavia as History*, 268; Leonid Gibianskii, "Soviet-Yugoslav Relations and the Hungarian Revolution of 1956." On Tito's effort to reassure the Soviets, see 8 November 1956, "Pis'mo . . . na sobytiia v Vengrii," from APRF f. 3, op. 64, d. 486, l. 61–67, in Orekhova et al., *Sovetskii soiuz i vengerskii krizis 1956 goda*, 622–25.

16. 19 April 1958, "Zapis besedy," P. F. Iudin and Liu Shaoqi, Wang Jiaxiang, and Yang Shangkun, AVPRF f. 0100, op. 51, p. 432, d. 6, l. 122.

17. 6 February 1958, N. Sudarikov to N. T. Fedorenko, Iu. V. Andropov, and M. V. Zimianin, AVPRF f. 0100, op. 45, p. 281, d. 16, l. 9.

18. 18 August 1958, "Aktenvermerk: Besprechung der Genossen Chruschtschow und Mao Tse-tung im Juli 1958," König and Liu Xiao, SAPMO DY 30/3603/87.

19. 19 November 1958, "Zapis' besedy," P. Iudin and Chen Yi, AVPRF f. 0100, op. 51, p. 432, d. 6, l. 178.

20. 30 August 1960, "Zapis' besedy," S. V. Chervonenko and Chen Yi, ibid., op. 53, p. 454, d. 8, l. 215.

21. 9 September 1960, "Zapis' besedy," S. V. Chervonenko and Ferenc Martin, ibid., l. 223.

22. 27 February 1959, "Zapis' besedy," P. F. Iudin and Chen Yi; 20 May 1959, "Zapis' besedy," P. F. Iudin and Chen Yi, ibid., op. 51, p. 435, d. 25, l. 4, 48.

23. 18 February 1960, "O sostoianii obmena informatsiei mezhdu sovetskoi i kitaiskoi

storonami cherez posol'stvo SSSR v KNR v 1959 g.," V. Lazarev, ibid., op. 53, p. 457, d. 24, l. 20.

24. See Lüthi, *The Sino-Soviet Split*, 143–44.

25. 18 February 1960, "O sostoianii obmena informatsiei mezhdu sovetskoi i kitaiskoi storonami cherez posol'stvo SSSR v KNR v 1959 g.," V. Lazarev, AVPRF f. 0100, op. 53, p. 457, d. 24, l. 14–20; Lüthi, *The Sino-Soviet Split*, 109.

26. 9 July 1960, "Nekotorye voprosy sovetsko-kitaiskikh otnoshenii i lichnye kontakty," V. Lazarev, AVPRF f. 0100, op. 53, p. 457, d. 24, l. 69; 30 January 1960, "Zapis' besedy," S. V. Chervonenko, Chen Yi, and Li Fuchun, ibid., p. 454, d. 8, l. 28–41.

27. 24 January 1959, "Heluxiaofu zai baogao zhong tandao zhongsu wenti," WJBDAG 109-01919-09, 100.

28. See Pu Guoliang, *Zouxiang bingdian*, 78–79, 232–33; Dali Yang, "Surviving the Great Leap Famine"; Li Jie, *Mao Zedong yu xin zhongguo de neizheng waijiao*, 100–105, 148; Shen Zhihua, *Sulian zhuanjia zai zhongguo*, 352; and Radchenko, *Two Suns in the Heavens*, 175.

29. *Jiangguo yilai Mao Zedong wengao*, 8:390–92, 600–602; Li Jie, *Mao Zedong yu xin zhongguo de neizheng waijiao*, 121.

30. 16 October 1959, "Sulian duiyu woguo nongcun renmin gongshehua yundongde faying," WJBDAG 109-01010-01, 21.

31. 11 October 1958, "Stenogramma," GARF f. 9324, op. 1, d. 7, l. 10.

32. 13 December 1957, "Kampaň za nápravu stylu práce v závodech," Ján Bušniak, 022.105/57, MZV TO—T 1955–59, ČLR, krabice 6, obal 3.

33. 1 April 1959, "Zpráva o situací v zásobování trhu v Kantonu a provincii Kwantung," Koubek Vlastimil, 033/59, ibid., krabice 9, obal 1.

34. 13 October 1959, "Záznam o rozhovoru," Antonov and Ján Bušniak, 00410/59, NA KSČ–AN-II, krabice 84, folder "Čína: Ruzné materiály, 1956–1967."

35. 21 November 1959, "Záznam z rozhovoru," J. Melničak, 0495/59, MZV TO—T 1955–59, ČLR, krabice 2, obal 9.

36. 17 October 1952, 508-D/52, and 12 December 1957, "Zpráva o cestě členů dipl. sboru-zaslání," 5966/57, MZV TO—O 1945–59, ČLR, krabice 3, obal 1.

37. 1 March 1955, "Záznam o rozhovoru," 413.700/55, MZV TO—T 1945–55, Čína, krabice 1, obal 2.

38. 29 August 1956, "Information über den gegenwärtigen Stand der Beziehungen zwischen der DDR und der VR China," SAPMO DY 30-IV 2/20/115/19.

39. 23 May 1956, "Besprechung mit indischen Botschafter," Gyptner, SAPMO DY 30-IV 2/20/119/38; 23 November 1956, "Bericht über den Aufenthalt des indonesischen Präsidenten Sockarno," Fr. Everhartz, SAPMO DY 30-IV 2/20/120/11.

40. 11 September 1959, "Záznam z oběda," Rejmán, 4366/59, MZV TO—T 1955–59, ČLR, krabice 2, obal 9.

41. 12 September 1959, "Záznam," Štětina, 4363/59, ibid.

42. 13 September 1959, 4367/59, ibid.

43. 15 October 1959, Ladislav Rejmán, 4417/59, ibid.

44. 21 October 1959, "Záznam," J. Štětina, 4401/59, ibid.

45. 10 March 1960, "Zapis' besedy," S. V. Chervonenko and Erik Dons, AVPRF f. 0100, op. 53, p. 454, d. 8, l. 84.

46. 11 June 1958, "Telegram z Pekingu," 017.408/58, and 8 December 1958, "Telegram z Pekingu," Vasek, 025.368/58 MZV TO—T 1955–59, ČLR, krabice 1, obal 1; 22 October 1959, "Záznam ze společenského podniku," 0454/59, MZV TO—T 1955–59, ČLR, krabice 2, obal 9; 16 December 1958, "Lidové komuny v ČLR," Anton Vasek, 026.185/58, MZV TO—T 1955–59, ČLR, krabice 6, obal 3.

47. 27 July 1959, Ambassador Wandel to CC SED, SAPMO DY 30/3603/98-100.

48. 10 March 1960, "Aktenvermerk," Wenning and Deng, SAPMO DY 30-IV 2/20/122/66.

49. 30 December 1958, "O výsledcích . . . kampaně za likvidaci negramotnosti," Ján Bušniak, 016.586/59, MZV TO—T 1955–59, ČLR, krabice 8, obal 1.

50. 28 January 1959, "Řadná politická zprava," 017.879/59, Ján Bušniak, ibid., krabice 6, obal 2.

51. 17 June 1959, "Telegram z Pekingu," Ján Bušniak, 024.974/59, ibid., krabice 1, obal 1.

52. 31 December 1959, "Výpis ze záznamu o rozhovorech," 033.652/59, NA KSČ–AN-II, krabice 84, folder "Čína: Ruzné materiály, 1956–1967."

53. 20 June 1959, "Problematika rozvoje hospodářských styků s ČLR v letech, 1961–65," 0.12.574/59, MZV TO—T 1955–59, ČLR, krabice 3, obal 6.

54. 27 September 1960, "Zpráva obchodního přidělenie S. Šimká v Pekingu o současné situaci ve stycích mezi ČSSR a ČLR," NA KSČ–AN-II, krabice 85, folder "Čína," 1959–61.

55. 9 January 1961, "Aktenvermerk über ein Gespräch zu Fragen der inneren Entwicklung der VR China," Wandel, SAPMO DY 30-IV 2/20/123/23. See also 12 January 61, "Kurzinformation über einige neue Fakten zur Lage in der Industrie und Landwirtschaft der Volksrepublik China," Mostertz, SAPMO DY 30-IV 2/20/123/29-33.

56. Chan, *Mao's Crusade*, 4; see also Becker, *Hungry Ghosts*.

57. 25 September 1958, "Beschluß des ZK der KP Chinas und des Staatsrates der Volksrepublik China über die Teilnahme der Kaderfunktionäre an der Körperlichen Arbeit," SAPMO DY 30/3603/91.

58. 1 July 1960, "Bericht der Delegation des Ministeriums für Volksbildung und des Staatssekretariats für das Moch- und Fachschulwesen in die Volksrepublik China," SAPMO DY 30/3605/4.

59. January 1958, "Information . . . über die Entsendung von Kadern auf dem Dorf," SAPMO DY 30-IV 2/20/121/325.

60. 22 January 1959, "Zpráva o návštěvě čs. delegace sociálního zabezpečení," 101.811/59, MZV TO—O 1945–59, krabice 14, obal 22.

61. 28 February 1959, "O dosavadním průběhu nástupu kulturní revoluce v Číně," Jaromír Štětina, 020.328/59, MZV TO—T 1955–59, ČLR, krabice 8, obal 1.

62. 21 October 1958, "Hodnocení výsledku hnuti za nápravu stylu práce," Anton Vasek, 023.115/58, ibid., krabice 6, obal 2.

63. 28 February 1959, "O dosavacním průběhu nástupu kulturní revoluce v Číně," Jaromír Štětina, 020.328/59, ibid., krabice 8, obal 1.

64. 7 December 1959, "Průběh oslov 10. výročí ČLR," Jaromír Štětina, 033.946/59, ibid., krabice 6, obal 1.

65. Lin Fang, "Gongchanzhuyi zhifeng," *Xinmin wanbao* (19 October 1958): 1.

66. 26 June 1959, "Závěry XXI. Sjezdu KSS pro práci KS Činy a jejich projednaní," Ján Bušniak, 025.654/59, NA KSČ–AN-II, krabice 86, folder "Čína," 1959.

67. 14 October 1959, "Závěry XXI. Sjezdu KSS pro práci KS Činy a jejich projednaní," 027.671/59, MZV TO—T 1955–59, ČLR, krabice 1, obal 1; 5 December 1960, "Information zu einigen wirtschaftlichen und politischen Problemen in der VR China," SAPMO DY 30-IV 2/20/123/19.

68. 11 October 1960, "Zpráva s. Fierlíngera ze Šanghaje," NA KSČ–AN-II, krabice 84, folder "Telegramy, sífry, depresè, zpravy."

69. 20 July 1959, "O kulturních stycích ČLR s kapitalistickými zeměmi," Ján Bušniak, 025.421/59, MZV TO—T 1955–59, ČLR, krabice 8, obal 1.

70. 30 September 1959, "Zpráva o čínské exportní výstavě I/1959 v Kantonu," V. Koubek, 031456/59, ibid., krabice 7, obal 1.

71. 22 March 1958, "Zasedání nejvyšší státní conference," Ján Bušniak, 014.227/58, ibid., krabice 6, obal 3.

72. 26 September 1958, "Telegram z Pekingu," Vasek, 029.693/58, ibid., krabice 1, obal 2.

73. 3 February 1959, "Telegram z Pekingu," 017.797/59, ibid., obal 1.

74. 21 May 1960, "Aktenvermerk über eine Unterredung mit dem Botschafter der Sowjetunion," Chernonenko and Wandel, SAPMO DY 30/3604/13.

75. Lüthi, The Sino-Soviet Split, 104.

76. 2 October 1958, "Zapis' besedy," GARF f. 9576, op. 18, d. 26, l. 312-322.

77. 9 November 1957, "Záznam z besedy čs. parlamentní delegace u předsedy ČLR Mao Ce-tunga," J. Busňiak, 0423/57, MZV TO—T 1955–59, ČLR, krabice 2, obal 10.

78. Lüthi, The Sino-Soviet Split, 107–8; Chan, Mao's Crusade, 99–108.

79. 25 November 1958, "Telegram z Pekingu," Vasek, 024.719/58, MZV TO—T 1955–59, ČLR, krabice 1, obal 2. See also 26 June 1959, "Závěry XXI. Sjezdu KSS pro práci KS Činy a jejich projednaní," Ján Bušniak, 025.654/59, NA KSČ–AN-II, krabice 86, folder "Čína," 1959.

80. 16 December 1958, "Záznam o informaci," J. Melničak, 024.816/58, MZV TO—T 1955–59, ČLR, krabice 2, obal 2.

81. Chan, Mao's Crusade, 31–47, 134.

82. 7 October 1960, "CC CCP an das Zentralkomitee der Polnischen Vereinigten Arbeiterpartei," SAPMO DY 30/3605/151.

83. 26 June 1959, "Závěry XXI. Sjezdu KSS pro práci KS Činy a jejich projednání," Ján Bušniak, 025.654/59, MZV TO—T 1955–59, ČLR, krabice 6, obal 1.

84. 25 May 1959, "Řodná pololetní hospodářská zpráva," Ján Bušniak, 023.844/59, MZV TO—T 1955–59, ČLR, krabice 7, obal 1.

85. 20 May 1959, "Zapis' besedy," P. F. Iudin and Zeng Xisheng, AVPRF f. 0100, op. 51, p. 435, d. 25, l. 4.

86. 26 June 1959, "Závěry XXI. Sjezdu KSS pro práci KS Činy a jejich projednaní," Ján Bušniak, 025.654/59, NA KSČ–AN-II, krabice 86, folder "Čína," 1959.

87. 8 June 1961, Vladimír Koucký, 00431/61, ibid., krabice 84, folder "Čína: Ruzné materiály, 1956–1967." The notion of the "two lines" within the CCP was of course well-developed in Western scholarship. See MacFarquhar, The Origins of the Cultural Revolution, vol. 3.

88. 12 October 1962, 0772/62, and 4 January 1963, 010/63, NA KSČ–AN-II, krabice 84, folder "Čína: Ruzné materiály, 1956–1967"; 4 October 1966, "Informační zpráva o pobytu posádky LO MV v ČLR," Josef Pása, NA KSČ–AN-II, krabice 85, folder "Čína," 1961–65.

89. 4 October 1960, "Zpráva s. Šedivého z Pekingu," NA KSČ–AN-II, krabice 84, folder "Telegramy, sífry, depresè, zpravy."

90. 8 October 1960, "Propaganda und Studium der Lehren Mao Tse-tungs in der Volksrepublik China," 9 October 1960, Wandel to Peter Florin, SAPMO DY 30-IV 2/20/122/184-198.

91. 1967, "Vývoj Korejsko-Čínských vztahů a hodnócaní situace v ČLR Korejskými představiteli," 1911.9/67, NA KSČ–AN-II, krabice 85, folder "Čína," 1967; 18 August 1966, Helmut Liebermann to Hegen, SAPMO DY 30/11515/190. See also Hershberg et al., "The Interkit Story."

92. Zubok, *A Failed Empire*, 126.

93. 19 November 1958, "Zapis' besedy," P. Iudin and Chen Yi, AVPRF f. 0100, op. 51, p. 432, d. 6, l. 179.

94. Pu Guoliang, *Zouxiang bingdian*, 42.

95. 25 May 1956, "Zapis' besedy," P. F. Iudin and Mao Zedong, AVPRF f. 0100, op. 49, p. 410, d. 9, l. 126.

96. 9 February 1955, "Priem," V. A. Zorin and Liu Xiao, ibid., op. 48, p. 393, d. 6, l. 9. See also Zhihua Shen and Yafeng Xia, "Hidden Currents during the Honeymoon," 112–14.

97. 11 November 1958, "Zhou zongli tong aulian zhuhua dashi," WJBDAG 107-00103-23, 4.

98. 27 March 1956, "Moluotuofu tongzhi jiejian suoyou renmin minzhu guojia zhu sulian dashiguan suo shuoming wenti," WJBDAG 109-01617-03, 18.

99. 1956, "Ustav," WJBDAG 109-00752-01, 7-34. The Chinese representative was Wang Ganchang, a nuclear physicist. See Zhihua Shen and Yafeng Xia, "Between Aid and Restriction," 12–13.

100. Shen Zhihua, *Sulian zhuanjia zai zhongguo*, 312; Zhihua Shen and Yafeng Xia, "Hidden Currents during the Honeymoon," 85; Zhihua Shen and Yafeng Xia, "Between Aid and Restriction," 9, 19. Nie Rongzhen and Li Yueran make a similar claim in their memoirs. See Lewis and Xue Litai, *China Builds the Bomb*, 62; and Li Yueran, *Zhongsu waijiao qinliji*, 99.

101. 24 October 1956, "Renda daibiaotuan fangwen wenti," WJBDAG 109-01101-01, 46.

102. Holloway, *Stalin and the Bomb*, 354; 7 April 1955, "Zapis' besedy," P. F. Iudin and Zhou Enlai, AVPRF f. 0100, op. 48, p. 393, d. 9, l. 54; 24 August 1957, P. Abrasimov to Zhang Wentian, WJBDAG 109-00752-03, 20; Liu Yanqiong and Liu Jifeng, "Analysis of Soviet Technology Transfer in the Development of China's Nuclear Weapons," 71–73.

103. Lewis and Xue Litai, *China Builds the Bomb*, 62–63. Chen Geng and Song Renqiong were both former Yunnan Province officials and facilitators of Chinese aid to the Vietminh in the Indochina conflict. See Zhai, *China and the Vietnam Wars*, 22–33.

104. Gobarev, "Soviet Policy toward China," 18–21; Zubok and Pleshakov, *Inside the Kremlin's Cold War*, 217; Lewis and Xue Litai, *China Builds the Bomb*, 41; Lüthi, "The Sino-Soviet Split," 72, 126; Li Danhui, "Mao Zedong dui su renshi yu zhongsu guanxi de yanbian," in Li Danhui, *Beijing yu Mosike*, 322–23.

105. Shen Zhihua, *Sulian zhuanjia zai zhongguo*, 282–84.

106. 9 February 1950, "Zapis' besedy," A. Gromyko and General Liu Yaolou, AVPRF f. 0100, op. 43, p. 302, d. 8, l. 12.

107. 25 September 1957, "Stenogramma," RGAE f. 8157, op. 1, d. 1991, l. 161–70.

108. 5 June 1956, WJBDAG 109-00745-03, 22–23; 16 July 1956, "Tongyi sulian tu-104 ji jing woguo bian chu yindu you," WJBDAG 109-00745-04, 37.

109. April 1956, N. A. Bulganin to Zhou Enlai, WJBDAG 109-00751-03, 13; 24 March 1956, to Zhou Enlai, WJBDAG 109-00746-01, 1.

110. Chen Jian, *Mao's China and the Cold War*, 73–74; Kuo, *Contending with Contradictions*, 148–49; Shu Guang Zhang and Chen Jian, "The Emerging Disputes between Beijing and Moscow," 156–59.

111. 9 July 1956, WJBDAG 109-00751-01, 4.

112. 10 August 1956, "Guanyu tongyi ling xinde youkuang kantan de xieding de fujian," WJBDAG 109-00751-01, 9.

113. Minaev, *Sovetskaia voennaia moshch' ot Stalina do Gorbacheva*, 157–58; Zubok, *A Failed Empire*, 131.

114. 11 September 1957, "Protokol No. 1," RGAE f. 8157, op. 1, d. 1991, l. 114.

115. Lewis and Xue Litai, *China Builds the Bomb*, 212.

116. Zhang Shu Guang and Chen Jian, "The Emerging Disputes between Beijing and Moscow," 154; Shen Zhihua, *Sulian zhuanjia zai zhongguo*, 285.

117. 4 April 1958, Nikita Khrushchev to Zhou Enlai, AVPRF f. 0100, op. 45, p. 181, d. 15, l. 2.

118. 1 June 1958, "Priem," A. Gromyko, GARF f. 9518, op. 1, d. 143, l. 77–78.

119. 15 September 1958, "Su dui wo yu meidi douzheng de zhichi qingkuang," WJBDAG 109-01213-09, 75.

120. 11 September 1958, "Susiluofu zai baoguan yanhui shang jianghua zhong qiangdiao sulian zhichi zhongguo," WJBDAG 109-01213-09, 68.

121. Zubok, "Khrushchev's Nuclear Promise to Beijing during the 1958 Crisis," 227.

122. 7 October 1958, "Guanyu taiwan wenti," WJBDAG 109-01213-09, 81; also 10 October 1958, "Su baokan dali zhichi wo dui 'meijiang de douzheng,'" WJBDAG 109-01213-09, 89.

123. 2 June 1960, "Predlozheniia sovetskogo pravitel'stva ob osnovnykh polozheniiakh dogovora o vseobshchem i polnom razoruzhenii," AVPRF f. 0100, op. 47, p. 194, d. 4, l. 8. See also Gobarev, "Soviet Policy toward China," 21; Zubok and Pleshakov, *Inside the Kremlin's Cold War*, 228; and Chen Jian, *Mao's China and the Cold War*, 78–79.

124. 17 October 1959, "Heluxiaofu tongzhi 1959 nian 10 yue 12 ri gei Aisenhaochengre de fuxin," WJBDAG 109-00873-19, 100–105.

125. 29 August 1959, "Chen Yi fuzongli jiejian sulian zhuhua dashi daiban Andongluofu tanhua jilu," WJBDAG 109-00874-01, 3.

126. 12 September 1960, "Chen Yi fuzongli tong sulian fuwaizhang Puxijin de tanhua jilu," WJBDAG 109-00933-15, 136.

127. 2 December 1960, "Záznam," J. Melničak and Jie Zhusheng, NA KSČ–AN-II, krabice 84, folder "Čína: Ruzné materiály, 1956–1967."

128. 14 November 1960, "Liecheng wo liuxuesheng fanying qingkuang jianbao," WJB-DAG 109-01098-02, 38.

129. 14 December 1959, "O návštěvě ústřední konservatoře hudby v Pekingu," Jaromír Štětina, 033.355/59, MZV TO—T 1955–59, ČLR, krabice 8, obal 1.

130. 4 December 1958, "Zpráva o návštěvach čsl. hudebních činitelů v Šanghaji," J. Fierlínger, 2130/58, MZV TO—O 1945–59, ČLR, krabice 8, obal 17.

131. "Dogovor druzhby i bratstva," *Novoe vremia*, no. 7 (12 February 1960): 1–2.

132. 17 December 1959, "O zájezdu české filharmonie do čínské lidové republiky," Jaromír Štětina, 033.351/59, MZV TO—T 1955–59, ČLR, krabice 8, obal 1.

133. 10 December 1959, "Zpráva o zájezdu české filharmonie," 073/59, ibid., krabice 2, obal 4; 21 November 1959, "Záznam z návštěvy," J. Melničak, 4409/59, ibid., krabice 2, obal 9.

134. 17 December 1959, "O zájezdu české filharmonie do čínské lidové republiky," Jaromír Štětina, 033.351/59, ibid., krabice 8, obal 1.

135. 9 September 1959, "Záznam z rozhovoru," Ladislav Rejmán and Brie, 0455/59, ibid., krabice 2, obal 9.

136. 16 January 1957, Liang Hanguang to Mikhail Chulaki, RGALI f. 648, op. 7, d. 256, l. 72.

137. 1958, "Materialy o kul'turnom sotrudnichestve," S. Iutkevich, RGALI f. 2936, op. 1, d. 1245, l. 2.

138. 28 November 1956, Chinese Youth Artistic Theater to Galina Nikolaeva, RGALI f. 2292, op. 1, d. 201, l. 1.

139. Wu Lengxi, *Shinian lunzhan*, 522. See also Wu Xiuquan, *Eight Years in the Ministry of Foreign Affairs*, 30–31.

140. Zhou Yizhi, "Zai Mao Zedong wenyi sixiang de qizhi xia," *Renmin ribao* (12 October 1960): 7.

141. "Gongren jieji shehuizhuyi jiaoyu xuezhe cunke," *Gongren ribao* (29 January 1958): 3.

142. "Quanmin de jieri quanmin de shengli," *Xinmin ribao* (1 October 1958): 3.

143. 1 August 1958, Jindřich Pech to B. Handla, 019.299/58-7, MZV TO—T 1955–59, ČLR, krabice 2, obal 5.

144. 3 July 1958, "Připomínky čínské strany k cs. Filmu 'Bratr ocean," 018.219/58, ibid.

145. 13 November 1958, "Telegram z Pekingu," Vasek, 024.211/58, ibid.

146. 10 December 1959, "Zpráva o zájezdu české filharmonie," 073/59, ibid., obal 4.

147. 20 July 1959, "O kulturních stycích ČLR s kapitalistickými zeměmi," Ján Bušniak, 025.421/59, ibid., krabice 8, obal 1.

148. 17 December 1959 "O zájezdu české filharmonie do čínské lidové republiky," Jaromír Štětina, 033.351/59, ibid. Czechoslovak officials on occasion pushed the Soviets to support more cultural exchange within the bloc on a commercial basis. See 8 October 1958, "Zapis' besedy," I. Vclenko and L. L. Barak, GARF f. 9518, op. 1, d. 143, l. 134.

149. 15 October 1959, Ladislav Rejmán, 4417/59, MZV TO—T 1955–59, ČLR, krabice 2, obal 9.

150. 1961, Jing Longjing, RGALI f. 2077, op. 1, d. 1953, l. 2.

151. 1958, "Materialy o kul'turnom sotrudnichestve," S. Iutkovich, RGALI f. 2936, op. 1, d. 1245, l. 1; 31 December 1959, "Perepiska s soiuzom kompozitorov Kitaia," G. Zhukov and Liu Xiao, RGALI f. 2077, op. 1, d. 1842, l. 2; 1961, "Perepiska s soiuzom muzykantov Kitaia," ibid., d. 1953, l. 24–25.

152. 20 January 1961, "Perepiska s soiuzom muzykantov Kitaia," S. Skrebkov, ibid., l. 8–9.

153. 22 July 1961, "Perepiska s soiuzom muzykantov Kitaia," Lu Zi, ibid., l. 70.

154. 20 March 1961, "Materialy o kul'turnykh sviaziakh OSKD s OKSD," I. Rogachev, GARF f. 9576, op. 18, d. 113, l. 20–23.

155. 16 January 1960, D. Shostakovich, Shi Leming, Yang Yinliu, RGALI f. 2077, op. 1, d. 1842, l. 26.

156. 7 March 1962, "Perepiska s Kitaem," Iu. Osadchii, GARF f. 9576, op. 18, d. 143, l. 116.

157. 25 May 1959, "Perspektivní plan kulturních styků," Ján Bušniak, 0233/59, MZV TO—T 1955–59, ČLR, krabice 2, obal 4.

158. 23 December 1961, "Materialy o kul'turnykh sviaziakh OSKD s OKSD," S. Chervonenko, GARF f. 9576, op. 18, d. 113, l. 212–13.

159. 1961, "Tvorcheskie i obshchestvennye organizatsii," RGALI f. 2077, op. 1, d. 1953, l. 24–25.

160. 31 May 1961, P. Kriukov to Iu. I. Mozhaev, ibid., l. 50.

161. 29 December 1961, "Perepiska s Kitaem," G. Grushetskii, GARF f. 9576, op. 18, d. 143, l. 1.

162. July 1961, "Perepiska s soiuzom muzykantov Kitaia," RGALI f. 2077, op. 1, d. 1953, l. 72.

163. 5 December 1960, "Information zu einigen Problemen auf den Gebieten der kulturellen Entwicklung in der VR China," SAPMO DY 30-IV 2/20/123/4-8.

164. January 1962, "Abschrift zu Übersetzung und Herausgabe Chinesischer Literatur in der DDR," SAPMO DY 30-IV 2/20/115/53.

Chapter Six

1. For Mao's views, see MacFarquhar, Cheek, and Wu, *The Secret Speeches of Chairman Mao*, 413–15; Leung and Kau, *The Writings of Mao Zedong*, 444; *Mao Zedong waijiao wenxuan*, 254; *Jianguo yilai Mao Zedong wengao*, 390–92, 600–602; and MacFarquhar and Schoenhals, *Mao's Last Revolution*, 356.

2. 15 March 1958, "Zapis' besedy," P. Iudin and Mao Zedong, AVPRF f. 0100, op. 51, p. 432, d. 6, l. 93.

3. Ledovskii, "Stalin, Mao Tszedun i Koreiskaia voina," 81–83; Chen Jian, *China's Road to the Korean War*, 19–21, 74–75.

4. 4 July 1959, "Daibiao zhonggong zhongyang lianxi gong (bu) zhongyang Sidalin de baogao," *Jianguo yilai Liu Shaoqi wengao*, 1:17.

5. Yang Kuisong, *Mao Zedong yu Mosike de enen yuanyuan*, 280.

6. 16 November 1949, "Zai yazhou aozhou gonghui huiyi shangde kaimu ci," *Jianguo yilai Liu Shaoqi wengao*, 1:133.

7. Zhai, *China and the Vietnam Wars*, 21. See also Xu Zehao, *Wang Jiaxiang zhuan*, 508.

8. Chen Jian, "Bridging Revolution and Decolonization," 141–45.

9. July 1954, "Joint Statement of Prime Ministers of China and India," WJBDAG 102-00171-02, 30.

10. "Russia had no defenders at Bandung," reported Richard Wright. Wright, *The Color Curtain*, 157; see also Hopf, *Social Construction of International Politics*, 102; and Pei Jianzhang, *Zhonghua renmin gongheguo waijiaoshi*, 7–18.

11. Xu Zehao, *Wang Jiaxiang zhuan*, 530.

12. 8 August 1958, "Guanyu Mao Zedong zhuxi tong Heluxiaofu huitan gongbao," WJBDAG 107-00152-03, 29.

13. Friedman, "Reviving the Revolution," 14; Zhihua Shen and Danhui Li, *After Leaning to One Side*, 247–48.

14. Richardson, *China, Cambodia, and the Five Principles of Peaceful Coexistence*; Kuo, *Contending with Contradictions*, 57.

15. 30 October 1956, "Deklaratsiia," 12; 30 October 1956, "Zhonghua renmin gongheguo zhengfu guanyu sulian zhengfu yijiuwuliu nian shiyue sanshi ri xuanyan de shengming," 6; also 1 November 1956, "Sulian zhengfu xuanyan de shengming," 1, all WJBDAG 109-00744-01.

16. 15 May 1957, "1957 nian 5 yue jiebo tanpan qingkuang," WJBDAG 109-01138-03, 30.

17. Ilya V. Gaiduk, "The Second Front of the Soviet's Cold War: Asia in the System of Moscow's Foreign Policy Priorities, 1945–1956," in Hasegawa, *The Cold War in East Asia*, 63–80.

18. 25 May 1956, "Zapis' besedy," P. F. Iudin and Mao Zedong, AVPRF f. c100, op. 49, p. 410, d. 9, l. 126.

19. 8 November 1956, "Zai su guoqing yanhui zhong Heluxiaofu deng jianghua yaodian," WJBDAG 109-01615-05, 26.

20. 18 July 1958, "Zhonghua renmin gongheguo zhengfu dui yingguo zhengfu de kangyi," WJBDAG 107-00152-05, 1.

21. 17 July 1958, "Gao Chen buzhang zhaojian yafei guojia shijie tan ya, leibanan qingkuang," WJBDAG 107-00152-02, 12–13.

22. 3 October 1957, "Mao zhuxi jiejian bolan junshi daibiaotuan tanhua jilu," WJBDAG 109-01129-07, 73.

23. 8 August 1958, "Guanyu Mao Zedong zhuxi tong Heluxiaofu huitan gongbao," WJBDAG 107-00152-03, 29; 8 August 1958, "Meizhou tongbao di 141 qi," ibid., 27.

24. 14 September 1959, M. Nesterov to A. I. Mikoian, RGANI f. 5, op. 30, d. 307, l. 87.

25. 19 September 1959, M. Zimianin; 29 April 1959, "O deiatel'nosti . . . KNR," 27 January 1960, all ibid., l. 65, 33; d. 335, l. 31.

26. 12 February 1958, "Wahua sichang jiejian sulian sudaliwafu canzan, WJBDAG 107-00103-01, 1.

27. C. Chen, *China and the Three Worlds*, 23; Li Jie, *Mao Zedong yu xin zhongguo de neizheng waijiao*, 37–39, 56–59, 137; Westad, *The Global Cold War*, 163; Friedman, "Reviving the Revolution," 151–99.

28. 13 November 1958, "Jishenweite tan deyi tanpan qingkuang," WJBDAG 107-00155-06, 23.

29. 29 January 1957, "Zhude shiguan 1956 nian gongzuo zongjie baogao," WJBDAG 109-00755-01, 3.

30. 19 June 1958, "Ma Geluotiwu zongli tanhua yaodian," Wang Guoquan, WJBDAG 107-00286-07, 63.

31. 10 May 1965, "Stenografische Niederschrift," Kurt Hager, et al., SAPMO DY30/11398/31.

32. 30 January 1961, "Aktenvermerk," Wandel and Chen Yi, SAPMO DY30-IV 2/20/123/85.

33. 24 May 1962, Stenzel, SAPMO DY30-IV 2/20/115/312.

34. 27 May 1962, Hegen, SAPMO DY 30-IV 2/20/125/84.

35. 28 November 1959, "Su dui zhongyin bianjie wenti de taidu," WJBDAG 109-01354-03, 50.

36. 18 December 1960, "Tong lao fuzongli Qidiluolin tanhua baogao," WJBDAG 109-01500-03, 37.

37. 26 November 1961, "Guanyu meiguo jiajin ganshe he qinlue yuenan nanfangde shengming, WJBDAG 106-00600-05, 25; 7 July 1961, "Yue jiang jinyibu kaizhan fan mei douzheng shi," WJBDAG 106-00608-01, 3.

38. 16 December 1961, "Guanyu dui yuenan guohui de huyu shu fuxin zhichi wenti yijian de baogao," WJBDAG 106-00600-03, 9.

39. 4 November 1963, "Sulian li qiu tingzhi gongkai taolun," WJBDAG 109-03341-01, 35–37.

40. 1960, "Bemerkungen zur Aussenpolitik der VR China im Jahre 1960," SAPMO DY 30-IV 2/20/122/308.

41. 6 July 1963, "Rech' . . . Suslova," SAPMO DY 30/11925/14.

42. 27 August 1963, "Su fanhua yundong de yixie zhide zhuyi de dongxiang," WJBDAG 109-03341-03, 107.

43. 9–13 December 1963, "Plenum TsK KPSS," N. S. Khrushchev, RGANI f. 2, r. 6312, op. 1, d. 664, l. 101.

44. 28 January 1969, "Stenografische Niederschrift einer internen Beratung über die Lage in der Volksrepublik China," SAPMO DY 30/11927/75.

45. Chen Jian, "A Crucial Step toward the Breakdown of the Sino-Soviet Alliance," 249.

46. 9 July 1960, S. Chervonenko to Iu. V. Andropov, I. I. Tugarinov, F. I. Golikov, AVPRF f. 0100, op. 53, p. 457, d. 24, l. 96–97. The 18 July 1960 communication, noted above, referred directly to Fu Zhong and this episode.

47. 22 June 1960, "Vystuplenie," Fu Zhong, ibid., l. 100.

48. 14 December 1960, "Osnovnye sobytiia v sovetsko-kitaiskikh otnosheniiakh v 1960 godu," G. Grushetskii, ibid., l. 267; 18 October 1960, "Zapis' besedy," S. V. Chervonenko, ibid., d. 9, l. 35.

49. 18 October 1960, "Zapis' besedy," S. V. Chervonenko and Tran Du Binh, ibid.

50. 9 August 1960, "Ban yue lai sulian junshi zhuanjia dongtai," Xiao Xiangrong, WJB-DAG 109-02085-07, 23–26; 10 August 1960, "Xiang sulian junshi zhuanjia xuanchuan liang guo zhengfu zhaohu qingkuang," ibid., 28–29.

51. 30 August 1960, "Zapis' besedy," S. V. Chervonenko and Chen Yi, ibid., p. 454, d. 8, l. 205; 13 August 1960, "Záznam," Bruno Köhler, 5823/8, NA KSČ–AN-II, krabice 86, folder "Čína," 1960.

52. 27 August 1960, "Guanyu su chetui zhuanjia shi," WJBDAG 109-02085-05, 20.

53. 27 November 1960, "Guanyu qu liu guo xieding lai hua," Zhou Enlai, WJBDAG 109-02085-08, 52.

54. 17 August 1960, "Zpráva s. Štětiny z Pekingu," NA KSČ–AN-II, krabice 84, folder "Telegramy, sífry, depresè, zpravy."

55. 27 September 1960, "Zpráva s. Šedivého z Pekingu," ibid. For Chinese complaints to the Soviets, see 4 November 1960, AVPRF f. 0100, op. 53, p. 457, d. 24, l. 224–29.

56. 24 September 1960, "Zpráva s. Dvořáka z Moskvy," NA KSČ–AN-II, krabice 84, folder "Telegramy, sífry, depresè, zpravy."

57. 17–22 September 1960, "Výpis z protokolu o dvoustranných jednáních mezi delegací KSSS a KS Číny ve dnech 17.—22 září v Moskve," ibid., krabice 86, folder "Čína," 1960.

58. 12 December 1960, Wang Guoquan, SAPMO DY 30-IV 2/20/122/291-92.

59. 2 April 1963, "Záznam z rozhovoru s. velv. radou ZÚ MLR," 003731/63, NA KSČ–AN-II, krabice 84, folder "Čína: Ruzné materiály, 1956–1967."

60. 22 August 1960, "Zpráva s. Štětiny z Pekingu," ibid., folder "Telegramy, sífry, depresè, zpravy."

61. 16 August 1960, "Zpráva s. Štětiny z Pekingu," and 22 August 1960, "Zpráva s. Štětiny z Pekingu," ibid.

62. 14 September 1960, "Zpráva s. Štětiny z Pekingu," ibid.

63. 15 August 1960, "Zaznam o odvolání sovětských specialist z ČLR," 31/2/22, VÚA MNO, krabice 37.

64. 27 September 1960; 29 September 1960; 12 October 1960; 13 October 1960, all in "Zpráva s. Šedivého z Pekingu," NA KSČ–AN-II, krabice 84, folder "Telegramy, sífry, depresè, zpravy."

65. 31 March 1962, "Telegram z Pekingu," Šedivý, ibid.

66. 3 March 1960, "Záznam," 022.314/60, ibid., folder "Čína," 1960.

67. 25 January 1962, "Telegram z Pekingu," Šedivý, ibid., folder "Telegramy, sífry, depresè, zpravy."

68. "De dashiguan wuguan juxing zhaodaihui," *Renmin ribao* (2 March 1961): 4.

69. January 1964, "Rozhovory velvyslance NDR v ČLR s činskými představiteli před odjezdem," 2900/7, NA KSČ–AN-II, krabice 85, folder "Čína," 1964.

70. Hershberg et al., "The Interkit Story," 9, 79.

71. 22 March 1962, "Záznam o rozhovoru," 10.309/8, NA KSČ–AN-II, krabice 85, folder "Čína," 1962; also 22 October 1959, "Záznam," J. Štětina, 4399/59, MZV TO—T 1955–59, ČLR, krabice 2, obal 9.

72. 7 March 1961, "Aktenvermerk," Wandel and Šedivý; 22 March 1961, "Aktenvermerk," Wenning and Szigeti; 10 March 1961, "Aktenvermerk," Wandel and Chervonenko, SAPMO DY 30-IV 2/20/123/195-203; 1 February 1962, "Aktenvermerk," Hegen and Martin; 22 February 1962, "Aktenvermerk," Hegen and Flato, SAPMO DY 30-IV 2/20/124/99-101.

73. 17 December 1959, "O zájezdu české filharmonie do čínské lidové republiky," Jaromír Štětina, 033.351/59; 25 July 1959, "O pobytu československé kulturní delegace v ČLR," Jaromír Štětina, 027.487/59, both MZV TO—T 1955–59, ČLR, krabice 8, obal 1.

74. 4 March 1961, "Interview dopisovatele 'Nepszabadsag,'" 7481/61, NA KSČ–AN-II, krabice 85, folder "Čína," 1961; 22 March 1961, "Aktenvermerk," Wenning and Szigeti, SAPMO DY 30-IV 2/20/123/186-89

75. 22 August 1962, "Záznam o návětěvě," 011277/62, NA KSČ–AN-II, krabice 84, folder "Čína," 1965–67.

76. 15 August 1961, "Informace pro soudruha Hendrycha," Josef Kudrna, ibid., folder "Čína: Ruzné materiály, 1956–1967."

77. 11 January 1962, "Informace o současné situaci v postoji čínských soudruhů k výsledkům XXII. Sjezdu KSSS," V. Podzimek, ibid., krabice 86, folder "Čína."

78. 5 October 1963, "Telegram z Pekingu," Šedivy, ibid., krabice 84, folder "Telegramy, sífry, depresè, zpravy."

79. 11 November 1965, and 18 December 1965, "Telegram z Pekingu," Křístek, ibid.

80. 12 November 1963, "Návštěvy madarského velvyslance v ČLR na rozloučenou," 2297/7, ibid., krabice 85, folder 118: Čína.

81. 23 January 1964, "Zhu deguo shiguan wenhuachu 1964 nian gongzuo guihua," WJBDAG 109-03535-02, 36.

82. 7 April 1964, "Liu zhuxi zai de dashi chengdi guoshu shide da ci," WJBDAG 117-01668-01, 1; 24 April 1964, "Jieshou jie dashi guoshu de daci," WJBDAG 117-01668-02, 17; 22 September 1964, "Guanyu dui de buchang huiyi zhuxi," WJBDAG 117-01720-01, 4–5.

83. 6 March 1963, "Sulian qun dui wo wenzhang de fanying," WJBDAG 109-03319-01, 1.

84. 16 August 1963, "Shiguan guanyu sulian qun dui hexiu changkuang fanhua de banfa," ibid., 14.

85. 6 April 1964, "Sugong fanhua wenxian fabiaohou de fanying," WJBDAG 109-02705-01, 85.

86. 15 August 1963, "Wo fang sufang xingzu jiechu de sulianren fanying de yixie qingkuang," WJBDAG 109-03319-01, 10–11.

87. 6 April 1964, "Sugong fanhua wenxian fabiaohou de fanying," WJBDAG 109-02705-01, 85.

88. 22 July 1963, "Wo liening geqin tongxue fanying qingkuang," WJBDAG 109-03319-01, 8.

89. 4 May 1964, "Wo liuxuesheng fanying de qingkuang," WJBDAG 109-02705-02, 135.

90. 27 November 1963, "Guanyu yierkucike shichang gongying he sulian ren dui zhongsu tiaoyue fanying deng qingkuang," WJBDAG 109-03319-01, 46.

91. 15 August 1963, "Wo fang sufang xingzu jiechu de sulianren fanying de yixie qingkuang," WJBDAG 109-03319-01, 10.

92. 22 July 1963, "Wo liening geqin tongxue fanying qingkuang," WJBDAG 109-03319-01, 8.

93. 22 August 1963, "Aerkuxiefusiji tan zai su liangyue jianwen," WJBDAG 109-03319-01, 28–30.

94. 6 November 1963, "Wo lai autaijin zhuanjia fanyi yilushang dao de qingkuang," WJBDAG 109-03319-01, 39.

95. 15 August 1963, "Wo fang sufang xingzu jiechu de sulianren fanying de yixie qingkuang," WJBDAG 109-03319-01, 10–11.

96. 23 April 1964, "22 ri dao Mosike guoji liejun yantu qingkuang," WJBDAG 109-02705-2, 121.

97. 10 March 1964, "Sugong zai eryue quanhuihou de yixie fanhua huodong," WJBDAG 109-02705-01, 43.

98. 6 April 1964, "Sugong fanhua wenxian fabiaohou de fanying," ibid., 89.

99. 15 August 1963, "Wo fang sufang xingzu jiechu de sulianren fanying de yixie qingkuang," WJBDAG 109-03319-01, 11.

100. 22 August 1963, "Aerkuxiefusiji tan zai su liangyue jianwen," ibid., 26.

101. 10 March 1964, "Sugong zai eryue quanhuihou de yixie fanhua huodong," WJBDAG 109-02705-01, 43.

102. 6 April 1964, "Sugong fanhua wenxian fabiaohou de fanying," WJBDAG 109-02705-01, 83.

103. Ibid., 87, 85.

104. 1 October 1964, "Mao zhuxi jiejian sulian dang zheng daibiaotuan," WJBDAG 204-01537-05, 1–3.

105. 19 October 1964, "Heluxiaofu xiataihou de yixie qingkuang," WJBDAG 109-02708-02, 99.

106. 24 October 1964, "Sugong xinde xuanchuan dongxiang," ibid., 129–32.

107. 24 October 1964, "Liange sulian ren dui woxuesheng tan de yixie qingkuang," WJBDAG 109-02708-05, 41. Aleksei Adzhubei was the editor-in-chief of *Izvestiia*.

108. 22 October 1964, "Sulian ren zui he xiatai de fanying," ibid., 31.

109. 27 October 1964, "Lie cheng jiuxuesheng fanying de qingkuang," ibid., 53.

110. 27 October 1964, "Sulian qunzhong dui he kuatai de fanying," ibid., 35–38.

111. Troianovskii, *Cherez gody i rasstoianiia*, 222, 349; Aleksandrov-Agentov, *Ot Kollontai do Gorbacheva*, 254; Radchenko, *Two Suns in the Heavens*, 138–40.

112. Aleksandrov-Agentov, *Ot Kollontai do Gorbacheva*, 168.

113. Radchenko, *Two Suns in the Heavens*, 130.

114. 30 October 1964, "Telegram z Pekingu," Křístek, NA KSČ–AN-II, krabice 84, folder "Telegramy, sífry, despresè, zpravy."

115. 1 November 1964, "Guanyu shiyue geming jie sishiba zhounian qingzhu banfa," WJBDAG 109-02840-02, 24.

116. S. A. Mel'chin et al., eds., "Kak snimali N. S. Khrushcheva," *Istoricheskii arkhiv*, no. 1 (1993): 13.

117. 23 October 1964, "Su zhengzhi jiaoyuan zai hang xuexiao tong xuesheng de tanhuo qingkuang," WJBDAG 109-02708-05, 49–50.

118. 24 October 1964, "Sugong xinde xuanchuan dongxiang," WJBDAG 109-02708-02, 129–32.

119. 30 October 1964, "Telegram z Pekingu," Křístek, NA KSČ–AN-II, krabice 84, folder "Telegramy, sífry, despresè, zpravy."

120. 10 November 1964, "Stenographische Niederschrift," Walter Ulbricht and Zhou Enlai, SAPMO DY30/11397/69.

121. 21 November 1964, "Lie cheng dengde qunzhong dui he xiatai, wo hewuqi de fanying," WJBDAG 109-02708-05, 63.

122. Radchenko, *Two Suns in the Heavens*, 132; Mingjiang Li, *Mao's China and the Sino-Soviet Split*, 120. In a toast at a military reception hosted by General He Long, Malinovsky reportedly offered: "Now that we've kicked out our Nikita, why don't you do the same to your Mao Zedong?" See Troianovskii, *Cherez gody i rasstoianiia*, 350; and Arbatov, *The System*, 114. In Aleksandrov-Agentov's rendition, the drunken Malinovsky says to Zhou Enlai, "Well, look what we've done—we threw away our old galoshes, Khrushchev. Now you can shed your old galoshes—Mao, and then we'll get along fine." Aleksandrov-Agentov, *Ot Kollontai do Gorbacheva*, 169. See also Fedotov, *Polveka vmeste s Kitaem*, 329–30.

123. 7 May 1964, "Pan dashi chuxi dashi zhaodaihui qingkuang," WJBDAG 109-02705-02, 125.

124. 16 January 1963, "Fandui wo jinxin zaoyao wumie chuxianle xin qingkuang," WJBDAG 109-03341-03, 113.

125. Aleksandrov-Agentov, *Ot Kollontai do Gorbacheva*, 168–71; Troianovskii, *Cherez gody i rasstoianiia*, 351; Radchenko, *Two Suns in the Heavens*, 140–51.

126. 12 May 1965, "Liu Xiao fubuzhang jiejian sulian zhuhua dashi Labin tanhua jiyao," WJBDAG 106-01516-06, 3.

127. Lüthi, "The Origins of Proletarian Diplomacy."

128. Cited in MacFarquhar and Schoenhals, *Mao's Last Revolution*, 356.

129. Lin Biao, "Why a Cultural Revolution," in Schoenhals, *China's Cultural Revolution*, 14–16.

130. 6 August 1966, "Telegram z Pekingu," Křístek, NA KSČ–AN-II, krabice 84, folder "Telegramy, sífry, depresè, zpravy."

131. Medvedev, *Neizvestnyi Andropov*, 105; Radchenko, *Two Suns in the Heavens*, 177–80, 188–95.

132. 3 February 1967, 020.898/67, NA KSČ–AN-II, krabice 84, folder "Čína," 1965–67.

133. 3 February 1967, 021.017/67, ibid.

134. 27 July 1967, "Záznam," 025.403/67, ibid.

135. 31 January 1967, "Telegram z Pekingu," Křístek, ibid., folder "Telegramy, sífry, depresè, zpravy."

136. 6 April 1964, "Sugong fanhua wenxian fabiaohou de fanying," WJBDAG 109-02705-01, 88.

137. 5 January 1959, "Pis'mo Kommunista," Dneprov, RGANI f. 5, op. 30, d. 320, l. 52–58.

Chapter Seven

1. 9 April 1953, Edwin Smith to Georgii Zarubin, RGANI f. 5, op. 28, d. 46, l. 39–46, 53–54, 71; 23 March 1954, N. Pal'gunov to G. M. Malenkov, ibid., op. 30, d. 51, l. 57; Rósa Magnúsdóttir, "Mission Impossible? Selling Soviet Socialism, 1955–1958," in Gienow-Hecht and Donfried, *Searching for a Cultural Diplomacy*, 50–72.

2. David-Fox, *Showcasing the Great Experiment*, 323; Mazov, *A Distant Front in the Cold War*, 26; 1958, "Spravka," T. Mamedova, GARF f. 9576, op. 8, d. 48, l. 237.

3. On VOKS and Soviet cultural programs in North Korea, see Kan In Gu, *Kul'turnoe sotrudnichestvo sovetskogo soiuza i severnoi Korei vo vtoroi polovine 40-kh godov*; and Armstrong, "The Cultural Cold War in Korea." See also Nikol'skaia, *Mezhdunarodnye kul'turnye sviazi SSSR v pervoe desiatiletie sovetskoi vlasti*; and Naimark, *The Russians in Germany*, 398–440.

4. 31 January 1944, T. Skvortsov to S. A. Novikov and N. M. Lifanov, GARF f. 5283, op. 18, d. 33, l. 49–52.

5. 9 March 1943, V. Valin, ibid., d. 35, l. 1–8.

6. Westad, *Decisive Encounters*, 128. For a Soviet treatment of the Northeast, see Borisov [former embassy official Oleg Rakhmaninin], *Sovetskii soiuz*.

7. 1 September 1949, "Anotatsiia," GARF f. 5283, op. 18, d. 91, l. 90.

8. "Kitaiskii narod ne zabudet sovetskoi armii–osvoboditel'nitsy," *Russkoe slovo* (17 August 1948): 2, ibid., d. 62, l. 15.

9. Shu Li, "When Writing History and Gazetters, Make a Critical Reassessment of the Sources (Excerpts)," 19.

10. Ibid., 24; Wolff, *To the Harbin Station*, 41.

11. L. V. Grigor'eva, "O kul'turnom nasledii rossiiskoi emigratsii v kharbine."

12. Clausen and Thøgersen, *The Making of a Chinese City*, 31–39.

13. 23 February 1948, Li Junfu, "Kratkaia istoriia obshchestva," GARF f. 5283, op. 18, d. 62, l. 54; 1947, "Informatsiia," l. 82–83; Clausen and Thøgersen, *The Making of a Chinese*

City, 152–53. For an account from a former Soviet military official, see Laboda, "History of the Sino-Soviet Friendship Society in Harbin."

14. 23 February 1948, Li Junfu, "Kratkaia istoriia obshchestva," GARF f. 5283, op. 18, d. 62, l. 53–57; 1950, ibid., d. 106, l. 12.

15. "Deiatel'nost' obshchestva kitaisko-sovetskoi druzhby," *Russkoe slovo* (1 February 1948): 8, ibid.

16. 1 September 1949, "Anotatsiia," ibid., d. 91, l. 88.

17. "Deiatel'nost' obshchestva kitaiskoi-sovetskoi druzhby," *Russkoe slovo* (1 February 1948): 8, ibid., d. 62, l. 12.

18. 1950, Qian Junrui, ibid., d. 106, l. 75.

19. 1947, "Informatsiia o sobraniiakh," ibid., d. 62, l. 82–83.

20. September–October 1950, "Doklad severno-vostochnogo otdela," ibid., d. 91, l. 231.

21. 29 April 1949; 1949, ibid., d. 86, l. 20–31, 45.

22. 1949, "Zapiska," Savinich, ibid., l. 32–33.

23. 13 April 1949, "Doklad," Krivtsov, ibid., d. 86, l. 34–37.

24. 27 February 1948, Union of Film Theaters in Harbin to OKSD, ibid., d. 62, l. 31.

25. September–October 1950, "Doklad severno-vostochnogo otdela," Dal'nyi, ibid., d. 91, l. 262, 257.

26. 1949, "Informatsiia," ibid., d. 86, l. 165.

27. "Kitaiskii narod ne zabudet sovetskoi armii–osvoboditel'nitsy," *Russkoe slovo* (17 August 1948): 2, ibid., d. 62, l. 15.

28. Brooks, *Thank You, Comrade Stalin!*

29. "Kitaiskii narod ne zabudet sovetskoi armii–osvoboditel'nitsy," *Russkoe slovo* (17 August 1948): 2, GARF f. 5283, op. 18, d. 62, l. 15.

30. September–October 1950, "Doklad severno-vostochnogo otdela," ibid., d. 91, l. 237.

31. "Sidalin dayuanshuai Jinricheng shouxiang zhuhe," *Suiyan ribao* (17 August 1952): 1.

32. 23 June 1950, "Anotatsiia," GARF f. 5283, op. 18, d. 91, l. 120.

33. N. A. Pankov, "Obshchestvo sovetsko-kitaiskoi druzhby," *Problemy dal'nego vostoka*, no. 3 (1972): 207–8.

34. 3 September 1955, "O nekotorykh nedostatkakh v organizatsii kul'turnykh i nauchnykh sviazei mezhdu SSSR i stranami narodnoi demokratii," S. Rumiantsev, RGANI f. 5, op. 28, r. 5136, d. 286, l. 188.

35. 26 November 1956, B. Polevoi, ibid., r. 5200, d. 506, l. 89.

36. 31 December 1959, "Zapis' besedy," A. I. Elizavetin and Liu Shuzhou, GARF f. 9576, op. 18, d. 26, l. 346;

37. 12 April 1957, "Zapis' besedy," N. Fedorenko and Liu Xiao, AVPRF f. 0100, op. 50, p. 423, d. 3, l. 26.

38. Kenez, *The Birth of the Propaganda State.*

39. 10 December 1957, P. Kriukov, V. Rogov, K. Ianbukhtin, GARF f. 9324, op. 1, d. 1, l. 2.

40. 15 October 1957, N. P. Zakharov and Lin Lang, ibid., d. 2, l. 1; 10 January 1958, "Doklad," ibid., d. 5, l. 2–6.

41. 4 May 1958, "Zapis' besedy," S. L. Tikhvinskii and Li Zhuang, ibid., d. 9, l. 7.

42. 4 May 1958, "Zapis' besedy," S. L. Tikhvinskii, ibid., l. 12.

43. 13 March 1958, P. Iudin to M. V. Zimianin, A. A. Andreev, G. A. Zhukov, ibid., l. 18.

44. 12 December 1958, "Priem," ibid., l. 16.

45. 4 April 1958, "Tezisy doklada," ibid., d. 8, l. 10.

46. 6 June 1958, "Vypiska iz pis'mo," Zakharov, ibid., d. 10, l. 2.

47. 11 October 1958, "Stenogramma," ibid., d. 7, l. 6.

48. 24 October 1958, "Zasedanie redkollegii," ibid., d. 6, l. 12.

49. 11 October 1958, "Stenogramma," ibid., d. 7, l. 5, 7.

50. 20 June 1958, "Doklad," V. D. Kudriavtsev, ibid., d. 12, l. 42.

51. 11 October 1958, "Stenogramma," ibid., d. 7, l. 16–21.

52. Ba Jin, "Ezhenedel'nik 'Sovetsko-Kitaiskaia druzhba,'" *Jiefang ribao*, and Wu Jingyou, "Pyst' vechno rastsvetaiut tsvety druzhby," *Guangming ribao* (30 March 1959): 1957–59, ibid., d. 3, l. 15–27.

53. July 1959, "Materialy chitatel'skoi konferentsii v Tianjin," ibid., d. 84, l. 19.

54. 24 October 1958, "Beseda," ibid., d. 11, l. 14–18.

55. 30 March 1958, "Kratkoe reziume vystupleniia na konferentsii chitatelei," ibid., d. 13, l. 55.

56. July 1959, "Materialy chitatel'skoi konferentsii v Tiantszine," ibid., d. 84, l. 24.

57. 23 May—29 May 1960, "Svodka pisem," ibid., d. 148, l. 76–78.

58. 8–15 May 1960, "Svodka pisem chitatelei," ibid., l. 93; 18–24 August 1958, "Svodka pisem," ibid., d. 16, l. 215.

59. 22–27 December 1958, "Svodka pisem," ibid., d. 85, l. 246.

60. He Bizhang, "Khoroshii uchitel' i blizkii drug," *Fuxian ribao* (27 May 1959): 1957–59, ibid., d. 3, l. 126.

61. "Sovetskie rabochie boriutsia za pretvorenie v zhizn' semiletnego plana," *Zhongguo gongren*, no. 10 (1959): ibid., l. 51.

62. 24 October 1958, "Beseda," ibid., d. 11, l. 17.

63. 31 October 1958, "Beseda," ibid., l. 45.

64. March–April 1958, "Materialy chitatel'skikh konferentsii," ibid., d. 13, l. 20, 38.

65. 28 October 1958, "Kratkaia zapis' o konferentsii chitatelei," ibid., d. 14, l. 15; also 25–30 January 1958, "Svodka pisem chitatelei zhurnala 'Sovetsko-kitaiskaia druzhba,'" ibid., d. 16, l. 11.

66. March–April 1958, "Materialy chitatel'skikh konferentsii," ibid., d. 13, l. 22. On Deng Tuo, see Cheek, *Propaganda and Culture in Mao's China*.

67. 7–13 March 1960, "Svodka pisem chitatelei," GARF f. 9324, op. 1, d. 148, l. 146.

68. March–April 1958, "Materialy chitatel'skikh konferentsii," ibid., d. 13, l. 14.

69. 28 October 1958, "Kratkaia zapis' o konferentsii chitatelei," ibid., d. 14, l. 6.

70. 5 October 1958, "Mnenie o zhurnale," ibid., d. 11, l. 30–32; also 1960, "Zhurnal 'Sovetsko-kitaiskaia druzhba,'" ibid., d. 145, l. 36; 1–7 February 1960, "Svodka pisem chitatelei," ibid., d. 148, l. 178.

71. 1958, "Beseda o zhurnale," ibid., d. 11, l. 36.

72. 11–17 April 1960, "Svodka pisem chitatelei," ibid., d. 148, l. 116.

73. De Grazia, *Irresistible Empire*.

74. "Zhongguo xuesheng zai Mosike daxue," *Suzhong youhao*, no. 6 (1958): 31; "Youyi," *Suzhong youhao*, no. 6 (1958): 32; "Women shenghuo zai youyi zhong," *Suzhong youhao*, no. 13 (1958): 33; "Mosike xuesheng xue zhongwen," *Suzhong youhao*, no. 12 (1958): 24, GARF f. 9324, op. 1, d. 19, l. 118–19, 258, 234; Li Wen, "Xilin gongchengshi xianzai de gongzuo he shenghuo," *Suzhong youhao*, no. 7 (1959): 9, ibid., d. 87, l. 9.

75. 20 June 1958, "Doklad," V. D. Kudriavtsev, ibid., d. 12, l. 30–34.

76. 6 June 1958, "Vypiska iz pis'mo," Zakharov, ibid., d. 10, l. 3.

77. 10 July 1958, "Konferentsiia chitatelei zhurnala 'Druzhba,'" ibid., d. 12, l. 3–17.

78. 11 October 1958, "Stenogramma," ibid., d. 7, l. 10.

79. 26 January 1959, N. Sudarikov to G. A. Zhukov, ibid., d. 81, l. 4.

80. 24 October 1958, "Zasedanie redkollegii," ibid., d. 6, l. 14.

81. 4 June 1960, "O rabote redaktsii zhurnala 'Sovetsko-Kitaiskaia druzhba,'" ibid., d. 145, l. 3–4.

82. "Wo you qinian jihua," Suzhong youhao, no. 7 (1959): 5–6, ibid., d. 87, l. 5.

83. "Zuotian, jintian, mingtian," Suzhong youhao, no. 2 (1959): 15, ibid., l. 15.

84. "Sulian chushengye chanpin shengchan yiding chaoguo meiguo," Suzhong youhao, no. 3 (1959): 5, ibid., l. 5.

85. Kalaxiefu, "Gongchanzhuyi yiding neng jiancheng," Suzhong youhao, no. 4 (1959): 3–4, 1960, ibid., d. 149, l. 3–4.

86. 9 September 1958, "Protokol," ibid., d. 6, l. 1.

87. 26 January 1959, N. Sudarikov to G. A. Zhukov, ibid., d. 81, l. 6.

88. 1958, "Vypiska iz otcheta posol'stva SSSR v KNR za 1958 g.," ibid., l. 11.

89. Kalaxiefu, "Gongchanzhuyi yiding neng jiancheng," Suzhong youhao, no. 4 (1959): 4, ibid., d. 149, l. 4.

90. June 1959, "Spravka," B. Gurevich and Iu. Lysenko, ibid., d. 145, l. 18–20.

91. 4–9 May 1959, "Svodka pisem," ibid., d. 85, l. 198.

92. June 1959, "Spravka," B. Gurevich and Iu. Lysenko, ibid., d. 145, l. 18–20.

93. Ibid.; see also 24 October 1958, "Zasedanie redkollegii," ibid., d. 6, l. 15.

94. Ibid., l. 13.

95. 13 November 1958, "Protokol zasedaniia," ibid., l. 27.

96. "1965 niande sulian jichuang zhizaoye," Suzhong youhao, 3 (1959): 28, 1960, ibid., d. 149, l. 28.

97. Ge Lizhong, "Sulian gonghui he qinian shili," Suzhong youhao, no. 13 (1959): 3, ibid., l. 3.

98. Václav Kotyk, "Výkum vztahů mezi socialistickymi státy v ústavu pro mezinárodní politiku a ekonomii," in Drulák and Kratochvíl et al., 50 let českého výzkumu mezinárodních vztahů, 40.

99. 25 May 1960, "Iz zapisi besedy," N. G. Sudarikov, GARF f. 9324, op. 1, d. 146, l. 4.

100. "Mosike xuesheng xue zhongwen," Suzhong youhao, no. 12 (1958): 24, 1958, ibid., d. 19, l. 234; 9–14 February 1959, "Svodka pisem," ibid., d. 85, l. 262; Bu Cheng, "Zai sulian shoudu xinangu shenghuode yinian," Suzhong youhao, no. 4 (1959): 29–31, 1960, ibid., d. 149, l. 29–31; "Yong hasa kewen chubian de zhongguo zuopin," Suzhong youhao, no. 3 (1959): 25, ibid., l. 25; "Youyi, jinbu, heping," Suzhong youhao, no. 7 (1959): 7–8, ibid., d. 87, l. 7.

101. "1965 niande hasakesidan," Suzhong youhao, no. 3 (1959): 30, 1960, ibid., d. 149, l. 30.

102. Ibid.; also Kalaxiefu, "Gongchanzhuyi yiding neng jiancheng," Suzhong youhao, no. 4 (1959): 4, ibid., l. 4.

103. "Hasake baleiwu zai Mosike," Suzhong youhao, no. 3 (1959): 24–25, ibid., l. 24–25.

104. 14 December 1960, "Osnovnye sobytiia v sovetsko-kitaiskikh otnosheniiakh v 1960 godu," G. Grushetskii, AVPRF f. 0100, op. 53, p. 457, d. 24, l. 264.

105. 12 September 1960, "Beseda s tov. Du Po," GARF f. 9324, op. 1, d. 146, l. 9.

106. 30 April 1959, "Doklad," GARF f. 9576, op. 18, d. 26, l. 33.

107. 28 January 1960, L. Kubasov, ibid., l. 326.

108. 8 April 1960, "Vypiska," ibid., l. 337.

109. 20 December 1958, "Zapis' besedy," N. G. Sudarikov, F. V. Mochul'skii, and Xiang Yan, ibid., l. 5.

110. Goncharov, Lewis, and Xue Litai, *Uncertain Partners*, 75.

111. 23 January 1959, N. G. Sudarikov, GARF f. 9576, op. 18, d. 26, l. 8.

112. 30 March 1959, "Zapis' besedy," N. G. Sudarikov, S. A. Zima, Zhang Zhixiang, Lu Ming, ibid., l. 19–20.

113. 31 December 1959, "Zapis' besedy," Liu Shuzhou and A. Elizavetin, ibid., l. 341, 345.

114. 8 April 1960, "Zapiski," ibid., l. 336.

115. 1 April 1960, E. Sharov, ibid., l. 98.

116. 1960, "Informatsiia," Iu. V. Novgorodskii, ibid., l. 131–34.

117. Ibid., l. 134.

118. 19 August 1960, "Zapiski," ibid., l. 155.

119. 8 January 1963, G. Grushetskii, ibid., d. 217, l. 18–21.

120. 23 January 1962, O. Rakhmanin and G. Grushetskii, ibid., d. 143, l. 69.

121. 15 August 1961, "Informace pro soudruha Hendrycha," Josef Kudrna, NA KSČ–AN-II, krabice 84, folder "Čína: Ruzné materiály, 1956–1967."

122. 1961, V. Danilov, GARF f. 9576, op. 18, d. 113, l. 52.

123. 6 March 1962, V. Feoktistov, ibid., d. 143, l. 143.

124. 23 January 1962, O. Rakhmanin and G. Grushetskii, ibid., l. 75.

125. 6 March 1962, V. Feoktistov, ibid., l. 145.

126. 23 October 1962, P. A. Zagrebel'nyi, ibid., l. 272, 275.

127. 16 December 1963, "Doklad," G. F. Kungurov, ibid., d. 217, l. 378.

128. 30 March 1959, N. G. Sudarikov and S. A. Zima, ibid., d. 26, l. 21.

129. 28 April 1961, F. V. Konstantinov, ibid., d. 113, l. 31.

130. 8 January 1963, G. Grushetskii, ibid., d. 217, l. 22–26.

131. 1 February 1963, "Zapis' besedy," ibid., l. 32, 36.

132. 28 March 1962, G. Grushetskii, ibid., d. 143, l. 145.

133. 8 January 1963, ibid., d. 217, l. 26.

134. 7 July 1962, T. Skvortsov-Tokarii, ibid., d. 143, l. 199, 209.

135. 24 September 1963, "Otchet," T. Skvortsov-Tokarin and Iu. Ushakov, ibid., d. 217, l. 274–75.

136. 25 September 1963, G. Kungurov, ibid., l. 287–88.

137. 7 June 1961, P. Bazarov, ibid., d. 113, l. 91.

138. 24 September 1963, "Otchet," T. Skvortsov-Tokarin and Iu. Ushakov, ibid., d. 217, l. 276.

139. 23 January 1959, N. G. Sudarikov, ibid., d. 26, l. 13.

140. 11 February 1961, Cheng Yunshan, ibid., d. 143, l. 157–58.

141. 30 November 1961, M. Titarenko, ibid., d. 113, l. 199.

142. 25 September 1963, "Otchet," G. Kungurov, ibid., d. 217, l. 291.

143. 9 December 1960, "Jianbao liuxuesheng fanying de qingkuang," WJBDAG 109-02098-02, 46–47.

144. 24 September 1963, "Otchet," T. Skvortsov-Tokarin and Iu. Ushakov, GARF f. 9576, op. 18, d. 217, l. 275–78.

145. 23 November 1963, V. Feoktistov, ibid., l. 352.

146. Ibid., l. 280–81.

147. 25 September 1963, "Otchet," G. Kungurov, ibid., l. 298.

148. 15 November 1963, S. Chervonenko, ibid., l. 341.

149. 2 July 1963, V. Feoktistov, ibid., l. 401.

150. 24 October 1962, A. Elizavetin and V. Lazarev, ibid., d. 113, l. 189.

151. *O kitaisko-sovetskoi druzhbe*, 5.

Conclusion

1. 22 November 1919, "Doklad na II vserossiiskom s'ezde kommunisticheskikh organisatsii narodov vostoka," Lenin, *Polnoe sobranie sochinenii*, 318–31.

2. 31 March 1959, "Zpráva ministra zahraničního obchodu k návrhu na konání VII. Zasedání československo—čínské komise," 020.905/59, MZV TO—T 1955–59, ČLR, krabice 3, obal 6.

3. 19 February 1956, "Gongyehua fang gong tanhua gongchengshi," BMA 125-001-01201, 2.

4. Spence, *To Change China*, 290–92.

5. 20 January 1965, "Polozhenie o zemliachestvakh," GARF f. 9518, op. 1, d. 69, l. 5.

6. Shen Zhihua, *Sulian zhuanjia zai zhongguo*, 105–9; 21 April 1953, "Zapis' besedy," V. V. Kuznetsov and Zhu De, AVPRF f. 0100, op. 46, p. 362, d. 12, l. 49.

7. September–October 1950, "Doklad severno-vostochnogo otdela," GARF f. 5283, op. 18, d. 91, l. 231.

8. Guo Moruo, "Guanyu wenhua jiaoyu gongzuo de baogao," *Renmin ribao* (20 June 1950): 1.

9. 17 September 1946, "Otchet," Savost'ianov, RGAE f. 8002, op. 3, d. 1, l. 30; 19 November 1953, BMA 001-004-00143, 6.

10. 12 November 1962, "Informatsiia," A. Krachun, GAPK f. P-68, op. 30, d. 392, l. 19.

11. Zhou Yizhi, "Zai Mao Zedong wenyi sixiang de qizhi xia," *Renmin ribao* (12 October 1960): 7; "Gongren jieji shehuizhuyi jiaoyu xuezhe cunke," *Gongren ribao* (29 January 1958): 3; "Quanmin de jieri quanmin de shengli," *Xinmin ribao* (1 October 1958): 3.

12. 10 December 1959, "Zpráva o zájezdu české filharmonie," 073/59, MZV TO—T 1955–59, ČLR, krabice 2, obal 4; 20 July 1959, "O kulturních stycích ČLR s kapitalistickými zeměmi," Ján Bušniak, 025.421/59, ibid., krabice 8, obal 1.

13. 26 December 1957, "Spravka," RGAE f. 9493, op. 1, d. 21, l. 7–10.

14. Li Yueran, *Zhongsu waijiao qinliji*, 51.

15. 31 October 1960, "Spravka," Rusalenko, GAPK f. P-68, op. 30, d. 359, l. 72–77.

16. 9 October 1955, "Otzyvy posetitelei," RGAE f. 635, op. 2, d. 247, l. 112.

17. 12 December 1955, N. D. Purtsev, RGAE f. 3527, op. 13, d. 2537, l. 43.

18. 24 June 1957, "Osveshenie v KNR poezdki delegatsii," V. Lazarev, AVPRF f. 0100, op. 50, p. 426, d. 32, l. 27.

19. 17 February 1954, "Informatsiia o prebyvanii v Kitae gruppy sovetskikh profsoiuznykh rabotnikov," V. Berezin, RGANI f. 5, op. 28, r. 7960, d. 255, l. 4–14.

20. 12 November 1954, Komzala, NA KSČ–AN-II, krabice 84, folder "Telegramy, sífry,

depresè, zpravy"; 7 April 1955, "Zapis' besedy," P. F. Iudin and König, AVPRF f. 0100, op. 48, p. 393, d. 9, l. 66.

21. 27 September 1957, "Sovetsko-kitaiskoe ekonomicheskoe i kul'turnoe sotrudnichestvo," AVPRF f. 0100, op. 50, p. 426, d. 29, l. 62.

22. 15 October 1957, "Informatsiia," N. Pridybailo, ibid., op. 44, p. 176, d. 17, l. 28.

23. 4 November 1960, ibid., op. 53, p. 457, d. 24, l. 224; 10 November 1964, "Stenographische Niederschrift," Walter Ulbricht and Zhou Enlai, SAPMO DY 30/11397/66. More recently, see Wang Ji, *Erzhanhou zhongsu (zhonge) guanxi de yanbian yu fazhan*, 22, 90–91; and Meng Xianzhang, *Zhongsu maoyi shi ziliao*, 604–5.

24. 10 September 1956, "Stenogramma," RGAE f. 3527, op. 13, d. 2577, l. 196.

25. 18 October 1959, "Otchet," N. A. Kononov, RGAE f. 9493, op. 1, d. 1098, l. 62.

26. Hunt, *The Genesis of Chinese Communist Foreign Policy*, 102. For a treatment of the comparative successes of Soviet industrialization in historic and global context, see Allen, *Farm to Factory*.

27. Shen Zhihua, *Sulian zhuanjia zai zhongguo*, 103–7.

28. 21 September 1950, "Zapis' besedy," N. V. Roshchin and Liu Shaoqi, AVPRF f. 0100, op. 43, p. 302, d. 10, l. 164; 27 July 1951, "Zapis' besedy," N. V. Roshchin and Zhou Dapeng, ibid., op. 44, p. 322, d. 13, l. 41.

29. October 1954, "Sulian zhuanjia Andeluoanfu tongzhi zai beshi diyi fu xiao deng sange xiaoxue de tanhua jilu," BMA 153-004-2166, 5.

30. 2 January 1953, "Zapis' besedy," A. S. Paniushkin and Wu Xiuquan, AVPRF f. 0100, op. 46, p. 362, d. 12, l. 6; February 1957, PLA to N. A. Bulganin, WJBDAG 109-00794-01, 3; 25 June 1957, Huang Kecheng to Zhou Enlai, ibid., 14; 13 October 1958, "Minzhu deguo dui zhongde jingji hezuo de yixie yijian," WJBDAG 109-01827-02, 29.

31. 9 March 1960, "Liu Dingyi fuzongli jiejian sulian zhuhua dashi Qierwonianke tanhua jilu," WJBDAG 109-00933-04, 14–20.

32. 14 December 1960, "Osnovnye sobytiia v sovetsko-kitaiskikh otnosheniiakh v 1960 godu," G. Grushetskii, AVPRF f. 0100, op. 53, p. 457, d. 24, l. 267; 18 October 1960, "Zapis' besedy," S. V. Chervonenko and Chang Tubing, ibid., p. 454, d. 9, l. 35.

33. 30 August 1960, "Zapis' besedy," S. V. Chervonenko and Chen Yi, ibid., p. 454, d. 8, l. 205; 13 August 1960, "Záznam," Bruno Köhler, 5823/8, NA KSČ–AN-II, krabice 86, folder "Čína," 1960.

34. 19 June 1959, "Bao Qing Chengrui tongxue ting fanying zhi wenti," WJBDAG 109-01919-01, 26.

35. 5 September 1956, "Spisok," WJBDAG 109-00984-13, 117–20; 9 August 1956, WJBDAG 109-00984-12, 75; 9 October 1956, WJBDAG 109-00984-16, 126.

36. 29 October 1959, "Moda jiaoshou shewei Mao, He dui meiguo wenti you fenqi," WJBDAG 109-01919-01, 29.

37. 30 December 1959, "Puxijin tan suguo neiwai xingshi," WJBDAG 109-02064-01, 2.

38. 22 August 1959, "Zapis' besedy," G. M. Pushkin and Liu Xiao, AVPRF f. 0100, op. 52, p. 442, d. 5, l. 33.

39. 1959, "Vsemerno uluchshat' kul'turno-bytovye obsluzhivanie naseleniia," GAPK f. P-68, op. 30, d. 383, l. 6.

40. 13 April 1956, "Woguo tong sulian he dongzhou renmin minzhu guojia youhao

hezuo de jiben qingkuang, cunzai de wenti he jintian yijian," WJBDAG 109-00736-01, 2–7.

41. 18 January 1955, "Otnosheniia mezhdu SSSR i KNR s 1950 g.," N. Fedorenko and M. Kapitsa, AVPRF f. 0100, op. 48, p. 377, d. 39, l. 6; 1962, "Spravka," F. Kleimenov, RGAE f. 9493, op. 5, d. 60, l. 59.

42. 20 October 1956, "Bodang bazhong quanhui qingkuang," WJBDAG 109-00762-03, 27; 8 December 1956, "Dui bolan shijian de chubu guji," WJBDAG 109-00762-01, 5–8.

43. 14 June 1957, "Zapis' besedy," P. Iudin and Zhou Enlai, AVPRF f. 0100, op. 50, p. 423, d. 5, l. 32.

44. 1954, "Al'bom," RGAE f. 1184, op. 31b, d. 16, l. 38–39.

45. Xiao Yu, *Sidalin pailai bangzhu women de renmin*; Shen Zhihua, *Sulian zhuanjia zai zhongguo*, 130.

46. Bo Yibo, "The Making of the 'Leaning to One Side' Decision."

47. 7 March 1950, "Zapis' besedy," P. A. Shibaev, Liu Shaoqi, and Li Kenong, AVPRF f. 0100, op. 43, p. 302, d. 10, l. 70. The Beijing Hotel off Mayakovsky Square today features a casino on the first floor.

48. "Delegace komunistické strany Československa na XXI. sjezd KSSS přibyla do Moskvy," *Rudé právo*, no. 24 (25 January 1959): 1; Stanislav Oborský "V pevném svazku," *Rudé právo*, no. 27 (28 January 1959): 1; "Z projevu soudruha Čou En-laje," *Rudé právo*, no. 28 (29 January 1959): 5.

49. 7 April 1955, "Zapis' besedy," P. F. Iudin and Peng Dehuai, AVPRF f. 0100, op. 18, p. 393, d. 9, l. 33.

50. 20 December 1955, "Zapis' besedy," Lu Dingyi and P. F. Iudin, ibid., op. 48, p. 393, d. 9, l. 191.

51. 27 September 1957, B. Kulik and G. Zverev, "Sovetsko-kitaiskoe ekonomicheskoe i kul'turnoe sotrudnichestvo," AVPRF f. 0100, op. 50, p. 426, d. 29, l. 62.

52. Franz Gabriel, "Die ökonomische Zusammenarbeit und gegenseitige Hilfe der Deutschen Demokratischen Republik, der Tschechoslowakischen Republik und der Volksrepublik Polen," *Deutsche Aussenpolitik*, no. 12 (December 1959): 1266–76.

53. "Cestovní zpráva," L. Sadecký, 1958, *Expo '58: Z cestovních zpráv*, 23.

54. *La Tchécoslovaquie à Bruxelles 58*, no. 5, NA ČSOK, Folder La Tchécoslovaquie, 9, cover.

55. 16 October 1956, "Aufzeichnungen über eine Unterredung zwischen den Genossen Mao Tse-tung, Liu Schao-tschi und Wang Tschia-hsiang," in Meissner, *Die DDR und China 1949 bis 1990*, 87.

56. 18 October 1963, "Program komise ÚV KSČ pro otázky životní úrovně," NA KSČ, Komise ÚV KSČ pro otázky životní úrovně, 1963–1968 (10/2), krab. arch. jednotka, 1.

57. 15 March 1958, "Zapis' besedy," P. Iudin and Mao Zedong, AVPRF f. 0100, op. 51, p. 432, d. 6, l. 88–94.

58. Zubok and Pleshakov, *Inside the Kremlin's Cold War*, 228; Jian, *Mao's China and the Cold War*, 78–79.

59. 2 June 1960, "Predlozheniia sovetskogo pravitel'stva ob osnovnykh polozheniiakh dogovora o vseobshchem i polnom razoruzhenii," AVPRF f. 0100, op. 47, p. 194, d. 4, l. 8.

60. "Sulian huifu heshiyan," *Xinmin wanbao* (3 October 1958): 1.

61. 8 January 1955, "Zapis' besedy," P. V. Iudin and Mao Zedong, RGANI f. 5, r. 5142, op. 28, d. 307, l. 9–10; 1 November 1957, "Zapis' besedy," P. Iudin and Chairman Mao, AVPRF f. 0100, op. 50, p. 423, d. 5, l. 44; 16 October 1950, "Zapis' besedy," N. V. Roshchin and Liu Shaoqi, ibid., op.43, p. 302, d. 10, l. 266; 21 February 1955, "Informatsiia otnositel'no vedeniia propagandy po voprosu amerikanskoi agressii na Taivane," RGANI f. 5, r. 5142, op. 28, d. 307, l. 51–55.

62. 30 June 1952, "Záznam o rozhovore," 122.254/52, Viliam Široký and Tan Xilin, MZV TO—T 1955–59, ČLR, krabice 4, obal 1.

63. 12 January 1955, "Zapis' besedy," K. V. Vlasov, I. P. Gusev, Liu Fang, Zhao Bing, RGAE f. 8115, op. 3, d. 1003, l. 12.

64. Gao, The Communist Takeover of Hangzhou, 217. On the eventual Chinese defense program of "third-line defense planning" (relocation from first-line [coastal and border] locations to the interior) on the eve of the Cultural Revolution, see Lüthi, "The Vietnam War and China's Third-Line Defense Planning before the Cultural Revolution."

65. Zolotarev, Istoriia voennoi strategii rossii, 403–57; Uhl, "Sovietization and Missileization of the Warsaw Pact."

66. April 1960, "Primery," F. Kleimenov; April 1960, "Spravka," F. Klemenov, RGAE f. 9493, op. 5, d. 59, l. 33–47, 49–52; 7 December 1957, N. Busygin to N. T. Stepanov, ibid., op. 1, d. 983, l. 85–96; 22 September 1959, N. Siluianov and A. Polozhenkov, ibid., d. 1003, l. 26–46.

67. 28 May 1957, "Plan," AVPRF f. 0100, op. 50, p. 46, d. 29, l. 39.

68. 18 October 1962, I. Ruzhichka to D. Gvishiani, RGAE f. 9493, op. 5, d. 183, l. 122.

69. Reid, "Cold War in the Kitchen," 217.

70. 9 September 1963, "Zápis z komise předsednictva ÚV KSČ pro životní úroveň"; 24 October 1963, "Zápis," NA KSČ, Komise pro otázky životní úrovně, 1963–1968, krabice 1, folders 1, 2. See Bren and Neuberger, Communism Unwrapped.

71. 24 March 1954, "Rekomendatsii," RGANI f. 5, r. 5119, op. 28, d. 211, l. 5.

72. 1960, "Erklärung der Beratung von Vertretern der Kommunistischen und Arbeitesparteien," SAPMO DY 30/11757/31, 17.

73. 18–19 January 1965, "Referat," SAPMO DY 30/360/3-4; 9 May 1969, "Stenografische Niederschrift der Beratung des Genossen Hermann Axen," SAPMO DY 30/11351/8; 12 July 1965, "Information," SAPMO DY 30/3726/50. On what Mary Fulbrook calls the GDR version of "consumer socialism," see Fulbrook, The People's State, 66–67. See also Heldmann, "Negotiating Consumption in a Dictatorship"; and Landsman, Dictatorship and Demand, 75, 178.

74. Nguyen, Hanoi's War; Mazov, A Distant Frontier in the Cold War, 227–31; Friedman, "Reviving the Revolution," 157–89; 16 May 1963, "Rech' Liu Shaoqi na prieme v Khanoe," NA KSČ–AN-II, krabice 85, folder "Čína."

75. 4 March 1963, WJBDAG 108-00905-02, 9.

76. 14 June 1957, "Zapis' besedy," P. Iudin and Zhou Enlai, AVPRF f. 0100, op. 50, p. 423, d. 5, l. 32.

77. Kocharian, Druzhba i sotrudnichestvo SSSR i Indii, 20–58; 4 January 1962, I. Ershova, GARF f. 9576, op. 18, d. 188, l. 3–5.

78. 8 December 1959, "Zapis' besedy," S. V. Chervonenko and Deng Xiaoping, AVPRF f. 0100, op. 51, p. 435, d. 25, l. 104; 14 December 1960, "Osnovnye sobytiia v sovetsko-

kitaiskikh otnosheniiakh v 1960 godu," G. Grushetskii, ibid., op. 53, p. 457, d. 24, l. 268; 5 December 1963, "Guanyu zhongsu bianjie wenti de yixie qingkuang," WJBDAG 109-03341-03, 110; 16 January 1963, "Fandui wo jinxin zaoyao wumie chuxianle xin qingkuang," ibid., 113. On the armed exchanges at Damanskii/Zhenbao Island along the Ussuri River in March 1969, see Riabchenko, *KNR-SSSR*; Radchenko, *Two Suns in the Heavens*, 202–3; Yang Kuisong, "The Sino-Soviet Border Clash of 1969"; Tai Sung An, *The Sino-Soviet Territorial Dispute*; Wishnick, *Mending Fences*; "Zhonghua renmin gongheguo zhengfu shengming," *Beijing ribao* (8 October 1969): 1; and Bubenin, *Krovavyi sneg damanskoi*.

79. 10 July 1985, "Niederschrift," Hu Yaobang and Gerhard Schürer, SAPMO DY 30/11399/5.

80. Pun Ngai and Chris Smith, "Putting Transnational Labour Process in Its Place."

81. Li Duo, "Rossisko-kitaiskoe sotrudnichestvo: dostizheniia i problem," *Vostok*, no. 4 (July–August 2008): 120–28; Erica S. Downs, "Sino-Russian Energy Relations: An Uncertain Courtship," in Bellacqua, *The Future of China-Russia Relations*, 146–75.

82. Aleksandr Orlov, "Ekho tskhinvala," *Mezhdunarodnaia zhizn'*, no. 10 (2008): 18–25; Igor' Chikin, "Beskonechna li voina imperii?" *Rossiia*, no. 13 (9 April 2009): 4; *Strategiia Rossii*, no. 11 (November 2008).

83. V. I. Zhukov, "Rossiia v global'noi sisteme sotsial'nykh koordinat: sotsiologicheskii analiz i prognoz," *Sotsiologicheskie issledovaniia*, no. 12 (2008): 3–14; V. V. Kirillov, "Rossiia i nato: kogo nado opasat'sia?" *Sotsiologicheskie issledovaniia*, no. 12 (2008): 112–16.

BIBLIOGRAPHY

Archives

CZECH REPUBLIC

Archiv Ministerstva zahraničních věci České republiky (Archive of the
    Ministry of Foreign Affairs of the Czech Republic, Prague)
    Teritoriální odbory—Obyčejne
      Čínská Lidová Republika (People's Republic of China), 1945–59
      Kuba, 1960–64
      SSSR, 1945–59
    Teritoriální odbory—Tajné
      Čínská Lidová Republika, 1945–55, 1955–59
Národní archiv (National Archive, Prague)
    Československá obchodní komora (Kancelář gen. komisaře EXPO 58)
    Úřad předsednictva vlády, 1945–53
    Ústřední výbor komunistické strany československa, 1945–89, Praha
      Antonín Novotný II. Část
      Komise pro otázky životní úrovně, 1963–68 (10/2)
      Oddělení kulturně-propagační a ideologické (19/7)
Vojenský ústřední archiv (Central Military Archive, Prague)
    Ministerstvo národní obrany

GERMANY

Stiftung Archiv der Parteien und Massenorganisationen der DDR im Bundesarchiv
    (Archive of Parties and Mass Organizations of the GDR in the German Federal
    Archive, Berlin)
    DY 30, Büro Walter Ulbricht im ZK der SED, 1946–73
    DY 30/IV 2/20, Abteilung Internationale Verbindungen des ZK der SED, 1947–64

PEOPLE'S REPUBLIC OF CHINA

Beijing shi danganguan (Beijing Municipal Archive, Beijing)
    001-014-00627, Haidian qu dengdeng danwei guanyu Zhu De tongzhi, February
      1960
    002-008-00066, Beijing shi renmin zhengfu daibiaotuan fangwen Mosike shi xuexi
      ge xiang gongzuo de baogao, 1956
    017-001-00659, Banfa youguan yuan meng yuan yue ji sulian zhuanjia de chaifangfei
      zhifu de queding he tongzhi, 2 January–29 May 1958
    125-001-01198, Beijing shi jianzhu yede qingkuang, 1956
    125-001-01200, Sulian zhuanjia Shelahaikefu tanhua jiyao, 1956

125-001-01201, Sulian zhuanjia Shelahaikefu guanyu fanggong gongyi guicheng qi bianzhi fangfa, 1956

125-001-01207, Sulian zhuanjia jianyi, tan hua jiyao, 1955

142-001-00212, Sulian zhuanjia dui qinghe, 1 June–16 September 1955

151-001-00007, Sulian zhuanjia canguan hehu wuran shuiyuanguang qingkuang jiyao, 7–31 October 1955

153-004-02166, Sulian zhuanjia Andeluoanfu zai beishi yifu xiaoxue sange xiaoxue de tanhua jilu, October 1954

Zhonghua renmin gongheguo waijiaobu danganguan (Archive of the Ministry of Foreign Affairs of the PRC, Beijing)

102-00071-01, Sulian zhuanjia tan wuxiandian tongxun wenti, 1 December 1956–31 October 1957

102-00171-02, Waijiaobu guanyu song "Zhongmian liangguo zongli lianhe shengming," 29 June–30 July 1954

105-00021-01, Menggu renmin gongheguo waijiaobu buzhang, 26 September 1951

105-01066-06, Zhou Enlai zongli jiejian minzhu deguo zhuhua dashi yao heipen, 9 June 1961

106-00003-01, Zhongguo yu menggu guanyu jianli waijiao guanxi de wanglai zhaohui (zhongwen, mengwen), 6–20 October 1949

106-00527-05, Guanyu meiguo dui nianyue de yixie zuofa wenti, 15 October 1960

106-00600-03, Guanyu dui yuenan guohui jiu meiguo zai nanyue jiajin junshi ganshe huyu shu biaozhi zhichi de qingshi ji youguan funhan, 16–23 December 1961

106-00600-05, Guanyu jiu meiguo zai yuenan jiajin junshi ganshe wo ying zuohe biaotai de qingshi ji wo waijiaobu youguan shengming deng, 26 November 1961

106-00608-01, Guanyu jinyibu kaizhan huodong zhichi yuenan renmin fandui meiguo, 7–18 July 1961

106-01516-06, Liu Xiao fuwaizhang jiejian sulian zhu hua dashi Labin tanhua jiyao, 11 May 1965

107-00103-01, Sulian shiguan canzan tan dui waiguo kaizhan wenhua hezuo, 4–18 February 1958

107-00103-03, Zhou Enlai zongli tong aulian dashi tan woguo nei jianshe deng wenti, 11 November 1958

107-00152-01, Guanyu shengyuan yilake geming zhengfu he leibanan renmin qiyi qi baodao shi, 16–17 July 1958

107-00152-02, Chen Yi buzhangdeng zhaojian yafei guojia shijie tan yalike he leibanan jushi, 17 July 1958

107-00152-03, Guanyu Mao Zedong zhuxi tong Heluxiaofu huitan gongbao, 8 August 1958

107-00152-05, Zhongguo zhengfu kangyi yingguo zhengfu chu lezhenya yuedan renmin, 18 July 1958

107-00155-06, Minzhu deguo waijiaobu guanyuan tantong yilake guanxi, 3 October –9 December 1958

107-00286-07, Minzhu deguo zongli fangwen aulian deng guoshi, 19 June–10 October 1958

107-00286-13, Nansilafu zongtong Tituo fangwen aulian, 31 October–9 December 1958

107-00611-01, Minzhu deguo guowu weiyuanhui zhuxi Niaobulixi fangwen aulian, 31 January–30 March 1965

107-00712-19, Yilake yu minzhu deguo guanxi, 26 May 1962

108-00213-02, Chuxi diliuci feizhou guoji ziyou gongliande minzhu deguo daibiaotuan guanyu meiguo, yingguo dui feizhou zhengce de baogao, 21 December 1959

108-00905-02, Jineiya dui sulian gongchangdang zong shuji Heluxiaofu de kanfa, sulian dui feizhou zhengce, minzhu deguo fuwaizhang Wenninger fang fei, nansilafu zai ji he feizhou huodong qingkuang ji dui zhongsu bie de fanying deng, 14 January–22 November 1963

109-00002-01, Sulian fangmian tongzhi geng yong dianxin gongzhen, 1–30 November 1949

109-00004-03, Liu Shaoqi zhi han Malinkefu tongzhi wo zai xinjiang ge danwei lianjie yuan wenti (ewen), 1 January–31 December 1949

109-00009-01, Zhongguo bolan jianli waijiaobu guanxi ji bolan renmin zou hua, dashi daibande youguan wenjian, 5–31 October 1949

109-00145-07, Bao aulian waijiaobu zhaohui neirong, 4–16 December 1958

109-00145-12, Aulian baokan dui Mao Zedong budang guojia zhuxi de fanying, 15–17 December 1958

109-00146-01, Guanyu pingqing sulian zhuanjia shi gei sulian zhuhua shiguan de zhaohui, 18 January–8 December 1951

109-00403-01, Mao Zedong zhuxi jiejian bolan zhengfu daibiaotuan de jihua jilu, 28 September 1954

109-00562-01, Liuping, Zengping wenjiao liuxue sulian zhuanjia shi, 1 January 1953–22 February 1954

109-00736-01, Woguo tong sulian he dongzhou guojia youhao hezuo jiben qingkuang, cunzai wenti jinian hou yijian, 13 April 1956

109-00743-05, Liu Shaoqi weiyuanchang jiejian sulian qingnian daibiaotuan tanhua jilu, 19 June 1956

109-00744-01, Zhongguo zhengfu guanyu yijiuwuliu nian shiyue sanshi ri sulian zhengfu xuanyan, 30 October–1 November 1956

109-00745-03, Guanyu wo pizhun sulian kaipi cong Yierkucike jing zhongguo lingkong, 5 June–6 July 1956

109-00745-04, Guanyu wo pizhun kaipi cong Mosike jing zhongguo lingkong zhi deli hangxian shi, 11 July–17 October 1956

109-00746-01, Guanyu sulian feiji dao zhongguo dongnan yidai jinxing da fei guancha shi, 24 March–7 April 1956

109-00747-01, Guanyu sulian tongyi pai feiji lai zhongguo jinxing hangkong diqiu, 4 January–18 July 1956

109-00749-01, Guanyu zhongguo jieshou she zai dalian, 24 September–30 November 1955

109-00751-01, Guanyu sulian jiangyi qiandong xin de you kuang kantan xieding de zhulai wendian, 9 July–17 August 1956

109-00751-02, Chen Yun fuzongli jiu tiaozheng 1957 du wo xiang sufang dinggou junpin, 12 December 1956

109-00751-03, Sulian buchang huiyi zhuxi Buerjianing jiu zhongguo xiang su dinggou wuxiandian tancezhan shi zhi Zhou Enlai zongli han, 1–30 April 1956

109-00752-01, Waijiaobu jiu sulian ni gongbu guanyu jianli lianhe hezi yanjiu suo xieding shi, 25 May 1956

109-00754-01, Guanyu zhongguo qing sulian daiyin xin renminbi wenti, 22 September 1952–14 June 1956

109-00755-01, Zhu minzhu deguo shiguan 1956 nian gongzuo zongjie ji 1957 nian gonzuo jihua, 29 January 1957

109-00757-03, Zhou Enlai zongli jiu zhongde youhao hezuo tiaoyue qianding yi zhounian zhi minzhu deguo zongli Geluotiwu de diangao, 24–25 December 1956

109-00759-07, Zhu De fuzhuxi zai jiekesiluofake bulajisila fahuo jun zhan qunzhong huanying hui shangde jianghuo, 17 January 1957

109-00761-04, Zhu bolan dashi Wang Bingnan dui bozinan shijian yuanyin de fenxi baogao, 5 July 1958

109-00762-01, Zhu bolan shiguan guanyu dui bolan shijian de chubu guji baogao, 8–11 December 1956

109-00762-03, Zhu bolan shiguan, Wang Bingnan dashi, xinhuashe fenji jizhe guanyu bolan shijianhou bolan dangnei, junnei maodun he shehui laodong qingkuang de baogao, 19 October–13 December 1956

109-00792-03, Sulian zhu hua shiguan dashi daiban Aoerlabumofu jiu sulian tongyi jiedai zhongguo yuanzi neng gongye he konggong gongye zhengfu tanpan daibiaotuan fang su zhi Zhang Wentian fuwaizhang de zhaohui, 24 August 1957

109-00794-01, Guanyu zhongguo renmin jiefanjun paobing xuexiao yi pingqing sulian zhuanjia de qingshi, pi jian ji wo waijiaobu zhi sulian zhuhua shiguan de zhaohui, 2 February–6 March 1957

109-00794-02, Guanyu heerbin junshi xuexiao he zhongguo renmin jiefang jun huaxue fanghu yanjiu guoji pingqing sulian zhuanjia de qingshi, 25 June–6 September 1957

109-00871-09, Sulian zhuhua dashi Youjin huijian Chen Yi fuzongli jianlun waizhang tongbao sulian zhengfu yijiu beiyue wenti fazhan shengming, 27 March 1959

109-00873-01, Sulian zhu hua dashi Youjin jiu renmin ribao fabiao, 7 May 1959

109-00873-10, Sulian zhu hua shiguan dashi daiban Andongluofu huijian zhonggong zhongyang shuji chu shuji Peng Zhen he zhong lianbu buzhang Wang Jiaxiang, 23 August 1959

109-00873-19, Sulian lingdao ren Heluxiaofu jiu sulian zhengfu guanyu taiwan wenti, 12 October 1959

109-00874-01, Guanyu Mao Zedong zhuxi jiu sulian lingdao ren Heluxiaofu fangwen meiguo fu Heluxiaofu xin de qingshi ji xinjian neirong, 10–25 August 1959

109-00874-02, Sulian lingdao ren Heluxiaofu jiu yu meiguo zongtong Aisenhaochenger hufang zhi Mao Zedong zhuxi de xin yi ji he, ai liangren guanyu hufang riqi de xinhan, 11 July–9 August 1959

109-00875-01, Zhou Enlai zongli zhi dian sulian buzhang huiyi zhuxi Heluxiaofu zhuhe sulian chengjiu, 5 January 1959

109-00876-01, Guanyu wo renyuan bu canjia meiguo zai sulian juben de ge xiang huodong wenti de qingshi ji dianwen, 2 July–1 August 1959

109-00876-03, Guanyu yaoqiu meiguo tuichu Mosike zhanlanhui shang wuru woguo zhaopian de laiwang dianwen, 30 July–19 August 1959

109-00933-02, Sulian zhu hua dashi Qierwonianke xiang Ji Pengfei fubuzhang jieshao sulian sugong zhongyang shier yue quanhui de qingkuang, 13 January 1960

109-00933-04, Liu Dingyi fuzongli huijian sulian zhuhua dashi Qierwonianke de tanhua jilu, 26 February 1960

109-00933-15, Chen Yi fuzongli huijian waizhang tong sulian fuwaizhang Puxijin de tanhua jilu, 20 August 1960

109-00971-01, Guanyu xuexi he taolun renmin ribao shelun 'guanyu wuchanjieji zhuanzheng de lishi jingyan' de tongzhi ji shouji waiguo baokan fanying de dianwen, 4–25 April 1956

109-00971-02, Guanyu souji ge guo dui sulian gongchandang ershici daibiaodahui Heluxiaofu ping Sidalin fanying de biaozhi dian, 31 March–24 June 1956

109-00977-01, Zhongguo he minzhu deguo, bolan deng qi guo liunian lai wenhua jiaoliu qingkuang (1949 nian zhi 1956 nian), 17 April 1956

109-00977-02, Zhongsu youhao xiehui dui sulian wenhua, youhao huodong qita fazhan de qingkuang, 20 April 1956

109-00981-01, Guanyu xiang sulian tigong 'Guanyu guonei qiaowu gongzuode ruogan zhengce' wenjian shi, 8 June–13 August 1956

109-00983-01, Zhu sulian shiguan daibiao Wenning baihui suwaijiaobu Gudefu tanhua jiyao, 3 January 1956

109-00983-06, Zhu sulian shiguan daibiao jiu zhongguo zhengfu niyu 1956 nian pai 136 ge junshi ganbu yue su xuexi shizhi su fuwaizhang Feidelin hanji sufang fuhan, 23 January–24 March 1956

109-00984-06, Sulian caizhengbu hanbao woguo ying chang qing sulian zai hua zhuanjia 1955 nian xiaban nian feiyong, 11 July 1956

109-00984-07, Sulian caizhengbu hangao woguo yingceng qing wo liusu xuesheng 1955 nian xia ban nian feiyong, 11 July 1956

109-00984-10, Zhu sulian shiguan Wenning baihui suwaijiaobu, 24 July 1956

109-00984-11, Zhu sulian dashiguan Wenning baihui suwaijiaobu Gudefu, 3 August 1956

109-00984-12, Sulian waijiaobu jiu suyituyunhe ziyou tonghang wenti, 9 August–15 September 1956

109-00984-13, Sulian qianshu duobian tiaoyue, 1–30 September 1956

109-00984-16, Zhu sulian shiguan daiban Chen Chu baihui suwaijiaobu yuandongsi, 9 October 1956

109-00985-01, Zhu De fuzhuxi fang sulian he chudi sulian gonchangdang diershi ci daibiao dahui jishi, 3 February–27 March 1956

109-01040-01, Guanyu xiongyali fasheng fan gemin shijian qian guonei qingkuang de dianbao, 9 February–22 October 1956

109-01100-01, Mao Zedong zhuxi jiu Mosike huiyi ji guonei xingshi tong minzhu dangpai rentu tanhua jiyao, 26 December 1957

109-01101-01, Peng Zhen tongzhi fenbie yi guan guo ren dachang weihui fuweiyuanchang he beijing shi shichang shenfan shuaituan fangwen sulian, 24 February–13 December 1956

109-01111-01, Guanyu minzhu deguo tong sulian guanxi de wendian, 5 July–4 December 1957

109-01112-06, Minzhu deguo guojia renmin jun qingkuang, 22 November 1957

109-01124-02, Jiekesiluofake dui waimaoyi de jiben qingkuang, 31 July 1957

109-01124-05, Guanyu jiekesiluofake duiwai guanxi qingkuang de wendian, 8 January–2 August 1957

109-01124-08, Zhu jiekesiluofake shiguan dianguo jie dui sulian gongchandang zhongyang quanhui guanyu kaichu Malinkefu dengran de juiyi de fanying, 3–6 July 1957

109-01129-06, Bolan junshi daibiaotuan fanghua qingkuang tongbao, 19 September–19 October 1957

109-01129-07, Mao Zedong zhuxi huijian bolan junshi daibiaotuan tanhuo jilu, 3 October 1957

109-01129-08, Guanyu bolan junshi daibiaotuan fanghuahou fanying de wendian, 12 December 1957–6 January 1958

109-01129-09, Guofang buzhang Peng Dehuai huijian bolan junshi daibiaotuan tanhuo jiyao, 20 September 1957

109-01130-01, Guanyu bolan dui renmin ribao 'Zailun wuchanjieji zhuanzheng lishi jingyan' wenzhang fanying de dianbao, 2–8 January 1957

109-01130-02, Zhu bolan shiguan diangao bo waichang Lapasiji dui Wang Bingnan dashi de tanhua neirong, 9 January 1957

109-01138-01, Bolan dui sulian gongchandang zhongyang quanhui guanyu Moluotuofu deng ren fandang jituan jueyi de fanying qingkuang, 5–19 July 1957

109-01138-03, Guanyu bolan tong minzhu deguo, yuenan, xiongyali, luomaniya, chaoxia qi jiekesiluofake guanxi qingkuang de dianbao, 9 January 1957

109-01138-04, Guanyu bolan tong nansilafu guanxi qingkuang de wendian, 16 March–8 October 1957

109-01138-05, Zhu bolan shiguan dianbao bolan tong meiguo guanxi qingkuang, 29 December 1956–17 August 1957

109-01154-01, Zhu xiongyali shiguan dianbao xiong dui renmin ribao 'zai lun wuchanjieji zhuanzheng de lishi jingyan' wenzhang de fanying, 1–14 January 1957

109-01154-03, You guan xiongyali dui Mao Zedong zhuxi jianghua, zhengfeng, fanpai yundong deng zhongguo qingkuang fanying de wendian, 24 May–24 December 1957

109-01200-04, Waijiaobu suosi guanyu minzhu deguo 1958 nian xingshi he zhongde guanxi de nian zhong zongjie, 1–31 December 1958

109-01213-01, Yijiuwuba nian sulian qingkuang he zhongsu guanxi, 24 December 1958

109-01213-02, Yijiuwuqi nian shiyiyue zhongguo he sulian guanxi jianxun, 30 November 1957

109-01213-09, Sulian baokan guanyu taiwan jushi de baoling qingkuang (dianwen),
6 September–23 October 1958

109-01216-01, Zhongguo tong minzhu deguo shuangfang guanxi de fazhan he wenti,
27 June 1958

109-01337-02, Guanyu bolan, xiongyali, minzhu deguo xiang jiuneiya tigong
bangzhu de qingkuang, 22–26 February 1959

109-01354-02, Sulian baokan dui xizang wenti de baodao qingkuang, 2 April–
25 October 1959

109-01354-03, Sulian meiti dui zhongyin bianjing wenti de fanying, 10 September–
23 December 1959

109-01361-01, Wo zhu minzhu deguo shiguan diangao 1958 nian gongzuo guihua,
30 November–21 December 1958

109-01393-03, Meiguo fuzongtong Nikesong fangwen bolan ji bomei guanxi,
7 March–8 December 1959

109-01500-03, Youguan minzhu deguo dui wo 'Lieningzhuyi wansui' san bian
wenzhang fanying de wandian, 26 April–18 December 1960

109-01615-01, Zhu sulian shiguan guanyu sulian dui fandui gerenchongbai fanying
de dianwen, 9 April–7 July 1956

109-01615-03, Zhu sulian shiguan guanyu sulian dui 'guanyu wuchanjieji
zhuanzheng de lishi jingyan' yiwen fanying de dianwen, 10–13 April 1956

109-01615-04, Zhu sulian shiguan guanyu sulian lingdao ren Heluxiaofu zai qingzhu
wuyi guoji laodong jie yanhui shang jianghua de dianwen, 3 May 1956

109-01615-05, Zhu sulian shiguan guanyu Heluxiaofu deng sulian lingdao ren zai
sulian guoqing zhaodaihui shang jianghua de dianwen, 8 November 1958

109-01617-03, Zhu sulian shiguan guanyu sulian waizhang Moluotuofu huijian
ge renmin minzhu guojia zhu sulian shijie daobao dui guoji xingshi kanfa de
dianwen, 27 March 1956

109-01617-07, Zhu sulian shiguan guanyu sulian buzhang huiyi diyi fuzhuxi
Migaoyang tan sulian yu bolan guanxi de dianwen, 20–28 November 1956

109-01617-08, Zhu sulian shiguan guanyu sulian 'zhenli bao' zong bianji,
7 December 1956

109-01617-09, Zhu nansilafu shiguan guanyu nansilafu dui sulian yu bolan huitan
qingkuang baodao de dianwen, 1 December 1956

109-01617-15, Zhu sulian shiguan guanyu sugong zhongyang quanhui qingkuang de
dianwen, 20–21 December 1956

109-01617-16, Zhu sulian shiguan guanyu sulian xuanchuan he sixiang gongzuo
zhong ruogan wenti de dianwen, 3 February–16 July 1956

109-01748-03, Zhongguo tong jiexesiluofake liangguo kexueyuan 1957 nian zhi 1958
nian hezuo xueyi, 7 November 1956

109-01824-03, Guanyu minzhu deguo jingji lingdao jigou gaizu de ziliao, 13 March
1958

109-01827-02, Guanyu zhongguo tong minzhu deguo jingji maoyi guanxi de ziliao,
13 October 1958

109-01828-02, Guanyu minzhu deguo wenhua qingkuang de ziliao, 24 January–
2 December 1958

109-01919-01, Zhu sulian shiguan jiu sufang dui woguo renmin gongshe, dalujin deng dui neizhengce jidui waizhengce de fanying fahui de wendian, 25 December 1958–29 October 1959

109-01919-02, Sulian baozhi dui woguo neiwai huodong ji dui sumei jiaozhu pinglun de fanying, 21 August–7 December 1959

109-01919-03, Guanyu sulian xinwen daibiaotuan jiu woguo guonei qingkuang tingma de baodao, 20 December 1958–16 January 1959

109-01919-04, Guanyu sulian waijiaobu yuangdong sifu sichangyuan bu cai zai Mosike daxue qingzhu woguo jianguo shizhounian wanhui shang baogao neirong de wenti, 10–19 October 1959

109-01919-05, Sulian dui woguo wenyi fangce de fanying he zhongsu wenhua hezuo zhongde wenti, 2 April–9 December 1959

109-01919-09, Heluxiaofu zai sugong 21 da baogao zhong tan dao zhongsu guanxi wenti, 4 December 1959

109-01940-01, Waimaobu guanyu zhongguo tong minzhu deguo 1959 nian du maoyi tanpan de qingshi baogao, 2–5 February 1959

109-01940-02, Waimaobu guanyu zhongguo tong minzhu deguo 1960 nian zhi 1962 nian changqi maoyi tanpan jieguo de qingshi baogao, 25 December 1959–18 January 1960

109-01940-03, Woguo tong minzhu deguo maoyi qingkuang de cankao ziliao, 26 December 1959

109-02064-01, Sulian lingdao ren he zhuwaisi shijie tan guoji xingshi qi su duiwai zhengce, 31 December 1959–24 December 1960

109-02077-02, Sulian qunzhong dui Heluxiaofu he guonei qingkuang de fanying, 25 July–5 November 1960

109-02077-03, Guanyu sulian qunzhong zhongde yixie qingkuang, 28 October–29 November 1960

109-02078-01, Guanyu sugong zhongyang jiaqiang sixiang xuanzhuai gongzuo de yixie qingkuang, 11 January–13 October 1960

109-02085-05, Guanyu zai waijiao yang he tan ji sulian chetui zhuanjia wenti de chuli yuanze, 27 August–12 September 1960

109-02085-07, Guanyu sulian junshi zhuanjia de dongtai, 9 August 1960

109-02085-08, Guanyu sulian che zou anli guo xieding lai hua zhuanjia shide chuli, 26 November 1960–7 January 1961

109-02087-03, Sulian lingdaoren he xiongdi guojia zhu waishiguan renmin tan zhongyin bianjie wenti, 8 January–3 May 1960

109-02098-02, Sulian renyuan dui zhongsu guanxi de fanying, 4 July–9 December 1960

109-02098-03, Sulian guanyuan zai waishi huodong zhong dui wode taidu, 9 July–6 December 1960

109-02098-04, Sulian dui "suzhong youhao" tiaozhi de bianji, 8 January–27 December 1960

109-02705-01, Sulian lingdao ceng zai dui hua guanxi wenti shangde dongxiang, 10 March–7 April 1964

109-02705-02, Sulian minzhong dui zhongsu guanxi de yixie yilun, 14 April–18 May 1964

109-02708-01, Waijiaobu suousi fenxi Heluxiaofu xiatai hou sulian neiwai zhengce bianhuade dongxiang, 23–29 December 1964

109-02708-02, Heluxiaofu xiataihou sulian guonei de yixie ren shi biandong he sulian lingdao de dongxiang, 19 October–5 December 1964

109-02708-05, Sulian guoneidu Heluxiaofu xiatai yishi de fanying he subaokan de baodao qingkuang, 19 October 1964

109-02834-02, Heluxiaofu xiataihou sulian guonei yixie fanying he women de gongzuo, 17 December 1965

109-02840-02, Guanyu sulian shiyue geming jie 48 zhounian qingzhu banfa de waijiao tongbao, 1 November 1956

109-03319-01, Sulian renmin qunzhong dui zhongsu fenbie de fanying, 24 March–17 December 1963

109-03341-01, Sulian fanhua xuanchuan qingkuang, 31 January–8 October 1963

109-03341-02, Sulian jundui neibu fanhua qingkuang, 17 July–6 December 1963

109-03341-03, Sulian jiu xianggang aumen wenti ji zhongsu bianjie wenti jinxing fanhua xuanchuan, 21 January–8 August 1963

109-03346-02, Sulian guonei dui Heluxiaofu taidu, 5 June–30 September 1963

109-03535-02, Zhu minzhu deguo shiguan wenhuachu gongzuo zongjie, 23 January 1964–21 January 1965

109-03903-01, Zhong lianbu, waijiaobu guanyu yu sulian gongchen dang lingdaoren zhankai yizhi xingtai douzheng de zhibiao, 21 February–8 September 1964

117-00405-02, Baojialiye, jiekesiluofake, auerbaniya, chaoxian, nansilafu, menggu, yuenan lingdao ren zhi wo guo qingzhu dianji wo fudian, 28 September–24 October 1955

117-00471-04, Jiekesiluofake zhu hua dashi Geligeerfunu de he han ji wo fuhan, 30 September 1955

117-00761-01, Qingzhu zhongsu youhao tongmeng huzhu tiaoyue qianding shizhounian zhongsu shuangfang qingzhu zhongguo zhu wailingguan juxing baochihui qingkuang 1 January–28 February 1960

117-01668-01, Minzhu deguo zhu hua dashi Waerte guoshu, 11 March–7 April 1964

117-01668-02, Jiekesiluofake zhu hua dashi Kerisiteke guoshu, 16 March–24 April 1964

117-01718-04, Zhou Enlai zongli diangao minzhu deguo buchang huiyi zhuxi Geluotiwu qishi shouchen jidui fang ganxie dian, 4–26 March 1956

117-01720-01, Minzhu deguo buchang huiyi zhuxi Geluotiwu shishi, 21 September–9 October 1964

204-00005-23, Mao Zedong zhuxi yu xiongyali deguo, yuenan, menggu zhengfu daibiaotuan de tanhua jilu, 26–27 September 1954

204-00148-04, 1950 nian zhi 1954 nian 9 yue meiguo feiji qinfan wo lingkong tongji, 1 June 1950–30 September 1954

204-00242-02, Zhongguo he jiekesiluofake youguan wenxian qianzi yishi anpai, 9–20 March 1957

204-01537-01, Sulian dang zhengfu daibiaotuan zai jing huodong qingkuang he jiedai gongzuo zonghe huibao, 5–10 October 1964

204-01537-02, Dui sulian dang zhengfu daituan de yaoqing he sufang dafu, 16–28 September 1964

204-01537-04, Dui sulian dang zhengfu daibiao de zhengzhi jiedai fangan he jihua, 25–26 September 1964

204-01537-05, Mao Zedong zhuxi, Peng Zhen jiejian Gelishen shuailing de sulian dang zheng daibiaotuan tanhua jilu, 30 September 1964

RUSSIAN FEDERATION

Arkhiv vneshnei politiki rossiiskoi federadtsii (Archive of Foreign Policy of the Russian Federation, Moscow)

0100/100, Referentura po kitaiu

Gosudarstvennyi arkhiv Primorskogo kraia (State Archive of Primorsk Region, Vladivostok)

P-68, Primorskii kraevoi komitet KPSS

P-2550, Pervichnaia organizatsiia KPSS Grodekovskoi tamozhni, st. Grodekovo ogranichnogo raiona

R-25, Ispolnitel'nyi komitet Primorskogo oblastnogo soveta rabochikh, krest'ianskikh i krasnoarmeiskikh deputatov, g. Vladivostok

R-46, Upravlenie Dal'nevostochnogo gosudarstvennogo morskogo parokhodstva Ministerstva morskogo flota, g. Vladivostok

R-179, Grodekovskii ispolnitel'nyi komitet raionnogo soveta deputatov trudiashchikhsia, r. Grodekovo

Gosudarstvennyi arkhiv rossiiskoi federatsii (State Archive of the Russian Federation, Moscow)

5283, Vsesoiuznoe obshchestvo kul'turnoi sviazi s zagranitsei (VOKS)

5673, Sovetskaia sektsiia mezhdunarodnoi vystavki v n'iu-iorke v 1939g.

9324, Glavnaia redaktsiia zhurnala 'Sovetsko-kitaiskaia druzhba'

9396, Ministerstvo vysshego obrazovaniie SSSR

9401, Narodnyi komissariat vnutrennikh del SSSR

9499, Sovetskaia sektsiia mezhdunarodnoi vystavki v 1937

9469, General'nyi pravitel'stvennyi komissar vsemirnoi vystavki 1967

9470, Sovetskaia sektsiia vsemirnoi vystavki 1958

9518, Komitet po kul'turnym sviaziam s zarubezhnymi stranami pri sovete ministrov SSSR

9539, Sovetskii komitet zashchity mira

9576, Soiuz sovetskikh obshchestv druzhba i kul'turnoi sviazi s zarubezhnymi stranami

Rossiiskii gosudarstvennyi arkhiv ekonomiki (Russian State Archive of the Economy, Moscow)

51, Gosudarstvennyi komitet soveta ministrov SSSR po radioelektronike

635, Vsesoiuznaia torgovaia palata i ee predshestvenniki

1884, Ministerstvo putei soobshcheniia

3527, Ministerstvo sviazi SSSR

7604, Ministerstvo legkoi promyshlennosti SSSR

8002, Pravlenie sovetsko-kitaiskogo obshchestva kitaisko-chanchunskoi zheleznoi dorogi (1945–52)

8115, Narkomaty i ministerstva srednego avtomobil'nogo, traktornogo i sel'skokhoziaistvennogo mashinostroeniia SSSR

8123, Ministerstvo mashinostroeniia SSSR

8469, Ministerstvo traktornogo i sel'skokhoziaistvennogo mashinostroeniia

8848, Ministerstvo elektrotekhnicheskoi promyshlennosti SSSR

9493, Upravlenie po delam nauchno-tekhnicheskogo sotrudnichestva s sotsialisticheskimi stranami

Rossiiskii gosudarstvennyi arkhiv ekonomiki (Annex)

8157, Ministerstvo oboronnoi promyshlennosti

Rossiiskii gosudarstvennyi arkhiv literatury i iskusstvo (Russian State Archive of Literature and Culture, Moscow)

618, Redaktsiia zhurnala "Znamia"

648, Gosudarstvennyi akademicheskii bol'shoi teatr SSSR

652, Gosudarstvennoe uzdevatel'stvo "Iskusstvo"

1038, Vishnevskii, Vsevolod Vital'evich

1072, Inber, Vera Mikhailovna

1397, Redaktsiia zhurnala "Internatsional'naia literatura"

1433, Reginin, Vasilii Aleksandrovich

1816, Tvardovskii, Aleksandr Trifonovich

2064, Chirkov, Boris Petrovich

2077, Soiuz kompozitorov SSSR

2226, Bulgakov, Valentin Fedorovich

2292, Nikolaeva, Galina Evgen'evna

2358, Petrov, Nikolai Vasil'evich

2499, Soiuznoe ob'edinenie gosudarsvennykh tsirkov ministerstva kul'tury SSSR (Soiuzgostsirk)

2720, Gol'dina, Mariia Solomonova

2732, Obraztsov, Sergei Vladimirovich

2751, Butorin, Nikolai Nikolaevich

2876, Apletin, Mikhail Iakovlevich

2936, Soiuz kinomatorgov SSSR

Rossiiskii gosudarstvennyi arkhiv noveishii istorii (Russian State Archive of Contemporary History, Moscow)

1, S'ezdy kommunisticheskoi partii sovetskogo soiuza

2, Plenumy TsK VKP(b)

5, Apparat TsK KPSS

11, Komissiia TsK KPSS po voprosam ideologii, kul'tury i mezhdunarodnykh partiinykh sviazei

72, Ideologicheskaia komissiia pri TsK KPSS

Rossiiskii gosudarstvennyi arkhiv sotsial'no-politicheskoi istorii (Russian State Archive of Social-Political History, Moscow)

82, Molotov, V. M.

Rossiiskii gosudarstvennyi istoricheskii arkhiv (Russian State Historical Archive, St. Petersburg)
  821, Departament dukhovnykh del inostrannykh ispovedanii MVD
  1268, Kavkazskii komitet

UNITED STATES

National Archive II (College Park, Maryland)
  RG 43, Records of International Conferences, Commissions, and Expositions
  RG 306, Office of Research: Special Reports, 1953–63
  RG 306, Records Relating to the American National Exhibition, Moscow, 1957–59
  RG 306, Records Relating to Trade Fairs, 1958–66

Newspapers and Journals

CHINESE

Beijing ribao
Fuxian ribao
Gongren ribao
Guangming ribao
Jiefang ribao
Renmin ribao
Suiyan ribao
Suzhong youhao
Xinmin ribao
Xinmin wanbao
Zhongguo gongren

CZECH

Historický obzor
Mezinárodní dělnické hnuti
Mezinárodní otázky
Mezinárodní politika
Nová mysl: Theoretický a politický časopis ÚV KSČ
Odbrorář
Rudé právo
Slezký sborník

GERMAN

Deutsche Aussenpolitik
Jahrbücher für Geschichte Osteuropas

RUSSIAN

Bol'shevik
Don
Istoricheskii arkhiv
Istoriia SSSR
Krasnoe znamia
Mezhdunarodnaia zhizn'
Narodnyi Kitai
Novaia i noveishaia istoriia
Novoe vremia
Novyi mir
Oktiabr'
Otechestvennaia istoriia
Pravda
Problemy dal'nego vostoka
Rossiia
Russkoe slovo
Sotsiologicheskie issledovaniia
Sovetskaia kul'tura
Sovetskaia torgovlia
Strategiia Rossii
Tvorchestvo
Vecherniaia moskva
Vneshniaia torgovlia
Voprosy ekonomiki
Voprosy istorii
Vostok
Zvezda
Zvezda vostoka

English-Language Scholarship and Translations

Abrams, Bradley F. *The Struggle for the Soul of the Nation: Czech Culture and the Rise of Communism*. Lanham, Md.: Rowman & Littlefield, 2004.

Acheson, Dean. *Present at the Creation: My Years in the State Department*. New York: W. W. Norton, 1969.

Allen, Robert C. *Farm to Factory: A Reinterpretation of the Soviet Industrial Revolution*. Princeton, N.J.: Princeton University Press, 2003.

Ambroz, Oton. *Realignment of World Power: The Russo-Chinese Schism under the Impact of Mao Tse-Tung's Last Revolution* vol. 1. New York: Robert Speller & Sons, 1972.

"A New 'Cult of Personality': Suslov's Secret Report on Mao, Khrushchev, and Sino-Soviet Tensions, December 1959." *CWIHPB*, nos. 8–9 (Winter 1996–97): 244, 248.

Apor, Balázs, Péter Apor, and E. A. Rees, eds. *The Sovietization of Eastern Europe: New Perspectives on the Postwar Period*. Washington, D.C.: New Academia, 2008.

Arbatov, Georgi. *The System: An Insider's Life in Soviet Politics*. New York: Random House, 1992.

Armstrong, Charles K. "The Cultural Cold War in Korea, 1945–1950." *Journal of Asian Studies* 62, no. 1 (February 2003): 71–99.

———. "'Fraternal Socialism': The International Reconstruction of North Korea, 1953–62." *Cold War History* 5, no. 2 (May 2005): 161–87.

Bailes, Kendall E. *Technology and Society under Lenin and Stalin: Origins of the Soviet Technical Intelligentsia, 1917–1941*. Princeton, N.J.: Princeton University Press, 1978.

Ball, Alan M. *Imagining America: Influence and Images in Twentieth-Century Russia*. Lanham, Md.: Rowman & Littlefield, 2003.

Banac, Ivo. *With Stalin against Tito: Cominformist Splits in Yugoslav Communism*. Ithaca, N.Y.: Cornell University Press, 1988.

Barany, Zoltan D. *Soldiers and Politics in Eastern Europe, 1945–90*. New York: St. Martin's, 1990.

———. "Soviet Takeovers: The Role of Advisers in Mongolia in the 1920s and in Eastern Europe after World War II." *East European Quarterly* 28, no. 4 (Winter 1994): 409–33.

Barnouin, Barbara, and Yu Changgen. *Zhou Enlai: A Political Life*. Hong Kong: Chinese University Press, 2006.

Bass, Robert, and Elizabeth Marbury, eds. *The Soviet-Yugoslav Controversy, 1948–58: A Documentary Record*. Intro. Hans Kohn. New York: Prospect, 1959.

Bassin, Mark. *Imperial Visions: Nationalist Imagination and Geographical Expansion in the Russian Far East, 1840–1865*. Cambridge: Cambridge University Press, 1999.

Bayly, C. A., et al. "AHR Conversation: On Transnational History." *American Historical Review* 111, no. 5 (December 2006): 1440–64.

Becker, Jasper. *Hungry Ghosts: Mao's Secret Famine*. New York: Free Press, 1996.

Beissinger, Mark R. "Soviet Empire as 'Family Resemblance.'" *Slavic Review* 65, no. 2 (Summer 2006): 294–303.

Békés, Csaba. "Soviet Plans to Establish the COMINFORM in Early 1946: New Evidence from the Hungarian Archives." *CWIHPB*, no. 10 (March 1998): 135–36.

Békés, Csaba, Malcolm Byrne, and János M. Rainer, eds. *The 1956 Hungarian Revolution: A History in Documents*. Budapest: Central European University Press, 2002.

Bellacqua, James, ed. *The Future of China-Russia Relations*. Lexington: University Press of Kentucky, 2010.

Benson, Linda. *The Ili Rebellion: The Moslem Challenge to Chinese Authority in Xinjiang, 1944–1949*. Armonk, N.Y.: M. E. Sharpe, 1990.

Berend, Ivan T. *Decades of Crisis: Central and Eastern Europe before World War II*. Berkeley: University of California Press, 1998.

Bernstein, Thomas P. "Mao Zedong and the Famine of 1959–1960: A Study in Wilfulness." *China Quarterly*, no. 186 (June 2006): 421–45.

Bernstein, Thomas P., and Hua-yu Li, eds. *China Learns from the Soviet Union, 1949–Present*. Boston: Lexington, 2010.

Bittner, Stephen V. *The Many Lives of Khrushchev's Thaw: Experience and Memory in Moscow's Arbat*. Ithaca, N.Y.: Cornell University Press, 2008.

Borhi, László. "Empire by Coercion: The Soviet Union and Hungary in the 1950s." *Cold War History* 1, no. 2 (January 2001): 47–72.

———. *Hungary in the Cold War, 1945–1956: Between the United States and the Soviet Union*. Budapest: Central European University Press, 2004.

Boterbloem, Kees. *The Life and Times of Andrei Zhdanov, 1896–1948*. Montreal: McGill-Queen's University Press, 2004.

Bo Yibo. "The Making of the 'Leaning to One Side' Decision." Trans. Zhai Qiang. *Chinese Historians* 5, no. 1 (Spring 1992): 57–62.

Braddick, C. W. *Japan and the Sino-Soviet Alliance, 1950–1964*. New York: Palgrave Macmillan, 2004.

Braester, Yomi. "'A Big Dying Vat': The Vilifying of Shanghai during the Good Eight Company Campaign." *Modern China* 31, no. 4 (October 2005): 411–47.

Bren, Paulina, and Mary Neuberger, eds. *Communism Unwrapped: Consumption in Cold War Eastern Europe*. Oxford: Oxford University Press, 2012.

Brooks, Jeffrey. *Thank You, Comrade Stalin! Soviet Public Culture from Revolution to Cold War*. Princeton, N.J.: Princeton University Press, 2000.

Brower, Daniel R., and Edward J. Lazzerini, eds. *Russia's Orient: Imperial Borderlands and Peoples, 1700–1917*. Bloomington: Indiana University Press, 1997.

Brown, Jeremy, and Paul G. Pickowicz, eds. *Dilemmas of Victory: The Early Years of the People's Republic of China*. Cambridge, Mass.: Harvard University Press, 2007.

Brus, W. "1957 to 1965: In Search of Balanced Development." In M. C. Kaser, ed., *The Economic History of Eastern Europe, 1919–1945*, vol. 3, *Institutional Change within a Planned Economy*, 71–138. London: Clarendon, 1986.

Brzezinski, Zbigniew K. *The Soviet Bloc: Unity and Conflict*. New York: Frederick A. Praeger, 1960.

Burbank, Jane, Mark Von Hagen, and Anatolyi Remnev, eds. *Russian Empire: Space, People, Power (1700–1930)*. Bloomington: Indiana University Press, 2007.

Burlatsky, Fedor. *Khrushchev and the First Russian Spring: The Era of Khrushchev through the Eyes of His Advisor*. Trans. Daphne Skillen. New York: Charles Scribner's Sons, 1991.

Burr, William, and Jeffrey T. Richelson. "Whether to 'Strangle the Baby in the Cradle': The United States and the Chinese Nuclear Program, 1960–64." *International Security* 25, no. 3 (Winter 2000–2001): 54–99.

Castillo, Greg. "East as True West: Redeeming Bourgeois Culture, from Socialist Realism to *Ostalgie*." *Kritika: Explorations in Russian and Eurasian History* 9, no. 4 (Fall 2008): 747–68.

Caute, David. *The Dancer Defects: The Struggle for Cultural Hegemony during the Cold War*. Oxford: Oxford University Press, 2003.

Chan, Alfred L. *Mao's Crusade: Politics and Policy Implementation in China's Great Leap Forward*. Oxford: Oxford University Press, 2001.

Chang, Gordon H. *Friends and Enemies: The United States, China, and the Soviet Union, 1948–1972*. Stanford, Calif.: Stanford University Press, 1990.

Chang, Julian. "The Mechanics of State Propaganda: The People's Republic of China and the Soviet Union in the 1950s." In Timothy Creek and Tony Saich, eds., *New Perspectives on State Socialism*, 76–124. Armonk, N.Y.: M. E. Sharpe, 1997.

Cheek, Timothy. *Propaganda and Culture in Mao's China: Deng Tuo and the Intelligentsia*. Oxford: Clarendon, 1997.

Chen, C., ed. *China and the Three Worlds: A Foreign Policy Reader*. White Plains, N.Y.: M. E. Sharpe, 1979.

Chen, Tina Mai. "Internationalism and Culture Experience: Soviet Films and Popular Chinese Understandings of the Future in the 1950s." *Cultural Critique* 58 (Fall 2004): 82–114.

———. "Socialism, Aestheticized Bodies, and International Circuits of Gender: Soviet Female Film Stars in the People's Republic of China, 1949–1969." *Journal of the Canadian Historical Association* 98, no. 2 (2007): 53–80.

Chen Jian, Vojtech Mastny, Odd Arne Westad, and Vladislav Zubok. "Stalin's Conversations with Chinese Leaders." *CWIHPB*, nos. 6–7 (Winter 1995–96): 4–29.

Chen Jian. *China's Road to the Korean War: The Making of the Sino-American Confrontation*. New York: Columbia University Press, 1994.

———. "A Crucial Step toward the Breakdown of the Sino-Soviet Alliance: The Withdrawal of Soviet Experts from China in July 1960." *CWIHPB*, nos. 8–9 (Winter 1996–97): 246, 249–50.

———. *Mao's China and the Cold War*. Chapel Hill: University of North Carolina Press, 2001.

———. "Bridging Revolution and Decolonization: The 'Bandung Discourse' in China's Early Cold War Experience." In Christopher E. Goscha and Christian F. Ostermann, eds., *Connecting Histories: Decolonization and the Cold War in Southeast Asia, 1945–1962*, 137–71. Washington, D.C.: Woodrow Wilson Center Press, 2009.

———. "Mao's China and 1956 as a Turning Point in Cold War and Chinese History." Conference on Mao's China, Non-communist Asia, and the Global Setting, 1949–1976, University of Hong Kong, 14–15 February 2012.

Cheng, Yinghong. "Sino-Cuban Relations during the Early Years of the Castro Regime, 1959–1966." *Journal of Cold War Studies* 9, no. 3 (Summer 2007): 78–114.

Chou Tse-tung (Zhou Cezong). *The May Fourth Movement: Intellectual Revolution in Modern China*. Cambridge, Mass.: Harvard University Press, 1960.

Christensen, Thomas J. *Worse than a Monolith: Alliance Politics and Problems of Coercive Diplomacy in Asia*. Princeton, N.J.: Princeton University Press, 2011.

————. *Useful Adversaries: Grand Strategy, Domestic Mobilization, and Sino-American Conflict, 1947–58*. Princeton, N.J.: Princeton University Press, 1996.

Chu-Yuan Cheng. *Economic Relations between Peking and Moscow, 1949–63*. New York: Frederick A. Praeger, 1964.

Ciesla, Burghard, and Patrice G. Poutrus. "Food Supply in a Planned Economy: SED Nutrition Policy between Crisis Response and Popular Needs." In Konrad H. Jarausch, ed., Eve Duffy, trans., *Dictatorship as Experience: Towards a Socio-cultural History of the GDR*, 143–62. Oxford: Berghahn, 1999.

Clausen, Søren, and Stig Thøgersen, eds. *The Making of a Chinese City: History and Historiography in Harbin*. Armonk, N.Y.: M. E. Sharpe, 1995.

Cohen, Deborah, and Maura O'Connor. *Comparison and History: Europe in Cross-national Perspective*. New York: Routledge, 2004.

Congdon, Lee, Béla K. Király, and Károly Nagy, eds. *1956: The Hungarian Revolution and War for Independence*. Trans. Paul Bödy et al. Boulder, Colo.: Social Science Monographs, 2006.

Connelly, John. *Captive University: The Sovietization of East German, Czech, and Polish Higher Education, 1945–1956*. Chapel Hill: University of North Carolina Press, 2000.

Craig, Campbell, and Fredrik Logevall. *America's Cold War: The Politics of Insecurity*. Cambridge, Mass.: Harvard University Press, 2009.

Crews, Robert D. *For Prophet and Tsar: Islam and Empire in Russia and Central Asia*. Cambridge, Mass.: Harvard University Press, 2006.

Crowley, David. "Paris or Moscow? Warsaw Architects and the Image of the Modern City in the 1950s." *Kritika: Explorations in Russian and Eurasian History* 9, no. 4 (Fall 2008): 769–98.

Crowley, David, and Susan E. Reid. "Style and Socialism: Modernity and Material Culture in Post-war Eastern Europe." In Susan E. Reid and David Crowley, eds., *Style and Socialism: Modernity and Material Culture in Post-war Eastern Europe*. Oxford: Berg, 2000, 1–24.

Dandan Zhu. "The Hungarian Revolution and the Origins of China's Great Leap Policies, 1956–57." *Cold War History* 12, no. 3 (2012): 451–72.

Danhui Li and Yafeng Xia. "Competing for Leadership: Split or Detente in the Sino-Soviet Bloc, 1959–1961." *International History Review* 30, no. 3 (2008): 545–74.

Daunton, Martin, and Matthew Hilton, eds. *The Politics of Consumption: Material Culture and Citizenship in Europe and America*. Oxford: Berg, 2001.

David-Fox, Michael. "The Implications of Transnationalism." *Kritika: Explorations in Russian and Eurasian History* 12, no. 4 (Fall 2011): 885–904.

————. *Showcasing the Great Experiment: Cultural Diplomacy and Western Visitors to the Soviet Union, 1921–1941*. Oxford: Oxford University Press, 2012.

David-Fox, Michael, Peter Holquist, and Alexander Martin, eds. *Orientalism and Empire in Russia*. Bloomington, Ind.: Slavica, 2006.

Dedijer, Vladimir. *The Battle Stalin Lost: Memoirs of Yugoslavia, 1948–1953*. New York: Viking, 1971.

De Grazia, Victoria. *Irresistible Empire: America's Advance through Twentieth-Century Europe*. Cambridge, Mass.: Harvard University Press, 2005.

Deng, Yong. "Remolding Great Power Politics: China's Strategic Partnership with Russia, the European Union, and India." *Journal of Strategic Studies* 30, no. 4–5 (August–October 2007): 863–901.

Dikötter, Frank. *Mao's Great Famine: The History of China's Most Devastating Catastrophe, 1958–1962*. New York: Walker, 2010.

Dimitrov, Vesselin. *Stalin's Cold War. Soviet Foreign Policy, Democracy and Communism in Bulgaria, 1941–48*. New York: Palgrave Macmillan, 2008.

Dittmer, Lowell. *Sino-Soviet Normalization and Its International Implications, 1945–1990*. Seattle: University of Washington Press, 1992.

Dobson, Miriam. *Khrushchev's Cold Summer: Gulag Returnees, Crime, and the Fate of Reform after Stalin*. Ithaca, N.Y.: Cornell University Press, 2009.

Dragomir, Elena. "The Formation of the Soviet Bloc's Council for Mutual Economic Assistance: Romania's Involvement." *Journal of Cold War Studies* 64, no. 1 (Winter 2012): 34–47.

Dunbabin, J. P. D. *The Cold War: The Great Powers and Their Allies*. London: Longman, 1994.

Dunham, Vera S. *In Stalin's Time: Middleclass Values in Soviet Fiction*. Durham, N.C.: Duke University Press, 1990.

Elleman, Bruce A. "The Final Consolidation of the USSR's Sphere of Interest in Outer Mongolia." In Stephen Kotkin and Bruce A. Elleman, eds., *Mongolia in the Twentieth Century: Landlocked Cosmopolitan*, 123–36. Armonk, N.Y.: M. E. Sharpe, 1999.

Engerman, David C. "The Romance of Economic Development and New Histories of the Cold War." *Diplomatic History* 28, no. 1 (January 2004): 23–54.

English, Robert D. *Russia and the Idea of the West: Gorbachev, Intellectuals, and the End of the Cold War*. New York: Columbia University Press, 2000.

Fairbank, John King, and Merle Goldman. *China: A New History*. 2nd ed. Cambridge, Mass.: Harvard University Press, 2006.

Fallenbuchl, Zbigniew M. "East European Integration: COMECON." In Joint Economic Committee, *Reorientation and Commercial Relations of the Economies of Eastern Europe*, 79–134. Washington, D.C.: U.S. Government Printing Office, 1974.

Fejtö, François. *A History of the People's Democracies: Eastern Europe since Stalin*. Trans. Daniel Weissbort. New York: Praeger, 1971.

Feng-Hwa Mah. "The Terms of Sino-Soviet Trade." *China Quarterly* 17 (January–March 1964): 174–91.

Fitzgerald, John. *Awakening China: Politics, Culture, and Class in the Nationalist Revolution*. Stanford, Calif.: Stanford University Press, 1996.

Fitzpatrick, Sheila. *The Cultural Front: Power and Culture in Revolutionary Russia*. Ithaca, N.Y.: Cornell University Press, 1992.

———. *Everyday Stalinism: Ordinary Life in Extraordinary Times: Soviet Russia in the 1930s*. New York: Oxford University Press, 1999.

Fitzpatrick, Sheila, ed. *Stalinism: New Directions*. New York: Routledge, 2000.

"FORUM: Mao, Khrushchev, and China's Split with the USSR: Perspectives on the Sino-Soviet Split." *Journal of Cold War Studies* 12, no. 1 (Winter 2010): 120–65.

Freeze, Gregory L. "The *Soslovie* (Estate) Paradigm and Russian Social History." *American Historical Review* 91, no. 1 (February 1986): 11–36.

Frommer, Benjamin. *National Cleansing: Retribution against Nazi Collaborators in Postwar Czechoslovakia.* Cambridge: Cambridge University Press, 2005.

Fulbrook, Mary. *The People's State: East German Society from Hitler to Honecker.* New Haven, Conn.: Yale University Press, 2005.

Funigiello, Philip S. *American-Soviet Trade in the Cold War.* Chapel Hill: University of North Carolina Press, 1988.

Fursenko, Aleksandr, and Timothy Naftali. *"One Hell of a Gamble": Khrushchev, Castro, and Kennedy, 1958–1964.* New York: W. W. Norton, 1997.

———. *Khrushchev's Cold War: The Inside Story of an American Adversary.* New York: W. W. Norton, 2006.

Gaddis, John Lewis. *The Cold War: A New History.* New York: Penguin, 2005.

Gaiduk, Ilya V. *Confronting Vietnam: Soviet Policy toward the Indochina Conflict, 1954–1963.* Washington, D.C.: Woodrow Wilson Center Press, 2003.

Ganshin, G., and T. Zazerskaya. "Pitfalls along the Path of 'Brotherly Friendship.'" *Far Eastern Affairs,* no. 6 (1994): 63–70.

Gao, James Z. *The Communist Takeover of Hangzhou: The Transformation of City and Cadre, 1949–1954.* Honolulu: University of Hawai'i Press, 2004.

Garver, John W. *Chinese-Soviet Relations, 1937–1945: The Diplomacy of Chinese Nationalism.* New York: Oxford University Press, 1988.

Gati, Charles. *Failed Illusions: Moscow, Washington, Budapest, and the 1956 Hungarian Revolt.* Washington, D.C., and Stanford, Calif.: Wilson Center Press and Stanford University Press, 2006.

Gelb, Michael. "An Early Soviet Ethnic Deportation: The Far-Eastern Koreans." *Russian Review* 54, no. 3 (July 1995): 389–412.

Gibianskii, Leonid. "The Soviet Bloc and the Initial Stage of the Cold War: Archival Documents on Stalin's Meetings with Communist Leaders of Yugoslavia and Bulgaria, 1946–1948." *CWIHPB,* no. 10 (March 1998): 112–34.

———. "Soviet-Yugoslav Relations and the Hungarian Revolution of 1956." *CWIHPB,* no. 10 (March 1998): 139–48.

Gienow-Hecht, Jessica C. E., and Mark C. Donfried, eds. *Searching for a Cultural Diplomacy.* New York: Berghahn, 2010.

Gilbert Rozman, Gilbert. *A Mirror for Socialism: Soviet Criticisms of China.* Princeton, N.J.: Princeton University Press, 1985.

Ginsburgs, George, and Carl F. Pinkele. *The Sino-Soviet Territorial Dispute, 1949–64.* New York: Praeger, 1978.

Gittings, John. *Survey of the Sino-Soviet Dispute: A Commentary and Extracts from the Recent Polemics, 1963–1967.* London: Oxford University Press, 1968.

Gobarev, Viktor M. "Soviet Policy toward China: Developing Nuclear Weapons, 1949–1969." *Journal of Slavic Military Studies* 12, no. 4 (December 1999): 1–53.

Goldstein, Steven M. "Nationalism and Internationalism: Sino-Soviet Relations." In Thomas W. Robinson and David Shambaugh, eds., *Chinese Foreign Policy: Theory and Practice*, 224–65. Oxford: Clarendon, 1994.

Goncharov, Sergei. "The Stalin-Mao Dialogue." *Far Eastern Affairs*, no. 2 (1994): 94–111.

Goncharov, Sergei N., John W. Lewis, and Xue Litai. *Uncertain Partners: Stalin, Mao, and the Korean War*. Stanford, Calif.: Stanford University Press, 1993.

Gorodetsky, Gabriel. *Grand Delusion: Stalin and the German Invasion of Russia*. New Haven, Conn.: Yale University Press, 1999.

Gorsuch, Anne E., and Diane P. Koenker, eds. *Turizm: The Russian and East European Tourist under Capitalism and Socialism*. Ithaca, N.Y.: Cornell University Press, 2006.

Goscha, Christopher E., and Christian F. Ostermann, eds. *Connecting Histories: Decolonization and the Cold War in Southeast Asia, 1945–1962*. Washington, D.C.: Woodrow Wilson Center Press, 2009.

Granville, Johanna. *The First Domino: International Decision Making during the Hungarian Crisis of 1956*. College Station: Texas A&M University Press, 2004.

———. "'Caught with Jam on Our Fingers': Radio Free Europe and the Hungarian Revolution of 1956." *Diplomatic History* 29, no. 5 (November 2005): 811–39.

———. "Blame the Messenger? Bucharest and Its Bungling Diplomats in 1956." *Canadian Slavonic Papers* 52, nos. 3–4 (September–December 2010): 299–330.

Gray, William Glenn. *Germany's Cold War: The Global Campaign to Isolate East Germany, 1949–1969*. Chapel Hill: University of North Carolina Press, 2003.

Gregory, Paul R., ed. *Behind the Facade of Stalin's Command Economy: Evidence from the Soviet State and Party Archives*. Stanford, Calif.: Hoover Institution Press, 2001.

Gross, Jan. "War as Revolution." In Norman Naimark and Leonid Gibianskii, eds., *The Establishment of Communist Regimes in Eastern Europe, 1944–1949*, 17–40. Boulder, Colo.: Westview, 1997.

Harrison, Hope. *Driving the Soviets up the Wall: Soviet-East German Relations, 1953–1961*. Princeton, N.J.: Princeton University Press, 2003.

Harrison, Mark, ed. *The Economics of World War II: Six Great Powers in International Comparison*. Cambridge: Cambridge University Press, 1988.

Hasegawa, Tsuyoshi. *Racing the Enemy: Stalin, Truman, and the Surrender of Japan*. Cambridge, Mass.: Harvard University Press, 2005.

———, ed. *The Cold War in East Asia, 1945–1991*. Washington, D.C., and Stanford, Calif.: Woodrow Wilson Center Press and Stanford University Press, 2011.

Heinzig, Dieter. *The Soviet Union and Communist China, 1945–1950: The Arduous Road to the Alliance*. Armonk, N.Y.: M. E. Sharpe, 2004.

Heldmann, Philipp. "Negotiating Consumption in a Dictatorship: Consumption Politics in the GDR in the 1950s and 1960s." In Martin Daunton and Matthew Hilton, eds., *The Politics of Consumption: Material Culture and Citizenship in Europe and America*, 185–202. Oxford: Berg, 2001.

Hershberg, James, Sergey Radchenko, Péter Vámos, and David Wolff. "The Interkit Story: A Window into the Final Decades of the Sino-Soviet Relationship." CWIHP Working Paper no. 63. Washington, D.C.: CWIHP, February 2011.

Hessler, Julie. *A Social History of Soviet Trade: Trade Policy, Retail Practices, and Consumption, 1917–1953.* Princeton, N.J.: Princeton University Press, 2004.

Hinton, Harold C., ed. *The People's Republic of China, 1949–1979: A Documentary Survey*, vol. 2. Wilmington, Del.: Scholarly Resources, 1980.

Hoffmann, David L. *Stalinist Values: The Cultural Norms of Soviet Modernity, 1917–1941.* Ithaca, N.Y.: Cornell University Press, 2003.

Holloway, David. *Stalin and the Bomb: The Soviet Union and Atomic Energy, 1939–1956.* New Haven, Conn.: Yale University Press, 1994.

Hopf, Ted. *Social Construction of International Politics: Identities and Foreign Policies, Moscow, 1955 and 1999.* Ithaca, N.Y.: Cornell University Press, 2002.

Hosking, Geoffrey. *Russia and the Russians: A History.* Cambridge, Mass.: Harvard University Press, 2001.

Hua-yu Li. "The Political Stalinization of China: The Establishment of One-Party Constitutionalism, 1948–1954." *Journal of Cold War Studies* 3, no. 2 (2001): 28–47.

———. *Mao and the Economic Stalinization of China, 1948–1953.* Lanham, Md.: Rowman & Littlefield, 2006.

Hung, Chang-tai. *Mao's New World: Political Culture in the Early People's Republic.* Ithaca, N.Y.: Cornell University Press, 2011.

Hunt, Michael H. *The Genesis of Chinese Communist Foreign Policy.* New York: Columbia University Press, 1996.

Jersild, Austin. "The Soviet State as Imperial Scavenger: 'Catch Up and Surpass' in the Transnational Socialist Bloc, 1950–1960." *American Historical Review* 116, no. 1 (February 2011): 109–32.

———. "The Great Betrayal: Russian Memories of the 'Great Friendship.'" *Cold War History* 12, no. 1 (February 2012): 159–69.

Johnson, Lonnie R. *Central Europe: Enemies, Neighbors, Friends.* 2nd ed. New York: Oxford University Press, 2002.

Jones, Polly, ed. *The Dilemmas of De-Stalinization: Negotiating Cultural and Social Change in the Khrushchev Era.* London: Routledge, 2006.

Kang Chao and Feng-hwa Mah. "A Study of the Rouble-Yuan Exchange Rate." *China Quarterly*, no. 17 (January–March 1964): 192–204.

Kaplan, Karel. *The Overcoming of the Regime Crisis after Stalin's Death in Czechoslovakia, Poland and Hungary.* Cologne: "Projekt," 1986.

Kaple, Deborah A. *Dream of a Red Factory: The Legacy of High Stalinism in China.* New York: Oxford University Press, 1994.

Kappeler, Andreas. *La Russie: Empire multiethnique.* Trans. Guy Imart. Paris: Institut d'études slaves, 1994.

Kaser, M. C., ed. *The Economic History of Eastern Europe, 1919–1975.* Vol. 3, *Institutional Change within a Planned Economy.* London: Clarendon, 1986.

Kaser, Michael. *Comecon: Integration Problems of the Planned Economies.* London: Oxford University Press, 1965.

Kelly, Catriona. *Refining Russia: Advice Literature, Polite Culture, and Gender from Catherine to Yeltsin.* Oxford: Oxford University Press, 2001.

Kemp-Welch, Tony. "Khrushchev's 'Secret Speech' and Polish Politics: The Spring of 1956." *Europe-Asia Studies* 48, no. 2 (1996): 181–206.

Kenez, Peter. *The Birth of the Propaganda State: Soviet Methods of Mass Mobilization, 1917–1929*. Cambridge: Cambridge University Press, 1985.

Khrushchev, Nikita S. "On Peaceful Coexistence." *Foreign Affairs* 38, no. 1 (October 1959): 1–18.

———. *For Victory in Peaceful Competition with Capitalism*. New York: E. P. Dutton, 1960.

Kim, Donggil. "The Crucial Issues of the Early Cold War: Stalin and the Chinese Civil War." *Cold War History* 10, no. 2 (May 2010): 185–202.

Kirby, William C. "China's Internationalization in the Early People's Republic: Dreams of a Socialist World Economy." *China Quarterly* 188, no. 4 (2006): 870–90.

Kornai, János. *The Socialist System: The Political Economy of Communism*. Princeton, N.J.: Princeton University Press, 1992.

Kozlov, Vladimir A. *Mass Uprisings in the USSR: Protest and Rebellion in the Post-Stalin Years*. Trans. and ed. Elaine McClarnand MacKinnon. Armonk, N.Y.: M. E. Sharpe, 2002.

Kramer, Mark. "The USSR Foreign Ministry's Appraisal of Sino-Soviet Relations on the Eve of the Split, September 1959." *CWIHPB*, nos. 6–7 (Winter 1995–96): 170–85.

———. "New Evidence on Soviet Decision-Making and the 1956 Polish and Hungarian Crises." *CWIHPB*, nos. 8–9 (Winter 1996): 358–84.

———. "The Soviet Union and the 1956 Crises in Hungary and Poland: Reassessments and New Findings." *Journal of Contemporary History* 33, no. 2 (April 1998): 163–214.

———. "Declassified Materials from CPSU Central Committee Plenums." *Cahiers du monde russe* 40, nos. 1–2 (January–June 1999): 271–306.

———. "The Early Post-Stalin Succession Struggle and Upheavals in East Central Europe: Internal-External Linkages in Soviet Policy Making (Part 1)." *Journal of Cold War Studies* 1, no. 1 (1999): 3–55; (Part 2) 1, no. 2 (1999): 3–38; (Part 3) 1, no. 3 (1999): 3–66.

Kraus, Charles. "Creating a Soviet 'Semi-Colony'? Sino-Soviet Cooperation and Its Demise in Xinjiang, 1949–1955." *Chinese Historical Review* 17, no. 2 (Fall 2010): 129–65.

Kuchins, Andrew C. "Limits of the Sino-Russian Strategic Partnership." In Andrew C. Kuchins, ed., *Russia after the Fall*, 205–20. Washington, D.C.: Carnegie Endowment for International Peace, 2002.

Kuo, Mercy A. *Contending with Contradictions: China's Policy toward Soviet Eastern Europe and the Origins of the Sino-Soviet Split, 1953–1960*. Lanham, Md.: Lexington, 2001.

Laboda, Ivan. "History of the Sino-Soviet Friendship Society in Harbin." *Far Eastern Affairs*, no. 1 (1990): 215–20.

Lahusen, Thomas. *How Life Writes the Book: Real Socialism and Socialist Realism in Stalin's Russia*. Ithaca, N.Y.: Cornell University Press, 1997.

Lampe, John R. *Yugoslavia as History: Twice There Was a Country*. Cambridge, Mass.: Cambridge University Press, 1996.

Landsman, Mark. *Dictatorship and Demand: The Politics of Consumerism in East Germany*. Cambridge, Mass.: Harvard University Press, 2005.

Lankov, Andrei. *Crisis in North Korea: The Failure of De-Stalinization, 1956.* Honolulu: University of Hawai'i Press, 2005.

Lees, Lorraine M. *Keeping Tito Afloat: The United States, Yugoslavia, and the Cold War.* University Park: Pennsylvania State University Press, 1997.

Leung, John K., and Michael Y. M. Kau, eds. *The Writings of Mao Zedong, 1949–1976,* vol. 2. Armonk, N.Y.: M. E. Sharpe, 1992.

Lewis, John Wilson, and Xue Litai. *China Builds the Bomb.* Stanford, Calif.: Stanford University Press, 1988.

Liu Yanqiong and Liu Jifeng. "Analysis of Soviet Technology Transfer in the Development of China's Nuclear Weapons." *Comparative Technology Transfer and Society* 7, no. 1 (April 2009): 66–110.

Lovell, Stephen. *The Shadow of War: Russia and the USSR, 1941 to the Present.* Oxford: Wiley-Blackwell, 2010.

Lukin, Alexander. *The Bear Watches the Dragon: Russia's Perception of China and the Evolution of Russia-Chinese Relations since the Eighteenth Century.* Armonk, N.Y.: M. E. Sharpe, 2003.

Lüthi, Lorenz. *The Sino-Soviet Split: Cold War in the Communist World.* Princeton, N.J.: Princeton University Press, 2008.

———. "The Vietnam War and China's Third-Line Defense Planning before the Cultural Revolution, 1964–1966." *Journal of Cold War Studies* 10, no. 1 (Winter 2008): 26–51.

———. "The Origins of Proletarian Diplomacy: The Chinese Attack on the American Embassy in the Soviet Union, 4 March 1965." *Cold War History* 9, no. 3 (October 2009): 411–26.

Lynch, Allen. *The Soviet Study of International Relations.* Cambridge: Cambridge University Press, 1987.

MacFarquhar, Roderick. *The Origins of the Cultural Revolution.* Vol. 3, *The Coming of the Cataclysm, 1961–1966.* New York: Columbia University Press, 1997.

MacFarquhar, Roderick, Timothy Cheek, and Eugene Wu, eds. *The Secret Speeches of Chairman Mao: From the Hundred Flowers to the Great Leap Forward.* Cambridge, Mass.: Council on East Asian Studies/Harvard University, 1989.

MacFarquhar, Roderick, and Michael Schoenhals. *Mao's Last Revolution.* Cambridge, Mass.: Harvard University Press, 2006.

Machcewicz, Paweł. *Rebellious Satellite: Poland, 1956.* Trans. Maya Latynski. Washington, D.C.: Woodrow Wilson Center Press, 2009.

Mah, Feng-Hwa. "The Terms of Sino-Soviet Trade." *China Quarterly,* no. 17 (January–March 1964): 174–91.

Maier, Charles S. "The Cold War as an Era of Imperial Rivalry." In Silvio Pons and Federico Romero, eds., *Reinterpreting the End of the Cold War: Issues, Interpretations, Periodizations,* 18–43. London: Frank Cass, 2005.

Major, Patrick. *Behind the Berlin Wall: East Germany and the Frontiers of Power.* Oxford: Oxford University Press, 2010.

Mancall, Mark. *Russia and China: Their Diplomatic Relations to 1728.* Cambridge, Mass.: Harvard University Press, 1971.

Marer, Paul. "Soviet Economic Policy in Eastern Europe." In Joint Economic Committee, *Reorientation and Commercial Relations of the Economies of Eastern Europe*, 135–63. Washington, D.C.: U.S. Government Printing Office, 1974.

Martin, Terry. *The Affirmative Action Empire: Nations and Nationalism in the Soviet Union, 1923–1939*. Ithaca, N.Y.: Cornell University Press, 2001.

Mastny, Vojtech. *The Cold War and Soviet Insecurity: The Stalin Years*. New York: Oxford University Press, 1996.

Mazov, Sergey. *A Distant Frontier in the Cold War: The USSR in West Africa and the Congo, 1956–1964*. Washington, D.C., and Stanford, Calif.: Woodrow Wilson Center Press and Stanford University Press, 2010.

Mëhilli, Elidor. "Defying De-Stalinization: Albania's 1956." *Journal of Cold War Studies* 13, no. 4 (Fall 2011): 4–56.

Menon, Rajan. "The Limits of Chinese-Russian Partnership." *Survival* 51, no. 3 (June–July 2009): 99–130.

Mingjiang Li. "Ideological Dilemma: Mao's China and the Sino-Soviet Split, 1962–63." *Cold War History* 11, no 3 (2011): 387–419.

———. *Mao's China and the Sino-Soviet Split: Ideological Dilemma*. London: Routledge, 2012.

Mirovitskaya, Raisa, and Yuri Semyonov. *The Soviet Union and China: A Brief History of Relations*. Moscow: Novosti Press Agency Publishing, 1981.

Mirunovic, Veljko. *Moscow Diary*. Trans. David Floyd, intro. George Kennan. Garden City, N.Y.: Doubleday, 1980.

Molotov Remembers: Inside Kremlin Politics. Conversations with Felix Chuev, ed. and intro. Albert Reis. Chicago: Ivan R. Dee, 1993.

Naimark, Norman M. *The Russians in Germany: A History of the Soviet Zone of Occupation, 1945–1949*. Cambridge, Mass.: Harvard University Press, 1995.

———. "Post-Soviet Russian Historiography on the Emergence of the Soviet Bloc." *Kritika: Explorations in Russian and Eurasian History* 5, no. 3 (Summer 2004): 561–80.

Nairmark, Norman, and Leonid Gibianskii, eds. *The Establishment of Communist Regimes in Eastern Europe, 1944–1949*. Boulder, Colo.: Westview, 1997.

Narkiewicz, Olga A. *Eastern Europe, 1968–1984*. Totowa, N.J.: Barnes & Noble, 1986.

Näth, Marie-Luise, ed. *Communist China in Retrospect: East European Sinologists Remember the First Fifteen Years of the PRC*. Frankfurt am Main: Peter Lang, 1995.

Nation, R. Craig. *Black Earth, Red Star: A History of Soviet Security Policy, 1917–1991*. Ithaca, N.Y.: Cornell University Press, 1992.

Nguyen, Lien-Hang T. *Hanoi's War: An International History of the War for Peace in Vietnam*. Chapel Hill: University of North Carolina Press, 2012.

Nielsen, Waldemar A., and Zoran S. Hodjera. "Sino-Soviet Bloc Technical Assistance: Another Bilateral Approach." *Annals of the American Academy of Political and Social Science* 323 (May 1959): 40–49.

Niu Jun. *From Yan'an to the World: The Origin and Development of Chinese Communist Foreign Policy*. Ed. and trans. Steven I. Levine. Norwalk, Conn.: EastBridge, 2005.

Northrup, Douglas. *Veiled Empire: Gender and Power in Stalinist Central Asia.* Ithaca, N.Y.: Cornell University Press, 2004.

Ostermann, Christian F., ed. *Uprising in East Germany, 1953: The Cold War, the German Question, and the First Major Upheaval behind the Iron Curtain.* Budapest: Central European University Press, 2001.

Ouimet, Matthew J. *The Rise and Fall of the Brezhnev Doctrine in Soviet Foreign Policy.* Chapel Hill: University of North Carolina Press, 2003.

Paine, S. C. M. *Imperial Rivals: China, Russia, and Their Disputed Frontier.* Armonk, N.Y.: M. E. Sharpe, 1996.

Pantsov, Alexander. "Stalin, Khrushchev and Modernization of the People's Republic of China in the 1950s." In *Russia and China: Traditional Values and Modernization,* 152–76. Taibei: Tamkang University Press, 2001.

Péteri, György. "The Occident Within—or the Drive for Exceptionalism and Modernity." *Kritika: Explorations in Russian and Eurasian History* 9, no. 4 (Fall 2008): 929–37.

———, ed. "Nylon Curtain: Transnational and Transsystemic Tendencies in the Cultural Life of State-Socialist Russia and East-Central Europe." *Slavonica* 10, no. 2 (November 2004): 113–23.

———. *Imagining the West in Eastern Europe and the Soviet Union.* Pittsburgh: University of Pittsburgh Press, 2010.

Platt, Kevin M. F., and David Brandenberger, eds. *Epic Revisionism: Russian History and Literature as Stalinist Propaganda.* Madison: University of Wisconsin Press, 2006.

Plokhy, S. M. *Yalta: The Price of Peace.* New York: Viking Penguin, 2010.

Poiger, Uta G. *Jazz, Rock and Rebels: Cold War Politics and American Culture in a Divided Germany.* Berkeley: University of California Press, 2000.

The Polemic of the General Line of the International Communist Movement. Peking: Foreign Languages Press, 1965.

Polevoi, Boris Nikolaevich. *A Story about a Real Man.* Moscow: Foreign Languages, 1952.

Pryor, Frederic L. *The Communist Foreign Trade System.* Cambridge, Mass.: M.I.T., 1963.

Pun Ngai and Chris Smith. "Putting Transnational Labour Process in Its Place: The Dormitory Labour Regime in Post-socialist China." *Work, Employment & Society* 21, no. 1 (2007): 27–45.

Radchenko, Sergey. *Two Suns in the Heavens: The Sino-Soviet Struggle for Supremacy, 1962–1967.* Washington, D.C., and Stanford, Calif.: Woodrow Wilson Center Press and Stanford University, 2009.

Radchenko, Sergey, and David Wolff. "To the Summit via Proxy-Summits: New Evidence from Soviet and Chinese Archives on Mao's Long March to Moscow, 1949." *CWIHPB,* no. 16 (Fall 2007–Winter 2008): 105–82.

Rádvanyi, János. "The Hungarian Revolution and the Hundred Flowers Campaign." *China Quarterly* 43 (1970): 121–29.

Rainer, János. "The New Course in Hungary in 1953." CWIHP Working Paper no. 38. Washington, D.C.: Woodrow Wilson Center, June 2002.

Rainer, János M., and Katalin Somla eds. *The 1956 Hungarian Revolution and the Soviet Bloc Countries: Reactions and Repercussions*. Budapest: Institute for the History of the 1956 Hungarian Revolution, 2007.

Rajak, Svetozar. *Yugoslavia and the Soviet Union in the Early Cold War: Reconciliation, Comradeship, Confrontation, 1953–1957*. New York: Routledge, 2011.

Rees, E. A. "Leaders and Their Institutions." In Paul R. Gregory, ed., *Behind the Facade of Stalin's Command Economy: Evidence from the Soviet State and Party Archives*, 35–60. Stanford, Calif.: Hoover Institution Press, 2001.

Reid, Susan. "Cold War in the Kitchen: Gender and the De-Stalinization of Consumer Taste in the Soviet Union under Khrushchev." *Slavic Review* 61, no. 2 (Summer 2002): 211–52.

———. "Who Will Beat Whom? Soviet Popular Reception of the American National Exhibition in Moscow, 1959." *Kritika: Explorations in Russian and Eurasian History* 9, no. 4 (Fall 2008): 855–904.

Reid, Susan E., and David Crowley, eds. *Style and Socialism: Modernity and Material Culture in Post-war Eastern Europe*. Oxford: Berg, 2000.

Richardson, Sophie. *China, Cambodia, and the Five Principles of Peaceful Coexistence*. New York: Columbia University Press, 2010.

Rieber, Alfred J. "The Crack in the Plaster: Crisis in Romania and the Origins of the Cold War." *Journal of Modern History* 76 (March 2004): 62–106.

Rip, Arie, Thomas J. Misa, and Johan Schot, eds. *Managing Technology in Society: The Approach of Constructive Technology Assessment*. London: Pintner, 1995.

Ross, Corey. "East Germans and the Berlin Wall: Popular Opinion and Social Change before and after the Border Closure of August 1961." *Journal of Contemporary History* 39, no. 1 (2004): 25–43.

Rothschild, Joseph. *Return to Diversity: A Political History of East Central Europe since World War II*. New York: Oxford University Press, 1989, 1993.

Rui, Huang, ed. *Beijing 798: Reflections on Art, Architecture and Society in China*. Beijing: Timezone 8 Ltd. and Thinking Hands, 2004.

Schoenhals, Michael, ed. *China's Cultural Revolution, 1961–1969: Not a Dinner Party*. Armonk, N.Y.: M. E. Sharpe, 1996.

Schram, Stuart R. *The Political Thought of Mao Tse-tung*. New York: Frederick A. Praeger, 1963.

Schultz, Kurt S. "Building the 'Soviet Detroit': The Construction of the Nizhnii-Novgorod Automobile Factory, 1527–1932." In Christopher Read, ed., *The Stalin Years: A Reader*, 70–83. New York: Palgrave Macmillan, 2003.

Seaborg, Glenn T., with the assistance of Benjamin S. Loeb. *Kennedy, Khrushchev and the Test Ban*. Berkeley: University of California Press, 1981.

Selected Works of Mao Tsetung, vol. 5. Beijing: Foreign Languages Press, 1977.

Seroka, Jim, and Maurice D. Simon, eds. *Developed Socialism in the Soviet Bloc: Political Theory and Political Realty*. Boulder, Colo.: Westview, 1982.

Shen Zhihua. "The Discrepancy between the Russian and Chinese Versions of Mao's 2 October 1950 Message to Stalin on Chinese Entry into the Korean War: A Chinese Scholar's Reply." Trans. Chen Jian. *CWIHPB*, nos. 8–9 (Winter 1996–97): 237–42.

———. "Sino–North Korean Conflict and Its Resolution during the Vietnam War." Trans. Dong Gil Kim and Jeffrey Becker. *CWIHPB*, nos. 14–15 (Winter 2003–Spring 2004): 9–24.

———. *Mao, Stalin and the Korean War: Trilateral Communist Relations in the 1950s.* Trans. Neil Silver. London: Routledge, 2012.

Shu Guang Zhang. *Economic Cold War: America's Embargo against China and the Sino-Soviet Alliance, 1949–1963.* Washington, D.C.: Woodrow Wilson Center Press, 2003.

Shu Guang Zhang and Chen Jian. "The Emerging Disputes between Beijing and Moscow." *CWIHPB*, nos. 6–7 (Winter 1995–96): 148–63.

Shu Li. "When Writing History and Gazetters, Make a Critical Reassessment of the Sources (Excerpts)." In Søren Clausen and Stig Thøgersen, eds., *The Making of a Chinese City: History and Historiography in Harbin*, 17–21. Armonk, N.Y.: M. E. Sharpe, 1995.

Simei Qing. *From Allies to Enemies: Visions of Modernity, Identity, and U.S.-China Diplomacy, 1945–1960.* Cambridge, Mass.: Harvard University Press, 2007.

Sin-Lin. *Shattered Families, Broken Dreams: Little-Known Episodes from the History of the Persecution of Chinese Revolutionaries in Stalin's Gulag.* Trans. Steven I. Levine. Portland, Me.: MerwinAsia, 2012.

Slezkine, Yuri. "The USSR as a Communal Apartment, or How a Socialist State Promoted Ethnic Particularism." *Slavic Review* 53, no. 2 (Summer 1994): 414–52.

———. *The Jewish Century.* Princeton, N.J.: Princeton University Press, 2004.

Smith, Steve, and Catriona Kelly. "Commercial Culture and Consumerism." In Catriona Kelly and David Shepherd, eds., *Constructing Russian Culture in the Age of Revolution: 1881–1940*, 106–55. Oxford: Oxford University Press, 1998.

Smith, Tony. "New Bottles for New Wine: A Pericentric Framework for the Study of the Cold War." *Diplomatic History* 24, no. 4 (Fall 2000): 567–91.

Smula, Johann. "The Party and the Proletariat: Škoda, 1948–53." *Cold War History* 6, no. 2 (May 2006): 153–75.

Spence, Jonathan D. *The Gate of Heavenly Peace: The Chinese and Their Revolution, 1895–1980.* New York: Viking, 1981.

———. *To Change China: Western Advisers in China, 1620–1960.* Boston: Little, Brown, 1969.

Spulber, Nicolas. "Soviet Undertakings and Soviet Mixed Companies in Eastern Europe." *Journal of Central European Affairs* 14 (1954–55): 154–73.

Stalin, Joseph. *Economic Problems of Socialism in the U.S.S.R.* New York: International Publishers, 1952.

Stephan, John J. *The Russian Far East: A History.* Stanford, Calif.: Stanford University Press, 1994.

Stitziel, Judd. "On the Seam between Socialism and Capitalism: East German Fashion Shows." In David Crew, ed., *Consuming Germany in the Cold War*, 51–85. Oxford: Berg, 2003.

Stokes, Raymond G. *Constructing Socialism: Technology and Change in East Germany, 1945–1990.* Baltimore: Johns Hopkins University Press, 2000.

Stone, David R. "CMEA's International Investment Bank and the Crisis of Developed Socialism." *Journal of Cold War Studies* 10, no. 3 (Summer 2008): 48–77.

Stone, Randall W. *Satellites and Commissars: Strategy and Conflict in the Politics of Soviet-Bloc Trade*. Princeton, N.J.: Princeton University Press, 1996.

Strauss, Julia. "Morality, Coercion and State Building by Campaign in the Early PRC: Regime Consolidation and After, 1949–1956." *China Quarterly* 188, no. 4 (December 2006): 891–912.

Stueck, William. *Rethinking the Korean War: A New Diplomatic and Strategic History*. Princeton, N.J.: Princeton University Press, 2002.

Sunderland, Willard. *Taming the Wild Field: Colonization and Empire on the Russian Steppe*. Ithaca, N.Y.: Cornell University Press, 2004.

Suri, Jeremi. *Power and Protest: Global Revolution and the Rise of Détente*. Cambridge, Mass.: Harvard University Press, 2003.

———. "America's Search for a Technological Solution to the Arms Race: The Surprise Attack Conference of 1958 and a Challenge for 'Eisenhower Revisionists.'" *Diplomatic History* 21, no. 3 (Spring 2007): 417–51.

Szalontai, Balázs. *Kim Il Sung in the Khrushchev Era: Soviet-DPRK Relations and the Roots of North Korean Despotism, 1953–1964*. Washington, D.C.: Woodrow Wilson Center Press, 2005.

Szporluk, Roman, ed. *The Influence of East Europe and the Soviet West on the USSR*. New York: Praeger, 1975.

Tai Sung An. *The Sino-Soviet Territorial Dispute*. Philadelphia: Westminster, 1973.

Taubman, William. *Khrushchev: The Man and His Era*. New York: W. W. Norton, 2003.

Taubman, William, Sergei Khrushchev, and Abbott Gleason, eds. *Nikita Khrushchev*. New Haven, Conn.: Yale University Press, 2000.

Taylor, Jay. *The Generalissimo: Chiang Kai-shek and the Struggle for Modern China*. Cambridge, Mass.: Harvard University Press, 2011.

Teiwes, Frederick C. *Politics at Mao's Court: Gao Gang and Party Factionalism in the Early 1950s*. Armonk, N.Y.: M. E. Sharpe, 1990.

Teiwes, Frederick C., with Warren Sun. *China's Road to Disaster: Mao, Central Politicians, and Provincial Leaders in the Unfolding of the Great Leap Forward, 1955–1959*. Armonk, N.Y.: M. E. Sharpe, 1999.

Thornton, Richard C. *Odd Man Out: Truman, Stalin, Mao, and the Origins of the Korean War*. Washington, D.C.: Brassey's, 2000.

Tooze, Adam. *The Wages of Destruction: The Making and Breaking of the Nazi Economy*. New York: Viking, 2006.

Toranska, Teresa. *"Them": Stalin's Polish Puppets*. New York: Harper & Row, 1987.

Trachtenberg, Marc. *A Constructed Peace: The Making of the European Settlement, 1945–1963*. Princeton, N.J.: Princeton University Press, 1999.

Tucker, Robert C. "The Cold War in Stalin's Time: What the New Sources Reveal." *Diplomatic History* 21, no. 2 (Spring 1997): 273–81.

Tudda, Chris. "'Reenacting the Story of Tantalus': Eisenhower, Dulles, and the Failed Rhetoric of Liberation." *Journal of Cold War Studies* 7, no. 4 (Fall 2005): 3–35.

Tyrrell, Ian. "American Exceptionalism in an Age of International History." *American Historical Review* 96, no. 4 (October 1991): 1031–55.

Uhl, Matthias. "Sovietization and Missile-ization of the Warsaw Pact, 1958–1965." In Balázs Apor, Péter Apor, and E. A. Rees, eds., *The Sovietization of Eastern Europe:*

New Perspectives on the Postwar Period, 65–74. Washington, D.C.: New Academia, 2008.

Waley-Cohen, Joanna. *The Sextants of Beijing: Global Currents in Chinese History*. New York: W. W. Norton, 1999.

Weathersby, Kathryn, intro. and trans. "New Russian Documents on the Korean War." *CWIHPB*, nos. 6–7 (Winter 1995–96): 30–93.

Werth, Alexander. *Russia under Khrushchev*. Westport, Conn.: Greenwood, 1961.

Westad, Odd Arne. "Mao on Sino-Soviet Relations: Conversations with the Soviet Ambassador." *CWIHPB*, nos. 6–7 (Winter 1995–96): 157, 164–67.

———. "Fighting for Friendship: Mao, Stalin, and the Sino-Soviet Treaty of 1950." *CWIHPB*, nos. 8–9 (Winter 1996–97): 224–36.

———. "Secrets of the Second World: The Russian Archives and the Reinterpretation of Cold War History." *Diplomatic History* 21, no. 2 (Spring 1997): 259–71.

———. "The New International History of the Cold War: Three (Possible) Paradigms." *Diplomatic History* 24, no. 4 (Fall 2000): 551–65.

———. *Decisive Encounters: The Chinese Civil War, 1946–1950*. Stanford, Calif.: Stanford University Press, 2003.

———. *The Global Cold War: Third World Interventions and the Making of Our Times*. Cambridge: Cambridge University Press, 2005.

———. "Struggles for Modernity: The Golden Years of the Sino-Soviet Alliance." In Tsuyoshi Hasegawa, ed., *The Cold War in East Asia, 1945–1991*, 35–62. Washington, D.C., and Stanford, Calif.: Woodrow Wilson Center and Stanford University, 2011.

———. *Restless Empire: China and the World since 1750*. New York: Basic Books, 2012.

Westad, Odd Arne, ed. *Brothers in Arms: The Rise and Fall of the Sino-Soviet Alliance, 1945–1963*. Washington, D.C.: Woodrow Wilson Center Press, 1998.

Wettig, Gerhard. *Stalin and the Cold War in Europe: The Emergence and Development of East-West Conflict, 1939–1953*. Lanham, Md.: Rowman & Littlefield, 2008.

Whiting, Allen S. "The Sino-Soviet Split." In Roderick MacFarquhar and John K. Fairbank, eds., *The Cambridge History of China*, 14:478–538. Cambridge: Cambridge University Press, 1987.

Wishnick, Elizabeth. *Mending Fences: The Evolution of Moscow's China Policy from Brezhnev to Yeltsin*. Seattle: University of Washington Press, 2001.

Wolff, David. *To the Harbin Station: The Liberal Alternative in Russian Manchuria, 1898–1914*. Stanford, Calif.: Stanford University Press, 1999.

———. "'One Finger's Worth of Historical Events: New Russian and Chinese Evidence on the Sino-Soviet Alliance and Split, 1948–1959." CWIHP Working Paper no. 30. Washington, D.C.: Woodrow Wilson International Center for Scholars, August 2000.

Wright, David. *Translating Science: The Transmission of Western Chemistry into Late Imperial China, 1840–1900*. Leiden, the Netherlands: Brill, 2000.

Wright, Richard. *The Color Curtain: A Report on the Bandung Conference*. Cleveland: World, 1956.

Wu Xiuquan. *Eight Years in the Ministry of Foreign Affairs (January 1950–October 1958)*. Beijing: New World, 1985.

Xue Mouhong and Pei Jianzhang, eds. *Diplomacy of Contemporary China*. Hong Kong: New Horizon, 1990.

Yang, Dali L. "Surviving the Great Leap Famine: The Struggle over Rural Policy, 1958–1962." In Timothy Cheek and Tony Saich, eds., *New Perspectives on State Socialism in China*, 262–302. Armonk, N.Y.: M. E. Sharpe, 1997.

Yang Kuisong. "The Sino-Soviet Border Clash of 1969: From Zhenbao Island to Sino-American Rapprochement." *Cold War History* 1, no. 1 (August 2000): 21–52.

Yen-lin Chung. "The Witch-Hunting Vanguard: The Central Secretariat's Roles and Activities in the Anti-Rightist Campaign." *China Quarterly*, no. 206 (June 2011): 391–411.

Zagoria, Donald S. *The Sino-Soviet Conflict, 1956–1961*. Princeton, N.J.: Princeton University Press, 1962.

Zauberman, Alfred. *Economic Imperialism: The Lesson of Eastern Europe*. London: Ampersand LTD, 1955.

Zhai, Qiang. *China and the Vietnam Wars, 1950–1975*. Chapel Hill: University of North Carolina Press, 2000.

———. "Coexistence and Confrontation." In Kenneth Osgood, ed., *The Cold War after Stalin's Death: A Missed Opportunity for Peace?*, 177–92. Lanham, Md.: Rowman & Littlefield, 2006.

Zhihua Shen and Danhui Li. *After Leaning to One Side: China and Its Allies in the Cold War*. Washington, D.C., and Stanford, Calif.: Woodrow Wilson Center Press and Stanford University Press, 2011.

Zhihua Shen and Yafeng Xia. "Hidden Currents during the Honeymoon: Mao, Khrushchev, and the 1957 Moscow Conference." *Journal of Cold War Studies* 11, no. 4 (Fall 2009): 74–117.

———. "New Evidence for China's Role in the Hungarian Crisis of October 1956: A Note." *International History Review* 31, no. 3 (2009): 558–75.

———. "The Whirlwind of China: Zhou Enlai's Shuttle Diplomacy in 1957 and Its Effects." *Cold War History* 10, no. 4 (November 2010): 513–35.

———. "The Great Leap Forward, the People's Commune and the Sino-Soviet Split." *Journal of Contemporary China* 20 no. 72 (November 2011): 861–80.

———. "Between Aid and Restriction: Changing Soviet Policies toward China's Nuclear Weapons Program, 1954–1960." NPIHP Working Paper no. 2. Washington, D.C.: Woodrow Wilson International Center for Scholars, May 2012.

Zinner, Paul E., ed. *National Communism and Popular Revolt in Eastern Europe: A Selection of Documents on Events in Poland and Hungary, February–November 1956*. New York: Columbia University Press, 1956.

Zubok, Vladislav M. "Khrushchev's Nuclear Promise to Beijing during the 1958 Crisis." *CWIHPB*, nos. 6–7 (Winter 1995–96): 218, 225–26.

———. "'Look What Chaos in the Beautiful Socialist Camp!' Deng Xiaoping and the Sino-Soviet Split, 1956–1963." *CWIHPB*, no. 10 (March 1998): 152–62.

———. *A Failed Empire: The Soviet Union in the Cold War from Stalin to Gorbachev*. Chapel Hill: University of North Carolina Press, 2007.

———. "Stalin's Plans and Russian Archives." *Diplomatic History* 21, no. 2 (Spring 1997): 295–305.

Zubok, Vladislav, and Constantine Pleshakov. *Inside the Kremlin's Cold War: From Stalin to Khrushchev*. Cambridge, Mass.: Harvard University Press, 1996.

Russian-Language Scholarship, Memoirs, and Primary Sources

Adamishin, A. L., et al. *Istoriia vneshnei politiki SSSR*. Vol. 2, *1945–1980 gg*. Moscow: "Nauka," 1981.

Aimermakher, K., et al. *Kul'tura i vlast': Doklad N. S. Khrushcheva o kul'te lichnosti stalina na XX s'ezde KPSS: Dokumenty*. Moscow: ROSSPEN, 2002.

Aksiutin, Iurii. *Khrushchevskaia 'ottepel'' i obshchestvennye nastroeniia v SSSR v 1953–1964 gg*. Moscow: ROSSPEN, 2004.

Aleksandrov-Agentov, A. M. *Ot Kollontai do Gorbacheva: Vospominaniia diplomata*. Moscow: "Mezhdunarodnye otnosheniia," 1994.

Apro, Antal. *Sotrudnichestvo stran-chlenov SEV v ekonomicheskikh organizatsiiakh sotsialisticheskikh stran*. Moscow: Izdatel'stvo "Ekonomika," 1969.

Aristov, A. *Sberezhennye milliony: Iz opyta novatorov promyshlennykh predpriatii Moskovskogo oblastnogo ekonomicheskogo raiona*. Moscow: "Moskovskii rabochii," 1958.

Arnol'dov, A. I. *Sotsializm i kul'tura: Kul'turnaia revoliutsiia v evropeiskikh stranakh narodnoi demokratii*. Moscow: Izdatel'stvo akademii nauk USSR, 1962.

Barkovskii, A. N., and B. N. Ladygin. *SEV: Istoriia i sovremennost'*. Moscow: Sovet ekonomicheskoi vzaimopomoshchi secretariat, 1989.

Bogatkin, V. V., V. I. Zabashta, A. I. Konstantinovskii, A. A. Kotukhina, and S. I. Selikhanov. *Sto dnei v Kitae (dekabr' 1956–fevral' 1957): Katalog*. Moscow: Soiuz khudozhnikov SSSR, 1957.

Bogush, E. Iu. *Maoizm i politika raskola v natsional'no-osvoboditel'nom dvizhenii*. Moskva: "Mysl'," 1969.

Borisov, O. [Oleg Rakhmaninin]. *Sovetskii soiuz: Man'chzhurskaia revoliutsionnaia-baza (1945–1949)*. Moscow: "Mysl'," 1985.

Brezhnev, A. A. *Kitai: Ternistyi put' k dobrososedstvu: vospominaniia i razmyshleniia*. Moscow: "Mezhdunarodnye otnosheniia," 1998.

Brodskii, Boris. *Ves' mir na iugo-zapade*. Moscow: "Znanie," 1961.

Brutents, Karen N. *Tridtsat' let na staroi ploshchadi*. Moscow: "Mezhdunarodnye otnosheniia," 1998.

Bubenin, Vitalii. *Krovavyi sneg damanskoi: Sobytiia, 1966–1969 gg*. Vladivostok: Russkii ostrov, 2009.

Budkin, V. S. *Ekonomicheskoe sotrudnichestvo chekhoslovatskoi sotsialisticheskoi lageria*. Kiev: Akademmiia nauk ukrainskoi SSR—institut ekonomiki, 1961.

Burlatskii, Fedor. *Maoism ili Marksizm?* Moscow: Izdatel'stvo politicheskoi literatury, 1967.

Bystrova, Nina. *SSSR i formirovanie voenno-blokovogo protivostoianie v evrope (1945–1955 gg.)*. Moscow: "Giperboreia," "Kuchkovo pole," 2007.

Cherviakov, P. A. *Vsemirnaia vystavka 1958 goda v Briussele*. Moscow: Izdatel'stvo "Znanie," 1958.

Chubar'ian, A. O., ed. *Stalinskoe desiatiletie kholodnoi voiny: fakty i gipotezy*. Moscow: "Nauka," 1999.

Danilov, A. A., and A. V. Pyzhikov. *Rozhdenie sverkhderzhavy: SSSR v pervye poslevoennye gody*. Moscow: ROSSPEN, 2001.

Edemskii, A. B. *Ot konflikta k normalizatsii: Sovetsko-iugoslavskie otnosheniia v 1953–1956 godakh*. Moscow: "Nauka," 2008.

Fateev, A. V. *Obraz vraga v sovetskoi propagande, 1945–1954 gg*. Moscow: Rossiiskaia akademiia nauk institut rossiiskoi istorii, 1999.

Fedotov, V. P. *Polveka vmeste s Kitaem: Vospominaniia, zapisi, razmyshleniia*. Moscow: ROSSPEN, 2005.

Filatov, L. V. *Ekonomicheskaia otsenka nauchno-tekhnicheskoi pomoshchi sovetskogo soiuza kitaiu, 1949–1966*. Moscow: "Nauka," 1980.

Firsov, B. M. *Raznomyslie v SSSR, 1940–1960-e gody: Istoriia, teoriia i praktika*. St. Petersburg: Izdatel'stvo evropeiskogo universiteta v Sankt-Peterburge: Evropeiskii dom, 2008.

Fridman, V. G., ed. *Druzhba naveki*. Irkutsk: Irkutskoe knizhnoe izdatel'stvo, 1959.

Fursenko, A. A., ed. *Prezidium TsK KPSS, 1954–1964*. Vol. 1, *Chernovye protokol'nye zapisi zasedanii*. Moscow: ROSSPEN, 2004.

Galenovich, Iu. M. *Rossiia i Kitai v XX veke: Granitsa*. Moskva: "Izograf," 2001.

———. *Rossiia-Kitai: Shest' dogovorov*. Moscow: "Muravei," 2003.

———. *Rossiia—Kitai—Amerika: Ot sopernichestva k garmonii interesov?* Moscow: "Russkaia panorama," 2006.

Garbuzov, V. "20 let postoiannoi komissii SEV po valiutno-finansovym voprosam." In S. Karavastev et al., eds., *20 let postoiannoi komissii SEV po valiutno-finansovym voprosam*, 5–25. Sofia: Redaktsiia zhurnala 'financy i kredit' NRB, 1983.

Gibianskii, L. Ia. *U istokov 'sotsialisticheskogo sodruzhestva': SSSR i vostochnoevropeiskie strany v 1944–1949 gg*. Moscow: "Nauka," 1995.

Girenko, Iu. S. *Stalin—Tito*. Moscow: Politizdat, 1991.

Golubev, A. V., et al. *Rossiia i zapad: Formirovanie vneshnepoliticheskikh stereotipov v soznanii rossiiskogo obshchestva pervoi poloviny XX veka*. Moscow: Rossiiskaia akademiia nauk institut rossiiskoi istorii, 1998.

Grigor'eva, L. V. "O kul'turnom nasledii rossiiskoi emigratsii v kharbine." *Vestnik mezhdunarodnogo tsentra aziatskikh issledovanii*, no. 2 (1999): 140–42.

Iarskaia-Smirnova, E. R., and P. V. Romanov, eds. *Sovetskaia sotsial'naia politika: stseny i deistvuiushchie litsa, 1940–1985*. Moscow: Tsentr sotsial'noi politiki i gendernykh issledovanii, 2008.

Kan In Gu. *Kul'turnoe sotrudnichestvo sovetskogo soiuza i severnoi Korei vo vtoroi polovine 40-kh godov*. St. Petersburg: Avtoreferat, 1995.

Karavastev, S., et al., eds. *20 let postoiannoi komissii SEV po valiutno-finansovym voprosam*. Sofia: Redaktsiia zhurnala 'financy I kredit' NRB, 1983.

Khachatriants, I. T. *Voprosy ekonomiki stroitel'nogo proizvodstva v zhilishchnom stroitel'stve*. Minsk: Redaktsionno-izdatel'skii otdel BPI im. I. V. Stalina, 1959.

Knyshevskii, Pavel. *Dobycha: Tainy germanskikh reparatsii*. Moscow: "Soratnik," 1994.

Kocharian, M. A. *Druzhba i sotrudnichestvo SSSR i Indii*. Moscow: Izdatel'stvo vostochnoi literatury, 1959.

Kudrina, T. A., ed. *Aktual'nye voprosy kul'turnogo stroitel'stva v period razvitogo sotsializma*. Moscow: Ministerstvo kul'tury RSFSR, 1977.

Kulik, B. T. *Sovetsko-kitaiskii raskol: prichiny i posledstviia*. Moscow: Institut dal'nego vostoka RAN, 2000.

Kutakov, L. N. *Ot pekina do n'iu-iuorka: Zapiski sovetskogo uchenogo i diplomata*. Moscow: "Nauka," 1983.

Lartsev, F. F. *Torgovlia pri sotsializme*. Moscow: Izdatel'stvo VPSh i AON pri TsK KPSS, 1959.

Ledovskii, A. M. *SSSR i Stalin v sud'bakh Kitaia: Dokumenty i svidetel'stva ychastnika sobytii, 1937–1952*. Moscow: "Pamiatniki istoricheskoi mysli," 1999.

———. "Stalin, Mao Tszedun i Koreiskaia voina, 1950–1953 godov." *Novaia i noveishaia istoriia*, no. 5 (September–October 2005): 79–113.

Lenin, V. I. *Polnoe sobranie sochinenii*. 5th ed. Moscow: Izdatel'stvo politicheskoi literatury, 1981.

Loginov, V. T., ed. *XX s'ezd: Materialy konferentsii k 40-letiiu XX s'ezda KPSS*. Moscow: "Aprel'-85," 1996.

Medvedev, Roi. *Neizvestnyi Andropov*. Rostov-na-Donu: "Feniks," 1999.

Mezhdunarodnye i inostrannye vystavki v SSSR, 1946–1972gg. Moscow: Torgovo promyshlennaia palata SSSR, 1973.

Minaev, A. V., ed. *Sovetskaia voennaia moshch' ot Stalina do Gorbacheva*. Moscow: Izdatel'skii dom 'voennyi parad,' 1999.

Muranov, A. P. *Reka khuankhe (Zheltaia reka)*. Leningrad: Gidrometeorologicheskoe izdatel'stvo, 1957.

Murin, Iu. G., ed. *Iosif Stalin v ob'iatiiakh sem'i: Iz lichnogo arkhiva*. Moscow: "Rodina," 1993.

Nadzhafov, D. G. "Antiamerikanskie propagandistskie pristrastiia stalinskogo rukovodstva." In A. O. Chubar'ian et al. *Stalinskoe desiatiletie kholodnoi voiny: fakty i gipotezy*, 134–50. Moscow: "Nauka," 1999.

Nepomniashchii, A. *Druzhba, kotoroi vechno zhit'*. Leningrad: "Lenizdat," 1960.

Nezhinskii, L. N. *U istokov sotsialisticheskogo sodruzhestva i SSSR: Strany tsentral'noi i iugo-vostochnoi evropy vo vtoroi polovine 40-kh godov XX stoletiia*. Moscow: "Mezhdunarodnye otnosheniia," 1987.

Nikhamin, V. P. *Nerushimaia sovetsko-kitaiskaia druzhba—oplot mira i bezopasnosti na dal'nem vostoke i vo vsem mire*. Moscow: Vysshaia partiinaia shkola pre TsK KPSS, 1955.

Nikol'skaia, I. S. *Mezhdunarodnye kul'turnye sviazi SSSR v pervoe desiatiletie sovetskoi vlasti: K istorii VOKS i zarubezhnykh obshchestv kul'turnoi sviazi s SSSR*. Moscow: Avtoreferat dissertatsii, 1970.

Noskova, A. F. "Moskovskie sovetniki v stranakh Vostochnoi Evropy (1945–1953 gg.)." *Voprosy istorii* 1 (1998): 104–13.

Noskova, Al'bina. "Vozniknovenie sistemy sovetskikh sovetnikov v stranakh vostochnoi evropy (1949–1953 gg.)." In Vitka Toshkova et al., *Bolgariia v sverata na sovetskite interesi*, 39–52. Sofiia: Akademichno izdatelstvo "Prof. Marin Drinov," 1998.

Nosov, B. V., ed. *Slavianksie narody: obshchnost' istorii i kul'tury*. Moscow: Indrik, 2000.

O kitaisko-sovetskoi druzhbe. Beijing: Izdatel'stvo literatury na innostrannykh iazykakh, 1950.

Orekhova, E. D., et al., eds. *Sovetskii soiuz i vengerskii krizis 1956 goda: Dokumenty*. Moscow: ROSSPEN, 1998.

Orlik, I. I., ed. *Tsentral'no-vostochnaia evropa vo votoroi polovine XX veka*. Vol. 1, *Stanovlenie "real'nogo sotsializma" 1945–1965*. Moscow: "Nauka," 2000.

Pavlov, K. A. "Sovetskie universal'nye i spetsializirovannye vystavki za granitsei v period s 1946 po 1957 g." In M. V. Nesterov, ed., *Uchastie sovetskogo soiuza v mezhdunarodnykh iarmarkakh i vystavkakh*, 61–84. Moscow, 1957.

Pechatnov, V. O. "Strel'ba kholostym': Sovetskaia propaganda na zapad v nachale kholodnoi voiny (1945–1947)." In A. O. Chubar'ian et al. *Stalinskoe desiatiletie kholodnoi voiny: fakty i gipotezy*, 108–33. Moscow: "Nauka," 1999.

Pikhoia, R. G. "O vnutripoliticheskoi bor'be v sovetskom rukovodstve, 1945–1958 gg." *Novaia i noveishaia istoriia*, no. 6 (November–December 1995): 3–14.

Polevoi, Boris Nikolaevich. *Izbrannye proizvedeniia v dvukh tomakh*. Moscow: Khudozhestvennaia literatura, 1969.

Pyzhikov, A. V. *Politicheskie preobrazovaniia v SSSR (50–60-e gody)*. Moscow: RAN "Kvadrat S," 1999.

Rakhimov, T. *Natsionalizm i shovinizm—osnova politiki gruppy Mao Tse-duna*. Moscow: "Mysl'," 1968.

Riabchenko, N. P. *KNR-SSSR: Gody konfrontatsii (1969–1982)*. Vladivostok: Dal'nauka, 2006.

Semenov, G. G. *Tri goda v Pekine: Zapiski voennogo sovetnika*. Moscow: Glavnaia redaktsiia vostochnoi literatury izdatel'stva "Nauka," 1980.

Shavarina, N., ed. *Velikaia druzhba: Ocherki, stat'i, vospominaniia*. Chita: Chitinskoe knizhnoe izdatel'stvo, 1959.

Shevelev, Vladimir. *N. S. Khrushchev*. Rostov-na-donu: "Feniks," 1999.

Shmelev, N. P. *Vneshne-ekonomicheskie sviazi zrelogo sotsializma*. Moscow: "Znanie," 1981.

Shneerson, A. I. *Chto takoe zhilishchnyi vopros*. Moscow: Izdatel'stvo VPSh i AON pri TsK KPSS, 1959.

Shukletsov, V. T. *Organizatsionno-khoziaistvennoe ukreplenie kolkhozov i pod'em material'nogo blagosostoianiia kolkhoznogo krest'ianstva v 1953–1957 godakh*. Moscow: Izdatel'stvo VPSh i AON pri TsK KPSS, 1960.

Sladkovskii, M. I. *Istoriia torgovo-ekonomicheskikh otnoshenii SSSR s Kitaem (1917–1974)*. Moscow: Izdatel'stvo "Nauka," 1977.

Slavinskii, D. B. *Sovetskii Soiuz i Kitai: istoriia diplomaticheskikh otnoshenii, 1917–1937 gg*. Moscow: ZAO "Iaponiia segodnia," 2003.

Strazheva, Irina. *Tam techet iantszy: vospominaniia*. 2nd ed. Moscow: "Nauka," 1986.

Terent'ev, M. *Milliony novykh kvartir*. Moscow: Izdatel'stvo VTsSPS Profizdat, 1957.

Tikhomirov, Aleksandr N. *Iskusstvo sotsialisticheskikh stran.* Moscow: "Znanie," 1959.

Tikhvinskii, S. L. *Kitai v moei zhizhni (30–90-gody).* Moscow: "Nauka," 1992.

Toshkova, Vitka, et al. *Bolgariia v sverata na sovetskite interesi.* Sofiia: Akademichno izdatelstvo "Prof. Marin Drinov," 1998.

Tret'iakov, P. N. *Ekonomicheskaia i technicheskaia pomoshch' SSSR slaborazvitym v promyshlennom otnoshenii stranam.* Moscow: "Znanie," 1960.

Troianovskii, Oleg. *Cherez gody i rasstoianiia.* Moscow: Vagrius, 1997.

Velikaia druzhba velikikh narodov: Rasskazy Tuliakov o krepnushchikh sviaziakh mezhdu kitaiskim i sovetskim narodami. Tula: Tyl'skoe knizhnoe izdatel'stvo, 1959.

Vinogradov, A. *V strane velikoi iantszy: Ocherki.* Kurgan: Izdatel'stvo gazety "Sovetskoe zaural'e," 1959.

Volokitina, T. V., T. M. Islamov, G. P. Murashko, A. F. Noskova, and L. A. Pogovaia, eds. *Vostochnaia evropa v dokumentakh rossiiskikh arkhivov, 1944–1953 gg.* Vol. 1, *1944–1948 gg.* Moscow: "Sibirskii khronograf," 1997.

Volokitina, T. V., G. P. Murashko, A. F. Noskova, and T. A. Pokivailova. *Moskva i vostochnaia evropa: Stanovlenie politicheskikh rezhimov sovetskogo tipa.* Moscow: ROSSPEN, 2002.

Zaichikov, V. T. *Bluzhdaiushchaia reka khuankhe.* Moscow: Gosudarstvennoie izdatel'stvo geograficheskoi literatury, 1957.

Zanegin, B., A. Mironov, and Ia. Mikhailov. *K sobytiiam v Kitae.* Moscow: Izdatel'stvo politicheskoi literatury, 1967.

Zazerskaia, T. G. *Sovetskie spetsialisty i formirovanie voenno-promyshlennogo kompleksa Kitaia (1949–1960 gody).* St. Petersburg: NIIKH, 2000.

Zelenin, I. E. *Agrarnaia politika N. S. Khrushcheva i sel'skoe khoziastvo.* Moscow: Institut rossiiskoi istorii RAN, 2001.

Zolotarev, V. A. *Istoriia voennoi strategii rossii.* Moscow: Kuchkovo pole, 2000.

Chinese-Language Scholarship and Memoirs

He Ming. *Zhongsu guanxi zhongda shijian shushi.* Beijing: Renmin chubanshe, 2007.

Jianguo yilai Liu Shaoqi wengao, 7 vols. Beijing: Zhongyang wenxian chubanshe, 2005.

Jianguo yilai Mao Zedong wengao, vol. 8. Beijing: Zhongyang wenxian chubanshe, 1993.

Jianguo yilai Zhou Enlai wengao, vol. 1. Beijing: Zhongyang wenxian chubanshe, 2008.

Kong Hanbing. *Zouchu sulian: Zhongsu guanxi ji qidui zhongguo fazhan de yingxiang.* Beijing: Xinhua chubanshe, 2011.

Li Danhui, ed. *Beijing yu Mosike: Cong lianmeng zouxiang duikang.* Guilin: Guangxi shifan daxue chubanshe, 2002.

Li Jie. *Mao Zedong yu xin zhongguo de neizheng waijiao.* Beijing: Zhongguo qingnian chubanshe, 2003.

Li Xiaoming. *Mao Zedong shehuizhuyi shehui jianshe lilun yanjiu.* Shijiazhuang: Hebei jiaoyu chubanshe, 2011.

Li Yueran. *Zhongsu waijiao qinliji: Shouxi eyu fanyi de lishi xianzheng.* Beijing: Shijie zhishi chubanshe, 2001.

Lian Zhengbao et al. *Jiemi waijiao wenxian: Zhonghua renmin gong he guo jianjiao dangan, 1949–1955*. Beijing: Zhongguo huabao chubanshe, 2006.

Mao Zedong waijiao wenxuan. Beijing: Zhangyang wenxian chubanshe, 1994.

Meng Xianzhang. *Zhongsu maoyi shi ziliao*. Beijing: Zhongguo duiwai jingji chubanshe, 1991.

Pei Jianzhang. *Zhonghua renmin gongheguo waijiaoshi, 1949–1956*. Beijing: Shijie zhishi chubanshe, 1994.

Peng Zhuowu, ed. *Mao Zedong yu Sidalin, Heluxiaofu jiaowanglu*. Beijing: Dongfang chubanshe, 2004.

Pu Guoliang. *Zhongsu dalunzhan de qiyuan*. Beijing: Dangdai shijie chubanshe, 2003.

———. *Zouxiang bingdian: Zhongsu da lunzhan yu 1956–1965 nian de zhongsu guanxi*. Beijing: Guoji wenhua chubanshesi, 1999.

Quan Yanchi. *Mao Zedong yu Heluxiaofu*. Huhe: Nei menggu renmin chubanshe, 1998.

Shen Zhihua. *Sulian zhuanjia zai zhongguo (1948–1960)*. Beijing: Zhongguo guoji guangbo chubanshe, 2003.

Shen Zhihua and Li Danhui. *Zhanhou zhongsu guanxi ruogan wenti yanjiu*. Beijing: Renmin chubanshe, 2006.

Shen Zhihua et al. *Zhongsu guanxi shigang: 1917–1991 nian zhongsu guanxi ruogan wenti zai shenlun*. Beijing: Shehui kexue wenxian chubanshe, 2011.

Shi Zhe. *Zai lishi juren shenbian*. Beijing: Zhongyang wenxian chubanshe, 1991.

Sidalin pailai bangzhu women de renmin. Shenyang: Dongbei renmin chubanshe, 1952.

Sulian zhuanjia he women zai yiqi. Beijing: Gongren chubanshe, 1955.

Wang Ji. *Erzhanhou zhongsu (zhonge) guanxi de yanbian yu fazhan*. Beijing: Qinghua daxue chubanshe, 2000.

Wu Lengxi. *Shinian lunzhan, 1956–1965: Zhongsu lianxi huiyi lu*. Beijing: Zhongyang wenxian chubanshe, 1999.

Xiao Yu, ed. *Sidalin pailai bangzhu women de renmin*. Harbin: Dongbei renmin chubanshe, 1952.

Xu Zehao. *Wang Jiaxiang zhuan*. Beijing: Dangdai zhongguo chubanshe, 1996.

Xue Xiantian, ed. *Zhanhou zhongsu guanxi zouxiang (1945–1960)*. Beijing: Shehui kexue wenxian chubanshe, 1997.

Yang Kuisong. *Mao Zedong yu Mosike de enen yuanyuan*. Nanchang: Jiangxi renmin chubanshe, 1999.

Yang Zhenghui et al. *Zhengtan fengyur (1956–1978)*. Beijing: Dongfang chubanshe, 2010.

Zhang Xiangshan. *Weishenme yao fandui gerenchongbai*. Beijing: Zhongguo qingnian chubanshe, 1956.

Zhongguo yu sulian guanxi wenxian huilian (1949 nian 10 yue–1951 nian 12 yue). Beijing: Shijie zhishi chubanshe, 2009.

Czech-Language Scholarship and Document Collections

Bakešova, Ivana. *Čína ve XX století*, vol. 2. Olomouc: Univerzita Palackého v Olomouci, 2003.

Berounská, O., et al. *Mezinárodní vztahy 1960*. Prague: Státní nakladatelstvi politické literatury, 1961.

Blažek, Petr, Łukasz Kamiński, and Rudolf Vévoda, eds. *Polsko a Československo v roce 1968: Sborník příspěvků z mezinárodní vědecké conference Varšava, 4.-5 září 2003*. Dokořan: Ústav pro soudobé dějiny AV ČR, 2006.

Československo-sovětské vztahy, 1945–1960: Dokumenty a materiály. Prague: Státní pedagogické nakladatelství, 1971.

Dvořáková, Jiřina. *Státní bezpečnost v letech, 1945–1953*. Prague: Uřad dokumentace a vyšetřování zločinů komunismu, 2007.

Drulák, Petr, Petr Kratochvíl, et al., eds. *50 let českého výzkumu mezinárodních vztahu: od ÚMPE k ÚMV*. Prague: Ústav mezinárodnich vztahů, 2007.

Expo '58: Československá restaurace: Příběh československé účasti na Světové výstavě v Bruselu. Prague: Národní archiv, 2008.

Expo '58: Z cestovních zpráv: Příběh československé účasti na Světové výstavě v Bruselu. Prague: Národní archiv, 2008.

Kalinová, Lenka. *Společenské proměny v čase socialístického experimentu: K sociálním dějinám v letech, 1945–1969*. Prague: Academia, 2007.

Kaplan, Karel. *Československo v RVHP, 1949–1956*. Prague: Ústav pro soudobé dějiny AV ČR, 1995.

——. *Kořeny Československé reform 1968*. Brno: Doplněk, 2002.

Kaplan, Karel, and Pavel Paleček. *Komunistický režim a politické procesy v Československsku*. Prague: Nakladatelství Barrister & Principal s.r.o. 2001, 2008.

Knapík, Jiří. *Kdo spoutal naši kulturu: Portrét stalinisty Gustava Bareše*. Přerov: Nakladatelství šárka, 2000.

Pernes, Jiří. *Krize komunistického režimu v Československsku v 50. letech 20. století*. Brno: Centrum pro stadium demokracie a kultury, 2008.

Skřivan, Aleš. Vývoj československého vývozu do číny po druhé světové válce (1945–1959)." *Historický obzor* 19, nos. 11–12 (November–December 2008): 267–74.

Sommer, Karel. "Sovětská válečná kořist a československo." In Josef Krátoška et al., eds., *O sovětské imperíalní politice v československsku v letech, 1945–1968: Sborník příspěvků*, 9–23. Olomouc: Vydavatelství university palackého, 1995.

Tomek, Prokop. *Československý uran, 1945–1989: Těžba a prodej československého uranu v éře komunismu*. Prague: Úřad dokumentace a vyšetřování zločinžů komunismu, 1999.

——. *Dvě studie o československém vězeňství, 1948–1989*. Prague: Úřad dokumentace a vyšetřování zločinů komunismu, 2000.

Vencovský, František, and Karel Půlpán, eds. *Dějiny měnových teorií na českém území*. Prague: Vysoká škola ekonomická v Praze, 2005.

Vykoukal, Jiří, Bohuslav Litera, and Miroslav Tejchman. *Východ: Vznik, vývoj a rozpad sovětskéhó bloku, 1944–1989*. Prague: Nakladatelství libri, 2000.

German-Language Scholarship and Document Collections

Behrends, Jan C. *Die erfundene Freundschaft: Propaganda für die Sowjetunion in Polen und in der DDR.* Cologne: Böhlau Verlag, 2006.

Brenner, Christiane, and Peter Heumos. *Sozialgeschichtliche Kommunismusforschung: Tschechoslowakei, Polen, Ungarn und DDR, 1948–1968.* Munich: R. Oldenbourg Verlag, 2005.

Fischer, Alexander, and Günther Heydemann, eds. *Geschichtwissenschaft in der DDR.* Vol. 2, *Vor- und Frühgeschichte bis Neueste Geschichte.* Berlin: Duncker & Humblot, 1990.

Hacker, Jens. *Der Ostblock: Entstehung, Entwicklung und Struktur, 1939–1980.* Baden-Baden: Nomos Verlagsgesellschaft, 1983.

Halpap, Paul. *China: Land und Leute* Berlin: Berliner Verlag, n.d.

Heinemann, Winfried, and Norbert Wiggershaus, eds. *Das international Krisenjahr 1956: Polen, Ungarn, Suez.* Munich: R. Oldenbourg Verlag, 1999.

Jeschonnek, Emil. "Freundschaft und Zusammenarbeit mit China—einzig mögliche Politik für ganz Deutschland." *Deutsche Aussenpolitik* 5 (May 1957): 374–78.

Kircheisen, Inge, ed. *Tauwetter ohne Frühling: Das Jahr 1956 im Spiegel blockinterner Wandlungen und internationaler Krisen.* Berlin: Berliner Debatte, 1995.

Meissner, Werner, ed. *Die DDR und China 1949 bis 1990: Politik-Wirtschaft-Kultur.* Berlin: Adademie Verlag, 1995.

Rupprecht, Tobias. "Die sowjetische Gesellschaft in der Welt des Kalten Kriegs: Neue Forschungsperspektiven." *Jahrbücher für Geschichte Osteuropas* 58, no. 3 (2010): 381–99.

Schleinitz, Karl Heinz. *Reisebilder aus China.* Berlin: Kongress Verlag, 1956.

Ziebura, Gilbert, ed. *Nationale Souveränität oder übernationale Integration?* Berlin: Colloquium Verlag, 1966.

Dissertations

Friedman, Jeremy Scott. "Reviving the Revolution: The Sino-Soviet Split, the 'Third World,' and the Fate of the Left." PhD diss., Princeton University, 2011.

Harris, Steven E. "Moving to the Separate Apartment: Building, Distributing, Furnishing, and Living in Urban Housing in Soviet Russia, 1950s–1960s." PhD diss., University of Chicago, 2003.

Lüthi, Lorenz M. "The Sino-Soviet Split, 1956–1966." PhD diss., Yale University, 2003.

Stiffler, Douglas A. "Building Socialism at Chinese People's University: Chinese Cadres and Soviet Experts in the People's Republic of China, 1949–57." PhD diss., University of California, San Diego, 2002.

Varga-Harris, Christine. "Constructing the Soviet Hearth: Home, Citizenship and Socialism in Russia, 1956–1964." PhD diss., University of Illinois, 2005.

Changchun Automobile Factory, 28, 37, 53–55

Changchun Railway, 3–4, 180, 219

Changjiang (Yangtze) Bridge, 15

Chekashillo, Andrei M., 27, 39

Chen Duxiu, 3

Cheng Cutao, 55

Chen Geng, 263 (n. 103); and nuclear bomb, 146

Cheng Gongzheng, 50–51, 53

Cheng Guangrui, 190

Cheng Yunshan, 204

Chen Haoling, 4, 13

Chen Kezhai, 118

Chen Yi: and Yugoslavia, 135; on Mao's position in 1958, 142; and war, 144, 149; and Khrushchev's trip to America, 149; and "intermediate zone," 158; and GDR, 160; and withdrawal of advisers, 163–64, 216; and Hungary, 165–66; and ten-year anniversary of Friendship Society, 198; and Friendship Society, 201

Chen Yuanzhi, 206

Chen Yun, 245; and training of cadres, 13–14; on reduction of import of military equipment, 74; and communication network, 76

Chervonenko, Stepan V., 10, 21, 174, 215, 216; and Yugoslavia, 135; and culture, 154; and withdrawal of advisers, 162–64; and Friendship Society, 205; and learning from Soviet Union, 215

Chervov, Vadim S., 95

Chistiakov, N. I., 76

Chulaki, Mikhail, 151

Consumerism, 20, 81, 129, 149, 156, 223; and standard of living in Czechoslovakia, 84, 224; and rebellion in Hungary, 120; and Czechoslovak diplomats in China, 123, 139; and Khrushchev, 217, 221; and Mao, 221; and standard of living in GDR, 224

Cuban Missile Crisis, 201

Čuda, Bořivoj, 175

Cui Yunchang, 205

Cyrankiewicz, Józef, 123

Czechoslovak Film Festival, 93–94

Czech Philharmonic, 150–52, 211–12

"Declaration on Further Strengthening of the Foundation of Friendship and Cooperation between the Soviet Union and Other Socialist Countries," 69–70, 158, 219

Dedijer, Vladimir, 133

Deng Tuo: vacationing on Black Sea, 30; and Hungarian rebellion, 119; and ideology, 127; and *Suzhong youhao*, 190

Deng Xiaoping: on diplomacy, 10; and declaration, 69; and Hungarian rebellion, 69; at 20th Party Congress, 116; and GDR, 165

Deng Yingchao, 237

Dian Guochen, 51

Dian Youtong, 53

Ding Haode, 185

Ding Ling, 182

Di Zhaoding, 159

Dresden Philharmonic, 151

Dubna: Soviet Joint Institute for Nuclear Studies at, 145

Dudinskii, I., 47, 58

Dulles, John Foster, 141

Dvořák, R., 74

Efremin, I. A., 111

Elizavetin, A., 198

Erban, Evžen, 140

Erigin, D. D., 68

Ermolenko, V. G., 70–71

Everhartze, Franz, 113

E Weiming, 182

Fabian, Ferenc, 165

Fang Xian, 185

Fedorenko, Nikolai, 74, 184

Fedorov, A., 59, 63

Fedotov, V. P.: and Iudin, 2

Fedotova, Margarita S., 30

Hungarian rebellion, 6, 20–21, 22, 69, 110, 116–20, 218; Chinese interpretation of, 128; and Yugoslavia, 134

Hu Shouzhun, 181

Hu Yaobang, 226

Iudin, Pavel, 10, 98, 135, 136, 143, 219, 225; and Zhdanov, 1; and heritage of empire, 1–3, 8; and Mao as "Chinese Tito," 2; and advisers, 23, 69; and industrial exchange, 74; and Czechoslovakia, 84; and Stalin question, 111–12; and ideology, 120; and Yugoslavia, 123–24, 135; and leadership of bloc, 126, 220; and war, 144–45; in conversation with Mao about GLF, 156; and intermediate zone, 158; and Suzhong youhao, 186; and Hungarian rebellion, 197; in depiction of Fedotov, 229 (n. 5)

Ivanov, A. N., 180

Jiang Jieshi, 3, 86, 141, 181, 237

Jiang Qing, 30, 144

Jie Zhusheng, 149

Kádár, Janós, 120

Kaganovich, Lazar, 114, 122

Kalaše, Julia, 150

Kang Sheng: in wake of ouster of Khrushchev, 172

Kang Youwei, 3

Kania, Adolf, 140

Kapitsa, P. S., 186

Karpov, M. N., 76

Khoroshikh, P. P., 187

Khrushchev, Nikita, 6–7, 17, 20, 21, 23, 142–43, 161; and joint companies, 4–5; ouster of, 18, 171–76, 216; and advisers, 43, 170; and reform, 67; and Secret Speech, 109, 166; and Stalin question, 109–16, 122, 166, 169, 219; and paths to socialism, 117; and trip to America, 129–30, 178, 196, 217; and people's communes, 136; and nuclear bomb, 144–45, 147, 197; and nuclear

umbrella, 148; and revisionism, 149, 167–68; and Taiwan Strait, 159; and competition with America, 168, 176, 217; and closing of Suzhong youhao, 196; and Friendship Society, 204, 206; and consumerism, 217, 221

Kim Il Sung, 29

Kiryliuk, Stanisław, 122

Kleimenov, F., 46

Kohrt, Günter, 167

Kokashvili, B. G., 186, 193

Komandirovka, 3, 12–13, 23, 40, 56, 71, 80, 184, 209–10, 212, 226, 236 (n. 2); and relationship to internationalism, 19; and relationship to imperial Russia, 28, 32, 36; as transnational institution, 28–33; and selection of advisers, 35; and adviser misbehavior, 43–46; and Hungarians, 121

Komzala, František, 73

König, Johannes, 73; and Yugoslavia, 135

Kononov, N. A., 75, 214

Konstantinov, F. V., 201

Korienko, P. M., 70–71

Korotin, Ivan, 59

Korzhov, L. A., 44

Kosygin, Aleksei N.: in wake of ouster of Khrushchev, 172; and February 1965 trip to Beijing, 174

Koubek, V., 141

Koucký, Vladimír, 143

Kovalev, Ivan, 116; and negotiation of Soviet aid program, 15

Kovshova, Nastia, 152

Kozlov, F. R.: and Friendship Society, 198

Kraelov, S. G., 65

Křístek, Vaclav, 167, 173

Krutikov, K .A., 121

Kubiš, L., 98–100

Kudriavtsev, V. D., 191

Kuklina-Brana, Nina K., 95

Kungurov, G., 205

Kurdiukov, I., 112

Kurilko, M. I., 88

Kurky, K., 166

Kutakov, L., 14
Kuznetsov, A. N.: and weaknesses of cultural exchange, 97; and Friendship Society, 202
Kuznetsov, V. V., 14

Lapin, Sergei, 174
Laptev, S. F., 62
Laštovička, Bohuslav, 60
László, Nevai, 128
Lazarev, V., 135
"Leading people": Soviet Union as, 6, 63, 67–68, 80, 89–90, 142, 210; and Central Europeans, 58–63, 68; and description of bloc, 127–30
"Lean to one side," 9, 57
Lei Feng, 21
Liang Hanguang, 151
Liang Qichao, 3
Li Dequan, 59
Li En Kho, 122
Li Erzhuang, 191
Li Fuchun: and adviser pay, 35; and achievements of Central Europeans, 59; and reduction of Chinese exchange with bloc, 74; and Hungarian rebellion, 84
Li Haijiong, 189
Li He, 119; and ideology, 127
Li Junfu, 183
Li Kenong, 220
Li Lingfu, 206–7
Lin Biao, 144; and Korean War, 30; and revisionism, 175
Lin Fang, 140
Ling Xueqing, 66
Li Shangfu, 87
Liu Changsheng, 198
Liu Denyun, 54
Liu Dingzhu, 50–51, 53
Liu Fang, 55
Liu Jingcheng, 76
Liu Shaoqi, 21, 58, 237; and need for cadres, 1, 13, 209–10; and "lean to one side," 9; on internationalism, 10;

on similarities to Soviet Union, 11; and June 1949 trip to Soviet Union, 15, 35, 197; and son, 30; and adviser pay, 35; and declaration, 69; and potential curtailment of adviser program, 70, 215; and communication networks, 76; and Hungarian rebellion, 109; and "great-power chauvinism," 119; and ideology, 128; and campaigns, 141; and nuclear bomb, 145; and intermediate zone, 157; and Third World, 159; and withdrawal of advisers, 164; and Friendship Society, 183, 197
Liu Shimo, 191
Liu Shuzhou, 197–98
Liu Xiao, 10; and curtailment of Chinese exchange with bloc, 74; and transnational romance, 98; and Stalin question, 113–14; and Hungarian rebellion, 119–20; and Poles in China, 122; and ideology, 127; and Yugoslavia, 135; and nuclear war, 145; and intermediate zone, 158; and conversation with Sergei Lapin, 174; and Suzhong youhao, 184; and Khrushchev's trip to America, 217
Liu Yunbin, 30
Li Xigeng, 200–202
Li Yi, 188
Li Yueran, 5, 116, 263
Li Zhaolin: assassination of, 181
Li Zhuang, 185–86, 194
Li Zhuchen, 198
Long Yunqing, 189
Lu Dingyi, 220; and intermediate zone, 157; and learning from Soviet Union, 215–16
Lüe Saiyang, 119
Lu Ming, 197
Luo Ruiqing, 165
Lüshan Plenum, 136
Lu Xiangxiang, 190
Lu Zi, 153
Lu Zhuzhu, 40
Lysenko, Iu., 193
Lysov, P., 62

Machalous, Josef, 104
Makarov, General Stepan, 3
Malenkov, Georgii, 172; and Stalin question, 122; and nuclear war, 144; and Friendship Society, 204
Ma Licheng, 87
Malinovsky, Rodion, 174; and nuclear umbrella, 148; and 1964 toast, 271
Mao Zedong, ix, 2, 3, 8, 21, 43, 102, 122, 130, 132, 147, 148, 151, 156, 159, 168, 169, 172, 174, 177, 191, 209, 215, 218, 222, 225; and *Collected Works*, 2; comparison to Tito, 2, 81, 125, 133–35, 155; and Chinese resources, 5; and Sino-Soviet Treaty, 9–10, 21, 191, 214; and November 1957 Conference, 22, 126, 130, 141–42, 162; and debt, 48; and learning from Central Europe, 58–60, 84–85; and China's relationship to foreign learning, 82; and Hungarian rebellion, 84, 116–20, 130; and China's similarity to GDR, 85; and personality cult, 112, 144, 170, 173; and Stalin question, 112–14, 169; and Chinese conditions, 116; and Polish rebellion, 116–20, 130; and leadership of bloc, 126, 215; and ideology, 127; and Great Leap Forward, 139–42, 155, 223; and nuclear war, 144–45, 222; and shortwave radio station, 147; and intermediate zone, 157; and Friendship Society, 171, 201, 206; and Stalin's seventieth birthday, 219; and consumerism, 221
Martin, Ferenc, 165–66; and Yugoslavia, 135
Martsenitsen, S., 61–62
Ma Sazong, 96
May Fourth Movement, 3
Mazal, Ladislav, 104
Melničak, Ján, 137, 149
Mikhailov, N. A., 92
Mikoyan, Anastas: and industrial projects in China, 15; and SEV, 72; on America, 78; and Hungarian rebellion, 119; on Chinese contribution to resolution of situation in Hungary, 120;

and war, 145; at Xibaipo, 157; Chinese distrust of, 172; and Mao in 1949, 177
Molotov, Viacheslav, 20, 64, 171, 172; and SEV, 72; and links to western Slavs, 83; and Stalin question, 113–15, 122; and Hungarian rebellion, 119; and bloc unity, 124, 130; and leadership of bloc, 124, 220; and Yugoslavia, 134; and war, 145; and Friendship Society, 204
Mu Jiafan, 204
Muntian, Iu. S., 68
Mzhavanadze, V. P., 115

Nagy, Imre: and Hungarian rebellion, 109; and search for refuge in Yugoslav embassy, 121, 134
Nehru, Jawaharlal, 157
New Defense Technical Accord, 146
New Democratic Union of Youth, 14
Nicholas II, Tsar, 83
Nie Rongzhen, 263; and nuclear bomb, 146
Nikanorov, A. P., 79
Nikolaeva, Galina, 152
Novák, František, 64
November 1957 Conference: and leadership of bloc, 22, 126, 130; and Mao, 141–42, 162
Novgorodskii, Iu. V., 199
Novikov, A. G., 153
Nuclear umbrella, 148–49

Ochab, Edward, 255
October Revolution, 9, 125
"On the Historical Experience of the Dictatorship of the Proletariat," 113–14
Opium Wars, 3
Ordzhonikidze, Sergo, 78
Osadchii, Iu., 154

Panenky, Jana, 150
Paniushkin, A. S., 4, 15
Pan Zili, 156
Paris, Miloš, 101
Peaceful coexistence, 18, 21, 157–58, 192–93, 217

Peng Dehuai: and visiting Polish military delegation, 18, 58–59; and leadership of bloc, 124, 220; and criticism of Mao at Lüshan Plenum, 136; and defense collaboration, 146; CCP criticism of, 169; Soviet concern for, 173

Peng Zhen, 132; and Soviet imperialism, 5; on China's relationship to 1956 events in Poland and Hungary, 6; on technical intelligentsia, 14–15; on adviser misbehavior, 43; in Czechoslovakia, 84; and leadership of bloc, 124–26; and nuclear bomb, 144; and closing of Suzhong youhao, 196; and ten-year anniversary of Friendship Society, 198; and learning from Soviet Union, 213

Pichlík, Václav, 104

Pobedonostsev, M. S., 71

Podzimek, Václav, 103

Polevoi, Boris, 219; on inequality in cultural exchange, 41–43; and Friendship Society, 184

Polish rebellion, 6, 20–21, 22, 110, 116–20, 218

Popović, Koca: and Hungarians in China, 122; and criticism of Soviet Union, 123–24

Potanov, N. M., 186

Poteriaev, V. A., 44

Přibyl, Josef, 175

Prokof'iev, M. A., 201

Pumpianskii, I. M., 72

Pushkin, G. M., 149, 217

Qian Junrui: and criticism of Stalin, 112; as general secretary of central administration of Friendship Society, 181, 199

Qian Xuesen, 146

Qi He, 14

Qi Ke, 191

Qing Chenrui, 216

Rakhmanin, O. B., 111; and Friendship Society, 199–200

Razdukhov, Iu. I., 197

The Red Poppy, 86–88, 211

Rejmán, Ladislav, 138, 150

Revisionism, 17, 149, 175, 217; as betrayal of international communism, 156–59; and Third World, 159–61; and Chinese effort to appeal to Central Europeans, 163–67; and Chinese effort to appeal to Soviet citizenry, 167–71

Rogov, Vladimir N.: and Chinese theater, 92; and Suzhong youhao, 186, 189–90, 192, 194

Romanov, A., 34

Roshchin, Nikolai V., 1, 13–14

Rostov, Iurii D., 44

R-7 missile, 147

R-2 missile, 146–47

Rusakov, K. V.: in wake of ouster of Khrushchev, 172

Ruzhichka, I., 79

Sabolčík, Michal, 224

Sall, Ezhef: and "great-power chauvinism," 119; and impact of Hungarian rebellion on Hungarian advisers in China, 121–22

Savchenko, S. R., 44

Schleinitz, Karl Heinz, 86, 94–95

Schürer, Gerhard, 226

Scientific-Technical Commission: and blueprints, 46; and Chinese revisions to agreements, 48; and bloc planning, 72–75; and SEV, 79

Secret Speech, 109, 111–14, 117

Šedivý, Josef: and personality cult of Mao, 144; and withdrawal of advisers, 164–65

Self-reliance, 54–55, 66, 136, 215; and copying of blueprints, 27; and industrial exchange, 66; language of, 116–17

Self-strengthening, 82; Society for the Study of Self-Strengthening, 3

Sequens, Jiří, 152

SEV, 33, 72; criticism of, 71; and GLF, 73; in wake of Sino-Soviet split, 78–79, 222–23

Yu Aifun, 30
Yu Changfu, 191
Yu Kuang, 99

Zagrebel'nyi, P. A., 200
Zakharov, A. A., 77
Zakharov, P. V., 187, 192
Zao Dengwan, 193
Žemla, M., 84
Zemskov, M. G., 72
Zeng Xisheng, 143
Zeng Xiufu, 87–88
Zhang Jiangwuzhi, 203
Zhang Pinghua: and Stalin question, 111;
    and Soviet betrayal, 206
Zhang Wentian: and Yugoslavia, 123;
    and leadership of bloc, 126
Zhang Yunqi, 202
Zhang Yuquan, 189
Zhang Zhixiang, 197, 199–200
Zhang Zhizhong, 14
Zhao Bing, 54–55
Zhao Zhen, 204
Zhdanov, Andrei: and Iudin, 1
Zhdanov, G. A., 45
Zheltukhin, D. V., 62
Zhen Likang, 109, 114, 120
Zhen Peilu: and romance with Havlíček,
    97–102, 191
Zhen Tuoshan, 100–101
Zhiganov, Nazib G., 96
Zhong Xidong, 166

Zhou Enlai, 3, 13, 35, 37, 59, 76, 84, 122, 123,
    126, 147, 166, 167, 219, 225; and Chinese
    resources, 5; and Russian imperial-
    ism, 8; and Chinese self-reliance, 55;
    and economic planning, 74; and SEV,
    79; and Hungarian rebellion, 84, 128,
    219; and Stalin question, 111–14; and
    ideology, 128; and nuclear war, 144–45;
    and shortwave radio station, 147; and
    Bandung, 157; and intermediate zone,
    157; and Third World, 159, 161; and with-
    drawal of advisers, 163–64; in wake of
    ouster of Khrushchev, 172–73; and 1964
    trip to Moscow, 173–74; and ten-year
    anniversary of Friendship Society, 198;
    and Friendship Society, 201
Zhou Xinfang, 92
Zhou Yizhi, 132
Zhou Zhengmin, 36
Zhou Zhenyuan, 203
Zhou Zhuan, 122
Zhuai Huansan, 199
Zhu De, 30, 166; and training of military
    cadres, 14; in Georgia, 115–16; and Stalin
    question, 115–16; and withdrawal of ad-
    visers, 164; and Friendship Society, 198
Zhukov, G. A., 186
Zhu Wu, 153
Zhu Yaopao, 99
Zimianin, M. V., 186
Zong Kewen, 203
Zorin, V. A., 145